The Economics of the Frontier

Ronald Findlay • Mats Lundahl

The Economics of the Frontier

Conquest and Settlement

palgrave
macmillan

Ronald Findlay
Department of Economics
Columbia University
New York, USA

Mats Lundahl
Department of Economics
Stockholm School of Economics and
Institute of Latin American Studies
Stockholm University
Stockholm, Sweden

ISBN 978-1-137-60236-7 ISBN 978-1-137-60237-4 (eBook)
DOI 10.1057/978-1-137-60237-4

Library of Congress Control Number: 2016955981

Printed on acid-free paper

This Palgrave Macmillan imprint is published by Springer Nature
The registered company is Macmillan Publishers Ltd.
The registered company address is: The Campus, 4 Crinan Street, London, N1 9XW, United Kingdom

For Tin Tin Aye and Kicki

Preface

This book collects a number of articles and book chapters written since 1993. The first and last two chapters have been written especially for the present volume. The book revolves around the idea of the economically optimal frontier, a frontier that is established either through conquest or through putting land under the plow.

The book mixes economic theory and economic history, in the spirit of the great Swedish economist and economic historian Eli Heckscher, who spent his entire life reflecting on the question of how to marry theory and history, of how to let the two crossbreed one another. It uses simple economic theory of the general equilibrium kind, based mainly in trade theory, and it applies this theory to a wide variety of historical settings, ranging from the Plague of Justinian in the mid-sixth century to banditry in Brazil in the 1920s and 1930s. Hopefully the applications demonstrate both the usefulness of model-based 'historical economics' and the strength of the trade-based approach.

We are grateful to a number of individuals who have assisted us in various ways. They are listed in connection with each individual chapter. We also owe a debt of gratitude to the various original publishers of the essays and to other publishers for allowing us to use their material. They are listed either in the Sources section or in direct connection with the material employed.

Ronald Findlay
Mats Lundahl

Contents

List of Sources

1. **Introduction: Frontiers and Empires.** Original chapter for the present volume.
2. **Frontiers and Empires in Historical Perspective.** Original chapter for the present volume.
3. **Modeling Global Interdependence: Centers, Peripheries, and Frontiers.** *American Economic Review*, Vol 86, 1996, pp. 47–51. With kind permission of the American Economic Association.
4. **Towards a Model of Territorial Expansion and the Limits of Empire.** In Michelle R. Garfinkel and Stergios Skaperdas (eds), *The Political Economy of Conflict and Cooperation*. Cambridge: Cambridge University Press, 1996. Reprinted by permission.
5. **Demographic Shocks and the Factor Proportions Model: From the Plague of Justinian to the Black Death.** In Ronald Findlay, Rolf G. H. Henriksson, Håkan Lindgren and Mats Lundahl (eds), *Eli Heckscher, International Trade and Economic History*. Cambridge, MA and London: MIT Press, 2006. Reprinted by permission.
6. **The First Globalization Episode: The Creation of the Mongol Empire or the Economics of Chinggis Khan.** In Göran Therborn and Habibul Haque Khondker (eds), *Asia and Europe in Globalization: Continents, Regions, and Nations*. Leiden: E. J. Brill, 2006. Reprinted by permission.

7. **Towards a Factor Proportions Approach to Economic History: Population, Precious Metals, and Prices from the Black Death to the Price Revolution.** In Ronald Findlay, Lars Jonung and Mats Lundahl (eds), *Bertil Ohlin: A Centennial Celebration 1899–1999*. Cambridge, MA and London: MIT Press, 2002. Reprinted by permission.
8. **International Trade and Factor Mobility with an Endogenous Land Frontier: Some General Equilibrium Consequences of Christopher Columbus.** In Wilfred J. Ethier, Elhanan Helpman and J. Peter Neary (eds), *Theory, Policy and Dynamics in International Trade: Essays in Honor of Ronald W. Jones*. Cambridge University Press, 1993. Reprinted by permission.
9. **Natural Resources, 'Vent-for-Surplus' and the Staples Theory.** In Gerald M. Meier (ed.), *From Classical Economics to Development Economics. Essays in Honor of Hla Myint*. Houndmills, Basingstoke: Macmillan, 1994. Reprinted by permission.
10. **Resource-Led Growth: A Long-Term Perspective: The Relevance of the 1870–1914 Experience for Today's Developing Economies.** Working Paper No. 162, Helsinki: WIDER, 1999. Reprinted by permission from UNU-WIDER which commissioned the original research and holds copyright thereof.
11. **Lampião and the Colonels: On the Political Economy of Banditry.** Original chapter for the present volume.
12. **Epilogue: Frontiers—Theory and History.** Original chapter for the present volume.

List of Figures

1

Introduction: Frontiers and Empires

There are few words, at least in the English language, which have more positive connotations than 'frontier'. What scholar would not want to be at the frontier of knowledge in his discipline and who was not entranced by the crew of the starship *Enterprise* as they ventured into *Space: the Final Frontier* to 'boldly go where no man has gone before'? The frontier concept was first formally introduced into historical discourse by Frederick Jackson Turner (1861–1932) in his seminal 1893 essay on 'The Significance of the Frontier in American History' (Turner 1893; cf. also Turner 1920, for an extended treatment of the same theme), tracing the westward expansion of settlement on the North American continent and its profound influence on the character and institutions of the people of the United States. The frontier is the moving edge of the zone of the safe and the familiar, into the unknown realm of novelty and danger; hence the excitement and sense of adventure that it generates. The human elements beyond the frontier, to the extent that they are acknowledged at all, are generally conceived as existing at a more primitive level than the society expanding into their midst: a contrast between Greeks and Romans,

Original chapter for the present volume by Ronald Findlay and Mats Lundahl.

R. Findlay, M. Lundahl, *The Economics of the Frontier*,
DOI 10.1057/978-1-137-60237-4_1

on the one hand, and multitudes of 'barbarians' on the other, a distinction repeated many times in history as in the case of Germans and Slavs and the *Drang nach Osten*, or the Chinese and the nomads of Central Asia.

When asked by Oxford University to give the Romanes Lecture for 1907 the great British imperial statesman Lord Curzon (1859–1925) appropriately enough chose 'Frontiers' as his subject, and displayed in the course of it both the classical erudition he had acquired at his *alma mater* and his vast experience as an empire-builder, culminating in the 5,700 miles of land frontier he presided over as Viceroy of India. In opening his lecture Curzon declared of the literature on frontiers: 'You may ransack the catalogues of libraries, you may search the indexes of celebrated historical works, you may study the writings of scholars, and you will find the subject almost wholly ignored' (Curzon 2008, p. 2). Today, more than a century later, the situation is vastly different. Turner's essay not only led to a flood of work on the American frontier but inspired a massive outpouring of 'frontier studies' unbounded in space and time, from the Roman Empire and medieval Europe to Russian expansion to the Far East, the Chinese interaction with the nomads of Central Asia, the advance of both indigenous and colonial empires in Africa and Latin America, and European migration to what the League of Nations called the 'regions of recent settlement'. The Texas historian Walter Prescott Webb (1888–1963) extended the Turner thesis to take in the expansion of Europe overseas from the fifteenth century onwards in a 1952 work entitled *The Great Frontier* (Webb 1964), followed by William McNeill (1983) with a 1983 book bearing the same title. Another American, Owen Lattimore (1900–1989), did some of the most penetrating and widely influential work on this subject in his *Inner Asian Frontiers of China*, first published in 1940 (Lattimore 1940), and in a number of earlier deeply insightful essays and reviews published in 1962 as *Studies in Frontier History* (Lattimore 1962).

Unlike 'frontier' the word 'empire', at least since the middle of the last century, has had an almost entirely negative connotation. Empires are the product of 'imperialism' of one sort or another, all bearing the common feature of an unjust exploitation of native populations by political or economic entities associated with more technologically or militarily advanced societies, as exemplified by such otherwise diverse imperial agencies as the Roman legions, Mongol hordes or Dutch and British East India Companies. All empires create frontiers of conquest, marking the limits of expansion, which they then have to control and maintain to preserve what has been gained. In some cases the conquerors have a more advanced level of 'civilization' than the conquered, but at other times this can be reversed. The Romans were more advanced than the Gauls in the west of their empire, but acknowledged their cultural dependency on the Greeks in the east. The European colonial empires of the nineteenth century were more 'developed' than their subjects in Asia and Africa but the Mongols were superior to their Chinese or Persian subjects only in military organization and efficiency. While many frontiers have been created by conquest, others, while still depending to some extent on the exercise of force, have been formed by the extension of settlement by farmers or ranchers into relatively uninhabited forests or plains. Turner's frontier, for example, was the decentralized outcome of decisions to move west by thousands of individual families and small communities, rather than an organized state venture, though state support by Homestead Acts or the US Cavalry also played its part.

While it is essential to maintain this distinction between 'frontiers of conquest' and 'frontiers of settlement', it is also necessary to realize that they can to a large extent overlap in practice, with force often being exercised to protect settlement and settlement also being used to consolidate and support conquest. In addition, the same state or empire may have a frontier of conquest in one direction and a frontier of settlement in another. China, for example, had a frontier of conquest in the north against the formidable nomadic 'northern barbarians' of Central Asia and a frontier of settlement with the more sedentary 'southern barbarians' on the borders of what are now Myanmar, Laos and Vietnam. Lattimore (1962, p. 477) writes: 'Thus on the south and the north the Chinese created two contrasting frontiers.' After the formation of a unified imperial state in the third century BC he notes (Lattimore 1962, p. 98):

> Thereafter a limited range of action continued to constrict Chinese expansion along the northern frontier, but in the south the Chinese kept up throughout ensuing history and still keep up today a gradual but massive advance, carrying with them Chinese forms of agriculture and assimilating, socially, the non-Chinese peoples encountered.

Thus the northern frontier tended to be static, holding fixed defensive positions associated with the famous Great Wall, while in the south it was more dynamic in the Turner fashion, first absorbing the fertile Yangtze River valley and then extending rice cultivation ever further southward. The northern frontier of course also had to be settled, if only to provision the forces defending it, while the southern frontier required military intervention to secure the advancing zone of settlement from armed incursions by the indigenous peoples.

Concepts and Definitions

In 1928 the French historian Lucien Febvre (1878–1956), founder together with Marc Bloch of the hugely influential *Annales* school, wrote an article systematically deconstructing the word and concept '*frontière*' (see Febvre 1973, Chap. 9, for the English translation). He begins by pointing out that the word was used in two senses in the Middle Ages, both for the façade of a building and 'for the front line of troops disposed in battle formation facing the enemy' (Febvre 1973, p. 208). A text he cites from the year 1538, however, describing how the river Biesme 'separates the lands of France from those of the (Holy Roman) Empire' (Febvre 1973, p. 209) or Germany, clearly corresponds to our modern usage. As he says, 'the *frontières*[sic] here is still a front line, but it is no longer the front line of an army, it is that of a country' (Febvre 1973, p. 209). By 1690 *frontière* is explicitly defined in a dictionary as the 'extremity of a realm or a province which an enemy is faced with when it wants to enter' (Febvre 1973, p. 210), which neatly combines the narrow factual meaning of the word with its somewhat sinister military origins as the front line of an army or the façade of a fortress or stronghold.

Febvre briefly traces the evolution of frontiers between political entities from ancient to modern times. He notes that the clans or tribes of Gaul in pre-Roman times were separated from each other by stretches of forest, swamp and marsh just like in Africa during more recent times. In the Middle Ages fiefs and other feudal domains had overlapping jurisdictions, so that once again there were no clear lines of demarcation between the various socio-political units. Even as late as the seventeenth century, he writes (Febvre 1973, p. 214):

> We can read the great treaties negotiated by Louis XIV from one end to the other but we shall never find the word '*frontière*' or the word '*limite*' used in them. It was not territories that were annexed at that time. It was fiefs which were detached from one crown and attached to another, together with all that belonged to them and went with them, and which were not necessarily all one block.

It was not until the French Revolution that (Febvre 1973, p. 212)

> … the continuous demarcation line, the linear '*frontière*' which can be accurately identified, and all it is is the projection onto the ground of the external outlines of a nation fully conscious of itself, making it a point of honour, devoting all its might and power to ensuring the protection of a natural homogeneous territory, and in practice forbidding any foreign power … to violate its *frontière* …

As a consequence he states: 'In fact we should not study the frontier in itself. We should study and analyse it in relation to the state. Given a certain type of state we get a certain type of limit and, where necessary, a certain type of frontier in the military and political sense of the word' (Febvre 1973, p. 213).

Curzon also briefly considers the historical origins of frontiers. An important observation is that the Greek and Italian city-states developed in hilly regions with the different communities forming their bonds of citizenship in close proximity to one another, distinct from and often in conflict with the others. We may note, however, that this did not prevent them from forging a broader common cultural identity exemplified by the concept of *Hellas*, which was defined by a cultural and linguistic, rather than political, frontier. The great centralized empires of the east, in contrast, arose on plains or large river valleys, with no natural obstacles to restrain a successful conqueror from within the midst of the extensive region from unifying it under his control. When the Persian Empire attacked the Greek city-states even such mortal enemies as Athens and Sparta could unite to successfully oppose it. Ultimately, however, their lack of unity led them to all fall prey to a mountainous western frontier society, the Macedonian Empire of Philip and his son Alexander.

Both Curzon and Febvre devote considerable attention to the distinction between 'natural' and 'artificial' frontiers. The doctrine of natural frontiers as determinative of the boundaries of states is associated with the German political geographer Friedrich Ratzel (1844–1904). From this standpoint it is tempting to say, for example, that the Indian subcontinent, bounded by the Himalayas, the Baluchistan desert and the sea, is destined to constitute a single unified state; similarly, one could say that the kingdoms of England, Scotland and Wales would be combined eventually into a single 'United Kingdom' of Great Britain, bounded only by the sea, or that the Italian Peninsula would be a single sovereign state bounded by the Alps and the sea. This ignores the fact that for most of recorded history there was no such single sovereign state in any of these three areas. Furthermore there is the question of whether the incorporation of Ceylon, Ireland and Sicily into each of these potential unified states should be considered 'natural' or not. Febvre (1966, p. 309) emphatically states: 'The State is never Natural, but always Man-made.' He demolishes the popular notion that the natural frontiers of France were the Atlantic, the Rhine, the Alps and the Pyrenees by pointing out that these were the limits of ancient Gaul and thus not natural but historical frontiers (Febvre 1973, p. 215).

Curzon (2008, pp. 9–15) is more sympathetic to the idea of natural frontiers, in a careful consideration of seacoasts, rivers, mountain ranges and deserts as particular instances. He states that 'Of all natural frontiers the sea is the most uncompromising, the least alterable and the most effective', while also admitting that the sea in many cases, such as the Mediterranean, is 'not a barrier but a link' and that 'Indeed the Mediterranean in civilized times has never been the southern frontier of Europe; the latter has in reality been supplied by the Atlas Mountains and the great desert of Sahara' (Curzon 2008, p. 9). Deserts, he writes, were 'until modern times a barrier even more impassable than the sea' (Curzon 2008, p. 10), citing the instances of the Libyan and Sinai deserts protecting Egypt and the Nile valley from either side, the Gobi protecting China on its western frontier and the Sahara protecting Africa from European penetration until the circumnavigation of the Cape of

Good Hope. Mountain ranges, he claims, were the earliest, most durable and most imposing of barriers, but they of course are not impregnable because of the existence of passes. Mountain peoples from the Scots to the Afghans have also often been known for ravaging the lowlands of the states that have relied on the mountains themselves as barriers to more distant enemies. When it comes to rivers 'no frontiers are more natural' (Curzon 2008, p. 13), but then he also acknowledges that 'the teaching of history is that rivers connect rather than separate' (Curzon 2008, p. 14).

As far as 'artificial' frontiers are concerned, Curzon differentiates between ancient and modern. In the former category he places palisades or walls, such as the Great Wall of China and Hadrian's Wall, constructed to defend the inhabitants from potential enemies beyond and also to separate them from what might be regarded as pernicious foreign influences. He makes the important point that although these man-made barriers were not impregnable they were nevertheless for the most part and for long stretches of time effective in achieving their intended purpose. Another ancient example of an artificial frontier is the intermediary or neutral zone deliberately created between two powers to prevent unintended collisions between them. A related concept was the designation of 'marks' or 'marches' by a kingdom on its frontier areas with potentially hostile forces, ruled under a sort of martial law by specially appointed 'marcher lords' or 'wardens', from which various aristocratic titles such as marquis and margrave are derived. Notable examples are from the borders of England with Wales and Scotland, and of the Holy Roman Empire with the Slavs and Turks. Modern artificial frontiers have been largely determined by negotiation between the adjacent states, resorting to precise mathematical specification in terms of longitude and latitude, such as the 38th Parallel between North and South Korea or the 49th Parallel between Canada and the United States. Curzon (2008, p. 24) sums up his discussion of natural and artificial frontiers by stating that 'In practice the tendency of mankind has been to ignore or override nature' and that (Curzon 2008, p. 24)

> In Europe, apart from certain ranges of mountains (but few rivers), which being genuine barriers have exercised a permanent influence upon the formation of states and the distribution of men, the boundaries of the majority of states are purely political, and find their origin in the events of

> history although geographical conditions, such as the eligibility of elevated, or sterile or sparsely peopled tracts for frontier purposes, have not been without influence in their selection.

Curzon was thus basically in agreement with Febvre's later dictum that 'The State is never Natural, but always Man-made.'

Neither Curzon nor Febvre has much to say about the role of economics in the determination of frontiers. This gap in the literature on frontiers began to be filled with the work of W. K. Hancock on the economic history of the British Commonwealth during the interwar years 1918–1939. In his opening chapter, on what he calls a 'perspective view', he offers a brief but extremely valuable discussion of 'economic frontiers' (Hancock 1940, pp. 1–27). He opens by saying (Hancock 1940, pp. 2–3):

> In books dealing with European history, the frontier is something fixed. It is the sharp edge of a sovereign state. In books dealing with American history, the frontier is something moving. It is the advancing fringe of a dynamic society. The European frontier is fundamentally a political thing. The American frontier is primarily an economic thing.

Hancock here is referring not to the actual historical frontiers of Europe and America but to their representation in the literature of the frontiers, which is of course a very different thing. Clearly there are both economic and political frontiers on each continent, and both of them could be either fixed or moving, depending upon the particular moment in time at which they are being considered. Thus, the European frontier was clearly moving in the middle ages before it began to close, as is argued in a highly influential paper by Archibald Lewis (1958) on 'The Closing of the Medieval Frontier 1250–1350', while the American frontier was of course expanding rapidly westward until 1890, when it was closed by the consolidation of settlement on the Pacific coast, in the opinion of Turner himself. Hancock contrasts the landward extension by the Germans towards Poland and Russia of the medieval European frontier, which was primarily a frontier of cultivation backed up by the armed force of the Teutonic Knights, with the maritime frontier in the Mediterranean and the Atlantic that was first an Italian and then an Iberian enterprise motivated by the search for trading profits. As he is quick to note, however, Venice had to protect her trade by armed force as well as by settlement in Crete and other strategically located areas. He also compares Venetian pressure on the Byzantine Empire to British wringing of concessions out of China, in both cases to expand and secure trade.

Hancock's main subject, however, is the emergence of the British Empire after the 1815 victory in the Napoleonic Wars, which he traces ingeniously through the concept of a moving economic frontier generally advancing well ahead of the political one taking over the administration of the associated territories. The economic frontier is itself conceived as being driven by a *trading* frontier that by 1914 has covered the globe, pulling in its wake a mining frontier, a plantation frontier, an investment frontier, and a migration or settlement frontier far more restricted in scope to the temperate zones of both hemispheres; only when necessary to secure these other frontiers does the political frontier itself move. An instructive example is the Cape Colony of South Africa, taken from the Dutch to prevent it falling into French hands in order to secure the flow of intercontinental trade. When the Boers moved into the interior in search of land and native labor the colonial regime had to follow reluctantly to keep exploitation of the native population within tolerable limits. All the reluctance and grumbling about cost disappeared when diamonds and gold were discovered in the 1860s and 1880s, with the mining and investment frontiers jumping into the lead, much as had happened earlier in the United States with the 1849 gold rush in California when 'the miners' frontier reaches the Pacific coast in one long leap' (Hancock 1940, p. 4), with settlement only slowly catching up. In the case of Australia the settlement frontier briefly took the lead in response to the problems of coping with overpopulation and penal servitude before the trading frontier caught up with it by the expansion of wool exports based on the abundance of land for pasture. In the West Indies the lead was of course taken by the plantation frontier for sugar, with all the associated horrors of the slave trade—which Hancock calls a perversion of the migration frontier just as piracy is a perversion of the trading frontier—and then the plantation frontier moved to the cultivation of tea in Assam and Ceylon, rubber in Malaya and many other cash crops. All these various frontiers interact and overlap and to some extent compete with each other, and ultimately the economic frontier has to be considered as a whole, but Hancock's subdivision of the concept into these particular components is a valuable contribution to the literature of this subject.

While the study of frontiers has found its place in the fields of history, geography and political science, it has been almost completely ignored in economics. This is surprising since the extension of a frontier, whether 'political' or 'economic', always involves a use of scarce resources, providing both benefits and costs that have to be evaluated against each other, and is thus just another instance of the basic economic problem of 'the relationship between ends and scarce means that have alternative uses'. In Chapter 4 below the reader will find a 'Model of Territorial Expansion and the Limits of Empire' that formalizes the concept of a 'frontier of conquest' and in Chapter 8 a model of 'International Trade and Factor Mobility with an Endogenous Land Frontier' that does the same for the 'frontier of settlement'. Chapters 5, 6 and 7 essentially apply the 'conquest model' of Chapter 4 to three different historical episodes while the later chapters do similar things for the 'settlement model' of Chapter 8, but still reflecting the fact that the two types are complementary and not completely distinct from each other.

The Present Volume

The essays in the present volume have been written over a period of more than twenty years and from different perspectives, but they all have a common denominator: the frontier, established by conquest and/or settlement, and the explanations they offer are all based on economics. Our ambition has been to demonstrate how modern economic theory can be applied to a variety of historical situations and contribute to explaining different sequences of events in a rational way.

Chapter 2, *Frontiers and Empires in Historical Perspective*, serves to emphasize the applicability of the frontier concept in economic analysis. It presents a number of historical examples of empires and settlement episodes.

The first of our cases is Rome, the epitome of empire, as well as its rise and fall. It took more than 400 years just to rise from insignificant beginnings to the control of her immediate surroundings and the subsequent control over the entire Apennine Peninsula before Rome could embark on the expansion which converted the Mediterranean into the *Mare Nostrum*, finally extending into Britain in the northwest and Syria and Palestine in the east, to embrace a territory with 60 million people. The technically proficient Roman legions efficiently absorbed both land and people into the growing empire whose borders were anything but 'natural' and where in the end the centrifugal forces were greater than the centripetal.

The collapse of the Roman Empire eventually opened the road for the amazing Arab conquests ranging from the Atlantic coast into Central Asia in little more than a century, following the death of the Prophet in 632. In a situation full of tribal rivalry, head-on confrontation was avoided by turning the unified arms of the new religion outwards to conquer lands some of whose defenders had been weakened by the Plague of Justinian, imposing the Arab language and religion and building an efficient administration in the conquered territories. The end of the Arab expansion was marked by the battles of Poitiers, probably in 732, in the west, and of the Talas River, on the border between present-day Kazakhstan and Kyrgyzstan, in 751, in the east.

Beginning in 711 the Arabs conquered the Iberian Peninsula, without ever gaining complete control of it. They would remain in al-Andalus for almost eight centuries, but the territory they occupied was anything but static. They advanced northwards until the mid-eleventh century, establishing the Emirate (later Caliphate) of Córdoba. Thereafter the Spanish *Reconquista* began in earnest. The Arab territory gradually disintegrated into a large number of small *taifas* (party states) while the Christian part of the peninsula was consolidated and extended. By the mid-thirteenth century only the dependent kingdom of Granada remained in Moorish hands, until it fell in 1492. Two and a half centuries before, in 1250, Portugal had been reconquered.

Christian Europe also advanced on the northeastern frontier. By 1100 the Scandinavians and Saxons had been converted, which made it possible to advance in 'crusades' against Wends in the mid-twelfth century, against

Pomeranians and Livonians a few decades later, and against Prussians in the thirteenth century, the latter campaign carried out by the Teutonic Order. The Danes went into Estonia around the same time, while the Swedes had already begun their conquest of Finland, up to the Russian border, in the twelfth century. The last pagans to convert were the formidable Lithuanians, who did so on their own terms after the marriage of their Grand Duke Jogaila to Jadwiga, the heiress to the Polish throne, in 1386.

The Spanish Empire in America grew directly out of the *Reconquista.* Once the Moors had been expelled from the Iberian Peninsula in 1492 the Spanish momentum was directed overseas, spurred at first by the desire to obtain precious metals—in the Caribbean, in Mexico, in Peru and in Bolivia (but also by the desire to christen the pagans). Gold and silver were not, however, to be found everywhere, so with time conquest had to be followed by agricultural settlements, as in the Southern Cone of South America where the Argentine pampa was waiting to be exploited. At first, settlement was driven by the demand for foodstuffs in Upper Peru and on the Pacific coast. The Northwest was developed while the La Plata region remained undeveloped until European demand for animal products made for an expansion there as well. With the development of railroad transportation an efficient penetration became possible. Staple followed upon staple. Capital and immigrants flowed into the country. The frontier was pushed outwards until it was closed at the end of the nineteenth century.

North America constitutes another example of a settlement frontier. The British colonies on the Atlantic coast gradually expanded westwards, removing the Indians and outmaneuvering the French in the process. As European immigrants and African slaves arrived, first the Appalachians were reached and then the Mississippi. The Louisiana Purchase doubled the US territory and with the development of canals and railroads the West lay open for penetration, at the expense of the Indians, until the conquest was complete, the bison of the prairie had yielded to wheat fields and the frontier was closed at the end of the nineteenth century. The Canadian case differed from that of the United States. It built on cooperation between settlers and Indians in the beaver fur trade. With time, however, as lumber and wheat became the most important staples, penetration of the interior became inevitable in Canada as well, facilitated by the system of waterways extending across the continent. The Canadian Indians suffered the same fate as those further to the south.

The first frontier in South Africa was established by the arrival of the Dutch in 1652 and the foundation of the Cape Colony. The subsequent history of the European settlement is all about its north- and eastward movement, into African territory, spurred by the rift between Dutch and English which led to the Great Trek and the foundation of the Boer republics, before the discoveries of diamonds and gold turned the Transvaal into a magnet for both people and capital, strong enough to lead to the outbreak of the Boer War in 1899. Once that was over the South African frontier was more or less closed and the region was in British hands. As part of the same process Rhodesia was absorbed by Britain. Exactly as in South Africa, the land passed from the Africans to the Europeans.

The point of departure of Chapter 3, *Modeling Global Interdependence: Centers, Peripheries and Frontiers*, is the literature on convergence of the rates of economic growth of different economies. It is argued that this literature pays too little attention to the interaction and interdependence of these economies via trade, factor mobility and diffusion of technology. Convergence cannot be explained without reference to foreign direct investment, international migration and trade between different regions of the globe. Economic growth takes place in an international context and is influenced by it. By the same token, without an understanding of how the world economy was created and developed over time, our understanding of the convergence process is bound to be both incomplete and biased. Central to this process is the combination of a land (or sea) frontier that is being rolled back in a settlement process that involves capital movements and migration from more advanced economies to the frontier areas.

Chapter 4, *Towards a Model of the Territorial Expansion and the Limits of Empire*, presents the basic model of frontier expansion through conquest. The economic problem is how to maximize GDP in a situation where borders are not given but can be extended through the use of an army. The GDP is produced with the aid of labor and land, and labor can be used either for production or for fighting, in order to pull in more land. The optimum extension of empire is found when the marginal product of labor is the same in production and in fighting.

The basic model can be extended in various ways. One is by allowing for increasing returns to labor, in some interval, in fighting. This makes it possible to explain certain exceptional outbursts of military productivity and conquest. Another is by allowing not only land but also labor to be acquired through conquest, i.e. by letting the labor force be a function of the territory. A third extension consists in disaggregating production into agriculture and manufacturing, and making the manufactured good an input in the function determining the size of the empire, along with the size of the army. Again, equality of the values of the marginal product of labor is required, in three different uses. Finally, the fact that an army is fighting an enemy can be taken into account explicitly, by allowing the latter to have a similar economic structure. The extension of the empire will then be determined by the relative strength of the two combatants, as determined not only by their armies but also by the characteristics of their economies.

Chapter 5, *Demographic Shocks and the Factor Proportions Model: From the Plague of Justinian to the Black Death*, models the period in European history that extends from the Plague of Justinian in the mid-sixth century to the advent of the Black Death eight centuries later. It deals with the interplay of three empires: the Byzantine, the Arab and the Western European. The approach combines a Malthusian demographic mechanism with an endogenous land frontier. A long-run stationary state is defined which determines the available arable land as a function of the labor employed to establish the frontier and the population as a function of consumption, as well as the size of the labor force, total output and consumption. Since the arable land deteriorates over time, however, more land must be cleared for the stationary state to be maintained.

The stationary state of the model is subjected to four different shocks. The Plague of Justinian can be modeled as an instantaneous demographic collapse. This increases the wage and reduces the land rent. The amount of land cleared is reduced but increased output and consumption per capita ensure that both the labor force and the cultivated area grow back to their original level over time. Technological progress raises productivity and increases the rate of population growth, hence increasing both the labor force and the cultivated area. A lower cost of land clearance and a lower rate of depreciation of the land, in turn, have similar results.

A reduction of fertility, finally, will increase consumption and output per capita as a result of increased land abundance.

The model is used to shed some light on the performance of the three economic systems. In the Byzantine Empire the population reduction due to plague and loss of territory to the Arabs altered the wage/rent relation in favor of the workers and increased per capita income which translated into spending on defense. As the population started to grow back and recovery set in, the relative bargaining power began to shift in favor of the landowners and land concentration increased while the Fourth Crusade (with the sack of Constantinople) and new loss of land, to the Turks, pushed the frontier inwards, a process that ended with the fall of Constantinople in 1453.

The Islamic world expanded rapidly during the seventh and eighth centuries. The Arabs were not hit by the plague and could take advantage of this to extend their territory through northern Africa all the way to Spain in the west and into Central Asia and India in the east. Conquest was followed by cultivation and the introduction of new crops and new agricultural techniques in the conquered territories. This increased productivity, in turn, led to (modest) population growth and urbanization until the Mongol invasions opened a new chapter in the history of Islam.

In the longer run, the most successful of the three areas was Western Europe which in the fifteenth century had managed to christen the pagans in the north and east and drive the Muslims out of most of the Mediterranean area. Technological progress in agriculture made it possible to cultivate a larger area, pushing the forest back, and the merger of faith and warfare in the Christian military orders contributed to pushing the southern and eastern frontiers of Western Europe outwards. The Church took an active interest in both processes. The result was rapid population growth, and when both the cultivated area and the population grew, larger cities could be supported. During the thirteenth and fourteenth centuries both frontiers began to close, a famine hit an overpopulated territory in the early fourteenth century and a few decades later the Black Death struck.

Chapter 6, *The First Globalization Episode: The Creation of the Mongol Empire, or the Economics of Chinggis Khan*, attempts to explain how 1 million Mongols could create the world's largest contiguous empire. The first task was to create a Mongol nation from various nomadic tribes which were frequently in conflict with and preyed on one another. This situation called for the installation of a 'stationary bandit' ruler. Marauding bandits have no incentives to limit their take, but a stationary bandit who can tax the population has. For the bandit to be accepted, he must provide law and order through a bureaucracy which yields a positive contribution to production. He also distorts production incentives through taxation, however, which means that actual production falls short of the theoretical maximum. In order to maximize his tax revenue he must balance what he gets at the margin by increasing the tax rate against the loss of GDP generated by distorting taxation and balance the use of labor in direct production and in the bureaucracy.

The second question is whether law and order will be created at all. This is a public good which invites the citizens to be free riders. The amount of it is likely to be suboptimal from the point of view of society as a whole and it may not even pay to create it. A large number of individuals have to agree to cooperate and in the nomad Mongol society the risk that nothing would happen was high since no central power existed. It took the organizational talent of Chinggis Khan to create the institutions which made unification possible.

Once the Mongols had been united the conquests began. The marginal return to war was much higher than the marginal return to production on the inhospitable Mongolian steppe. Chinggis Khan organized his armies in such a way as to take advantage of the existence of the segment of increasing returns and he had access to the best war technology of his day—the Mongol bow—and superior tactics. The Mongols conquered a huge chunk of the then known world, a chunk which was too small in the sense that they could presumably have gone on even further had it not been for the death of Ögödei in 1241 and the necessity to elect a new khan, but too big in the sense that it was not possible to occupy it permanently.

Chapter 7, *Towards a Factor Proportions Approach to Economic History: Population, Precious Metals and Prices from the Black Death to the Price Revolution*, continues the analysis of Chapter 5. It presents a stock-flow model which is used to shed light on the consequences of the bubonic plague of the mid-fourteenth century and the inflow of silver to Europe from Spanish America during the fifteenth and sixteenth centuries.

The core of the chapter is a general equilibrium model specifically designed to be able to analyze demographic and monetary shocks. The model has two production sectors, one for goods and one for a commodity money such as silver. Labor and capital (accumulated stock of goods) are used to produce goods, and labor and a natural resource ('mines') to produce silver. Population and hence labor supply are endogenously determined by a Malthusian mechanism balancing fertility and mortality as functions of the real wage. Consumers demand not only the domestically produced good but also 'eastern luxuries' that have to be paid for with silver. The stocks of money and capital are endogenously determined by equations balancing their supply and demand. The relative price of silver and goods (the same as the price level of goods in terms of silver in this model) in the long-run steady state must be at a level that is consistent with equilibrium in the asset markets for both goods and silver as well as with the flow supplies and demands for each of them.

Suppose now that a considerable fraction of the population and hence the labor supply is lost as a result of a demographic shock such as the Black Death. At the outset there will be a rise in the real wage which will cause population to slowly start rising again by the Malthusian mechanism. Output of goods as well as silver falls because of the reduction in labor supply. Thus, real GDP falls. By quantity theory reasoning, MV is constant while Q (real GDP) falls, so p, the price level of goods in terms of silver, must rise, but this is equivalent to a fall in the relative price of silver in terms of goods, so the output of silver will fall even further. Since per capita incomes have risen, the demand for eastern luxuries and hence flow demand for silver will also rise, creating an excess flow demand for silver which has to be met by a reduction in the stock of silver, i.e. the money supply, resulting in what monetary historians have called the 'bullion famine of the fifteenth century'.

But with M now falling and Q rising (because of the recovery in labor supply) p must start falling. This means that the relative price of silver in terms of goods is rising, enhancing the recovery in the flow supply of silver. With per capita income now slowly falling, because of diminishing returns to the recovery of population, the initial excess demand for silver is slowly eroded until it turns into an excess supply and the money supply starts to expand again until it returns to its original level along with all the other variables of the model. The Price Revolution of the sixteenth century is modeled as an increase in 'mines', e.g. the 'silver mountain' of Potosí, in other words an extension of the 'mining frontier' across the Atlantic into the New World. It is shown that this will lead to inflation from the influx of American silver, consistently with the experience of the Price Revolution. In the new long-run steady state population, money supply and capital stock will all increase in the same proportion as the exogenous supply of 'mines'.

It is not possible to disentangle the relative importance of the Black Death and the inflow of silver on the long swings of the price level because the effects of the two partly overlap in time. Prices were already on the rise in Europe before the inflow of silver from the New World began, but, of course, the inflow reinforced the inflationary trend. This is precisely what our model indicates.

Chapter 8, *International Trade and Factor Mobility with an Endogenous Land Frontier: Some General Equilibrium Consequences of Christopher Columbus*, analyzes the impact of the European discovery of America. A general equilibrium model is constructed which allows for a characterization of the economy that had emerged as a result of this discovery by the end of the nineteenth century. In Europe two kinds of goods are produced: food (using land and labor, both in fixed supply) and manufactures (using labor, capital, in perfectly elastic supply, and a raw material, in fixed supply). The fixed supply of land and raw material acts as a constraint on production and makes for diminishing returns to labor and a declining income per capita. This is the situation before the discovery of the New World. In America, land is available but it can only be put under the plow at an increasing cost in terms of capital. Together with labor the 'improved' land can be used to produce food or the raw material. All labor is immigrant labor from Europe. Capital is also perfectly mobile, which means that factor prices will be equalized across the Atlantic. The price of food in terms of the raw material is given. The general equilibrium of the world economy can then be determined: production, factor employment and migration, as well as relative prices and factor rewards.

This equilibrium is subjected to two exogenous shocks. The first consists in an increase in the labor force. With a given relative price of food and raw material, the production of the latter in the New World will remain unchanged. For the same reason the wage rate in Europe does not change. Food production there remains constant. The European demand for raw material, however, will be affected. In the absence of migration the increase in the labor force must go into manufacturing, and capital will be added, which in turn calls for additional raw material, since the model assumes a constant relation between manufacturing output and raw material use. Raw material production will then increase in America, leading to emigration of workers from the Old to the New World. Raw material production, which is more labor-intensive than food production, expands and food production is reduced when the immigrants arrive. Since food production has not changed in Europe, the world production of food has declined, while the demand for it has increased because both the labor force and the capital stock have increased and factor prices have not changed. Hence the price of food will increase in terms of the raw material. The return to land (used intensively in food production) will increase and the wage rate will fall. More labor will be employed in European agriculture and world food output will increase. The increased return to land will in turn lead to an extension of the frontier in America.

The second shock is an industrial revolution in Europe, modeled as technological progress in manufacturing which increases the marginal productivity of labor and capital in the same proportion. It is shown that with a constant price of food in terms of the raw material and a constant real wage in terms of food this will increase the capital intensity in manufacturing and the price of the raw material in terms of manufactures. Output per worker increases in the sector but employment remains constant. Under the same assumption employment and production of food in Europe will remain constant. The higher output in manufacturing calls for more raw material. Again labor will emigrate from Europe to America where raw material production once more increases and food production falls. As a result of technical progress and a higher capital intensity in European manufacturing, world income has increased and this will increase the demand for food and hence the food price. The return to land increases and stimulates an expansion of the frontier.

Chapter 9, *Natural Resources, 'Vent-for-Surplus' and the Staples Theory*, merges three approaches to international trade with the aid of the endogenous land frontier: the vent-for-surplus approach of Adam Smith, revived by Hla Myint, where trade serves to stimulate an exploitation of hitherto idle resources; the staples theory of growth, where international trade in raw materials stimulates factor movements and growth; and the conventional Heckscher-Ohlin factor proportions approach. The chapter is based on a number of concrete staples cases, divided into three categories: regions of recent settlement, plantation economies, and peasant export economies. The first category consists of the 'European' settlements in North America, the Southern Cone of South America, Southern Africa, Australia and New Zealand. Our examples are Canada (cod and furs), the United States (cotton and grain), Argentina (meat and other foodstuffs) and Australia (gold and wool). The plantation economies may be exemplified by Malaya (rubber) and Costa Rica (coffee and bananas). The Gold Coast (cocoa) and Burma (rice) were staple-exporting peasant economies. In all cases, staples are defined as goods in high international demand based on a natural resource and with a value high enough to make transoceanic shipments feasible.

These cases provide the background for a formal specific factors model. Two goods are produced: primary products with the aid of land and labor; and manufactures, using capital and labor. Land can be used only after having been developed with the use of capital, and the frontier is fixed by the condition that the rate of return on clearing must equal the rate of interest. When this economy is opened to trade the price of primary products rises and their production increases while that of manufactures falls and the frontier is extended. The production of primary goods increases once more. Opening the economy may also lead to access to capital at a lower rate of interest, as it did during the nineteenth century. This serves to increase the capital-labor ratio in manufacturing and to raise the real wage which in turn increases the land-labor ratio in agriculture and depresses the land rent. If the latter falls less than proportionally to the rate of interest, however, it will be profitable to increase the land frontier.

When trade is opened, labor moves from manufacturing to primary production. Possibly the demand emanating from the latter sector will then be larger than the labor force in the former. The solution to this is immigration. The sequence where trade and extension of the frontier led to massive immigration was common in the historical perspective.

In many cases the manufacturing sector did not exist when trade was opened, for example in the tropical economies. Economic activities were limited to subsistence cultivation. In this case, when trade is opened and capital becomes available at a given rate of interest, a transition may take place to the production of a primary export commodity. This may entail clearing land before production can take place. The producer must then borrow to cover his consumption expenditure up to the point where the return from his cleared land equates the rate of interest at which he can borrow. The rational peasant will equate his marginal net income from cash crop production on cleared land with what he obtains at the margin in subsistence cultivation. This determines the frontier.

Chapter 10, *Resource-Led Growth—A Long-Term Perspective: The Relevance of the 1870–1914 Experience for Today's Developing Economies*, examines the experience of a number of staples-producing countries during the 'golden age' of Heckscher-Ohlin trade: exchange of European manufactures for primary products mainly from North America but also from other areas of the globe. Movements of labor and capital, mainly but not exclusively from Europe to North America and other 'regions of recent settlement', were an important part of the picture. The chapter examines fifteen different instances of staples exports, divided among the regions of recent settlement, three varieties of tropical countries—plantation economies, mixed economies and peasant economies—and finally, mineral economies.

The theoretical aspects of the regions of recent settlement story are mainly those covered by the 'Christopher Columbus model' of Chapter 8 and our staples model from Chapter 9. Our empirical cases from the regions of recent settlement are Canada, the United States, Australia and Argentina. The history of Canada is the history of the creation of linkages from cod fishing, furs and wheat to manufacturing. The United States provides another example of how linkages emanating from staples production created a diversified economy with cotton in the south, wheat in the west and manufactures in the east as the three main ingredients through a process that involved the extension of the frontier. In Australia the stimulus to the frontier extension on the outback came from gold and wool and their production also attracted a substantial number of immigrants. Argentina, finally, exported a number of staples from the livestock and farming sectors. In all four cases, economic expansion rested on the development of a frontier.

The growth process of the tropical economies may be thought of in terms of a dual economy with a hinterland with a given wage rate and a modern export sector with plantations, commercial farms or mines. The constraint on this system is the development of world demand for the exportables. If this grows too slowly, profits and capital accumulation will suffer. The high demand for staples that characterized the 1870–1914 period made it possible to escape this trap. Trade served as an engine of growth along the lines of our staples model in Chapter 9. The growth of Brazil rested on coffee, rapid immigration and quick development of the frontier. Costa Rica also produced coffee and when the decision was made to construct a railroad from the capital to the Atlantic coast, bananas were grown along the line to help finance it, a linkage from one staple to another. Colombia was a country where smallholders grew coffee which created a demand for simple domestic manufactures. In Ceylon the important staples of tea, coconut products and rubber yielded increasing incomes as the cultivated area of the colony was extended and immigrants arrived from India. In Malaya rubber was the main staple, grown on both large and small farms. It was complemented by tin.

Many but by no means all staples were introduced from the outside. Burma was a long-standing rice producer in the mid-nineteenth century when the British took over and the Suez Canal was opened. Cultivation could easily be extended to Lower Burma. Labor moved in from the north and from India. Moneylenders and Europeans provided the capital. Burma rapidly became the world's number one rice exporter. Nearby Siam was a parallel case, with migrant workers and unused land. In the Gold Coast cocoa—a foreign crop—was king. The colony became the world's leading cocoa exporter. Production rested on migrant labor and European capital.

In the case of mineral exporters the frontier is vertical. In Bolivia the first staple, silver, went through a crisis but revived during the period under consideration here. Silver mining created a backward linkage to agriculture—food—and another to railroad construction, which in turn played an important role in the development of Bolivia's second mineral staple: tin. Chile conquered the area where its future staple—nitrate—was located. Nitrate had linkages. Given the geographical shape of Chile and the location of nitrates in the north, food was needed and railways had to be developed; some of the proceeds of nitrate taxes were spent on education and nitrate incomes provided a market for domestic industrial goods. In South Africa, finally, diamonds and gold brought both people and capital from abroad and the transport network had to be extended to ensure that people and goods could be brought to the mineral fields and back. Mining incomes also provided the market for a growing manufacturing sector.

Staples-led growth as such was vulnerable to changing demand and did not always result in linkages that spread growth across a wider segment of the economy. It repeatedly led to enclave creation—export sectors without much contact with the rest of the economy. The staples approach allows for a variety of outcomes. Sectors interact in various ways and the interaction isn't always strong. Much depends on the institutional setting and the technical characteristics of the activities in question. Among the cases examined by us, by and large, the regions of recent settlements managed to develop an industrial sector while the other economies failed.

The 1870–1914 experience was unique. It built on a frontier, something that hardly exists today, on mass migration, also vastly more difficult these days, and on rapid development of transportation technology, not likely to be repeated either. Primary inputs play a much less important role today and time-honored primary specialization may make a switch into high-yielding manufacturing difficult. Primary specialization may even serve to put a brake on industrialization and it may stimulate conflict between different groups over natural resource rents. Moving into industry and from there climbing the industrial ladder requires a degree of increasing technical sophistication that usually does not exist in poor primary-producing economies. It has often been easier for low-income economies without natural resources to industrialize than for economies with abundant resources. The degree of success has, however, also been conditioned by the policy choices made. Foreign trade served to increase the rate of growth during the 1870–1914 period, given the circumstances that prevailed in the international economy during that period. Thereafter, however, a number of our cases made policy choices that either precluded industrialization or made the industrialization process inefficient.

Chapter 11, *Lampião and the Colonels: On the Political Economy of Banditry*, deals with the establishment of an 'interior' frontier—a state within the state, as it were. The setting is northeast Brazil in the 1920s and 1930s, when the greatest of the Brazilian *cangaceiros* (bandits)—Lampião—was able to dominate an area the size of Italy for close to twenty years. The chapter seeks an explanation of how it was possible for a relatively small band to hold such a large territory for so long. It questions some of the more common explanations of banditry, those which hold that the *cangaceiros* were 'social' bandits of the Robin Hood type or avengers of some past wrongdoing. Our alternative explanation rests on simple income maximization. The bandits were bandits in order to make a living, since in their physical environment, the sertão, the alternatives were few, and they chose a band size that fell short of maximum combat strength but which maximized their incomes.

The *cangaceiros* did not act in a social vacuum but interacted with other groups. The first consisted of the so-called *coronéis* (colonels), local political bosses who delivered votes to higher levels in the regional and national political system in exchange for pecuniary and political favors. They had good reasons for courting the *cangaceiros*. The latter constituted what in game theory is known as a credible threat to anybody in their immediate neighborhood and contracting them was a weapon in the political game which consisted in maximizing the number of votes for a certain candidate. They had no interest in getting rid of the bandits.

The general population was faced with a somewhat unpalatable choice: supporting the bandits or supporting the police. To what extent should it collaborate with either of these two groups? Both would prey on them and both would exact punishment for failing to cooperate. Usually the cost-benefit calculation of the common man resulted in more support for the bandits than for the police and the military. As the historical evidence demonstrates, the latter failed to protect the population. They yielded no benefits—only costs. The bandits occasionally did and, above all, their vengeance was worse than that of the police.

The fourth player was of course the police and their logic was more or less identical to that of the bandits. The fact that *cangaceiros* were around meant that funds would be provided, funds that could either be pocketed or spent on combat strength. The former turned out to be the preferred alternative with the result that the police tended to avoid fights with the bandits.

Thus, the support of the local political bosses and the population in general, in combination with the choice of both potential combatants to avoid potentially disastrous fighting, made for a low-intensity war situation where the police duly followed the tracks of the bandits but avoided direct contact whenever possible and the bandits avoided presenting major challenges.

In the end, however, the *cangaceiros* were wiped out. When the political situation in Brazil began to swing in favor of a strong central government and little local autonomy the bandits were seen as an anachronism and a nuisance in general. The modern state and society created by Getúlio Vargas in the 1930s had no room for them, and once the decision was made to fight them in earnest they stood no chance.

Chapter 12, *Epilogue: Frontiers—Theory and History*, finally, pulls together the threads that run through the book: the concepts, the historical episodes and the theoretical approaches employed to model the various frontier episodes dealt with in Chapters 2, 3, 4, 5, 6, 7, 8, 9, 10 and 11 and discusses how these episodes relate to each other.

References

Curzon, George N. (Lord Curzon of Kedleston). (2008). *Frontiers. The Romanes Lecture 1907*. Gloucester: Dodo Press.

Febvre, Lucien. (1966). *A geographical introduction to history*. New York: Barnes and Noble.

Febvre, Lucien. (1973). *A new kind of history from the writings of Lucien Febvre*. Edited by Burke, P. London: Routledge & Kegan Paul.

Hancock, W. K. (1940). *Survey of British commonwealth affairs, volume II: Problems of economic policy 1918–1939, Part I*. London: Oxford University Press.

Lattimore, Owen. (1940). *Inner Asian frontiers of China*. New York: American Geographical Society.

Lattimore, Owen. (1962). *Studies in frontier history. Collected papers 1928–1952.* London/New York: Oxford University Press.

Lewis, Archibald R. (1958). The closing of the medieval frontier 1250–1350. *Speculum, 33*, 475–483.

McNeill, William H. (1983). *The great frontier: Freedom and hierarchy in modern times*. Princeton: Princeton University Press.

Turner, Frederick Jackson. (1893). The significance of the frontier in American history. *Primary Sources. Workshops in American History.* https://www.learner.org/workshops/primarysources/corporations/docs/turner.html. Downloaded 1 Feb 2016.

Turner, Frederick Jackson. (1920). *The frontier in American history*. New York: Henry Holt.

Webb, Walter Prescott. (1964). *The great frontier*. Austin: University of Texas Press.

2

Frontiers and Empires in Historical Perspective

The aim of the present chapter is to point to a variety of historical frontiers in the Old and New Worlds in order to indicate that the applicability of the basic models that we present is global in scope and not confined to the particular cases examined later in this volume. Completeness is not the idea. It is obvious that there are innumerable historical frontier episodes: ancient Egypt, Assyria, Persia, the Macedonian Empire, China, the Byzantine and Ottoman Empires, the Portuguese and Dutch seaborne empires, the Russian expansion in Siberia as well as the latter-day expansion of the Communist bloc, Australia, the changing map of Europe, and the European colonization of India and East and West Africa, to mention but a few of the instances we will not attempt to cover here. That is hardly necessary. A few well-chosen examples should suffice.

Original chapter for the present volume by Ronald Findlay and Mats Lundahl.

R. Findlay, M. Lundahl, *The Economics of the Frontier*,
DOI 10.1057/978-1-137-60237-4_2

The Roman Empire

We begin our discussion with the Roman Empire not simply because it was so extensive in both space and time but because 'in some senses it was an archetypal one' (Woolf 2001, p. 312), inspiring all subsequent empires in the European and Islamic worlds, from Charlemagne and Charles V to Mussolini and Hitler. As we have seen from our references to Lord Curzon, British empire-builders, drawing on their classical education, consciously saw themselves as following in the footsteps of their Roman predecessors. Russian rulers, from the Romanovs to Putin, have seen their empire as the 'Third Rome'. Even the United States has long been seen as the modern successor to the Roman Empire.

The Romans traced the founding of their state by Romulus and Remus, the mythical 'sons of the she-wolf', to 753 BC (Grandazzi 1997, p. 151). Early Rome was small and weak, dominated by the powerful Etruscans from north of the Tiber, but it eventually grew into one of the more successful city-states of the Italian Peninsula (Cornell 1995). It was not until 338 BC, however, after she had subdued and absorbed the neighboring states of Latium and Campania, that Rome truly began her illustrious imperial career. The entire peninsula fell under her domination, and victory over the rival North African empire of Carthage in the Punic Wars gave her control of the western Mediterranean (David 1997; Bagnall 1999). Leadership in the early republic was in the hands of two elected consuls, subject to strict 'term-limits' of one year each. By the last century BC, however, power had fallen increasingly into the hands of wealthy oligarchs such as Crassus and Lepidus, and victorious generals like Pompey and Julius Caesar (Gruen 1974). The ultimate victor in the bloody power struggles between these individuals was Caesar's nephew and adopted son Octavian, who was eventually crowned as the Emperor Augustus. The empire that he founded was to last in one form or another for the next five centuries, covering all of Europe west of the Rhine and south of the Danube, the entire Mediterranean basin, Africa north of the edges of the Sahara, and Syria and Palestine in the east. The population at its height was about 60 million (Rosenstein 1999, p. 193):

> War and conquest were the hallmarks of Republican Rome. Nearly every year for almost five hundred years, the city's armies marched off to war;

> their efforts won Rome first hegemony in central Italy, then dominance within the peninsula, and finally rule over the length and breadth of the ancient Mediterranean.

'How and why was the small city-state on the Tiber able to successfully launch such a sustained expansion' (Findlay and O'Rourke 2012, p. 564)? Were the Romans 'born to be wolves', blindly following some innate predatory instinct defined by their mythical ancestry? Did their frontiers advance merely because they defended themselves against unprovoked attacks by a succession of powerful neighbors, as implausibly maintained by a long line of distinguished authorities?

Modern scholarship, largely following the lead of William Harris (1979), has convincingly demonstrated that the answers can be found in certain structural and institutional features of the socio-political system of the Roman Republic that created and sustained the drive for expansion, and innovations in military organization and tactics that gave them what Douglass North (1981, p. 21) called the 'comparative advantage in violence' necessary to overcome all rivals. The main avenue to *gloria*, *fama* and *dignitas* for the two consuls during their single annual terms would be to lead their fellow-citizens in a campaign against a neighboring state during the off-season, with victory bringing not only the crowning laurel leaves of the ceremonial 'triumph' but slaves and booty as well as land that could be distributed to the community. Since the conquered neighbors were in many cases not expelled or exterminated, but instead given Roman citizenship, the pool of farmer-soldiers was increased, creating a larger base of food supply and military manpower in an ever-expanding virtuous circle. Competition between ambitious individuals and families of the aristocratic elite ensured that this process would be continually sustained, while the redistributed land secured the support of the plebeian class as well.

A crucial feature of the alliance system between Rome and her Italian neighbors was that the only obligation placed on the latter was not payment of taxes or tribute but military assistance, the provision of troops whenever she went to war. Thus Rome had either to 'use or lose' this particular diplomatic asset in her possession. These potential additional military resources made war for additional land, slaves and booty an attractive option compared to the *status quo*, and since the gains would be shared with the allies—a 'win-win' proposition for the alliance as a whole—the bellicose bias imparted to the state by the structure of the internal political system was enhanced (Beard and Crawford 1999, p. 74).

This openness and inclusiveness with respect to citizenship was a unique attribute of Rome in the ancient world, in marked contrast to the rigid exclusiveness of all the Greek city-states, including Athens and Sparta. Citizenship granted to the allied people was not originally 'full' or exactly the same as that enjoyed by the Romans themselves. The various degrees of 'second-class citizenship' created simmering resentment that ultimately erupted into the fierce conflict known as the Social War, lasting from 91 to 89 BC. Rome defeated the rebellious allies in the war but found it expedient to grant them full citizenship rights in the end. The number of Roman citizens was increased threefold at a stroke, to 'something over a million' and 'Italy was now the closest thing to a nation state that the classical world ever knew' (Beard 2015, p. 239).

The basic Roman military unit, the famous 'legion', was a more flexible and adaptable version of the hoplite phalanx, inherited from the Greeks and the Macedonians. Whereas the phalanx was always a single collective entity the legion was sub-divided into smaller units, cohorts and maniples or 'handfuls', just as modern armies have their 'divisions' sub-divided into battalions, companies, platoons and squads. Each of these sub-units could either operate on its own, or combine into the legion as a whole, or form an intermediate unit, the cohort, generally consisting of three maniples. The cumbersome long spears and big shields of the phalanx were replaced by the smaller and lighter *scutum*, the short sword or *gladius* for thrusting and slashing at close quarters and the *pilum* or javelin as a missile weapon, thrown in a coordinated volley for maximum effectiveness (Webster 1998; Le Bohec 2000).

The Romans were also unrivaled as military engineers, their skill at building roads, bridges and fortified camps enabling them to secure the advantage of mobility even in difficult terrain. These advantages enabled them to defeat larger concentrations of Celtic and Germanic tribal warriors on their western and northern frontiers despite the individual courage and prowess of those warriors. On the eastern frontiers the mounted archers of the Parthians and other steppe peoples were more difficult opponents (Isaac 1992).

The legions in the early years of the republic were manned by citizen-soldiers, farmers serving unpaid during the off-season of the agricultural cycle, providing their own food and weapons. This worked only when wars were confined to nearby areas and were of short duration. As the empire expanded, soldiers had to serve on longer campaigns over greater distances, and this required monetary payment in the form of the *stipendium*, financed by a sort of war-tax, the *tributum.* Rosenstein (1999, p. 201) argues that this solution 'not only solved the immediate problem but also set in motion a series of changes that fundamentally altered the nature of Roman warfare'. The army evolved from being one based on citizen-soldiers owning their own small farms to one based on payment to men from the ranks of the landless rural proletariat, who were increasingly recruited not only from the rest of Italy but from distant western and eastern provinces of the empire. The Augustan legions consisted of professionals signing up for as long as twenty-five years, after which they could use their pensions to buy small farms if they so wished. The army became more skilled and specialized but at the expense of weakening the vital cohesion between army and society that had been a fundamental strength of the early republic. This process finally culminated in the 'outsourcing' of the military function to barbarian tribes that ultimately led to the decline and fall of the empire (Watson 1969; Southern and Dixon 1996; Le Bohec 2000).

At its maximum extent the Roman Empire stretched from the Atlantic in the west, to the Rhine and the Danube in the north, the Euphrates in the east, and the upper reaches of the Nile, the Sahara Desert and the Atlas Mountains in the south. Were the limits of the empire thus determined by these 'natural frontiers' of oceans, rivers, deserts and mountains? C.R. Whittaker (1994) devotes most of his book to a vigorous refutation of this idea. He points out that the ocean did not stop the Romans from taking Britain up to the border with Scotland marked by Hadrian's Wall which is an 'artificial' and not a natural frontier; the Rhine and the Danube were regularly patrolled on the far sides and frequently crossed, while it was the strength of the Parthian and Sassanid Empires and not the Euphrates and the Syrian Desert that confined the Roman Empire in the east. Augustus intended to drive deep into eastern Germany well beyond the Rhine and only pulled back after three legions were ambushed and destroyed in the Teutoburg Forest by the Romanized German chieftain Arminius in 9 AD (Wells 2003). Trajan went beyond the Danube to conquer Dacia in what is now Romania and beyond the

Euphrates in what is now Iran before again pulling back because these gains could not be sustained against formidable military opposition rather than because of any geographical obstacles.

The alternative hypothesis that Whittaker enthusiastically adopts is Owen Lattimore's idea that empires expand until the 'centripetal gain' of further expansion is offset by the 'centrifugal loss'. It is not that these geographical features are irrelevant or unimportant but that they influence the extent of empire through their effect on the calculus of benefit and cost and not as impassable or impenetrable obstacles in their own right. Whittaker also follows Lattimore in insisting that the frontier is not a linear boundary but a band or zone in which the empire exercises only a very loose or indirect control. Lattimore's approach is the basis of our 'conquest model' of Chapter 4. Luttwak (1976, pp. 22–23), in his two models of empire, in turn, distinguishes between a 'territorial empire' in which the entire area is directly administered, and a 'hegemonic empire' in which the 'zone of direct control' is bordered by an 'inner zone' of diplomatic influence over client states and an 'outer zone' of looser influence over client tribes, with the latter model corresponding to the Roman case.

Islam and the Arab Conquests

How are we to account for the speed and extent of the Arab conquests that spread Islam from its birthplace in the Arabian Peninsula to the Atlantic coasts of North Africa and Spain in the west to the heart of Central Asia in the east, in the short time span from 632 to 750? First, we can ask what structural features of the society of that region contributed to this astonishing success and, second, what were the weaknesses of the surrounding states from which the Arabs wrenched these vast territories, namely the Eastern Roman or Byzantine Empire and the Persian Sasanian Empire.[1]

The opposition between nomadic and sedentary life, or between the 'desert and the sown', is one of the central themes of world history.

[1] In attempting to answer these questions we rely in particular on the recent works of Hugh Kennedy (2007) and Robert Hoyland (2015).

Despite their opposition and frequent conflict it is apparent that the two modes of human existence are mutually complementary, each needing the other to develop its full potential. This was particularly true in the case of Arabia and the emergence of Islam. Mecca and Medina, the two poles of the Prophet Mohammed's life, were cities based on trade and agriculture. The Bedouin nomads of the interior depended on the cities for grain and manufactures in exchange not only for their livestock products but also for their military and long-distance transport services, based on their mobility provided by the horse and, in particular, by the single-humped camel or dromedary. The merchants and farmers of the settled communities also provided leadership and organization for the management of collective projects, such as shrines, fairs and caravan journeys. According to Hugh Kennedy (2007, p. 45), 'It was this symbiosis of settled leadership and nomad military power which formed the foundation of the armies of the early Muslim conquests.'

Another important aspect of Arabian society was its tribal nature. Competition and conflict between the tribes tended to be the norm, which made some of them dependent on the Byzantines, like the Ghassanids, or on the Sasanians, like the Lakhmids, each serving their respective patrons as auxiliaries and border guards. By the time of the Prophet's death in 632, however, the new religion of Islam had largely unified the Arab tribes after a number of intertribal conflicts known as the *ridda* wars (*ridda* meaning apostasy of the tribes that did not adhere to Islam) had been settled during the last years of his life. This unity was nevertheless very fragile, and the destructive divisions could easily have been resumed. The first four 'rightly guided' successors, or *caliphs,* Abu Bakr (632–634), Umar (634–644), Uthman (644–656) and Ali (656–660), all based in Medina, were able to avoid disintegration by turning the tribal energies outwards under the banner of Islam against the Christian Byzantines and the Zoroastrian Sasanians. As Kennedy (2007, p. 57) points out: 'The only way of avoiding an implosion was to direct the Muslims against the non-Muslim world.'

The Muslim armies were never large, seldom more than a few thousand strong. Their equipment was simple but effective. 'The principal weapon was the sword. The early Arab sword was not the curved scimitar of popular imagination but a broad, straight, two-edged blade with a small hilt' (Kennedy 2007, p. 58). Spears were used, on horseback and on foot. Unlike steppe warriors such as the Turks and the Mongols, the Arabs were not mounted archers. They rode camels and horses but the battles were usually fought on foot. Chain mail was available but it was beyond the means of most of the warriors, who provided their own weapons, mounts and even food. Their principal military asset was the mobility provided by horse and camel. In his article 'The Role of the Camel and the Horse in the Early Arab Conquests', Donald Routledge Hill (1975, p. 42) concludes that 'The superior mobility of the Arabs was … one of the most important factors in ensuring their success in the early conquests. In a wider context it can be stated with confidence that, without the domestication of the dromedary, the conquests could never have been undertaken at all.'

The Arab marching speed was remarkable, about forty miles a day for an army as a whole, with couriers and messengers covering up to 100 miles (Hill 1975, p. 34). They were used to moving at night, when the desert is cooler, and used this advantage to launch surprise attacks under cover of darkness. They also used the desert as a refuge into which to withdraw safely after reverses and defeats. The effective constraint on the size of the early armies appears to have been scarcity of mounts rather than of manpower itself, but their victories and spoils soon put more of the essential animals at their disposal. In addition they were able to equip themselves much better with the weapons they captured from their Byzantine and Sasanian opponents.

Motivation and morale seem to have been very strong in the early Arab armies. This is usually seen as resulting from the inspiration provided by Islam, but economic gain—booty and plunder—must also have been a strong motivating factor. The units of the army seem to have been organized along tribal lines, each fighting under its own standard, competing fiercely with one another in pursuit of the glory of victory. Central direction from the caliphs in Medina, and later Damascus and Baghdad, was always present and a unified command generally prevailed. The quick initial successes brought many Christians, Jews and adherents of other religions to their side. There are well-known instances of Slavs deserting from the Byzantine army and of elite Persian cavalry units deserting from the Sasanians.

Finally, we may note that the early Arab armies were led by a succession of extraordinarily able commanders, most of them drawn from the Quraysh tribe of the Prophet himself. Foremost among them was Khalid ibn al-Walid from Mecca, the 'Sword of God', who had led the armies that crushed the tribal opposition within Arabia during the *ridda* wars and consolidated Islamic rule among the Arab tribes living west of the Euphrates before joining the army that conquered Syria and Palestine.

Turning to the weaknesses of the surrounding states, as stressed in Chapter 5 below, a major factor was the devastation caused to the more settled communities by the Plague of Justinian in the sixth century, from which the far more sparsely populated Arabian Peninsula escaped largely unscathed. Perhaps even more important, however, was the enormous damage caused by the prolonged wars between the Byzantine Emperor Heraclius (610–641) and the Sasanian Shah Khusrau (Chosroes) II (590–628) during the first three decades of the seventh century (Treadgold 1997, pp. 287–307). The Persians were initially victorious, driving the Byzantines out of Syria, Palestine and Egypt before they recovered to impose a devastating defeat on Khusrau II in 628, after which he was murdered by an aristocratic faction at his court. Order in the empire was restored by his grandson Yazdgard III (632–651), who turned out to be the last ruler of the Sasanian Dynasty that had come to power in 224.

The Arab forces began the occupation of Syria and Palestine in 633 and had completed it by 641, when Caesarea, the last coastal city to hold out, fell. The military highlight of the campaign was the decisive victory over the Byzantines and their Christian Arab allies at the Battle of the Yarmuk in 636, a battle that 'had, without doubt, more important consequences than almost any other in all world history' (Gabrieli 1968, p. 150). Khalid ibn al-Walid is given the credit for this victory, set up by a spectacular march his forces made from Iraq across the Syrian Desert, to take Damascus by storm (Gabrieli 1968, Chap. 8). Command of the sea enabled the Byzantines to better defend the coastal cities such as Tyre, Sidon, Caesarea and Latakia, but eventually they all fell, along with Antioch, Homs and Jerusalem.

The Arab triumph over the Byzantines at the Yarmuk was quickly followed by the equally if not even more decisive victory in Iraq over the Sasanians and their Armenian and Albanian allies in the Battle of

Qadisiyya, west of the Euphrates, the exact date of which is uncertain—somewhere between 636 and 638. Yazdgard III was forced to flee after this defeat, and was eventually killed while on the run in 651, bringing the dynasty to an inglorious end. The Sasanian capital at Ctesiphon on the Tigris was looted of its vast treasures. The Arabs had now obtained all of Mesopotamia, the fertile lands between the Tigris and the Euphrates. Basra and Kufa were established as garrison towns that served as bases for further advances into Iran and ultimately beyond the Oxus into Central Asia. Qadisiyya was followed up by another decisive victory in 642 at Nihavand near Hamadan, the ancient Ecbatana, which was itself taken in 643. The famous towns of Isphahan, Qum, Qazvin, Shiraz and Rayy fell next, and by about 650 all of Iran proper, up to its eastern provinces of Kirman, Sistan and Khurasan, was occupied (Hoyland 2015, Chap. 3).

Egypt was conquered in another remarkable campaign, launched in 639 by an army of Yemeni tribesmen numbering no more than 4,000 under Amr ibn al-As. Egypt had been ruled by Greek speakers since the time of Alexander's successors, the Ptolemies—that is, for well over a thousand years. At the time of the Arab invasion the local people were mostly adherents of the Coptic Church (regarded as heretical by the official Orthodox Church of Constantinople). Their resentment at their Byzantine overlords made it easier for Amr to overcome the defenses and to take Alexandria and other rich prizes. Egypt had been the breadbasket for both Rome and Constantinople but now the grain surpluses would flow to Medina and the Muslim world instead. A new military base was established at Fustat in the Nile delta that would ultimately merge with the later Fatimid capital of Cairo (Kennedy 2007, Chap. 4).

The nature of the nascent Islamic state was changed drastically by the establishment of the Umayyad Caliphate in 661, which changed the leadership from the elective succession of the first four 'rightly guided' caliphs to a hereditary dynasty that lasted until 751 when it was replaced by that of the Abbasids. The founder was Muawiya ibn Abi Sufyan, appointed governor of Syria in 640, who used that influential position to secure the caliphate after the death of Ali in 661. During the next twenty years of his rule he consolidated the foundations of the Islamic state and laid the basis for further expansion by his successors both westward to the shores of the Atlantic and eastward beyond the Oxus into Central Asia (Hawting 2000, Chap. 2).

The shift of the capital from Medina in the far west of the Arabian Peninsula to the centrally located Syrian city of Damascus reflected the nature of the change. The remote holy city, not only so closely identified with the life of the Prophet and his spiritual message but also the homeland along with Mecca of his native tribe, the Quraysh, was now replaced by a prosperous commercial and administrative center that had a purely Roman and Byzantine past and no association at all with either the Arabs or Islam. The efficient civil and military administration of an empire had superseded the claims of both the Islamic religion and Arab ethnicity. It is not surprising that many of the various revolts that broke out during the rule of the Umayyads desired the return of the capital to Medina.

Despite their secular tendencies and lack of spiritual charisma the Umayyads imposed the supremacy of both the religion of Islam and the Arabic language on their empire. One has only to look at the Germanic invaders of the Roman Empire and the Mongols to see why the imposition of the conqueror's language or religion on the conquered people was not in any sense inevitable (Kennedy 1986, p. 117). Under the Umayyads, however, Arabic was the sole official language of law and administration and Islam the state religion, even though Christianity and Judaism could continue to be practiced. The incentives for converting to Islam and adopting the Arabic language were thus very strong and they grew steadily over time. As Kennedy (1986, p. 119) observes, 'Arabic, far from being overwhelmed, actually became essential; like English in India, it was the only common language in which the peoples of a vast empire could communicate with each other.'

The already wide frontiers of Islam were greatly extended both east and west under the Umayyads. In the west the occupation of Egypt in the 640s had been followed by some thrusts against the Byzantines in what are now Libya and Tunisia, but the systematic conquest of North Africa did not begin until 663 during the rule of the first Umayyad caliph. The leader was the flamboyant Uqba ibn Nafi. He occupied Tripolitania and much of what is now Tunisia between 663 and 670, establishing Qayrawan as a fortified camp and base for future operations. After being recalled, Uqba returned in 680, launching a deep thrust from Qayrawan all the way to the shores of the Atlantic, riding his horse belly-deep into the ocean, loudly lamenting that there was no more land for him to conquer in the name of Allah. He was, however, intercepted and killed by a strong Berber force on his return journey in 683. It was left to other Arab leaders to suppress the fierce Berber resistance and impose the Islamic religion and the Arabic language in North Africa just as they had in Syria and Iraq. The historic city of Carthage was taken from the Byzantines in 698. After subduing the surrounding area the Arab governor Musa ibn Nusair left a detachment of troops at Tangier under the command of a converted Berber named Tariq ibn Ziyad (Kennedy 2007, p. 223).

In 711 Tariq crossed the narrow straits to land on a rock on the opposite shore known ever since as *Jabal al-Tariq* (Rock of Tariq), i.e. Gibraltar. With him he brought about 7,000 men, some Arabs but mostly his fellow Berbers. Spain had been ruled since the fifth century by the Visigoths, a Germanic tribe that drove out the Vandals and established their own kingdom with its capital at Toledo. The king had been deposed and his place usurped by a nobleman named Rodrigo, who fought the Muslim invaders at a battle near the town of Medina Sidonia where his army, riven by dissension, was utterly defeated (Collins 1995). The victorious Tariq then easily took Toledo and Córdoba and soon had the entire country at his mercy.

Not to be outdone by his Berber lieutenant, Musa followed in 712 with a far larger force of 18,000 troops, this time mostly Arabs. The two commanders met at Talavera and subjugated most of the country except for some smaller Christian kingdoms located in more mountainous northern regions. They were then recalled to Syria by the caliph bringing loads of captives and treasure to Damascus, never to return. Musa left his son Abd al-Aziz as governor of the lands they called al-Andalus, and under his brief but vigorous rule from 714 to 716 the Arab conquests were extended to encompass Évora and Coimbra in what is now Portugal, and Málaga, Granada and Barcelona. His very success caused the new caliph in Damascus to suspect his loyalty and have him murdered in Seville. Despite its spectacularly rapid rise the new Muslim regime in Iberia was riven by dissension not only between Arabs and Berbers but between the various Arab tribes themselves. This allowed the upland Christian kingdoms to consolidate and prevent further losses. A great Berber revolt broke out in North Africa itself in 741 and the need to deal with this crisis across the straits further distracted the rulers of al-Andalus from any further conquests at the expense of their Christian enemies (Kennedy 2007, pp. 308–23).

The extension of the eastern frontier of Islam under the Umayyads was no less spectacular than their advances in the west. The Oxus (Amu Darya) had long been the boundary between 'Iran' and 'Turan', the settled lands of ancient high civilizations to the west and the vast spaces of Central Asia peopled only by wandering nomadic tribes. The Silk Roads connecting China and the west, however, ran through the fertile valleys and oases of the Oxus, Jaxartes (Syr Darya) and Zafarshan rivers and the cities of Paykand, Bukhara and Samarkand had long grown rich on this trade, supporting a number of small independent states at the turn of the eighth century.

The base of operations for the Muslim armies that crossed the Oxus was at Merv in the province of Khurasan. A large number of Arab settlers had been introduced into this province, mingling with the local population and providing a source for recruits (Gabrieli 1968, Chap. 11).

The Umayyads appointed as governor of Iraq and 'viceroy of the east' a remarkably talented and imaginative man, Hajjaj ibn Yusuf al-Thaqafi, who was 'the controlling mind behind Arab imperialism in the east' (Gabrieli 1968, p. 211). He in turn appointed another outstanding general, Qutaiba ibn Muslim, to command a series of annual invasions of the lands beyond the Oxus from bases at Merv and Balkh. These armies subdued vast stretches of land in present-day Afghanistan, Turkmenistan and Uzbekistan, including the wealthy Silk Road cities of Paykand, Bukhara and Samarkand, which fell in 712. Qutaiba's conquests went as far east as Shash on the site of what is now Tashkent.[2] (Kennedy 2007, pp. 255–76; Gibb 1970, Chap. 3).

After sending Qutaiba northeast across the Oxus into Central Asia the restless ambition of Hajjaj inspired the launching of another expedition,

[2] Qutaiba's victorious career was ended after the death of his great patron Hajjaj in 714 when he was recalled to Damascus. Thinking that his troops would be loyal to him he refused to obey, but they killed him and sent his head to Damascus.

this time to the southeast through the desolate Makran coast of southern Iran towards Sind and the Indus valley in 711. It was commanded by his kinsman Muhammad ibn al-Qasim. The young general defeated various Indian rulers and advanced up to Multan in the Punjab.[3] The incursion, however, had no enduring consequences. It was only some centuries later that much of India was to be conquered by Muslim armies, this time coming from the north commanded by Turkish or Turco-Mongol war-lords from bases in Afghanistan, setting up first the Delhi Sultanate and then the Mogul Empire (Gabrieli 1968, pp. 220–23).

The limits of Arab expansion in east and west can best be defined by two battles fought at the opposite extremities of their empire. In the west the Pyrenees were no barrier and the Arab and Berber forces launched frequent raids deep into France from bases in Barcelona and other places in Spain, sacking Bordeaux and reaching as far as Lyons and Autun in Burgundy. The Frankish warriors of the Merovingian kingdoms resisted vigorously. The most famous encounter took place, probably in 732, near Poitiers on the road to Tours between an Arab army led by the governor of al-Andalus and a Christian one led by the Merovingian 'mayor of the palace', subsequently known to history as Charles Martel, ancestor of the Emperor Charlemagne (Fouracre 2000). The Arab force was routed but the encounter was by far from the Armageddon between the contending faiths that subsequent western tradition, including even the usually skeptical Edward Gibbon, has maintained. Rather, as noted above, it was the great Berber revolt of 741 that distracted the Muslim rulers of al-Andalus from attempting to extend their frontiers further northward (Kennedy 2007, p. 323).

The eastern battle was fought some twenty years later in July 751 on the Talas River, on the border between the present states of Kazakhstan and Kyrgyzstan, deep in Central Asia. It seems that two local princes, the rulers of Farghana and Shash respectively, had a dispute that led to the former calling on the aid of China and the latter that of the governor of Samarkand. A Chinese force occupied Shash after a spectacular march along the route of the Karakorum highway, leading to a Muslim army

[3] The death of Hajjaj in 714, soon followed by that of the caliph al-Walid, led to his recall. He made no attempt to resist but returned to Syria and eventual execution.

from Samarkand being dispatched to meet it. The Kazakh allies of the Chinese switched sides and gave the victory to the Arabs. The defeat was not decisive and the Chinese could have attempted to avenge it but a major rebellion against the Tang dynasty was launched soon afterwards (Hoyland 2015, p. 187). There is thus an interesting symmetry in the fact that the two losers, the Arabs in the west and the Chinese in the east, were both prevented from returning to the fray by rebellions in their rear, in each case providing an instance of centrifugal loss exceeding centripetal gain in the further extensions of their respective frontiers, and thereby deciding their limits of these frontiers according to Lattimore's hypothesis.

The Medieval European Frontier

In 1958 Archibald Lewis (1958, p. 475) emphatically proposed that 'few periods can be better understood in the light of a frontier concept than western Europe between 800 and 1500 A.D.', and the medievalist Robert Bartlett closes his *The Making of Europe: Conquest, Colonization and Cultural Change 950–1350* with the statement that 'from the Iberian peninsula in a wide arc east across the Mediterranean and north to the Arctic Circle, Catholic Europe did have a frontier and, from the tenth century, a frontier that was moving outwards' (Bartlett 1993, p. 313). In this and the next section we will be concerned with two segments of this 'wide arc', the Christian-Muslim frontier in the Iberian Peninsula in the west and the Christian-pagan frontier that moved from the Elbe to the Vistula and beyond in the east, in other words the Spanish *Reconquista* and the German *Drang nach Osten* or *Ostsiedlung*. These two frontiers had many features in common despite the obvious difference that—in comparison with itself—Latin Christendom was contending with what was a more advanced civilization in the west and a more primitive one in the east.

The Western European society on both frontiers can perhaps best be described as a 'military-ecclesiastical complex' formed by the fusion of the institutions of feudalism and Roman Catholicism. The unsettled times in the aftermath of the barbarian invasions and the fall of the Roman

Empire led to the rural peasantry seeking and finding protection provided by local warlords, loosely organized in a hierarchical order by ascending ties of vassalage at the apex of which was a king or emperor (Bloch 1962; Duby 1974). Each level of this socio-political pyramid corresponded to a spiritual-cultural one provided by the Roman Catholic Church, at the apex of which was the pope. The physical manifestations of the military side were the stone castles of the feudal lords and of the ecclesiastical side the abbeys, monasteries and cathedrals administered by the corresponding bishoprics. An additional important institutional feature of medieval Europe was the independent charters of the small towns that played an essential role in the economic networks that sustained it (Pirenne 1956; Hodges 1989). The pagan east had no real towns but the Muslim west had sophisticated and advanced ones, which lacked, however, the relative political independence of their Christian counterparts.

The characteristic military technology of Western European society was summed up by Robert Bartlett (1993, p. 60) as 'knights, bowmen, castles'. The knights were the heavily armored cavalry, clothed in chain mail and riding specially bred and trained warhorses, large and strong enough to carry them and the twenty-five kilos of iron comprising their full equipment of armor, lance, sword and shield into battle. The cost was enormous, especially given that the relative price of steel in terms of wheat was more than fifty times as high as today in that pre-industrial age (Bartlett 1993, p. 61). Considering also the cost of the castles and cathedrals one wonders how even squeezing the maximum surplus out of an enserfed peasantry could have sustained such expenditure without the parallel innovations in agricultural technology of the horse collar, iron plowshare and water mill, as pointed out by Marc Bloch (1969, Chaps. 5–6) and Lynn White (1964, Chaps. 1–2). The heavy cavalry was supported by specialized companies of archers, including the very effective crossbowmen, and primitive artillery: engines to batter down walls with large stones or to fire volleys of smaller stones at massed enemy formations.

Since these characteristic institutions of the 'military-ecclesiastical complex' of Latin Christendom were developed in the Carolingian era it is perhaps useful to recall that Charlemagne (748–814) himself fought on both frontiers (Collins 1998). In 778 he crossed the Pyrenees in an unsuccessful attempt to assist the Muslim governor of Zaragoza who had rebelled against his overlord, the Emir of Córdoba. On his return march his rearguard was attacked and wiped out at Roncesvalles (Roncevaux) by a force of Basques in an incident immortalized in *The Song of Roland* (1976) around 1100. His campaigns on the eastern frontier against the heathen steppe nomads, the Avars and the Saxons, were far more successful, and immensely profitable. The pagan Saxon shrine of Irminsul and the fortified camps of the Avars both contained large treasure hoards. The extensive territory they controlled became the *Ostmark*, or Eastern March: Austria. The long wars against the Saxons were particularly bitter, with the execution of 4,500 prisoners in a single day being only the most egregious of the many atrocities committed by the supposedly Christian side. Given what amounted to a choice between genocide and conversion the Saxons eventually took the more sensible course, and as Charlemagne's biographer Einhard (1969, p. 63) somewhat unctuously declared, 'once they had adopted the sacraments of the Christian faith and religion, they were to be united with the Franks and became one people with them'.

The Spanish *Reconquista*

The Pyrenees marked the western frontier of Latin Christendom for several centuries before the *Reconquista*—the Christian advance in Spain—got fully under way.[4] There is no other episode that looms as large in the history of Spain as the struggle between Moors and Christians on the east–west frontier that divided the Iberian Peninsula. It gave rise not only to an enormous literature but also to one of the hottest and most important Spanish historiographical controversies, that between Américo Castro (1948, 1971) and Claudio Sánchez Albornoz (2000) about the relative influence of Muslim and Jewish versus Castilian and Germanic elements in the formation of the Spanish nation, identity and mentality.

Following the initial Arab crossing of the Strait of Gibraltar, from 756 onwards a powerful centralized state existed on the Muslim side,

[4] For overviews of the *Reconquista*, see e.g. Mínguez Fernández (2005) and Valderón Baruque (2006).

the Emirate (after 929 the Caliphate) of Córdoba. The emirate was established by Abd al-Rahman I (756–788), an Umayyad prince who fled from Syria to North Africa to escape death at the hands of the Abbasids when the dynasty fell in 750. He benefited from a lineage that had the Arab Umayyad royal family on the paternal side and Berber connections on the maternal side and was thus able to secure the support of both Arab and Berber troops when he crossed the straits in 755 and established his power base at Córdoba. The Abbasid caliphs in Damascus and later Baghdad were his mortal enemies but also his *de jure* overlords. In *de facto* terms, however, the Spanish Emirate was always independent of the Abbasids, and after Abd al-Rahman III (912–961) announced the Caliphate of Córdoba in 929, it regarded itself independent *de jure* as well until its own fall in 1031.

During most of the three centuries of its existence the Arab state in Spain was the richest and most highly sophisticated society in the entire geographical entity of Western Europe, ahead even of the Italian city-states that began to emerge a little later. With the Mediterranean a 'Muslim sea', Córdoba had virtually free trade, not only with the Islamic world of Syria, Iraq, Iran, Egypt and the Maghreb, but with Byzantium as well through various intermediaries, while Christian northern Europe was cut off, as argued by Henri Pirenne (1992) in his famous thesis that the feudal society created by Charlemagne was only possible because of Mohammed and Islam. Córdoba, and al-Andalus as a whole, played a major role in what Maurice Lombard (1975) evocatively called the 'Golden Age of Islam', with a very productive and highly diversified irrigation-based agriculture and industries such as paper-making in Játiva, Cordoban leather and Toledo steel to name only some of the most outstanding.[5] The most evident difference between the two socio-economic systems, however, was the much greater extent of urbanization, in terms of both the relative number and the size of cities such as Córdoba and Seville, and the extent of monetization, with gold and silver coins circulating freely in the Muslim zone and much less, or not at all, in most parts of the Christian one.

[5] See Findlay and O'Rourke (2007), pp. 48–60, for a convenient summary, that draws in particular on the important research of Chalmeta (1994) in 'An Approximate Picture of the Economy of al-Andalus'.

Unlike all of Christian Europe, at this time al-Andalus had both a functioning bureaucracy and a professional standing army. Arabic was the sole official language, known by all literate members of the community, Christians and Jews as well as Muslims. As is well known, the West was only able to read Latin translations of the original Greek works of Aristotle, Ptolemy and Galen from prior translations into Arabic (cf. e.g. Vernet 2000). The troops were Arabs and mostly Berbers but with many mercenary and slave soldiers of Slav, African or other non-Muslim origin as well. In addition to these institutional advantages, the Spanish Umayyads themselves 'produced an unbroken succession of fairly long-lived, vigorous, intelligent monarchs, each designated by his predecessor' (Lomax 1978, p. 18).

On the Christian side the main state that resisted the Muslim occupation from the outset was the kingdom of Asturias, in the mountainous northwest of the peninsula, founded by a nobleman named Pelayo who defeated the Muslims in what was probably no more than a skirmish but later became enshrined in the lore of the *Reconquista* as the battle of Covadonga, most probably in 722. Pelayo's descendants allied with neighboring mountain territories in Cantabria to drive the Muslims out of the valley of the Duero and to depopulate it deliberately to prevent their return, absorbing the Christian inhabitants within their own upland states of Asturias, flanked by Galicia in the west and Álava in the east. Encouraged by these developments, many Christian subjects of al-Andalus, the so-called Mozarabs, fled from there to join their co-religionists in the north (Ladero Quesada 2004, pp. 17, 20).

The Christian-Muslim frontier thus became not a line or a narrow band but a 'wide, inhospitable no-man's land' in the Duero valley (Lomax 1978, p. 27). The Muslims had no incentive to enter these lands to settle permanently since the terrain and climate were not as favorable as their own kingdom to the south, but Muslim armies advancing north from Zaragoza regularly raided the Christian land along the valley of the Ebro in search of plunder and slaves. Several castles were built to defend against them in this area, eventually called Castile, (Castilla—the 'land of the castles'). These western Christian kingdoms were to merge into the kingdom of León in 910. At the eastern end of the Pyrenees three states emerged in the region between Pamplona and Barcelona in the first half of the ninth century, the kingdoms of Navarre and Aragón and the region of Catalonia, ruled by counts technically appointed by the Carolingians in France but in practice increasingly independent.

The ideology of the *Reconquista* was greatly stimulated by the cult of Saint James, who became the patron saint of Spain with his shrine created by King Alfonso II of Asturias (791–842) at the site of Santiago de Compostela, which began to attract pilgrims from all over Europe. '¡*Santiago y cierra España*! (Saint James and charge Spain!)' became the Spanish war cry. Alfonso and the other Asturian kings consciously sought to cast themselves as the heirs of the Visigoths, once the rulers of all of Spain; hence the necessity of the *Reconquista* to restore the patrimony that had been lost.

It has been pointed out that the Middle Ages in Spain have been viewed not as beginning with the barbarian invasions and the fall of the Roman Empire in the west and ending with the Renaissance, as in the rest of Europe, but as beginning with the Muslim invasions of 711 and ending with the fall of the last remaining Muslim state, Granada, to Ferdinand and Isabella in 1492 (MacKay 1977, p. 1). The Middle Ages in the Iberian Peninsula therefore correspond to the ebb and flow of the Islamic conquests and the Christian *Reconquista* that inevitably developed in response. It will be convenient to divide these eight centuries of complex interaction into three phases. First, from the eighth to the mid-eleventh century, spanned by the rise and fall of the Emirate of Córdoba, we have essentially the period of expansion and consolidation of the Muslim empire, with the Christian kingdoms in the north largely on the defensive but slowly building up their demographic base and military capacity. The second period extends from the mid-eleventh to the mid-thirteenth century, with the Christians kingdoms of León, Castile and Aragón invading and ravaging a disunited al-Andalus, temporarily halted by new Muslim invasions from North Africa led by the Berber dynasties of the Almoravids and the Almohads. The final period, from the mid-thirteenth century to 1492, sees the fall of the last Muslim state: that of Granada.

The Emirate of Córdoba separated itself from the Christian states of the north by establishing three frontier zones or 'marches', the Upper March based on Zaragoza in the northeast, the Middle March between the Tagus and the Duero based on Toledo, and the Lower March based on Mérida. These three defensive centers all lie close to a straight line running from southwest to northeast across the peninsula, separating the realms of the two faiths. Of necessity the rulers of the Muslim cities and garrisons in these areas had to be given considerable latitude in matters of administration and military organization, so it is not surprising to find constant tension frequently breaking out into open warfare between Córdoba and these frontier governors and warlords. Abd al-Rahman I and his able successors were thus kept busy not just with hostilities against the Christians and with the development of Córdoba and its environs but with suppressing dissent and rebellion all over the realm as well. They were also actively involved in North Africa, particularly with the effort to contain the rising power of the Shiite Fatimid Caliphate based first in Tunisia and then in Egypt. It was largely to counter this Fatimid threat that the particularly able and energetic Abd al-Rahman III assumed the title of caliph in 929, enhancing the prestige and authority of the previous emirate. Generally victorious over both rebels and Christians he suffered a crushing defeat in a campaign against León in 939, after which he did not personally take to the field again during his life-time. He died in 961, still at the height of his own power and of the prosperous state that he ruled.

The great extent of his success over the Christians was even exceeded during the caliphate of his grandson Hisham II (976–1016). The man responsible was not the caliph himself but his *hajib* or chamberlain, known to history by his honorific title of al-Mansur (Almanzor) (the Victorious). Beginning as a scribe in the lower ranks of the bureaucracy he worked his way up to the height of power by a combination of remarkable ability and ruthless intrigue and personally took complete control of all civil and military affairs. He attacked the Christian states relentlessly every year, forcing them not only to pay massive amounts of tribute but also to accept humiliating treaties that placed them in the position of vassal states. He not only sacked Pamplona and Barcelona and several other major Christian cities but in 997 he besieged and sacked Santiago de Compostela itself, bringing back the bells of the shrine to be placed in the Great Mosque of Córdoba. He died in 1002 'after a brilliant career devoted to the interminable and fruitless demonstration of Christian military inferiority' (Lomax 1978, p. 47).

Brilliant as they were, his achievements proved to be completely ephemeral. With the caliphate itself reduced to a mere cipher there was no focus for the legitimacy of the state to hold together the competing military and civilian factions, and in 1031 the office of the caliphate itself was abolished by the citizens of Córdoba after it had lost all meaning. The unified Muslim state disintegrated into about thirty petty *taifa* or 'party' states, so called because they were each ruled by one of the various factions of the military and civilian elites contending for power, such as the Hispanic Arabs, the Berbers and the Slavs. The winners were the Christian states that now had the opportunity to finally realize the dream of the *Reconquista.*

The southward movement of the frontier was as much, and perhaps even more, a process of repopulation and settlement as it was of conquest (cf. Ladero Quesada 2004, for a wealth of detail). The reconquered space was reorganized, and with the population came the foundation of cities. An 'interior', consolidated frontier à la Owen Lattimore was established by the settlers. The first major step was the resettlement of the Duero valley from about the early ninth century, mostly by independent smallholding farmers ready to bear arms in the defense of their new homes and the progress of the *Reconquista,* the so-called *caballeros villanos* (villein-knights). The Duero itself became the new frontier with Islamic Spain for its entire length by the early eleventh century, rather than being in the 'no-man's land' as it had been previously. The lower Duero valley was under the kingdom of León but the upper valley and the lands between it and the upper reaches of the Ebro were in the increasingly powerful region of Castile, with its capital at Burgos. Castile had developed a distinct language, culture and ideology as a frontier warrior state by about the year 1000. The people of Castile owed allegiance to their own counts but the region itself was within the realms of the kingdom of León.

Alfonso VI (1065–1109) of León emerged as the most powerful ruler in the entire peninsula, dominating not only the Christian north but several of the *taifa* states as well that paid him tribute and allegiance. He secured the first great victory of the *Reconquista* when Toledo, the ancient capital of the Visigoths, fell to him in 1085, to the joy not only of Christian Spain but of all Latin Christendom.

The fall of Toledo convinced the rulers of the Muslim states that they needed a more effective collective response to the Christian advance. This consisted in inviting the Berber Almoravid dynasty that had just taken power in North Africa to intervene in Spain. This option did not come without severe risks. How could they be sure that the Almoravids would not simply take over all of their states after saving them from Alfonso VI? The ruler of Seville who took the lead in the invitation to the Almoravids was well aware of this problem but is reported to have said that if dispossessed he would 'prefer to be a camel-driver in Africa rather than a swineherd in Castile' (Lomax 1978, p. 69). The Islam adhered to by the Almoravids was far more puritanical and intolerant than that prevailing in al-Andalus and the regime far more despotic. The invitation to the Almoravids was hedged with the requirement for them to promise to return across the straits after the defeat of the Christians, leaving the *taifa* rulers in place.

The Almoravid emir Yusuf ibn Tashufin landed in Algeciras with a very large army in 1086, where he was joined by the kings of Seville, Granada, Málaga and Badajoz to march on Toledo. Alfonso VI met them with an army of his own vassals and some Aragonese and French contingents at Sagrajas, near Badajoz. The Christians were routed after a fierce battle, with Alfonso VI himself barely escaping with his life. The Muslim victory was mainly due to the Almoravid cavalry, with the Andalusians not distinguishing themselves at all. Yusuf returned to Morocco, presumably in response to his promise, but had to come back again in 1090 after the Christians counter-attacked. Yusuf besieged Toledo but a strong defense obliged him to lift the siege. This time he did not return to Morocco but took over Granada, Seville and many of the other *taifa* states as well. Andalusia (al-Andalus) was thus once more a unified Muslim state but not an independent one, as it was in effect a colony of the Almoravid Empire, with its capital at Marrakesh in Morocco.

In 1094 the Almoravids sent an army towards Valencia. This city had recently been seized from its Muslim *taifa* rulers by Rodrigo (Ruy) Díaz de Vivar, *El Cid*, the historical personage immortalized in myth and legend and as the protagonist of the first major literary work in Spanish, the *Cantar de Mío Cid* (2007), from around 1140. The real Rodrigo fought on both the Christian and Muslim sides depending on what was most advantageous to him at any given time. He was a commander of genius and he routed the Almoravid army outside Valencia. He continued to defend the city until his death in 1099, after which the Christian population led by his widow withdrew to Castile leaving the city in Muslim hands in 1102. Nevertheless, by delaying the fall of Valencia from 1094 to 1102, El Cid had given time for the Christian kingdoms to consolidate and recover from the Almoravid invasion (Fletcher 1989).

Alfonso I of Aragón (1104–1134), *El Batallador* (the Battler), was able with help from across the Pyrenees to lay siege to and occupy the city of Zaragoza, commanding the Upper March of the frontier of al-Andalus. With this victory his kingdom was doubled in size and quadrupled in population because of his new Muslim subjects (Reilly 1993, p 110). It not only shifted the balance of power significantly between Christians and Muslims in the peninsula but made Aragón a rival to León-Castile within the Christian realm itself until the two crowns merged in the second half of the fifteenth century with the marriage of Ferdinand and Isabella.

A major consequence of the Almoravid entry into the Iberian Peninsula was the intensification of the ideological conflict, with *jihad* on one side and crusade on the other. Pope Urban II was preaching the First Crusade to the Holy Land (Riley-Smith 2003, Chap. 1) at the same time as these events took place in the peninsula, and both sides tended to see the opposition as aspects of a single conflict. Knights from France and northern Europe crossed the Pyrenees and joined the fight against the Muslims in the service of the rulers of Navarre, Aragón and Catalonia (Riley-Smith 1987, p. 106). Spain itself saw the rise of the military orders of Calatrava (1157), Santiago (1171) and Alcántara inspired by the example of the Templars and the Hospitallers in the Holy Land. Combining the military with the monastic way of life, the orders played a major role in manning the castles that defended the Christian lands in the Extremaduras between the Tagus and the Guadalquivir as well as in attacks and raids into Andalusia (Martínez Díaz 2006).

The capture of Toledo and its successful defense had extended the Christian frontier from the Duero to the Tagus 'in a single bound' and the lands and cities in between were quickly resettled by both northern Christians and Mozarabs (Lomax 1978, p. 77). Thus, despite the success of the Almoravid armies in the field, the Christian side was able to sustain the pressure on Andalusia in the ongoing conflict. The Almoravid ruling class was meanwhile corrupted by the luxurious urban lifestyle of the Andalusians and their resources strained on both shores of their empire. It is therefore not surprising that a new Berber dynasty, the Almohads, arose in North Africa, displacing the Almoravids in 1145.

The two successive Berber dynasties were remarkably similar in their structure, though the first arose among the desert tribes, known as the Sanhaja, while the second emerged from the Masmuda tribe of the Atlas Mountains. Both espoused puritanical 'fundamentalist' versions of Islam despite some theological differences and both had very powerful military striking power using massed cavalry formations as the main arm. The Almohads took some time to appraise the political situation in the peninsula and it was not until 1171 that they entered in force, occupying Seville before moving on to Toledo, besieging it for a while before withdrawing. Toledo, because of its central position, was the key to Andalusia, and their inability to take it then or later prevented the Almohads from establishing a secure foothold in the peninsula. The military orders played a major role in keeping them at bay. According to Angus MacKay (1977, p. 32), they 'were invaluable in resisting the onslaught of the Almohads and in wresting and holding lands on the frontier'. Little by little the Almohad state fell apart. By 1229 nothing remained of it in al-Andalus (Ladero Quesada 2004, p. 29).

Before that, the Almohads, however, managed to inflict a crushing defeat on a large Christian army led by Alfonso VIII of Castile (1158–1214) at Alarcos in 1195. Coming soon after Saladin's great victory over the Crusaders at Hattin in 1187 the defeat caused consternation throughout Latin Christendom, but the Almohads were not able to take full advantage. Alfonso VIII lived not only to fight another day but to more than make up for his defeat when he crushed the Almohads in the decisive battle of Las Navas de Tolosa in 1212. He died soon afterwards in 1214 but his very able grandson Ferdinand III (1217–1252) went on to secure the triumphs of taking Córdoba in 1236 and Seville in 1248. Ferdinand was succeeded by his even more famous son, Alfonso X (1252–1284), 'El Sabio' (the Wise), who proceeded to extend the *Reconquista* further south. From the 1220s to the 1250s the area of Aragón increased from 85,000 to 106,000 square kilometers, that of Castile and León from 235,000 to 355,000 (and that of Portugal, cf. below, from 85,000 to 106,000) (Ladero Quesada 2004, p. 29). The only Muslim state that was able to survive was Granada but it could only do so by becoming a vassal-state of the kingdom of Castile and Léon in 1264 (Ferdinand III having succeeded to the crown of León in addition to that of Castile on the death of King Alfonso IX of León in 1230). Meanwhile another great conqueror, Jaume I of Aragón (1213–1276), was securing a string of victories on the east coast and the adjacent Balearic Islands, including Valencia in 1238 and Murcia in 1266 (Bisson 1986, Chap. 3). The Muslim defeat was comprehensive throughout the peninsula.

The frontier which had moved in a single bound from the Duero to the Tagus after the fall of Toledo in 1085 took another leap from the Tagus to the Guadalquivir following the fall of Córdoba and Seville. 'The Christians did not advance steadily, step-by-step; they took great leaps forward, to the Duero, the Tagus, the Guadalquivir and the south coast, and after each leap they waited for centuries to consolidate their position before making the next one' (Lomax 1978, p. 175).

The kingdom of Granada maintained a nominal independence from 1264 to 1492. The Marinid dynasty of Morocco that succeeded the Almohads intervened actively in the peninsula until 1340, providing a countervailing power to the pressure of the divided Christian kingdoms, improving the terms on which Granada was able to maintain its limited independence. Despite the frequent hostilities the economy of Granada was able to flourish due to its trade with North Africa that was the source of an influx of gold from south of the Sahara, enabling the rulers not just to sustain themselves but to provide to the world the glory of the Alhambra. The rise of the power of the Ottoman Empire after the fall of Constantinople in 1453 struck fear into the hearts of all the rulers of Europe. Having a Muslim state north of the Strait of Gibraltar substantially enhanced the geopolitical stakes involved. After the marriage of Ferdinand of Aragón and Isabella of León and Castile the power of both the *Reyes Católicos* (Christian kings) was turned against Granada, no doubt motivated at least in part by this threat, and the two monarchs entered Granada in triumph on 6 January 1492.

Portugal

In the foregoing we have concentrated exclusively on Spain, but the Arab invasion and the *Reconquista* of course affected Portugal as well. Around 714–716 Évora, Santarém and Coimbra were occupied, whereas in the northwest the number of Muslims was too low to go beyond the capitulation of the Visigothic governors (Livermore 1976, p. 33). Above the Mondego few garrisons were found. Virtually all of Galicia was reconquered in the 740s and from 751 to 754 the territory from the Minho to the Douro (Duero) was occupied, but only temporarily, since the resources needed for the repopulation of this area were lacking (Payne 1973, p. 114). A no-man's land was established, with the Christians north of the Minho and the Arabs south of the Douro (Payne 1973, p. 114; Marques 1972, p. 11, García de Cortázar 2005, p. 144). This area during the ninth century began to be referred to as the Provincia Portucalense (from the name of the port of Cale, subsequently Porto), later Portugalense and Portugal (Payne 1973, pp. 114–15). Coimbra was taken in 878, but al-Mansur once more pushed the frontier to the north, sacking the city in 987–988, putting it again under Arab control (Livermore 1976, p. 37), before the Coimbra-Mondego region was definitely reconquered in 1063–1064 (Marques 1972, p. 27; Payne 1973, p. 116).

In 1093 Lisbon, Sintra and Santarém were garrisoned by the Christians but were quickly lost again to the Arabs (Livermore 1976, p. 43). In 1135 Afonso Henriques, who had taken over as head of the territory of Portugal in 1128, broke loose from Castile-León and subsequently proclaimed himself king of Portugal. A new kingdom, officially recognized by the pope in 1179, had been created in the Iberian Peninsula (Marques 1972, pp. 39–43). The long reign of Afonso I, which did not end until his death in 1185, saw a further southward extension of the Christian sphere in the west. Lisbon fell in 1147 and much of the Alentejo region, including Évora, was conquered (Marques 1972, p. 74; Payne 1973, p. 119). However, the arrival of the Almohads in 1190 once more pushed the frontier northwards, to the Tagus (Marques 1972, p. 75; Livermore 1976, pp. 70–71) and it was not until the reign of Sancho II (1223–1246) that the expansion was renewed, this time all the way to the Algarve.

Only Silves in the extreme southwest and its immediate surroundings remained in Arab hands (Livermore 1976, p. 65). It remained for Afonso III (1246–1279) to complete the liberation of Portugal from the Moors in 1250 (Marques 1972, pp. 75–76).

The Northern Crusades and the Eastern Frontier

On the northeastern frontier of Latin Christendom around the year 1100 there were to the west of the Elbe recently converted Saxons and Scandinavians, while to the east there was a mass of still unconverted 'heathen' peoples. Moving from west to east these peoples were successively Wends, Pomeranians, Prussians, Lithuanians, Livonians, Estonians and Finns, each of which was further sub-divided by tribe and location. The Saxons, Danes and Swedes who had all raided and plundered the Christian lands to the west were now prevented from doing so by their own conversion. Surviving expansionist tendencies could, however, conveniently be turned to the east, which was abundantly endowed with both natural resources and a potential supply of slaves. The eastern peoples themselves were not reluctant to engage in land raids and piracy along the shores of the Baltic at the expense of their western neighbors, so a case could also be made for a pre-emptive war against them. Furthermore, Latin Christendom was gripped by the frenzy of the First Crusade at exactly this time, with Jerusalem having just been recovered from the Saracen infidels in 1099. The Church was not slow to generalize the concept of crusade from warfare against Islam, whether in Palestine or Spain, to warfare against the benighted pagans on Europe's eastern frontier.

The Wends were a western branch of the Slavs, akin to the Poles and the Czechs, both of whom had, however, already adopted Christianity and established their own kingdoms of Poland and Bohemia. The Wends had been partly converted in the tenth century but a great rebellion in 983 had made them abandon both the religion and the rule of their Saxon overlords. Their social structure was dominated by both a warrior and a priestly elite capable not only of effective resistance but of aggression by land and sea as well. The lead in preaching of a crusade against these threatening pagans was taken by the most influential cleric of the age, Bernard of Clairvaux. He contended that the only solution was to offer them the choice of baptism or death. The fall of Edessa to the Muslims in the Holy Land in 1144 resulted in the preaching of the Second Crusade, and the papacy agreed that subduing the pagans on Europe's eastern frontier was no less worthy of the declaration of Holy War.

Thus, what was called the Wendish Crusade was launched with considerable fanfare in 1147, led by the flower of the German and Danish nobility along with multiple bishops. Despite some initial successes, dissension within the Christian ranks and determined Wendish resistance under their war chief Nyklot held the crusaders at bay. Subsequently the Danish king Valdemar I (1157–1182) and the Saxon duke Henry the Lion conducted a joint operation in 1160 that killed Nyklot and divided his lands between them. Valdemar then launched a massive raid on the Wendish stronghold of the island of Rügen, destroying the elaborate temple complex and wiping out all resistance in 1168. Carrying their campaigns further east the Saxon-Danish forces subdued Pomerania by 1185, bringing the Wendish Crusade to a successful end, with new bishoprics, abbeys and monasteries to ensure that the now converted pagans would remain true to their new faith while the political leaders could enjoy the expanded revenues from trade and taxes now available to them (Lotter 1989).

Despite their defeat the Wendish ruling elite by no means disappeared. Once they agreed to convert they were allowed to retain their positions by entering the ranks of the Christian nobility. Thus, Nyklot's son Pribislav became duke of Mecklenburg, a position which his descendants held until 1918. The Christian leaders realized that accepting their allegiance was a better option than removing them and ruling their Slavic subjects directly and risking resistance and revolt in the future. The Slav elite, in turn, understood that the arrival of German settlers into their lands would raise productivity through the use of heavier plows and better farming methods, and that encouraging towns to be set up under German law would bring further prosperity. Christianization and 'Germanization' were therefore mutually reinforcing processes that together extended the frontier further east, with the Plow and the Book following in the wake of the Sword (Barraclough 1984, Chap. 10).

The next stage of the eastward Saxon thrust was not a gradual extension of the frontier but a leap from the Oder to the Dvina, into what was then known as Livonia and now corresponds to Latvia. The leap was not over land but by sea, from Lübeck, founded in 1158, to Riga, founded in 1186. The initiative was taken by Archbishop Hartwig II of Bremen (1185–1207) who from 1195 onwards sent a succession of merchants, settlers and warriors from western Germany and the Low Countries to pacify and settle the southern shores of the Gulf of Riga and the valley of the Dvina. A nephew was appointed bishop of Livonia to propagate the faith and trade in furs, wax and other valuable northern commodities in exchange for weapons and other manufactured goods and silver, expanding trade on the Riga-Lübeck run. The military task of subduing the natives and defending against incursions from Lithuanian and other hostile tribes was left to a detachment of soldier-monks known as the Swordbrothers, a particularly violent and undisciplined group that engaged in the most egregious atrocities but at the same time was sufficiently competent, with their heavy armor and large warhorses, to carry out the task assigned to them initially. Eventually, however, they ended up being routed by the Lithuanians in 1236 and the task of holding Livonia was transferred to the Teutonic Knights. Despite suffering many losses the Knights hung on to establish a stable frontier with the Lithuanians to the north and east by 1290 (Christiansen 1997, p. 104).

The official title of the body to which these knights belonged was the Teutonic Order of St Mary's Hospital in Jerusalem, formed at the end of the twelfth century in the Holy Land in the aftermath of Saladin's great victory over the Crusaders at Hattin in 1187. Originally founded like the Templars and the Hospitallers or Knights of St John to care for the sick and wounded, it soon became a military order *par excellence,* in which the brothers were monks sworn to chastity and poverty but also warriors pledged to sacrifice their lives in the perpetual war against Satan and his minions, in this case the pagans of eastern Europe. Their patron saint was the Virgin Mary, transformed into a war goddess.

The Order quickly won the full support of both Pope Honorius III (1216–1227) and the Emperor Frederick II (1212–1250) and gained vast amounts of land and wealth all over Europe from donations as well as, and more importantly, an eager supply of recruits from all over Germany.

Unlike the Templars and Hospitallers but like the orders of Calatrava, Santiago and Alcántara it concentrated on a single enemy within its home country rather than on generalized action against the infidel on all fronts including the Holy Land. The leaders of the Order also astutely ensured that they had full autonomy to conduct their operations without interference from other secular or religious authorities. As Eric Christiansen (1997, p. 83) puts it, 'they entered Prussia with a free hand'. While the Order itself concentrated on defeating the heathen Prussians at the invitation of the Polish duke Conrad of Mazovia it was by no means alone in its crusading task. Prominent nobles from Germany and Poland, and even the king of Bohemia, participated actively in the fighting from time to time, bringing their own forces with them.

The campaign to subdue the formidable Prussians began in 1230 and took about fifty years to complete. The Crusaders advanced steadily eastwards along the shore of the Baltic, securing a string of river forts that served as bases for thrusts into the interior, reaching Balga at the eastern end of the Vistula delta by 1239 (Christiansen 1997, Map 4). At this point the Christian duke of Danzig, fearing that his trade routes were being cut off, changed sides. This led to a ten-year war that ended with the duke agreeing to share the control of the Vistula delta with the Order. The advance proceeded to a point where a new fortress was constructed in 1255 and named Königsberg, in honor of the king of Bohemia who had joined in the crusade. In 1260, however, as noted earlier, the crusading position in Livonia collapsed and this led to an upsurge of Prussian resistance, with many forts destroyed and Königsberg itself barely surviving. Reinforcements from Germany between 1265 and 1272 were able to hold the line and by the end of the thirteenth century the Order had been able to grind the Prussians down to surrender and accept conversion. Prussia had become an *Ordenstaat*, a state ruled by an entity that exercised a political, economic, confessional and military monopoly over society as a whole.

Meanwhile the rulers of Denmark and their vigorous Archbishop Absalon of Lund (1178–1202), described as being 'as much pirate as prelate', were busy launching several raids against the heathens in Estonia. In 1219 the Danes founded a city on the site of a natural harbor on the southern shore of the Gulf of Finland that they and the Germans called

Reval but was known to the natives by its present name of Tallinn. The city was strongly fortified and populated by a number of mostly German merchants and craftsmen, in addition to Danish knights and priests. A bishopric was also established and a cathedral built. Reval therefore served both as a military-ecclesiastical base for the control and pacification of the surrounding countryside and as a flourishing port of the expanding Baltic trade. Despite these advantages, the Danish colony was exposed to constant attacks by native rebels, Lithuanians and Russians from Novgorod, and also had to contend with the designs on it of allied powers such as the Swedes and the Teutonic Knights; it survived largely on the strength of its sea power. Dissension and disunity in the Danish kingdom itself finally led to the winding up of the Estonian venture when it was sold to the Teutonic Knights in 1346, 'who loosely integrated it into Livonia' (Tyerman 2006, p. 696).

Separated by a mere 240 kilometers of water the peoples of Sweden and Finland have interacted since prehistoric times but their relationship became particularly acute during the period of the Northern Crusades. The Finns were allegedly converted to Christianity in the middle of the twelfth century by Sweden's King Erik Jedvardsson assisted by a Bishop Henry of Uppsala, who became the patron saint of Finland, as the result of a successful crusade. There seems to be little historical evidence for any such crusade but it has lived on as myth and legend (Tarkiainen 2008, pp. 72–84). In any case the people of southwestern present-day Finland appear to have been converted, perhaps peacefully, by Swedish settlers in that part of the country. Of more interest to the Swedish state, however, was the eastern end of the Gulf of Finland which was the outlet for furs and other northern commodities exported from Novgorod to the west. The Finnish tribes here, the Tavastians and the Karelians, were far less amenable to Latin Christianity and the Swedes. The Tavastians apparently rejected Christianity altogether, while the Karelians came under Greek Orthodox influence from Novgorod.

With force clearly necessary if anything was to be achieved, a Swedish fleet under the powerful Earl Birger Magnusson (Birger Jarl, the founder of Stockholm) was dispatched in 1249 to the Gulf of Finland, landing at a harbor that Christiansen (1997, p. 118) maintains may have been Helsinki. The Tavastians were defeated and forced to accept Christianity under the shadow of fortresses at Tavastehus and Turku (Åbo), which was also the site of a bishopric that ministered to the spiritual needs of both the Suomi and the Tavastians (Tarkiainen 2008, pp. 92–99). Another major operation launched by Marshal (Marsk) Torgils Knutsson set up the key fortress of Viborg at the northeastern end of the Gulf of Finland in 1293. This put the Swedes directly athwart the vital trade route from Novgorod to the Hansa ports lower down the Baltic, a position they were not slow to exploit. Despite many ups and downs the Swedes were to remain in Finland until 1809.

The last pagans to be converted were the most formidable of all, the Lithuanians. Like the Prussians they were Balts, an ancient people speaking an Indo-European language. Their social organization was based on a peasantry practicing agriculture and pasturage, but with a mounted warrior elite that carried out systematic plundering raids on their neighbors, deriving their incomes from the proceeds in booty, slaves and trade goods. Their original native habitat was in the forested basins of the Niemen and other rivers east of Prussia. According to Christiansen (1997, p. 139), 'Their strength lay in their inaccessibility, and in their horses'—giving them long-range striking power and the ability to withdraw back into their forests and fortified places. They also had the great advantage of a remarkable ruling dynasty founded by Mindaugas (d. 1263), who built up their strength through contacts with their more advanced neighbors, including the Teutonic Order. The core of their army was the cavalry which used javelins instead of bows as the main missile weapon but was supported by infantry and detachments of crossbowmen.

The wealth accumulated by the Lithuanian ruling class made them good customers for German and other merchants, including those of the city of Riga. Their vast hinterland connected them to the Ukraine, the Black Sea and the Byzantine world as well as to the Mongols of the Golden Horde to the east, providing them with silver from the sale of slaves that they used to buy weapons and consumer goods from the Hanseatic League. Their homeland which included much of what is now Belarus had its main centers at Vilnius and Trakai. It was also the source of many rivers that flowed both north and south and they could push down the valleys of these rivers to establish what Christiansen (1997, p. 141) calls 'a vast tributary system that absorbed the wealth of all the western Russian principalities'. He also says (p. 142) that at his death in 1263 Mindaugas' territory 'corresponded to a rough circle, centered on Vilnius, with a radius of some 120 miles'. This was greatly expanded by his descendants so that 100 years later the radius was 400 miles to the south and east, giving the Lithuanians a huge power base from which to threaten Poland and Prussia to their west and north. Throughout this expansionary process the Lithuanians retained their paganism but it was an asset instead of a handicap, since it allowed them 'to govern Latins, Greeks, Jews and Tartars impartially' (Christiansen 1997, p. 145), while maintaining their identity as an imperial race under their grand-princes.

The paganism of their great enemy enabled the Teutonic Order to call for the papacy and the Western European states to launch a continuing crusade against them. The nobility of not only Germany but also of France and England took up the cause, spending at least one summer or winter in the field against the heathen. Even Henry Bolingbroke, the future Henry IV, made two expeditions to Prussia in 1390 and 1392. The conflict between the Order and the Lithuanians was a long and grinding one, made particularly difficult for both sides by the thickly forested terrain and the harsh climate. The incessant raids into each other's territories along a frontier zone separated by a largely depopulated no-man's land made life miserable for the unfortunate civilian populations of both sides but produced little net advantage to either side.

The event that eventually broke the logjam was, strangely enough, a marriage. Jogaila, grand duke of Lithuania (1377–1434), was looking for a suitable bride in 1385 when one suddenly became available in the person of Jadwiga, heiress to the vacant Polish throne. A deal was struck at the Treaty of Krevo (1385) in which Jogaila (or Jagiello—the Polish version of his name) would become the king of Poland in return for his own baptism and the conversion of all his pagan subjects into the Roman Catholic faith and associating the grand duchy of Lithuania with the kingdom of Poland in a permanent union. In one instant the pagan grand duke of Lithuania, Jogaila, had become the Roman Catholic king of Poland Władysław II (1386–1434). A further deal struck later between the Lithuanians themselves put Jogaila's cousin and political rival Vytautas

(1350–1430), also known by his Polish name of Witold, in charge of the grand duchy while Władysław himself sat on the Polish throne.

The political consequences of the Treaty of Krevo were momentous. The Polish historian Oscar Halecki (1956, p. 69) has called it 'the most important treaty in the whole of Polish history' and surely in Lithuania's as well. It proved fatal to the Teutonic Order since it not only removed its very *raison d'être* when Lithuania ceased to be a pagan state but drastically shifted the balance of power by unifying its two most dangerous enemies, that could previously be played off against each other, into a single implacable one. Desperate efforts were made to separate the two cousins by diplomatic intrigues but to no avail. A Polish-Lithuanian army augmented by Czechs, Hungarians and even some Crimean Tartar cavalry annihilated the Knights at the Battle of Tannenberg in July 1410, leaving over 400 of the brothers dead on the field including the Grand Master himself, together with other top commanders. The Order continued to resist, however, and successfully defended its great castle of Marienburg from a prolonged siege, but it eventually had to accept humiliating peace terms at Torun in 1411, surrendering the vital province of Samogitia between Prussia and Livonia and paying an indemnity estimated at 850,000 pounds sterling, ten times the annual revenue of the king of England (Christiansen 1997, p. 228). The Order lingered on, before slowly fading away after it was secularized in 1525 during the course of the Reformation. In a sense it was the victim of its own success (Christiansen 1997, Chap. 9).

Tannenberg essentially brought the Northern Crusades to an end. If the objective was to convert all the heathens east of the Elbe they could be said to have been successful. Unlike all the other pagan peoples, however, the Lithuanians converted on their own terms and to their own great advantage.

Spain in the Americas

As Archibald Lewis (1958) has pointed out, between 1250 and 1350 the frontier was closed in Europe: both the external frontier and the internal, cultivation, frontier (for lack of virgin lands). 'Behind the moving frontiers of the Reconquista in the Iberian Peninsula, during the eleventh, twelfth, and early thirteenth centuries, historians are beginning to appreciate the role of a peasantry who settled much of the newly conquered land in Aragon, Castile, and Portugal and made the reconquest permanent for the future' (Lewis 1958, p. 475). As we have seen, in the mid-fourteenth century this process had by and large come to an end. The further expansion of Christian Spain would take place outside the peninsula.

The establishment of the Spanish Empire in the New World was an instance of both conquest and settlement. It grew organically out of the *Reconquista* (Sánchez-Albornoz 1970; Parry 1966; Braudel 1975; Elliott 1984), which is not at all surprising since Spain's entire medieval history is one of conquest and loss of territory, from the first penetration of Germanic peoples across the Pyrenees at the beginning of the fifth century (Collins 1995) until the fall of Moorish Granada in 1492 as well as the expansion by Aragón into the Mediterranean. Naples was taken over by the Spanish in 1504.

The westward overseas expansion of Spain began around the same time, with the incorporation of the Canary Islands in the 1490s, and by the crossing of the natural frontier of the Atlantic in the first of the four voyages of Columbus in 1492—the start of the process whereby the Europeans were to conquer much of the world by the means of 'guns and sails' (Cipolla 1965). This created a new artificial frontier on the other side of the Ocean Sea, the maximum extension of which was in the last instance regulated by a series of papal bulls in 1493 and the Treaty of Tordesillas with Portugal in 1494, which laid down the division of the globe between the two European maritime powers.

'The men who conquered America were the cultural heirs of *reconquistadores* of Iberia', writes H.B. Johnson (1970, p. 5). The *conquistadores* were motivated by economic factors. Conquest expeditions were often privately financed. The Spanish crown as well had a strong economic interest in the discovery of the New World. Public finances deteriorated gradually from the Catholic kings to Philip II, which led to the *quinto real* being levied from 1504 on all precious metals in the Americas (Lundahl 1991), as the principal measure to restore them.

Pecuniary forces were, however, not the only factor behind the overseas expansion. Another was religion. It must not be forgotten that the *Reconquista* was an episode with roots in the Crusades. The Arab invaders had brought an alien religion into the Iberian Peninsula, and the very same year that the episode was over, not only the Muslims but also the Jews were expelled from Spain. Ferdinand and Isabella, Charles V and Philip II were all deeply religious and the Church was enormously powerful in Spanish society. That Christendom was extending the religious frontier was an essential feature of the *Reconquista*, and this ethos carried over to the conquest of the New World. All expeditions of exploration and conquest included a priest, and a number of papal bulls forced the Castilian crown to undertake active conversion of the Indians (Lundahl 1991). With the military conquest of the Americas went the extension of the religious frontier.

The people who secured most of Latin America under Spain are known as *conquistadores*, but the extension of the Spanish frontier in the New World was a process that mixed conquest and settlement. 'Without settlement there is no good conquest, and if the land is not conquered, the people will not be converted. Therefore the maxim of the conqueror must be to settle', states Francisco López de Gómara (quoted by Elliott 1984, p. 149) in his 1552 *Historia general de las Indias*, a work based on information obtained directly from Hernán Cortés. As J. H. Elliott (1984, p. 149) has pointed out, this maxim was one of the pillars of the Spanish colonization in the sixteenth century, but it was not always adhered to, above all not in the early phases of the conquest; '... it might also mean to raid, plunder and move on' (Elliott 1984, p. 152).

Nowhere was this more true than in the case of Hispaniola. Columbus and his followers were attracted to the island in the hope of finding gold. The placer gold of the rivers was quickly exhausted, however, and when the news was out that gold had been found in Cuba as well, in 1512, the emigration began. By the time Cortés had conquered Tenochtitlán in 1521, finishing the Aztec Empire, the Caribbean islands were doomed.

Not even the introduction of capital punishment for leaving could prevent their virtual depopulation (Lundahl 1991). All the areas touched by Columbus during his four voyages were in a state of acute crisis. Carl Ortwin Sauer (1966, p. 294) has summed up the situation in a classic passage:

> By 1519 the Spanish Main was a sorry shell. The natives, whom Columbus belatedly knew to be the wealth of the land, were destroyed. The gold places or the islands were worked out. The gold treasures which the Indians of Castilla del Oro had acquired had been looted. What most Spaniards wanted was to get out and seek their fortunes in parts as yet untried and unknown.

Mexico suffered a similar fate. Cortés did not find enough gold in Tenochtitlán to make it worthwhile for all the conquerors to remain there, but gradually the latter began to move both northwards, to California, and southwards through Mexico and Panama and towards Colombia where gold was discovered. When Francisco Pizarro reached Peru and discovered the Inca riches in 1532 the centrifugal forces proved too strong. All the Spanish towns except Mexico City and possibly Vera Cruz lost their populations just a few years after their foundation (Davis 1973, p. 42).

The thirst for precious metals would not be easily slaked. 'The accumulated gold of centuries was looted during the two decades, 1520–40, which saw the Spanish conquest of Middle and South America. Thereafter, though gold was mined in varying and often substantial amounts, silver predominated in both volume and value produced' (Bakewell 1984, p. 105). The conquerors moved on to new virgin fields. The silver mountain of Potosí in Upper Peru was discovered in 1545 and quickly became the largest producer of this metal in the world and, together with Zacatecas and Guanajuato in Mexico, saw to it that a never-ending flow of bullion extended from Spanish America to Seville. Potosí had an estimated population of 100,000 to 150,000 at the beginning of the seventeenth century (Klein 1992, p. 55). It was the largest town in the New World and larger than any town in Spain (Kamen 2003, p. 286).

Argentina

With time, however, settlement became more important than mere conquest. Once the Spaniards moved into the Southern Cone of South America the agricultural potential of the land mattered more than the chance of new mineral discoveries.[6] The prime case here is Argentina. (Of course, the Spaniards hoped for precious metals there as well, but things did not turn out that way.) Argentina was penetrated from two directions: first from the northwest and thereafter from the Atlantic. The western frontier was penetrated from Peru and Chile. Tucumán, 1565, Córdoba, 1573, Salta, 1582, La Rioja, 1591, Jujuy, 1593 were founded from Peru, and Santiago del Estero, 1553, Mendoza, 1561, San Juan, 1562 and San Luis, 1596, from Chile (Pendle 1963, p. 11). The Northwest was the most important economic region of Argentina during the entire colonial period, responding above all to the demand emanating from Potosí for pack animals, foodstuffs, wine and cotton fabrics, and from the Spanish communities on the Pacific coast (Ferrer 1965, pp. 37–38). The Northwest became the most densely populated region in the Southern Cone (Sawers 1996, p. 51).

Compared to the northeast, the La Plata region remained an economic backwater during the same period. Buenos Aires had been founded in 1536, but the absence of gold and silver in the region made for a failure. The Spaniards were driven out by the Indians in 1541. In the meantime they had moved on also to Paraguay where Asunción was founded in 1537. Asunción became the hub of the eastern part of La Plata and it was from there that the Atlantic side of Argentina was settled: Corrientes in 1558, Santa Fe in 1573 and Buenos Aires for the second time in 1580 (Pendle 1963, pp. 12–13; Ferrer 1965, p. 35).

[6] The case of Chile is a mixture of both. It is also decidedly a frontier episode. It is no coincidence that the Chilean national epos, Alonso de Ercilla y Zúñiga's (1966) *La Araucana*, completed in 1589, deals with the frontier wars between the Spaniards and the Mapuches (Araucanos). They would extend way beyond Ercilla's times. The conquest of the south of Chile was not effectively completed until the dawn of the twentieth century (Villalobos et al. 1974; Bengoa 1987). Chile also expanded towards the north, in the War of the Pacific 1879–83 against Peru and Bolivia (Sater 1986; Collier and Sater 1996, Chap. 6) which deprived Bolivia of its coastal regions.

The development of the Atlantic side of Argentina was held back until the late 1770s by the Spanish trade monopoly which required goods from the La Plata area to go through Lima. At the end of the eighteenth century no more than 10 percent of the pampas was occupied by Europeans. The rest was in Indian hands for lack of incentives to penetrate any further (Ferrer 1965, p. 41). The economic center of Argentina was the northwest, while the Río de la Plata area was a backwater. In 1776 the Viceroyalty of Río de la Plata was established as a measure of defense against the Portuguese in Brazil and the English and two years later trade was liberalized. In the meantime the horses and the cattle brought from Spain and let loose on the pampas had multiplied. The ground had been laid for the *civilización de cuero*, the cattle economy, from the beginning very much a subsistence economy, but one which with time would turn the economic geography of Argentina completely around. The gaucho culture of the pampa developed, fueled by an increasing demand for cattle products. Hides could be sold in Europe, where the ongoing industrial revolution had created an increasing import demand. (Giberti 1970, Chaps. 2–3). Hunting of wild cattle little by little gave way to the establishment of *estancias* with tame herds.

After independence the Río de la Plata region was successively integrated into the world economy. Buenos Aires turned its back on the interior (Lynch 1985, p. 616). *Saladeros* (salting factories) were established from 1810 which allowed the entire animal to be used, not just the skin, and salted meat was exported to feed the slave populations in the United States, Cuba and Brazil (Lynch 1985, p. 620). The presence of Indians on the pampa, however, provided an obstacle to the expansion of cattle raising. Towards the end of the eighteenth century the approximate frontier extended in a line from east to west south of Buenos Aires, along the Río Salado, south of San Luis and Mendoza (Giberti 1970, p. 133). According to John Lynch (1985, p. 616),

> The Pampa Indians, immediately to the south and west of the Río Salado, were the fiercest of all the Indians of the plains. Irredeemably savage, they lived and fought on horseback, a mobile and elusive enemy, handling the lance and the *bola* with supreme skill in their swift raids against settlements, *estancias*, personnel and property.

With the expansion of the pastoral economy it was inevitable that sooner or later the Indians would be pushed back. In 1833 the ex-governor of Buenos Aires, Juan Manuel de Rosas, led an expedition which pushed the frontier to Bahía Blanca and Patagonia (Giberti 1970, p. 133; Cortés Conde 1985, p 324).

In the 1850s the expansion of European textile production led to the development of a sheep and wool economy in Argentina that began to threaten cattle raising. Immigrant shepherds began to replace the gauchos and the area between Buenos Aires and Río Salado was turned into sheep lands. In the 1870s Argentina still had a land frontier. There were few humans but many animals. The country was a pastoral economy. Sheep farming was increasingly taking over the better land, pushing cattle raising towards the south and the west, towards the existing frontier (Scobie 1964, pp. 83–84). When the prices of the main agricultural exports fell from the mid-1870s the solution was to push the land frontier outwards, obtaining enough land at a low enough cost to make up for the price decrease by increased output at low cost. In 1879–1880 the so-called conquest of the desert extended the frontier well into Patagonia, and during the last two decades of the nineteenth century, the last 'wastelands' were incorporated, namely the rest of Patagonia as well as the Gran Chaco (Giberti 1970, p. 157; Ferrer 1965, p. 62).

The military extension of the frontier was merely the first step. The conquered territories had to be consolidated as well. They had to be settled. '*Gobernar es poblar* (To govern is to populate)', stated the political theorist and diplomat Juan Bautista Alberdi (quoted by Scobie 1964, p. 107). In the model introduced in Chapter 4, the army serves to pull land, and with land, labor, into the empire. This was not the case in Argentina. The conquered areas were sparsely populated, often the Indians were brutally exterminated, and the economic activities that took place in the frontier regions required very few people. A handful of gauchos could handle thousands of animals (Slatta 1992, p. 30). Over time, however, the labor intensity increased as the products changed. 'During the last third of the nineteenth century, Argentina's gauchos ceased to be an identifiable social group. Traditional frontier life on the great Argentine pampas largely vanished', summarizes Richard Slatta (1992, p. 2) in his account of the decline of the gauchos.

Sheep farming required more labor per unit of land than cattle herding—in 1895 Argentina had more than 74 million sheep (Slatta 1992, p. 194)—and when cultivation (mainly wheat) began to seriously compete with animal husbandry, matching it in terms of export value in 1900 (Scobie 1964, p. 119), the ratio increased even more. In both cases the solution was immigration: Irish and to some extent Basque and Galician shepherds (Lynch 1985, p. 650), and from around 1890 the famous *golondrinas*, seasonal workers alternating between Italy or Spain and Argentina, working the harvest seasons of both the northern and the southern hemisphere (Mörner 1985, p. 43) who in the end often became outright immigrants. Between 1857 and 1924 5.5 million Europeans emigrated to Argentina (Slatta 1992, p. 163; for details see e.g. Jefferson 1971). After 1862 immigration obtained the status of national policy in Argentina (Lynch 1985, p. 658). Between 1890 and 1910 the population almost doubled (Di Tella and Zymelman 1967, p. 139). This was 'the age of mass migration' (Hatton and Williamson 1998).

Agriculture had remained insignificant on the pampas ever since the arrival of the first Spaniards. 'Where there is nothing but grass, there is nothing with which to build a fence. Without a fence, only nomadic pastoral activities are possible' (Sawers 1996, p. 17). The arrival of barbed wire in the late 1860s changed this. It meant a revolution on the pampa, for now cultivation could compete with animal husbandry. But you also had to get there. Transportation was another constraint on the consolidation process which had to be broken. There are few waterways in the pampas. After the end of the period of civil wars, foreign capital began to flow into Argentina, much of it going into railroad construction (Ferrer 1965, p. 96; Di Tella and Zymelman 1967, p. 138)

The first railroad line—eleven kilometers—was inaugurated in 1857 to be followed by more tracks linking the interior to the capital and facilitating both the transportation of imported commodities into the hinterland and the development of export products in the interior. In 1885 Argentina had 3,700 kilometers of railroads and in 1914 33,400 kilometers (Slatta 1992, p. 143; see Cuccorese 1969, for details). This made marginal lands worth exploiting (Pendle 1963, p. 62):

> The distant north, for example, could now send its sugar and *caña* (rum) to market by train. The sugar industry of Tucumán had languished because

> transport by ox-cart to Buenos Aires doubled the cost of the produce. In 1876 the railway arrived. Six years later the sugar fields had doubled in area, iron machinery and generators had been brought in. Thus the development of Tucumán's large modern sugar industry was made possible.

The most important crop, however, was wheat, stimulated by the combination of railroads and fences. Exports rose ninefold between 1888 and 1894 (Cortés Conde 1986, p. 348). The cultivated area of the pampas increased fifteen times between 1872 and 1895 (Scobie 1964, p. 119).

Wheat was the product that propelled the Argentine economy in the 1890s. After the turn of the century meat exports provided another stimulus. Again the reason was improved transportation—overseas. The 1880s saw the arrival of the steel-hulled steamship and when refrigeration techniques made it possible to transport frozen and chilled beef and mutton to Europe exports of these products increased rapidly (Scobie 1964, p. 120; Giberti 1970, pp. 176–90; Smith 1969, Chap. 2). Argentina entered its short-lived golden age (Ferns 1969, p. 119). It would end with the Depression.

All the above is related to the expansion of the frontier. The importance of the frontier for Argentine economic development up to World War I cannot be overestimated. This development was what Guido Di Tella and Manuel Zymelman has termed 'horizontal', i.e. it was built on an expansion of the land area in pastures or under cultivation. After the closing of the frontier the expansion had to be 'vertical', a combination of an intensification of agriculture and industrialization—a far more difficult enterprise (Di Tella and Zymelman 1967, pp. 139–41).

North America

Before the arrival of Columbus between 2.5 and 10 million Indians are estimated to have been living north of Mexico (Thompson and Lamar 1981, p. 19). The Indian population of North America was not homogeneous. The tribes in the southeast had developed a productive agriculture based on maize and vegetables and their area contained an abundance of game. In the northeast, from Virginia to Canada, agriculture, hunting and fishing were the main pursuits. On the eastern and central plains buffalo hunting and agriculture were the mainstays; around the Great Lakes, wild rice, hunting and fishing. In the semi-arid southwest a civilization of town-dwellers, the Pueblo Indians, had developed a highly efficient farming system, based on irrigation. In the Great Basin area (mainly Nevada and Utah) scattered desert bands survived on the gathering of seeds and wild vegetables, complemented by some hunting. The California peoples practiced hunting, gathering and fishing. The Pacific Northwest, finally, was wholly non-agricultural, based on fishing, whaling, hunting and wood products in a caste society with a wealthy aristocracy at the top and slaves at the bottom. The polities of these societies were usually small and leadership often diffused (Thompson and Lamar 1981, pp. 20–21; cf. Morison 1965, pp. 11–15).

The contact between Indians and Europeans on the North American frontier would prove fatal for the Indians. The European immigration and gradual push of the frontier into the interior of North America by the end of the nineteenth century had resulted in a close to complete substitution of European economy, society, religion and culture for the various Indian ones. By and large, Indian society had ceased to exist. European agriculture, cattle raising and manufacturing had been substituted for indigenous hunting, fishing, gathering and farming. Exactly like Argentina, as had been forcefully argued by Richard Hakluyt (1969) at the end of the sixteenth century (Brogan 1999, p. 13), North America had to be settled and cultivated in order to yield its riches. The English and the Americans conceived of the frontier lands as 'empty'. A clash between European and Indian conceptions of property rights was inevitable. '*Labranza mata crianza y viceversa* (farming kills ranching and vice versa)', states a Spanish proverb. Something similar occurred in the meeting of Europeans and Indians. European farming required private property rights and fencing which made Indian hunting activities difficult (Brogan 1999, p. 11):

> This fact implied four things about the European advance. It meant that the country would succeed most completely which could most easily export the largest number of people; which could most easily keep them supplied—in other words, which was strongest at sea over the longest period; which had colonists who brought with them the most appropriate

skills; and, lastly, which had the most adaptable culture, in the widest sense of that word.

That country turned out to be England.

But England was not alone. The French established a foothold in Canada (the New France colony) and during the reign of Louis XIV also claimed the Great Lakes and the Mississippi. In 1699 the Louisiana colony was established. The Dutch had founded New Netherland in the early 1600s. The Spanish held New Mexico and they settled Upper California as late as 1769. All three would be overtaken by the British (and the Americans), the Dutch colony as early as 1674. The other two would take longer.

Leonard Thompson and Howard Lamar (1981, pp. 23–26) have identified five phases in the extension of the frontier in North America. The earliest British colonies, those of Jamestown (1607) and Plymouth (1620) survived their first years with great difficulty—both came close to being wiped out. Soon, however, tobacco, grown with the aid of African slaves, turned the Virginia colony into a staple producer.[7] The first cargo was shipped in 1614 (Eccles 1972, p. 18). Plymouth was engulfed by the Massachusetts Bay colony, founded in 1629. Fishing and agriculture produced exports. Connecticut, New Hampshire and Maine were drawn into the same sphere. Between 1685 and 1688 New England was consolidated (Morison et al. 1980a, p. 81). It took a settler rebellion in Virginia (1676–1677), a bloody Indian uprising in New England in 1675–1676 and the peace with France in 1713 after the War of the Spanish Succession before the British Atlantic colonies could start a westward expansion. Clyde Milner (1981, p. 125) speaks of these frontiers as 'survival frontiers'.

By then the British had reached and settled the territory up to the Appalachians. The population of Boston reached the 17,000 mark in 1740 (Brogan 1999, p. 88) and twenty years later Philadelphia—the largest town in the British colonies in North America—had 23,750 inhabitants (Brogan 1999, p. 96). Cities began to be important. This expansion

[7] In the end, more than half a million slaves would be imported into the British colonies in North America and subsequently into the United States up to 1860 (Thomas 1997, p. 804; Klein 1999, pp. 210–11). Fogel (1989, p. 18) gives a figure of 693,000.

also involved the French and Indian War (1754–1763), part of the Seven Years' War between Britain and France in Europe, which ended with the Treaty of Paris and secured the expulsion of the French from the territory east of the Mississippi. By then the total population of the British colonies was around 1.5 million, one-third of whom were black slaves (Morison 1965, p. 173). The rate of immigration had been rapid. Fifty years earlier, in 1713, the population of the twelve colonies that had existed at that date had been 360,000 and the only colony that had been added since then, after a war with Spain, was Georgia (Morison et al. 1980a, p. 91).

The second phase of frontier extension went on up to 1760. The third phase of the European westward expansion extended from 1763 to 1815 and included the American Revolution (1775–1783) which established the United States and the renewed conflict between the latter country and Britain during the Napoleonic Wars. This was the period when what Felipe Fernández-Armesto (2004, p. 80) has called the landward turn took place. Immigrants poured in at an unprecedented rate (Fernández-Armesto 2004, pp. 84–85). During this phase the frontier was pushed through Tennessee, Kentucky and Ohio up to the Mississippi. It was, however, not until the end of the 1812 war with Britain—'one of the most unnecessary in history' (Brogan 1999, p. 253)—that US control of the entire area east of the Mississippi was assured.

The Louisiana Purchase in 1803, in turn, secured the first foothold west of the river. Its importance cannot be overestimated. The huge Louisiana territory, which extended from the Gulf of Mexico to the Canadian border and from the Mississippi River to the Rocky Mountains, had passed from French to Spanish hands in 1762 and back to France in 1800. The territory had proved extremely difficult to settle (Eccles 1972, pp. 158–66) but its importance loomed large because of the development of the Mississippi-Missouri waterway as a route into the interior (Fernández-Armesto 2004, p. 76). Its purchase by the United States finished France as a competitor in North America and doubled the US territory (Brogan 1999, p. 237).

During the fourth phase the Americans penetrated west of the Mississippi. The reason was simple. 'The quality of land and resources in the West was unmatched … it was the natural resource wealth of the

American West that served as the fundamental determinant of our extensive growth in attracting capital and labor to America', writes Douglass North (1956, pp. 493–94). A wholesale westward movement began across the entire continent (Brogan 1999, p. 220):

> Of course it had always been there, that vast, tempting, unexplored wilderness; but until the late eighteenth century the advance upon it had necessarily been slow. Demography, politics, diplomacy, economics, technology and the Indians had seen to that. By the second quarter of the nineteenth century the balance had been tipped dramatically to the other side, and the race for the Rockies and the Pacific was fairly begun. With it also began the great age of the Wild West.

The consequences for the Indians were devastating (Milner 1981, p. 144):

> Before the War of 1812, Indians inhabited and to some extent controlled much of the state of Georgia and nearly all of what was to become Alabama and Mississippi. Also large sections of western Tennessee and Kentucky, northwestern Ohio, and much of what remained of the Old Northwest [Ohio, Indiana, Illinois, Michigan, Wisconsin and Minnesota] could be called Indian land. By 1840, with the exception of a few small enclaves, none of this land could be labeled Indian … the overwhelming majority of native peoples had either been removed to the trans-Mississippi or had died in the process of moving.

The American government took an active interest in the expansion. Immediately after the Louisiana Purchase, President Thomas Jefferson sent an expedition led by the two army officers Meriwether Lewis and William Clark up the Missouri River across the American continent to map the new territory, find a negotiable water communication route across it and establish claims on what lay further west. They set out in May 1804 and returned to St Louis in September 1806, having descended the Columbia River to the Pacific Ocean, making contact with more than seventy Indian tribes (Lewis and Clark 1979). Some forty years later the West was well explored (Brogan 1999, p. 237) and well on its way to being conquered and settled. 'Go west, young man!' exhorted Horace Greeley in his *New York Tribune*.[8] Little by little, family farms spread across to Iowa, Wisconsin and Minnesota.

Further east, the conquest was consolidated. Florida was added in 1821, for the second and final time. (It had been in American hands for twenty years from 1763 before it was taken over again by Spain during the wars of the American Revolution.) In 1830 an Indian Removal Act was passed: an excuse for 'a series of shabby and dishonorable proceedings' (Morison 1965, p. 450) which served to remove 60,000 Indians from the Five Civilized Tribes (Cherokee, Choctaw, Creek, Chickasaw and Seminole) from their ancestral lands in the southeast to areas west of the Mississippi—the Indian Territory (present-day Oklahoma) (Brogan 1999, p. 67)—and north of the Ohio River, in the Old Northwest, removal was begun as well (Morison 1965, pp. 445–46).

As industrialization began and transportation into the interior improved, via canals and railroads, the pace of land alienation from the Indians was speeded up considerably. 'Thus the brief era of the canals and the railroad witnessed the expropriation of much more Indian lands than did the previous two and a quarter centuries of English and American expansion' (Berkhofer 1981, p. 55). Transportation into the interior was vastly improved by canals and railroads. The use of the steamboat on the Mississippi from 1816 made it possible to ship foodstuffs from the west to the south (North 1966b, p. 102), and the Erie Canal which linked the Hudson River to the Great Lakes, opened in 1825, stimulated west–east trade and triggered a canal boom (Brogan 1999, p. 271).

The fourth phase ended with the cession of California, Arizona, Utah, Colorado, Nevada and New Mexico by Mexico, after the Mexican War, 1846–1848. The Americans resettled all the major tribes east of the Mississippi in reservations west of the river and fought the Indians on the Great Plains all the way from the Dakotas to Texas. Land was taken over both from the Indians and the Spanish. Independent republics or regions were established in some instances before these were absorbed by the United States. Texas was wrung from Mexico in 1836 and became a state

[8] In 1859 Greeley did it himself, traveling by railroad and stage coach from New York to San Francisco (Greeley 1963).

in the union nine years later. It was the 'manifest destiny' of the United States to expand in the west (Brogan 1999, p. 297). The expansion rested on immigration. Canal (and later railroad) construction created a strong demand for labor and with this came the settlers. In the 1920s 129,000 immigrants were registered, in the 1830s 540,000 and in the 1850s more than 2,800,000 (Morison 1965, p. 479).

The fifth phase of the frontier expansion began with the California gold rush in 1848. A mining frontier was established and expanded (Thompson and Lamar 1981, p. 27). 'Forty-niners' poured into the mining camps. The white California population increased dramatically, from around 8,000 in 1846 (Osborne 2013, p. 40) to 92,000 in 1850 and 380,000 in 1860 (Brogan 1999, pp. 298–99). At the same time the Indian population there was drastically reduced, from 100,000 in 1850 to less than 35,000 ten years later (Morison 1965, p. 750). With time, the California population became permanent and dedicated itself to the development of farming. 'This process was to be repeated time and again in the decade of the "sixties": in Colorado, Nevada, Arizona, Idaho, Montana and Wyoming' (Morison et al. 1980b, p. 9)—mining followed by farming.

The canal boom was followed by the expansion of the railroad system across the American continent from the mid-nineteenth century. The railroad quickly rendered the canals obsolete (Morison 1965, p. 478). The acts providing for the creation of the Central Pacific and Union Railroads in 1862 and Union Pacific Railroads in 1864 triggered a wave of railroad construction. In 1869 the legendary junction of the Union Pacific and the Central Pacific was completed with a golden spike at Promontory Point, Utah. In 1900 almost 322,000 kilometers of railroad were available, more than in all of Europe (Morison et al. 1980b, p. 31). These developments contributed to carrying the center of the American population ever more into the interior, crossing the Mississippi in 1891 (Brogan 1999, p. 397). Farmers moved into the Great Plains and other areas in the west in their 'prairie schooners'. 'Everywhere between the Canadian border and the Rio Grande, between the Rockies and the valley of the Missouri, towns mushroomed, farms blossomed' (Brogan 1999, p. 422). From 1860 to 1910 the acreage of improved farm land in the United States trebled (Morison et al. 1980b, p. 120). The population in the west increased with amazing speed. Between 1870 and 1890, the population west of the Mississippi rose from 6.9 million to 18.8 million (Morison et al. 1980b, p. 24).

Much of the public domain of land was transferred to individuals between 1860 and 1900. The Homestead Act of 1862 provided for free acquisition of 65 hectares of land from the public domain in the west provided that it was cultivated for five years (Brogan 1999, p. 384). The railroad companies were given 73 million, the states were granted land from the public domain and 81 million hectares (much of it Indian) was put on the market to the highest bidder (Morison et al. 1980b, p. 123). This stimulated both farming and land speculation (North 1966a, Chap. 10). So did the arrival of new machines—the mechanical reaper, the harvester, the self-knotting binder, the steel-toothed cultivator, improved plows and steel-wire fences—as well as a dramatic increase of the price of wheat at the beginning of the 1850s (Morison 1965, p. 586). The conversion of the prairie to wheat land was 'arguably the biggest modification of the natural environment ever achieved in the course of human history' (Fernández-Armesto 2004, p. 112). And if it wasn't farms, it was the cattle kingdom on the open range, animals driven from Texas to Wyoming, Colorado and Montana to be fattened before embarking on the railroads to the east (Morison et al. 1980b, pp. 15–21). In both cases, Indian interests were trampled under the boot between 1860 and 1890. Tribe after tribe was driven from its ancient homelands. The 1887 Allotment (Dawes) Act, by which reservations were broken up into individual homesteads, made the Indians lose almost 35 million hectares between 1887 and 1934 (Brogan 1999, p. 70).

From 1869 American policy toward the Indians amounted to a complete onslaught (Thompson and Lamar 1981, p. 32):

> Beginning in 1869, a new American policy of *total* assimilation—the so-called Peace Policy—assigned Protestant missionaries as agents to Indian reservations in the West where they were expected to Christianize their charges and to teach them agriculture. Another aim of the policy was to break the power of the traditional chiefs so that the assimilation process could be accelerated … Seldom in history has an indigenous

> society been so subjected to a simultaneous attack on its religion, culture, economy, and political institutions as in the American West between 1867 and 1890.

At the end of the nineteenth century the frontier was closed. While it existed the demand for labor had been huge and its power of attraction tremendous. The last two phases had been rapid. During the century after 1820 33 million people emigrated from Europe to the United States (Hatton and Williamson 1998, p. 7).

New frontiers had to be opened up for the Americans, way up north through the Alaska Purchase from Russia in 1867, and outside the United States in Cuba, Puerto Rico and the Philippines during the 1898 Spanish-American War; in the same year Hawaii was annexed.

The Indian population had been decimated at a frightening rate, partly by war, but far more important was the extension of the 'virulent disease frontier': 'hepatitis, encephalitis, polio, and perhaps yellow fever, the Europeans introduced them to the contagions of smallpox, whooping cough, measles, chicken pox, bubonic plague, typhus, malaria, diphtheria, amoebic dysentery, influenza, and a number of helminthic infections' (Cook 1981, p. 189). By 1890 the Indian population had dwindled to a mere 250,000, its lowest point after the arrival of the Europeans, to be compared to 55 million whites—an estimated decline of from 60 to 98 percent of the population before the contact with the Europeans (Berkhofer 1981, pp. 48–49). The extension of the frontier served to pull in only land, not people. 'Indians in British areas of expansion were too poor to be worth exploiting for tribute. It was more economical to dispossess them and replace them with white farmers or black slaves', summarizes Felipe Fernández-Armesto (2004, p. 69).

At the end of the nineteenth century the European takeover was complete. In 1890, the Indian Territory was opened to settlement. The frontier was closed. At the end of the 1930s when the allotment of land had ended only 2 percent of the land area remained in Indian trust (Berkhofer 1981, p. 47). 'The ultimate outcome of frontier interaction … was the disappearance of the Indian from American history' (Berkhofer 1981, p. 75).

Canada

The pattern of frontier expansion in Canada was not the same as in the United States. As Harold Innis demonstrated in *The Fur Trade in Canada*, the creation of the former nation was largely a function of its geography (Innis 1999). Canada was crossed from west to east by a series of waterways (Winks 1999, p. xxxi):

> Rather than a series of regions each of which has more natural affinity with a like region in the United States than with other Canadian regions, she is a single, coherent unit, created by an east–west line of imperial communications, a line based on the St. Lawrence River, the Great Lakes, and the western waterways and trails, penetrating via the natural extension of the Atlantic Ocean into the capitals of Europe.

The existence of this natural communication system made it easy to move the frontier westwards. St John's in Newfoundland had been claimed by the English in 1583, and the French had founded Quebec in 1608 and Montreal in 1642. Staples production predated both, exported via trading posts on the coast. (Quebec was founded precisely to trade fur with the Indians.) The first Canadian staple was cod (Innis 1940). French fishermen had begun to frequent the rich fishing grounds on the Grand Banks outside Newfoundland less than a decade after John Cabot's first landfall on the North American coast in 1497 (Morison 1971, p. 225).

It was, however, the fur trade—beaver—that triggered the westward expansion. The vogue for wide-brimmed felt hats in Europe made for a high demand for beaver underfur to make the felt (Eccles 1972, p. 11), and the fur trade fitted well into an already established pattern. 'The *coureurs des bois* and buckskin-clad frontiersmen slotted into an existing framework, which linked hunting grounds and routes of trade and tribute' (Fernández-Armesto 2004, p. 73). The Canadian French could sell all the furs they could obtain at a fixed price (Eccles 1972, p. 84), and so they did. The beaver is a stationary animal, easy to kill, and once the beaver population of eastern Canada began to be exterminated it was both imperative and easy to move west. The expansion built on the cooperation of the competing French and English with the Indian hunters and trappers. The number of Europeans in Canada was never high: around 10,000 in 1680 (Eccles 1972, p. 77), a mere 18,000 in 1713 and about twice that figure in 1734 (Morison 1965, p. 157). The Indians became eager consumers of European manufactured goods (including alcohol) and played an essential role in the fur trade. As more sophisticated transportation facilities were developed the ground was prepared for the later development of lumbering and wheat production as the supply of animals began to dry up (Innis 1956, pp. 62–77, 220–32, 242–51, 273–79). As Ramsay Cook (1981, p. 195) has pointed out, the fur trade 'died of its own success, for success brought the depletion of resources'. It was a prime example of the 'tragedy of the commons' with no central authority present to enforce conservation of the beaver population.

In their exploitation of Canada and their territorial ambitions in North America the French clashed with the British. The New England colonies nearby presented a potential threat to New France. In 1668 an English ship made it into the Hudson Bay and two years later the Hudson's Bay Company was chartered and immediately started setting up trading posts in its territory (Eccles 1972, p. 87):

> What made this threat so dangerous was that the … cost of shipping goods from England to the Bay was far less than from France to Quebec, then a thousand miles by canoe to Lake Superior and beyond. These events, in the Hudson Bay and the Great Lakes region, marked the beginning of the Anglo-French struggle for the continent.

This struggle—which included the French strategic quest for Louisiana, the War of the Spanish Succession, thirty years of peace 1713–1744, and the inconclusive war of 1744–1748 before the French and Indian War broke out in 1754—ended only with the 1763 Treaty of Paris. New France came under British suzerainty, and Britain was to reign supreme on the continent until 1775.

Innis argues that it was the reliance on staples production that was responsible for keeping Canada within the British Empire when the United States seceded. The fur market was in Europe, it was Europe that supplied Canada with manufactures, and the borders of Canada coincide relatively well with those of the fur-trading area (Innis 1999, pp. 91–92).

Innis also alleges there was another interesting consequence of the fur trade: 'Canada has had no serious problems with her native peoples since the fur trade depended primarily on these races. In the United States no point of contact of such magnitude was at hand', he writes, 'and troubles with the Indians were a result' (Innis 1999, p. 392). Innis' statement is, however, a truth with modifications. When Columbus arrived in America for the first time perhaps as many as 1 million Indians were living in Canada, Alaska and Greenland. In 1911, the figure was 108,000 (Cook 1981, p. 189). In the end, the Canadian Indians suffered the same fate as their US brethren: 'wholesale removal of long-established tribes, and finally confinement on reservations' (Cook 1981, p. 204).

Southern Africa

When the first Dutch colonists under Jan van Riebeeck (Leipoldt 1936) moved into Table Bay in 1652, the purpose was to establish a provisioning station for Dutch ships going to Asia. The settlers, however, had other things in mind. Van Riebeeck had a hedge planted outside Cape Town to mark the border between the Dutch colony and the San and the Khoikhoi (Katzen 1969, pp. 189–90), but to no avail. The Dutch East India Company administration very much left the colonists to do things as they saw fit. In 1659–1660 they fought a war against the Khoikhoi. There was nothing the company could do to stop the *burghers* from expanding their activities into the territory occupied by the Africans. A process had been set in motion which culminated with the 1913 Natives Land Act which reduced the African share of the land to a mere 7 percent (Horwitz 1967, p. 134).[9] All the way from 1652 to World War I the conflict between Europeans and Africans in South Africa was a conflict over land, of how to draw the borders between European and African territory (Lundahl and Ndlela 1980).

Land was the most important production factor in Southern Africa when the Europeans arrived. The Nguni-, Sotho- and Shona-speaking

[9] Subsequently revised to 13.8 percent by the 1936 Natives Trust and Land Act (Thompson 1990, pp. 178–79).

peoples were herders and extensive agriculturalists, the Khoikhoi were nomadic herders and the San lived off hunting, fishing and collection in the veld. Cattle-raising was important and frequently led to land disputes. Shifting cultivation required large areas due to the necessity of periodic fallows (Lundahl and Ndlela 1980).

Land was as important for the Europeans as it was for the Africans. The Dutch were *boere*—farmers—and they were dependent on territorial expansion. Capital was scarce and the Dutch were few—no more than 4,000 not employed directly by the East India Company as late as 1740 (Houghton 1973, p. 3). Their economic activities were hence bound to be land-intensive. The Dutch became cattle raisers. It was inevitable that they would clash with the Africans in their quest for land.

Little by little the Dutch deprived the Khoikhoi of their territory and in the process obtained the labor necessary for tending their herds, in the manner envisaged in the empire model in Chapter 4. The European economy could expand in the simplest possible fashion: adding land and labor in fixed proportions, and when the native population began to be decimated, introducing slaves from Africa, Madagascar and Southeast Asia (Davenport and Saunders 2000, p. 25).

In 1795 Britain seized the Cape Colony from the Dutch. By that time the colony consisted of around 20,000 Dutch, 25,000 slaves, 15,000 Khoikhoi and a few thousand Bantu speakers in the east (Elphick and Giliomee 1979, p. 360). The change of government did not lead to any change of land policy. On the contrary (Saunders and Smith 1999, p. 597):

> The struggle between white settlers and African populations for control of the limited well-watered land was marked by recurrent warfare, in which British troops repeatedly intervened to play a crucial role in supporting settlers who were unable on their own to displace African farmers.

The first two of the so-called Xhosa wars had been fought before the arrival of the British. Seven more took place before the last one ended in 1879 with the final defeat of the Xhosa (Mostert 1992). In 1820 large-scale British settlement began with the arrival of 5,000 colonists who were settled on the borderlands from which the Xhosa had been evicted in the Eastern Cape (Saunders and Smith 1999, p. 598). The British were, however, outnumbered by the Dutch, which led to tension when the former set out to reorganize the colony and erode the institution of slavery until it was finally abolished in the British Empire in 1833. Boers and Britons did not intermarry other than exceptionally. The white populations remained divided.

The division led to what in South African history is known as the Great Trek (Walker 1948). *Trekboere* had for a long time been active on the frontier, extending it in bits and pieces, but when the abolition of slavery created an acute labor problem for the Boers, and land was growing increasingly scarce in the Cape Colony, they decided to make a radical break with Britain and trekked northeastwards in a fan-shaped movement, beginning in 1835 and 1836, founding the Orange Free State and Transvaal north of the Vaal and Orange rivers; the independence of both regions was recognized by Britain in the early 1850s. The supply of labor was ensured by the takeover of African land.

During their northward migration, the *voortrekkers* ran straight into the turmoil caused by the *difaqane*: the westward population movement resulting from the expansion of the Zulu kingdom from Natal. The Boers defeated both the Zulu and the Ndebele (1837–1840) (Davenport and Saunders 2000, pp. 78–79) and large land areas were taken over by the Dutch. In less than fifteen years they settled the best lands of South Africa (Lundahl and Ndlela 1980). The British also moved northeastwards. Following the 1838 victory at Blood River against the Zulu, the Boer Republic of Natalia had been founded, in 1839. In 1843 it was taken over by Britain and became the Natal colony.

The economy of South Africa had not changed much from the arrival of the first Dutch in the seventeenth century to the mid-nineteenth century. Livestock raising continued to be the dominant activity and the prospects for the colony were deemed to be poor in comparison with the situation elsewhere in the empire. South Africa failed to attract British immigrants (Saunders and Smith 1999, p. 604). This state of affairs changed completely with the discoveries of diamonds in Kimberley in 1867 (Worger 1987) and gold on the Witwatersrand in 1886 (Rosenthal 1970). These events led to a very strong increase in the demand for labor, especially for the gold mines where the economic problem consisted in extracting gold from low-grade ore with labor-intensive techniques. In order to secure the supply, extraordinary measures were resorted to—some of which led to the closing of the frontier at the end of the nineteenth century. All that remained thereafter was the formal racial division of the territory through the legislation to which we have already made reference.

The most important of these measures from the frontier point of view was the crushing of the remaining African chiefdoms and the continued takeover of the land to lower the reservation wage of African workers. In 1870 a number of such chiefdoms still existed, but thirty years later virtually all of them were gone, with or without violence: West Griqua, Southern and Natal Nguni, Southern Sotho, Tswana, Mpondo and East Griqua (Thompson 1975). The Zulu were defeated in 1879 (Morris 1966, Part Two). Independent African peasantries had been emerging since the 1830s as a response to the imposition of cash taxes and the development of new wants, working as tenants on 'European' land (Bundy 1979). A number of laws issued during the last decade of the nineteenth century and the first of the twentieth it more difficult for Africans to rent land, and the crowning achievement was the 1913 Natives Land Act which prohibited Africans from purchasing or renting land in areas that were not scheduled as African (Lundahl and Ndlela 1980, p. 112).

At the same time the British had settled their differences with the Boers. In 1871 they had secured Griqualand West, which contained the diamond fields. In 1877 the Transvaal was annexed as well. As could be expected this act provoked a reaction. Led by Paul Kruger, the Transvaalers rebelled against Britain at the end of 1880. After a British defeat at Majuba Hill the following year, a convention was signed which gave the Transvaal considerable autonomy under British suzerainty (Saunders and Smith, pp. 607–08).

The issue did not end there, however. The discovery of gold on the Witwatersrand dramatically increased the economic importance of the Transvaal. In 1890 Cecil Rhodes became prime minister of the Cape Colony. He was convinced that the future development of Southern Africa was crucially dependent on British leadership over a number of self-governing states in the area. We will soon come back to what this implied further north. For the Transvaal it resulted in the so-called Jameson Raid. The idea was that the British in the Transvaal should rise against the Boers and that British forces should thereafter 'restore order'. The insurrection attempt failed, but only after a British column had entered the Transvaal at the end of 1895. The affair turned out to be a complete fiasco and forced Rhodes to resign as prime minister (Rotberg 1988, Chap. 19).

Kruger and his people began their preparations for meeting a British invasion on a larger scale. They had good reasons to do so, for the British Secretary of State for the Colonies, Joseph Chamberlain, a convinced imperialist, moved to secure British supremacy in Southern Africa once and for all, and this included a British Transvaal. The Boer War broke out in 1899. The British had hoped for a short campaign, but the war dragged on for almost three years and involved no fewer than 450,000 British and Empire forces against a tenth of that number of adversaries (Saunders and Smith 1999, p. 617), before the two Boer republics were defeated (Pakenham 1979). In 1910 the Union of South Africa could be proclaimed.

The South African frontier had been closed and peace prevailed within the Union. An economy had been created which rested on European ownership of the land and African labor: a discriminatory economy and society that would be further developed during the nineteenth century until things began to be reversed in 1994 (Lundahl 1982). But that is another story.

Rhodesia

The discussion of the extension of the European frontier in Southern Africa will not be complete unless the story of the creation of Rhodesia is added. This is a much later story than that of South Africa and it is intimately bound up with the name of Cecil Rhodes: the man who more than any other personified British imperialism (Rotberg 1988). Rhodes was hoping to find a second Witwatersrand north of the Limpopo, in Matabeleland or Mashonaland. He obtained a royal charter for his British South Africa Company that allowed it to act on behalf of Britain both north of the Limpopo and north of the Zambezi. The so-called Pioneer Column was recruited and in

1890 began the conquest of the northern areas. No second Rand was found, but the Ndebele and the Shona were defeated and in 1897 their territories were finally secured for Britain. For the Africans, the end was the same as in South Africa. The land gradually passed from African to European hands, and force and taxation were resorted to in order to mobilize labor (Lundahl and Ndlela 1980). The 1930 Land Apportionment Act conceded 50 percent of the total land area of Southern Rhodesia to the whites (3 percent of the population) and 30 percent to the Africans (97 percent of the population), the rest remaining undistributed (Palmer 1977, p. 185).

***

As our journey—however selective—has, we hope, demonstrated, the frontier has always been an important part of human history: military, economic and cultural. No matter how you look at it, as soon as humans join together in groups they clash with other groups. They attempt to establish their domains or territories, i.e. they seek to stake out their claims and mark the borders of them—and other groups do the same. Sooner or later you are bound to have contending forces, competing for the same territory. Frontiers are seldom 'natural'. They are 'artificial' or 'political'. With time the competing units grow in size. Some territories are absorbed by others. Some civilizations are engulfed by their foes. Altogether, the game is one of attempting to push frontiers outwards.

As we hope also to have shown, the frontier issue is not just one of military conquest, however. On the contrary, in order to secure a conquest, the frontier must be settled, cultivated, mined or made subject to some other economic activity which ensures that it is permanently populated. (Claiming a no-man's land is difficult and likely to be conducive to counter-claims and conflict.) And with settlement come other human activities, activities that help to consolidate the frontier even further, like religion, culture, language and cross-border trade. Conquest and settlement are inseparable. The Sword and the Plow come together, and in periods when further expansion of the frontier is not at the top of the political agenda the Book may have a chance to thrive as well.

References

Bagnall, Nigel. (1999). *The Punic wars: Rome Carthage and the struggle for the Mediterranean*. London: Pimlico.

Bakewell, Peter. (1984). Mining in colonial Spanish America. In Leslie Bethell (Ed.), *The Cambridge history of Latin America, volume II: Colonial Latin America*. Cambridge: Cambridge University Press.

Barraclough, Geoffrey. (1984). *The origins of modern Germany* (2nd ed.). New York/London: W.W. Norton & Co.

Bartlett, Robert. (1993). *The making of Europe: Conquest, colonization and cultural change 950–1350*. Princeton: Princeton University Press.

Beard, Mary. (2015). *SPQR: A history of ancient Rome*. New York: Liveright.

Beard, Mary, & Crawford, Michael. (1999). *Rome in the late republic*. Bristol: Bristol Classical Press.

Bengoa, José. (1987). *Historia del pueblo mapuche (Siglo XIX y XX)* (2nd ed.). Santiago: Ediciones Sur.

Berkhofer, Robert F., Jr. (1981). The North American frontier as process and context. In Howard Lamar & Leonard Thompson (Eds.), *The frontier in history. North America and Southern Africa compared*. New Haven/London: Yale University Press.

Bisson, Thomas N. (1986). *The medieval crown of Aragon: A short history*. Oxford: Clarendon.

Bloch, Marc. (1962). *Feudal society*. London: Routledge & Kegan Paul.

Bloch, Marc. (1969). *Land and work in medieval Europe. Selected papers*. New York: Harper & Row.

Braudel, Fernand. (1975). *The Mediterranean and the Mediterranean world in the age of Philip II* (2nd ed., Vol. 2). London: Fontana/Collins.

Brogan, Hugh. (1999). *The Longman history of the United States of America* (2nd ed.). London/New York: Longman.

Bundy, Colin. (1979). *The rise and fall of the South African peasantry*. London: Heinemann.

Cantar de Mío Cid (2007). Barcelona: Galaxia Gutenberg.

Castro, Américo. (1948). *España en su historia: Cristianos, moros y judíos*. Buenos Aires: Losada.

Castro, Américo. (1971). *The Spaniards: An introduction to their history*. Berkeley: University of California Press.

Chalmeta, Pedro. (1994). An approximate picture of the economy of al-Andalus. In Salma Khadra Jayyusi (Ed.), *The legacy of Muslim Spain* (Vol. 2). Leiden: E.J. Brill.

Christiansen, Eric. (1997). *The Northern Crusades*. London: Penguin.

Cipolla, Carlo M. (1965). *Guns, sails, and empires: Technological innovation and the early phases of European expansion, 1400–1700*. New York: Pantheon Books.

Collier, Simon, & Sater, William F. (1996). *A history of Chile, 1808–1994*. Cambridge: Cambridge University Press.

Collins, Roger. (1995). *Early medieval Spain: Unity in diversity, 400–1000* (2nd ed.). Basingstoke: Macmillan.

Collins, Roger. (1998). *Charlemagne*. Basingstoke: Macmillan.

Cook, Ramsay. (1981). The social and economic frontier in North America. In Howard Lamar & Leonard Thompson (Eds.), *The frontier in history. North America and Southern Africa compared*. New Haven/London: Yale University Press.

Cornell, T. J. (1995). *The beginnings of Rome. Italy and Rome from the Bronze age to the Punic wars (c. 1000–264 BC)*. London/New York: Routledge.

Cortés Conde, Roberto. (1985). The export economy of Argentina 1880–1920. In Roberto Cortés Conde & Shane J Hunt (Eds.), *The Latin American economies: Growth and the export sector* (pp. 1880–1930). New York/London: Holmes & Meier.

Cortés Conde, Roberto. (1986). The growth of the argentine economy, c. 1870–1914. In Leslie Bethell (Ed.), *The Cambridge history of Latin America, volume V: c. 1870 to 1930*. Cambridge: Cambridge University Press.

Cuccorese, Horacio Juan. (1969). *Historia de los ferrocarriles en Argentina*. Buenos Aires: Ediciones Macchi.

Davenport, Rodney, & Saunders, Cristopher. (2000). *South Africa: A modern history* (5th ed.). Basingstoke: Macmillan.

David, Jean-Michel. (1997). *The Roman conquest of Italy*. Oxford/Malden: Blackwell.

Davis, Ralph. (1973). *The rise of the Atlantic economies*. Ithaca: Cornell University Press.

Di Tella, Guido, & Zymelman, Manuel. (1967). *Las etapas del desarrollo económico argentino*. Buenos Aires: Editorial Universitaria de Buenos Aires.

Duby, Georges. (1974). *The early growth of the European economy: Warriors and peasants from the seventh to the twelfth century*. London: Weidensfeld & Nicholson.

Eccles, William C. (1972). *France in America*. New York: Harper & Row.

Einhard. (1969). The life of Charlemagne. In Einhard and Notker the Stammerer, *Two lives of Charlemagne*. London: Penguin Books.

Elliott, J. H. (1984). The Spanish conquest and settlement of America. In Leslie Bethell (Ed.), *The Cambridge history of Latin America, volume I: Colonial Latin America*. Cambridge: Cambridge University Press.

Elphick, Richard, & Giliomee, Herman (Eds.). (1979). *The shaping of South African society, 1652–1820*. Cape Town: Longman.
Ercilla y Zúñiga, Alonso de. (1966). *La Araucana* (5th ed.). Madrid: Aguilar.
Fernández-Armesto, Felipe. (2004). *The Americas: The history of a hemisphere*. London: Phoenix.
Ferns, H. S. (1969). *Argentina*. London: Ernest Benn.
Ferrer, Aldo. (1965). *La economía argentina: Las etapas de su desarrollo y problemas actuales*. México/Buenos Aires: Fondo de Cultura Económica.
Findlay, Ronald, & O'Rourke, Kevin H. (2007). *Power and plenty: Trade, war, and the world economy in the second millennium*. Princeton/Oxford: Princeton University Press.
Findlay, Ronald, & O'Rourke, Kevin H. (2012). War, trade and natural resources: A historical perspective. In Michelle R Garfinkel & Stergios Skaperdas (Eds.), *The Oxford handbook of the economics of peace and conflict*. Oxford/New York: Oxford University Press.
Fletcher, Richard A. (1989). *The quest for El Cid*. London: Hutchinson.
Fogel, Robert William. (1989). *Without consent or contract: The rise and fall of American slavery*. New York: W.W. Norton & Co.
Fouracre, Paul. (2000). *The age of Charles Martel*. Harlow: Longman.
Gabrieli, Francesco. (1968). *Muhammad and the conquests of Islam*. London: Weidenfeld & Nicholson.
García de Cortázar, Fernando. (2005). *Atlas de historia de España*. Barcelona: Planeta.
Gibb, Hamilton A. R. (1970). *The Arab conquests in Central Asia*. New York: AMS Press.
Giberti, Horacio G. E. (1970). *Historia económica de la ganadería argentina*. Buenos Aires: Solar/Hachette.
Grandazzi, Alexandre. (1997). *The foundation of Rome: Myth and history*. Ithaca/London: Cornell University Press.
Greeley, Horace. (1963). *An overland journey: From New York to San Francisco in the summer of 1859*. London: Macdonald.
Gruen, Eric S. (1974). *The last generation of the Roman republic*. Berkeley: University of California Press.
Hakluyt, Richard. (1969). *The principal navigations voyages traffiques & discoveries of the English nation. Made by sea or over-land to the remote and farthest distant quarters of the earth at any time within the compasse of these 1600 yeeres* (3rd ed., Vol. 12). New York: Augustus M. Kelley.
Halecki, Oscar. (1956). *A history of Poland*. New York: Roy.

Harris, William V. (1979). *War and imperialism in republican Rome 327–70 BC*. Oxford: Oxford University Press.

Hatton, Timothy J., & Williamson, Jeffrey G. (1998). *The age of mass migration: Causes and economic impact*. New York/Oxford: Oxford University Press.

Hawting, G. R. (2000). *The first dynasty of Islam: The Umayyad caliphate AD 661–750* (2nd ed.). London/New York: Routledge.

Hill, Donald Rutherford. (1975). The role of the camel and the horse in the early Arab conquests. In V. J. Parry & M. E. Yapp (Eds.), *War, technology and society in the Middle East*. London: Oxford University Press.

Hodges, Richard. (1989). *Dark age economics: The origins of towns and trade AD 600–1000* (2nd ed.). London: Duckworth.

Horwitz, Ralph. (1967). *The political economy of South Africa*. London: Weidenfeld and Nicolson.

Houghton, Desmond Hobart. (1973). *The South African economy* (3rd ed.). Cape Town: Oxford University Press.

Hoyland, Robert G. (2015). *In god's path: The Arab conquests and the creation of an Islamic empire*. New York: Oxford University Press.

Innis, Harold A. (1940). *The Cod fisheries: The history of an international economy*. New Haven: Yale University Press.

Innis, Harold A. (1956). *Essays in Canadian economic history*. Toronto: University of Toronto Press.

Innis, Harold A. (1999). *The Fur trade in Canada: An introduction to Canadian economic history*. Toronto: University of Toronto Press.

Isaac, Benjamin. (1992). *The limits of empire: The Roman army in the East* (Revised ed.). Oxford: Clarendon.

Jefferson, Mark. (1971). *Peopling the Argentine Pampa*. Port Washington/London: Kennikat Press.

Johnson, H. B., Jr (Ed.). (1970). *From reconquest to empire: The Iberian background to Latin American history*. New York: Knopf.

Kamen, Henry. (2003). *Spain's road to empire: The making of a world power 1492–1763*. London: Penguin.

Katzen, M. F. (1969). White settlers and the origin of a new society, 1652–1778. In Monica Wilson & Leonard Thompson (Eds.), *The Oxford history of South Africa I: South Africa to 1870*. Oxford: Oxford University Press.

Kennedy, Hugh. (1986). *The prophet and the age of the Caliphates: The Islamic near East from the sixth to the eleventh century*. London/New York: Longman.

Kennedy, Hugh. (2007). *The great Arab conquests*. Philadelphia: Da Capo Press.

Klein, Herbert S. (1992). *Bolivia: The evolution of a multi-ethnic society* (2nd ed.). New York/Oxford: Oxford University Press.

Klein, Herbert S. (1999). *The Atlantic slave trade*. Cambridge: Cambridge University Press.

Ladero Quesada, Miguel Ángel. (2004). *La formación medieval de España: Territorios. Regiones. Reinos.* Madrid: Alianza Editorial.

Le Bohec, Yann. (2000). *The imperial Roman army*. London/New York: Routledge.

Leipoldt, C. Louis. (1936). *Jan van Riebeeck: A biographical study*. London: Longmans, Green and Co.

Lewis, Archibald R. (1958). The closing of the mediaeval frontier 1250–1350. *Speculum, 33*, 475–483.

Lewis, Meriwether, & Clark, William. (1979). In Elliott Coues (Ed.), *The history of the Lewis and Clark expedition* (Vol. 3). New York: Dover Publications.

Livermore, H. V. (1976). *A new history of Portugal* (2nd ed.). Cambridge: Cambridge University Press.

Lomax, Derek W. (1978). *The reconquest of Spain*. London/New York: Longman.

Lombard, Maurice. (1975). *The golden age of Islam*. Amsterdam: North-Holland.

Lotter, Friedrich. (1989). The crusading idea and the conquest of the region East of the Elbe. In Robert Bartlett & Angus MacKay (Eds.), *Medieval frontier societies*. New York: Oxford University Press.

Lundahl, Mats. (1982). The rationale of apartheid. *American Economic Review, 72*, 1169–1179.

Lundahl, Mats. (1991). Spain and the conquest of America: Profits, religion and forced labor in the fifteenth and sixteenth centuries. In Göte Hansson (Ed.), *Trade growth and development. The role of politics and institutions*. London/New York: Routledge.

Lundahl, Mats, & Ndlela, Daniel B. (1980). Land alienation, dualism, and economic discrimination: South Africa and Rhodesia. *Economy and History, 23*, 106–132.

Luttwak, Edward N. (1976). *The grand strategy of the Roman Empire: From the first century A.D. to the third*. Baltimore/London: Johns Hopkins University Press.

Lynch, John. (1985). The river plate republics from independence to the Paraguayan war. In Leslie Bethell (Ed.), *The Cambridge history of Latin America, volume III: From independence to c. 1870*. Cambridge: Cambridge University Press.

MacKay, Angus. (1977). *Spain in the Middle Ages: From frontier to empire, 1000–1500*. London: Macmillan.

Marques, A. H. de Oliveira. (1972). *History of Portugal. Vol.1: From Lusitania to Empire*. New York/London: Columbia University Press.
Martínez Díaz, Gonzalo. (2006). *Los templarios en los reinos de España*. Barcelona: Editorial Planeta.
Milner, Clyde A., II. (1981). Indulgent friends and important allies: Political process of the Cis-Mississippi frontier and its aftermath. In Howard Lamar & Leonard Thompson (Eds.), *The frontier in history. North America and Southern Africa compared*. New Haven/London: Yale University Press.
Mínguez Fernández, José María. (2005). *La reconquista*. Madrid: Historia 16.
Morison, Samuel Eliot. (1965). *The Oxford history of the American people*. New York: Oxford University Press.
Morison, Samuel Eliot. (1971). *The European discovery of America: The Northern voyages A.D. 500–1600*. New York: Oxford University Press.
Morison, Samuel Eliot, Commager, Henry Steele, & Leuchtenberg, William E. (1980a). *The growth of the American republic. Volume one* (7th ed.). New York/Oxford: Oxford University Press.
Morison, Samuel Eliot, Commager, Henry Steele, & Leuchtenberg, William E. (1980b). *The growth of the American republic. Volume two* (7th ed.). New York/Oxford: Oxford University Press.
Mörner, Magnus, with the collaboration of Harold Sims. (1985). *Adventurers and proletarians: The story of migrants in Latin America*. Pittsburgh: University of Pittsburgh Press and Paris: UNESCO.
Morris, Donald R. (1966). *The washing of the spears: A history of the rise and fall of the Zulu nation under Shaka and its fall in the Zulu war of 1879*. London: Jonathan Cape.
Mostert, Noël. (1992). *Frontiers: The Epic of South Africa's creation and the tragedy of the Xhosa people*. London: Jonathan Cape.
North, Douglass C. (1956). International capital flows and the development of the American West. *Journal of Economic History, 16*, 493–505.
North, Douglass C. (1966a). *Growth and welfare in the American past: A new economic history*. Englewood Cliffs: Prentice-Hall.
North, Douglass C. (1966b). *The economic growth of the United States 1790–1860*. New York: W. W. Norton & Co.
North, Douglass C. (1981). *Structure and change in economic history*. New York/London: W. W. Norton & Co.
Osborne, Thomas J. (2013). *Pacific Eldorado: A history of greater California*. Chichester: Wiley-Blackwell.
Pakenham, Thomas. (1979). *The Boer war*. Johannesburg/London: Jonathan Ball/Weidenfeld & Nicolson.

Palmer, Robin. (1977). *Land and racial domination in Rhodesia*. London: Heinemann.

Parry, J. H. (1966). *The Spanish seaborne empire*. London: Hutchinson.

Payne, Stenley G. (1973). *A history of Spain and Portugal*. Madison: University of Wisconsin Press.

Pendle, George. (1963). *Argentina* (3rd ed.). London: Oxford University Press.

Pirenne, Henri. (1956). *Medieval cities*. Garden City: Doubleday.

Pirenne, Henri. (1992). *Mohammed and Charlemagne*. New York: Barnes and Noble.

Reilly, Bernard F. (1993). *The Medieval Spains*. Cambridge: Cambridge University Press.

Riley-Smith, Jonathan. (1987). *The Crusades: A short history*. New Haven/ London: Yale University Press.

Riley-Smith, Jonathan. (2003). *The first crusade and the idea of crusading*. London/New York: Continuum.

Rosenstein, Nathan. (1999). Republican Rome. In Kurt Raaflaub & Nathan Rosenstein (Eds.), *War and society in the ancient and medieval worlds*. Cambridge, MA: Harvard University Press.

Rosenthal, Etic. (1970). *Gold! Gold! Gold! The Johannesburg gold rush*. New York: Macmillan.

Rotberg, Robert I., with the collaboration of Miles F. Shore. (1988). *The founder: Cecil Rhodes and the pursuit of power*. New York/Oxford: Oxford University Press.

Sánchez-Albornoz, Claudio. (1970). The continuing tradition of reconquest. In HB Johnson Jr (Ed.), *From reconquest to empire: The Iberian background to Latin American history*. New York: Knopf.

Sánchez-Albornoz, Claudio. (2000). *España, un enigma histórico* (Vol. 2). Barcelona: Edhasa.

Sater, William F. (1986). *Chile and the war of the pacific*. Lincoln/London: University of Nebraska Press.

Sauer, Carl Ortwin. (1966). *The early Spanish Main*. Berkeley/Los Angeles: University of California Press.

Saunders, Christopher, & Smith, Iain R. (1999). Southern Africa, 1795–1910. In Andrew Porter (Ed.), *The Oxford history of the British Empire. Volume III: The nineteenth century*. Oxford/New York: Oxford University Press.

Sawers, Larry. (1996). *The other Argentina: The interior and national development*. Boulder/Oxford: Westview Press.

Scobie, James R. (1964). *Argentina: A city and a nation*. New York: Oxford University Press.

Slatta, Richard W. (1992). *Gauchos and the vanishing frontier*. Lincoln/London: University of Nebraska Press.
Smith, Peter H. (1969). *Beef and politics in Argentina: Patterns of conflict and change*. New York: University of Columbia Press.
Southern, Pat, & Dixon, Karen Ramsey. (1996). *The late Roman army*. New Haven/London: Yale University Press.
Tarkiainen, Kari. (2008). *Sveriges Österland. Från forntiden till Gustav Vasa*. Atlantis: Stockholm.
The Song of Roland. Translated by Dorothy L. Sayers (1976). Harmondsworth: Penguin.
Thomas, Hugh. (1997). *The Slave trade. The story of the Atlantic slave trade: 1440–1870*. New York: Simon & Schuster.
Thompson, Leonard. (1975). The subjection of the African Chiefdoms, 1870–1898. In Monica Wilson & Leonard Thompson (Eds.), *The Oxford history of South Africa II: South Africa 1870–1966*. Oxford: Oxford University Press.
Thompson, Leonard. (1990). *A history of South Africa*. New Haven/London: Yale University Press.
Thompson, Leonard, & Lamar, Howard. (1981). The North American and South African frontiers. In Howard Lamar & Leonard Thompson (Eds.), *The Frontier in history. North America and Southern Africa compared*. New Haven/London: Yale University Press.
Treadgold, Warren. (1997). *A history of the Byzantine state and society*. Stanford: Stanford University Press.
Tyerman, Christopher. (2006). *God's war: A new history of the Crusades*. Cambridge, MA: Harvard University Press.
Valderón Baruque, Julio. (2006). *La reconquista: El concepto de España: unidad y diversidad*. Madrid: Espasa Calpe.
Vernet, Juan. (2000). *Lo que Europa debe al Islam de España*. Barcelona: El Acantilado.
Villalobos R., Sergio, Silva G., Osvaldo, Silva V., Fernando, & Estellé M., Patricio. (1974). *Historia de Chile*. Four volumes. (3rd–6th ed.). Santiago de Chile: Editorial Universitaria.
Walker, Eric A. (1948). *The great Trek*. London: Adam and Charles Black.
Watson, G. R. (1969). *The Roman soldier*. Ithaca: Cornell University Press
Webster, Graham. (1998). *The Roman imperial army of the first and second centuries A.D* (3rd ed.). Norman: University of Oklahoma Press.
Wells, Peter S. (2003). *The battle that stopped Rome: Emperor Augustus, Arminius, and the Slaughter of the Legions in the Teutoburg forest*. New York: W. W. Norton & Co.

White, Lynn, Jr. (1964). *Medieval technology and social change*. London: Oxford University Press.

Whittaker, C. R. (1994). *Frontiers of the Roman Empire: A social and economic study*. Baltimore: Johns Hopkins University Press.

Winks, Robin W. (1999). Foreword. In Harold A Innis (Ed.), *The Fur trade in Canada: An introduction to Canadian economic history*. Toronto: University of Toronto Press.

Woolf, Greg. (2001). Inventing empire in ancient Rome. In Susan E. Alcock et al. (Eds.), *Empires: Perspectives from archaeology and history.* Cambridge: Cambridge University Press.

Worger, William H. (1987). *South Africa's city of diamonds: Mine workers and monopoly capitalism in Kimberley, 1867–1895*. New Haven/London: Yale University Press.

3

Modeling Global Interdependence: Centers, Peripheries and Frontiers

It seems particularly appropriate that, at the start of the third millennium, economic growth should once again be at the forefront of the research agenda of economists. Beginning as an 'enquiry into the origin and nature of the wealth of nations' with Adam Smith, David Ricardo and John Stuart Mill, from about 1850 to 1950 economics turned its back on the study of long-run trends to focus on the static allocation of resources and the determinants of fluctuations in economic activity. The 1950s saw the first surge of growth theory, with Roy Harrod and Evsey Domar, Nicholas Kaldor and Joan Robinson, Robert Solow and Trevor Swan all making their seminal contributions. The 1960s saw refinements and extensions, but by and large the next two decades were marked by the disappearance of growth theory from the center of the stage. The 1990s, however, have seen a remarkable burst of new interest, fueled by the influential work of Lucas (1988), Romer (1990), Young (1991) and others. Mankiw et al. (1992) have revived the original Solow

---

Revised from 'Modeling Global Interdependence: Centers, Peripheries, and Frontiers' by Ronald Findlay, *American Economic Review*, Vol 86, 1996, pp. 47–51. With kind permission of the American Economic Association.

R. Findlay, M. Lundahl, *The Economics of the Frontier*,
DOI 10.1057/978-1-137-60237-4_3

model by explicitly incorporating human capital as an additional variable. 'Convergence', the one-word title of a major paper by Barro and Sala-i-Martin (1992), is now the focus of inquiry, and much progress has been made in analyzing and accounting for this phenomenon. The Penn World Table (Summers and Heston 1991), a carefully prepared data set for OECD countries since 1950, has provided the 'stylized facts' that the models have purported to explain.

Economic growth and decline have been features of human society ever since the species first learned to use fire and invented stone tools. Economic statistics, of course, are a relatively recent invention, but the work of historians, archeologists, and demographers has provided an extensive charting of the relative dimensions of population growth, urbanization, agricultural settlement, immigration and technical change. In the light of all this evidence going back so far and extending over so much of the globe, it is surely extremely parochial, in both space and time, to confine the study of 'convergence' to the last few decades in North America, Western Europe and Japan.

If it is acknowledged that the task of a theory of economic growth is to account for its occurrence, or non-occurrence, whenever and wherever on this planet, then I would submit that the formal apparatus of the highly aggregative growth models that have been used in the literature needs to be supplemented by a wide variety of concepts and models from other parts of the discipline: notably, trade theory, location theory, development economics, political economy, and perhaps above all, economic history.

In its purest and starkest form, the theory of convergence is exactly represented by the following analogy. Imagine a set of trains on parallel tracks. The initial positions of the trains correspond to per capita income levels at a certain date. The speed of the trains is inversely related to their initial position, with the train that is farthest behind moving the fastest, and the train in front moving the slowest. This corresponds to the effect of diminishing returns to capital accumulation in the neoclassical growth model. As time elapses, the disparity in their relative positions will diminish and become vanishingly small as the parallel lines of the tracks extend toward infinity. If technology and saving rates (or discount rates) are identical, no 'overtaking' will occur. The 'latecomers' will never catch up, but they can come arbitrarily close to the leader if sufficient time is allowed.

I think everyone would agree that economic growth in reality is a lot more interesting than this 'trains on parallel tracks' analogy, yet this analogy corresponds closely to the mechanism that is postulated in studies of convergence in growth theory. What is missing, in the models as well as in the analogy, is *interdependence*: the links of trade, factor mobility, and technological diffusion that connect the 'trains' to each other *across* the parallel tracks.

The idea that the last train runs the fastest is an old one, going back at least to Thorstein Veblen (1915). The same idea of the 'penalty of taking the lead' and its corollary 'advantages of relative backwardness' was also elaborated by Alexander Gerschenkron (1962). A formal treatment of the same idea is the Nelson and Phelps (1966) model of technological catching up. Suppose that one country, the leader, is the source of technological progress and that it proceeds at the same constant rate, n, so that its technological level at any time t can be denoted $A(t)$, equal to $A(0)e^{nt}$. Let the technological level of a 'backward' country be $B(t)$, and postulate that the rate of change of $B(t)$ is proportional to the relative 'technology gap' $[A(t) - B(t)]/B(t)$. Nelson and Phelps consider the speed of the catching-up process to be an increasing function of the level of human capital in the backward society. Return now to the railway-track analogy. Exactly the same results will follow for technological diffusion as for physical and human capital accumulation. The relative dispersion of technological levels will decrease over time toward some 'equilibrium gap', depending upon the magnitude of the exogenous growth rate (n) and the magnitude of the catch-up parameter that links the rate of change of $B(t)$ to the relative technology gap. Once again we have a rather mechanical story, though some interdependence has been introduced, of the followers on the leader.

Historically, technological diffusion has taken place through the migrations of artisans and merchants, who spread the information by a process of 'contagion', the benign equivalent of the way germs spread a disease. In the modern world the most active and vital carriers of technology are multinational corporations. Direct foreign investment not only brings capital, but more importantly it is an effective vehicle for the transfer of technology. Thus, in addition to the domestic availability of human capital, successful technology transfer can be enhanced by the presence of foreign corporations from advanced countries. In Findlay (1978) I presented a simple dynamic model in which the rate of technical progress in a developing country is an increasing function of both the relative technology gap and the share of foreign direct investment in the total capital stock. This hypothesis was extended into an elegant two-country growth model by Jian-ye Wang (1990). In his model, both leader and follower have aggregate production functions with physical and human capital as arguments. There is perfect mobility of physical capital, with the leader investing in the follower. The leader's rate of human-capital formation is exogenously fixed, but that of the follower is an increasing function of the relative gap in the levels of human capital and the share of the leader's investment in the follower. Under autarky, the follower's growth rate is less than the leader's, and the gap would therefore widen relatively and absolutely over time. Capital-market integration not only brings the familiar static gains to both regions, but also raises the growth rate of the follower, allowing for the possibility of catch-up. Wang and Blomström (1992) provide a game-theoretic model of a multinational corporation and a home country in which the ad hoc hypothesis of Findlay (1978) finds some microeconomic foundations. Borensztein et al. (1995) report empirical evidence in favor of the idea that foreign direct investment raises the rate of growth in the host country. They also find that the magnitude of the effect is greater, the greater the human capital in the host country. Thus there seems to be at least some support for the original hypothesis. The mechanism postulated in these models may also be behind some of the positive regressions that people have found between measures of 'openness' and growth.

Models of 'asymmetrical interdependence' that divide the world into a 'center' and a 'periphery', or *North-South models* as they have come to be called, also have a part to play in any account of convergence in the long run. They acknowledge the fact, ignored in standard growth theory, that the scientific and industrial revolutions were historically specific: they occurred in one part of the world, Western Europe, from which their influence has been radiating to the rest of the world ever since. It is true that other parts of the world have successfully adopted scientific methods and modern industrial technology, but the lags have been long and certainly not uniform. Latin America and East Asia have been industrialized but, with the exception of Japan, only in the last few decades. Most of Africa is still in the stage of exporting primary products in exchange for manufactured goods. In any case, the experience of the nineteenth century, in which most of the rest of the world was in a dependent position relative to Great Britain, is itself of major interest in any account of global convergence.

The North-South model of Findlay (1980) envisages the North as a Solow economy and the South as a labor-surplus dual economy à la Arthur Lewis (1954). The manufacturing output of the North is consumed by both regions, and also provides the capital goods for both regions. The primary products of the South are consumed in both regions, and there is balanced trade. The growth rates of the two regions are linked through the terms of trade. Thus, if the South's terms of trade are above the long-run equilibrium level, it will grow faster than the North, pulling the terms of trade down to the equilibrium level; conversely if the terms of trade are below the long-run equilibrium level. The model is consistent with the expansion of the world economy from the middle of the nineteenth century to 1914. As Dennis Robertson (1938) put it in a memorable phrase, trade was the 'engine of growth' in that period; manufactured goods and capital exported from Western Europe fueled the growth of primary exports, such as wheat and beef from Argentina, wool from Australia, rubber from Malaya, tea from Ceylon, and so on. When production in the industrialized North collapsed in the Great Depression of the 1930s, the impact on primary producers was devastating. Thus, when normal trade was resumed after World War II, most development experts, such as Arthur Lewis, Raúl Prebisch, and Ragnar Nurkse, were reluctant to count on a favorable external environment for the development of the primary-producing regions; hence their advocacy of 'balanced growth' and import substitution as development strategies. Only Hla Myint consistently advocated 'outward-looking' policies, which were of course vindicated by the great trade boom of the 1960s.

Labor-intensive manufactured exports have turned out to be the solution to the dilemma of whether to rely on primary product exports, with the volatility and risks associated with that option, or on import substitution, with its own drawbacks of inefficiency and stagnation. As argued in Findlay and Wellisz (1993), it was economies such as Hong Kong, Singapore and Malta, with no natural resources at all, that were among the earliest and most successful exporters of manufactures, while resource-rich Jamaica and the Philippines, for example, have floundered. Countries such as Indonesia and Malaysia, on the other hand, have wisely balanced primary exports with energetic industrialization measures that appear to have paid off handsomely.

Surprisingly, international trade has been relatively neglected in the recent convergence literature. This is a pity since it is apparent that the great trade boom of the last three decades, with brief interruptions due to the two oil shocks, has been an ideal environment for rapid growth at the national level. In particular the Four Dragons of East Asia (Hong Kong, Singapore, Korea and Taiwan) have clearly based their development strategy on exports of manufactured goods with an increasing degree of capital intensity and technical sophistication.

Alwyn Young (1995) and Paul Krugman (1994) have both stressed the fact that total factor productivity calculations attribute all the growth to increases in capital and other inputs, with no room left for factors such as technological change or trade. The growth accounting exercise and the associated concept of an aggregate production function, however, mask the role that trade plays in growth of these for economies. Thus, it is often recognized as a puzzle that their rapid growth since the 1960s has not led to a decline in the return to capital and hence to a slowing of their expansion.

Formally, the elasticity of substitution between capital and labor in the aggregate production function must be very high. Yet the aggregate production function for a highly open 'small' economy can be regarded as the envelope of the individual production function for tradable goods, as I have pointed out in Findlay (1973, Chap. 6) and Findlay (1984, p. 204). With a near infinity of potential products, this envelope is going to be almost linear (i.e. the elasticity of substitution is going to be very high). As the capital-labor ratio rises, resources switch into increasingly capital-intensive production sectors before diminishing returns appear in the original lines of specialization that were very labor-intensive. This continuous upgrading of export products, evident in all the four economies, is an important reason for their high growth having been so persistent. The fact that they are still relatively small in the world economy as a whole is also, of course, highly relevant, since otherwise the terms of trade would turn sharply adverse, leading to declines in the rate of return to capital and thus in the rate of growth.

Remarks by Krugman (1994, p. 71) that the East Asian economies are merely replicating the Soviet pattern of heavy capital investment, and that they will therefore meet the same dismal fate, seem to me to be perverse and wrongheaded. The Soviet economy was completely decoupled from world prices, whereas the East Asian Four have respected them. This makes all the difference.

Extensions of endogenous growth to the open economy by Grossman and Helpman (1991) and others stress the role of R&D and new inventions in boosting the rate of growth through international spillovers. In the East Asian case, however, it is doubtful that much innovation has been involved. For the most part, what they have done is to absorb successfully existing technology of an increasingly sophisticated type. While by no means easy, this activity is qualitatively different from pure invention as stressed in the endogenous growth models. The other strand of endogenous growth theory, learning by doing, as modeled in Young (1991), on the other hand, has the implication that the relatively backward country or region will be relegated to less progressive technologies as a result of trade with more advanced partners. Neither does this seem to fit the East Asian case very well. The dynamic extension of the familiar Heckscher-Ohlin model that I use in Findlay (1973, 1984) seems a simpler and more appropriate framework. An excellent recent paper by Jaume Ventura (1995) very effectively employs a similar factor proportions approach to growth and interdependence.

The analysis and description of the emergence and formation of the world economy should logically precede any study of convergence in the world economy. This implies, at the very least, some consideration of the impact and consequences of the European voyages of discovery at the end of the fifteenth century that brought the New World into contact with the Old and added the route around the Cape of Good Hope to the ancient trade routes that connected Europe to Asia. As noted by Eric Jones (1981) and other historians, these voyages added vast new reserves of natural resources to the stock available for exploitation by the economies of Europe. They also opened up the prospects of eventual mass migration from Europe in the second half of the nineteenth century. What Walter Prescott Webb (1952) called the 'Great Frontier' extended the domain of European settlement around the world to the Americas and Australia. Once again, the Heckscher-Ohlin model, suitably extended to incorporate factor proportions endogenously, as I have attempted to do in Findlay (1995, Chap. 5), can provide the appropriate conceptual framework. With Europe exporting manufactures in exchange for primary products and with perfect capital and labor mobility across the oceans, the New World can be modeled as a moving frontier, with each marginal acre of new land opened up earning just enough in rent as a proportion of the cost of clearing to be equal to the rate of interest. This model determines the equilibrium extent of the frontier in the New World, the cumulative level of migration, the capital stock in the world economy as a whole, and the volume and terms of trade. Further geographical discoveries, technical changes, and other shocks can then be analyzed. I am happy to see that Jeffrey Williamson and his former students Kevin O'Rourke and Alan Taylor have independently been exploring the economic history of what they call the Greater Atlantic Area with the aid of Heckscher-Ohlin and associated models. Growth theory and trade theory can both serve Clio, and in turn be inspired by her.

References

Barro, Robert, & Sala-i-Martin, Xavier. (1992). Convergence. *Journal of Political Economy, 100*, 223–251.

Borensztein, Eduardo, De Gregorio, Jose, & Lee, Jong-Wha. (1995, March). *How does foreign direct investment affect economic growth?*. Cambridge, MA: National Bureau of Economic Research Working Paper No. 5057.

Findlay, Ronald. (1973). *International trade and development theory*. New York: Columbia University Press.

Findlay, Ronald. (1978). Relative backwardness, direct foreign investment and the transfer of technology: A simple dynamic model. *Quarterly Journal of Economics, 92*, 1–16.

Findlay, Ronald. (1980). The terms of trade and equilibrium growth in the world economy. *American Economic Review, 70*, 291–299.

Findlay, Ronald. (1984). Growth and development in trade models. In Ronald W. Jones & Peter B. Kenen (Eds.), *Handbook of international economics* (Vol. 1). Amsterdam: North-Holland.

Findlay, Ronald. (1995). *Factor proportions, trade, and growth*. Cambridge, MA: MIT Press.

Findlay, Ronald, & Wellisz, Stanislaw (Eds.). (1993). *The political economy of poverty, equity and growth: Five small open economies. A world bank comparative study*. Oxford: Oxford University Press.

Gerschenkron, Alexander. (1962). *Economic backwardness in historical perspective*. Cambridge, MA: Harvard University Press.

Grossman, Gene, & Helpman, Elhanan. (1991). *Innovation and growth in the global economy*. Cambridge, MA: MIT Press.

Jones, Eric. (1981). *The European miracle*. Cambridge: Cambridge University Press.

Krugman, Paul R. (1994). The myth of Asia's miracle. *Foreign Affairs, 73*(6), 62–78.

Lewis, W. Arthur. (1954). Economic development with unlimited supplies of labour. *Manchester School of Economic and Social Studies, 22*, 139–191.

Lucas, Robert E. (1988). On the mechanics of economic development. *Journal of Monetary Economics, 22*, 3–42.

Mankiw, Gregory, Romer, David, & Weil, David. (1992). A contribution to the empirics of economic growth. *Quarterly Journal of Economics, 107*, 407–437.

Nelson, Richard, & Phelps, Edmund S. (1966). Investment in humans, technological diffusion and economic growth. *American Economic Review: Papers and Proceedings, 56*, 69–75.

Robertson, Dennis. (1938). The future of international trade. *Economic Journal, 48*, 1–14.

Romer, Paul M. (1990). Endogenous technological change. *Journal of Political Economy, 98, Part 2*, S71–S102.

Summers, Robert, & Heston, Alan. (1991). The Penn World Table (Mark 5): An expanded set of international comparisons, 1950–1988. *Quarterly Journal of Economics, 106*, 327–368.

Veblen, Thorstein. (1915). *Imperial Germany and the industrial revolution*. London: Macmillan.

Ventura, Jaume. (1995). *Growth and interdependence*. Mimeo. Cambridge, MA: Massachusetts Institute of Technology.

Wang, Jian-Ye. (1990). Growth, technology transfer and the long run theory of international capital movements. *Journal of International Economics, 29*, 255–271.

Wang, Jian-Ye, & Blomström, Magnus. (1992). Foreign investment and technology transfer. *European Economic Review, 36*, 137–155.

Webb, Walter Prescott. (1952). *The great frontier*. Lincoln: University of Nebraska Press.

Young, Alwyn. (1991). Learning by doing and the dynamic effects of international trade. *Quarterly Journal of Economics, 106*, 369–405.

Young, Alwyn. (1995). The tyranny of numbers: Confronting the statistical realities of the East Asian growth experience. *Quarterly Journal of Economics, 110*, 641–680.

4

Towards a Model of Territorial Expansion and the Limits of Empire

The question of the size of political units never seems to attract among historians and sociologists the attention which it deserves. What determines why states and empires have expanded to the limits which they have historically achieved? What are the conditions under which it has been possible to maintain those frontiers? Why have the larger states normally broken up into fragments after a certain period of time? As a general problem—distinct from the specific question of why particular units have disintegrated—this is still largely unexplored territory.

An earlier version of this chapter was presented at a conference on 'Conflict and Rent-Seeking' at the University of California, Irvine, in May 1994. I would like to thank the participants at the conference and at a Columbia University Political Economy Seminar in September 1994 for very helpful comments. Several friends and colleagues have also given me the benefit of their criticism. Though I cannot mention all of them, I must acknowledge in particular the comments of David Bloom, Alessandra Casella, Richard Clarida, Andrew Newman, Stanislaw Wellisz and Murray Wolfson. All remaining defects are, of course, my own responsibility.

Revised from 'Towards a Model of Territorial Expansion and the Limits of Empire' by Ronald Findlay, in Michelle R. Garfinkel and Stergios Skaperdas (eds), *The Political Economy of Conflict and Appropriation*, 1996, Cambridge University Press, pp. 41–56. With kind permission of Cambridge University Press.

R. Findlay, M. Lundahl, *The Economics of the Frontier*,
DOI 10.1057/978-1-137-60237-4_4

Adding economists to historians and sociologists in the first sentence of this quotation from the eminent sinologist Mark Elvin (1973, p. 17) only enhances its salience. Insofar as they are considered at all in economics, the boundaries of a given economic system or 'country' are generally regarded as given, along with the population living within those boundaries. Yet it is obvious that, however sanctified these boundaries may have become in international law, they were all at one time or another contested between rival claimants and determined ultimately by the balance of economic and military power between the contending parties. The process by which these boundaries are determined and defined clearly depends on the interplay of economic and military forces, which have, however, generally been regarded as independent factors.

Elementary textbooks frequently introduce the production possibilities frontier between 'guns' and 'butter' to illustrate the nature of the economic problem and the concept of opportunity cost. It is noteworthy, however, that they never, as far as I am aware, consider the question of how 'guns' might be used in a predatory fashion to acquire resources from neighboring peoples or states and thus push out the production possibilities frontier of the society itself. As Jack Hirshleifer (1987, p. 297) points out in his brief but penetrating survey of the little that we have on 'The Economic Approach to Conflict':

> The institutions of property and law, and the peaceful process of exchange, are highly beneficial aspects of human life. But the economist's inquiries should not be limited to such 'nice' behaviors and interactions. Struggle, imposing costs on others, and downright violence are crucial phenomena of the world as we know it. Nor is the opposition between the 'nice' and the 'not nice' by any means total. Law and property, and thus the possibilities of peaceful exchange, can only persist where individuals are ultimately willing to use violence in their defense.

While the literature on violence and coercion as 'rational' economic options, subject to the usual calculus of benefits and costs, is scarce, it is by no means devoid of insightful contributions, upon which I attempt to build in this paper. Kenneth Boulding (1963), in a work entitled *Conflict and Defense: A General Theory*, has many wise and interesting things to say about the subject. I find his Chapters 12 and 13, on international conflict, particularly stimulating. Other important references are Bush and Mayer (1974), Friedman (1977), Thompson and Faith (1981), Usher (1989), Hirshleifer (1991) and Skaperdas (1992). An interesting alternative to the approach taken here, through coercion and violence as rational activities, is the 'mergers and acquisitions' view of Wittman (1991).

The Basic Model

Consider, to begin with, a collective entity or 'tribe' such as the Romans, Han Chinese, or Ottoman Turks. The primary resource owned by the tribe is their labor, which we will assume to be initially fixed. We also suppose that there is only a single final output, that we can identify with agriculture, although a second 'crafts' or 'manufacturing' sector will be introduced later. Production of the final output requires land or 'territory', which is not simply given but has to be acquired and held against the tribe's enemies who surround it. To fix ideas, let us conceive of the labor of the tribe as concentrated at a single point on a 'featureless plain' so beloved by the location theorists. We can think of this central point as its 'home base'. To secure and hold territory, the tribe must devote some of its labor force to fighting. We can call those so engaged the 'army' of the tribe, with the remainder as the 'workers'.

Letting N denote the total size of the tribe, A the army, and L the workers we have the manpower constraint of the tribe as

$$L + A = N \tag{4.1}$$

while the production function for final output, denoted Q, has labor and 'territory', denoted T, as its arguments:

$$Q = Q(L,T) \tag{4.2}$$

We assume that the production function (4.2) exhibits constant returns to scale and diminishing returns to either factor with the other held fixed. The territory that the tribe can acquire and defend against its enemies, an undifferentiated mass of 'barbarians', is given by the function

$$T = \alpha\pi r(A)^2 \tag{4.3}$$

where r is the radius of a circle centered on the original point, the home base of the tribe, and α is a constant. We postulate that

$$r'(A) > 0, r''(A) < 0 \tag{4.4}$$

i.e. the larger the army, the greater is the radius of the tribe's 'sphere of influence'. But there is a diminishing returns effect of increases in the size of the army on the radius of the circular territory that it can control and defend. Since the area of the circle, $\alpha\pi r(A)^2$, is a convex function of the radius, the territory occupied could still increase more than proportionately to the size of the army. We shall initially assume, however, that the absolute value of the negative second derivative in Equation (4.4) is sufficiently high to give us T as a concave function of A, so that

$$d(dT / dA) / dA < 0 \tag{4.5}$$

What does the tribe want to maximize? Territory could conceivably be desired for its own sake, for the kind of pleasure that British schoolboys were supposed to derive from seeing so much of the map of the world painted red in the days when the sun never set on their empire. However, let us suppose initially that the tribe is narrowly 'rational' and desires territory only for its contribution to production. The economic problem of empire, then, is simply to maximize (4.2) subject to the manpower constraint (4.1) and the sphere of influence function (4.3).

The obvious trade-off is that each man added to the army adds economically valuable land that raises final output but withdraws a man from the labor force working on the land. Because of Equation (4.5), the extra land added as the army is extended declines at the margin, while the marginal productivity of the falling labor force on the increased land obtained by the expanding army is rising. When the marginal productivity of a warrior is equal to that of a worker, we have the optimal size of the army and associated extent of territory, which maximizes final output.

The first-order condition for the optimal size of empire is

$$\partial Q / \partial L = (\partial Q / \partial T)(\mathrm{d}T / \mathrm{d}A) = (\partial Q / \partial T) 2\alpha\pi r'(A) \qquad (4.6)$$

in which the left-hand side is the marginal productivity of a worker and the right-hand side the marginal productivity of a warrior. This condition can also be interpreted as stating that the marginal rate of substitution between land and labor in production is equal to the marginal product of a warrior in terms of territory, which is $2\alpha\pi r'(A)$.

The sphere of influence function $r(A)$ clearly depends on the *relative* military proficiency of the tribe and the barbarians. Fluctuations in the relative military efficiency variable, brought about, say, by diffusion of weapons or tactics from one side to the other, would lead to pulsations in the size of the empire in response. Thus adoption of iron for weapons by the steppe nomads, brought about by contact with China, led to a rise in their relative military efficiency and hence made the holding of the size of the Chinese empire at its original level more difficult. Technology could, however, flow in the other direction also. As pointed out by Herrlee Creel (1970), the sedentary Chinese were dependent on the steppe nomads not only for the provision of horses for cavalry, but also for techniques of riding and training these essential military assets for control of the frontier. Similarly the Germanic tribes north of the Roman frontier also learned from the imperial power, especially after many of them came to be employed as mercenaries in the Roman army.

Improvements in production technology, however, have an ambiguous effect on the size of the army and the empire. An additional acre of land is worth more, so that the marginal productivity of a warrior goes up, but so does his opportunity cost, which is the marginal productivity of a worker. Thus the effect of the technical improvement on the *relative* marginal products of land and labor in production is what determines the impact of the innovation on the size of the army and the extent of the empire.

By what means are resources allocated between farming and fighting, and how is the final output divided between warriors and workers on the one hand, and these and the 'ruling elite' of chiefs, priests, and officials on the other? Here a variety of outcomes is possible. The territory could be allocated by the leader of the tribe to his relatives and other privileged individuals, who then hire labor in a free market to work on the land at the going wage rate. The army could recruit soldiers in the same labor market, and the optimal result defined by Equation (4.6) could be brought about by giving just enough tax revenue to the army to hire the optimal A at the market-clearing wage w, equal to the marginal product of both warriors and workers. The taxes could be raised on rents of land distributed to the privileged elite or on the labor force as a whole, preserving efficiency in allocation. Taxes only on workers would equate the after-tax civilian wage to the army wage, implying too few civilian workers and too large an army.

At the other extreme we could imagine that all the land was the property of the tribe as a whole, with the surplus of output above subsistence for all distributed in some arbitrary fashion to the optimally determined members of the army and civilian workers and privileged elite. Since most historic empires had great difficulty collecting taxes, it could be that the optimal size of army could not be maintained because of a shortage of revenue. Thus the size of the empire would shrink below the optimal level just determined to whatever was possible, given the revenue constraint, minus luxury consumption by the elite. At the level of generality of the present paper, it would be a distraction to consider particular institutional alternatives in detail, though this would be an interesting subject for further research.

Absorption of Subject Populations

Up to now we have been assuming that it is only territory that the tribal army acquires. The alien population is either exterminated or expelled through 'ethnic cleansing', as we have come to call it in our enlightened age. While such horrors have certainly not been unknown in the records of historic empires, reason, if not compassion, dictated that the conquered populations, and not only the land that they lived on, were valuable assets that could be enslaved, enserfed, or simply taxed, at higher rates than the members of the tribe themselves. Cultural assimilation to the language and customs of the conquerors could ultimately result in such enlightened outcomes as the extension of Roman citizenship to all the subjects of the empire. Conversion to the religion of the conquerors was, of course, another major avenue of assimilation, as in the cases of the early Arab and Ottoman Turk Empires.

The model can be readily modified to take account of this important feature of all historic empires. We assume that the absorbed alien population increases as a function of the territory that the tribe acquires. Assuming complete assimilation for simplicity, we have N in the manpower constraint (4.1) as a positive function of the territory T, which of course is itself a positive but concave function of the size of the army. The marginal benefit of adding warriors is then not only the additional territory they bring in but the people along with it, valued at their shadow price, which is the marginal productivity of labor in production. The manpower constraint (4.1) now becomes

$$L + A = N\left[T\left(A\right)\right] \tag{4.7}$$

while the first-order condition (4.6) is now

$$\left\{\left(\partial Q / \partial L\right)\left(dN / dT\right) + \partial Q / \partial T\right\}\left(dT / dA\right) = \partial Q / \partial L \tag{4.8}$$

The empire has now not only territory but also an alien population absorbed within its borders. As already noted, there is a very wide array

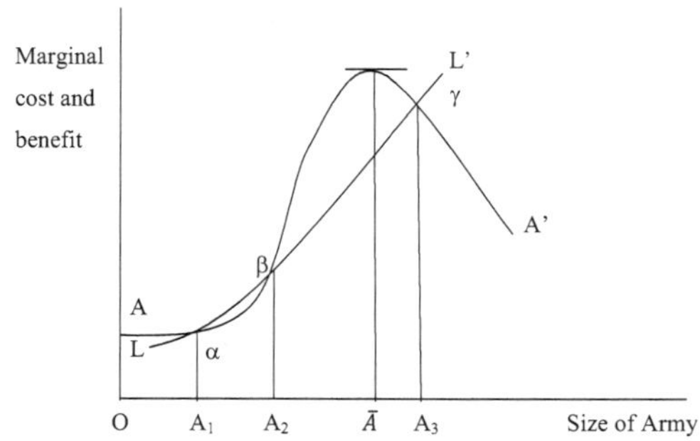

Figure 4.1 The optimal size of the army

of different practices known to history about the manner in which the subject population is treated relative to members of the original tribe. In the case of Sparta and the *helots*, the Spartans themselves did not follow any occupation other than warfare and the supervision of the *helots*, who did all the productive work. On the other hand we have the Mamelukes of Egypt and the Janissaries of the Ottoman Turks, exclusively alien-born military elites in the service of these respective realms.

Local and Global Optima

As we have seen, the concave function $r(A)$ and the extent of the territory associated to it by the factor of $\pi r(A)^2$ can interact to make territory T either a concave or a convex function of the size of the army. While in the case of the basic model we assumed that it was concave throughout, it is interesting to consider the possible implications of the $T(A)$ function being convex over an initial range and concave only after a certain critical size is passed.[1]

In Figure 4.1, the monotonically positive relation LL' depicts the rising opportunity cost of additional warriors in terms of their marginal productivity as workers with an increasing supply of land resulting from

[1] See Wolfson (1994) for an interesting extension of my original analysis along these lines.

increases in the size of the army. The function AA', however, depicts the marginal productivity of warriors $(\partial Q / \partial T)(dT / dA)$ as first rising and then falling only after the level of $\bar{A}$ is reached. The AA' function cuts the LL' at three points, denoted α, β and γ corresponding to army levels of A_1, A_2, and A_3. It is apparent, from Figure 4.1, that α and γ are stable equilibria, while β is unstable. This is because to the left of α and γ the marginal product of a warrior exceeds his marginal opportunity cost while to the right it falls short of it. The opposite is the case with β.

If there are no constraints on the level of the army that a unified decision-making process can determine and there is full information about the relevant functions, the outcome will, of course, be the global optimum at A_3 and the corresponding $T_3(A_3)$. If these conditions are not fulfilled, however, the situation could be analogous to the familiar 'low-level equilibrium trap' of development economics. There will be no incentive to expand beyond A_1 if the decision makers are 'myopic' and the equilibrium will therefore be at the locally stable point α in this case, with army level A_1 and associated territory $T_1(A_1)$. On the other hand, full information about the shapes of AA' and LL' might be available, but there could be a constraint on the possible size of the army at some point between A_1 and A_2, again leading to point α as the 'normal' solution.

Suppose that the original historical equilibrium is at α. There will be no incentive to expand further if only small incremental changes take place in the size of the army. Suppose, however, that under some very special circumstances a unique, charismatic leader arises who can organize an expansion in the size of the army to A_2 or beyond. Once this initial feat is performed, success will be cumulative since the marginal productivity of additional warriors will now exceed their marginal cost. Expansion can take place all the way to A_3, with the territory of the empire at the globally optimal level of $T_3(A_3)$.

Historical examples of such sudden explosive conquest are rare but not unknown. There are at least three of great interest and significance. The first is the establishment of the original Arab Empire after the tribes of the Arabian Peninsula had been united by the new religion of Islam preached by the Prophet. Ending their intensive feuding, banding together and exercising spectacular mobility across the deserts, these tribes conquered most of the land from Spain to India in a generation. Even more spectacular, though shorter-lived, was the unification of the

Mongols under Chinggis Khan. Their historic equilibrium was a 'tribal confederacy', a loosely knit association that subsisted on a parasitic relation with their more sedentary and wealthier neighbors. Chinggis Khan, by a mixture of ruthlessness and daring, welded the various tribes into a centralized steppe kingdom before launching his whirlwind conquests of the civilized world from China to the borders of Poland. A final example is that of the Zulu chief Shaka early in the nineteenth century in Southern Africa, with his combination of military innovations and terror against rival chieftains. The fact that all three great conquests were difficult to sustain shows how hard it was to establish them initially, dependent as they were on the emergence of truly extraordinary personalities.[2]

A Manufacturing Sector

Up to now we have identified production with land and agriculture. How will the introduction of a manufacturing sector alter the determinants of the optimal size of territory and population? We will suppose that the manufacturing does not require any land at all, only labor and a specific input capital. For simplicity, we will take this stock of specific manufacturing capital as fixed. The model will now have an additional production function for manufacturing:

$$M = M\left(L_M, \bar{K}\right) \tag{4.9}$$

where M is output of manufactures, $\bar{K}$ is the specific input of capital, and L_M is labor employed in manufacturing. The manpower constraint (4.7) is now

$$L_A + L_M + A = N\left[T\left(A\right)\right] \tag{4.10}$$

where L_A denotes labor in agriculture.

[2] On the rise of Islam and Arab conquests, see Crone (1987), Chapter 10; on Chinggis Khan and the Mongols, see Ratchnevsky (1991) and Barfield (1989); on Shaka and the Zulus, see Morris (1969) and Gluckman (1940).

We suppose that the relative valuation of the two goods Q and M, with Q as the *numéraire,* is a constant p. This constant could be thought of either as a relative price on a world market in which our economic system is imbedded, or a constant marginal rate of substitution in a linear utility function. National income will be

$$Y = Q + pM \tag{4.11}$$

The augmented model thus corresponds closely to the familiar Ricardo-Viner model of international trade theory, expounded in Jones (1971) and Samuelson (1971). The significant difference of course is that the supplies of the specific input land T and the overall labor force N are both endogenous instead of fixed, as a result of our hypotheses in Equations (4.3), (4.4), (4.5) and (4.7).

The objective of the empire is to maximize Equation (4.11), subject to the technology and the resource constraints. The first-order condition now becomes

$$p(\partial M / \partial L_M) = \partial Q / \partial L_A = \{(\partial Q / \partial L_A)(dN / dT) + \partial Q / \partial T\}(dT / dA) \tag{4.12}$$

which is the same as Equation (4.8) except for the fact that the marginal productivity of labor must now be equal in *three* uses—the army, agriculture, and manufacturing—instead of in just two as before.

It is apparent that the higher the relative price p, holding N, A and T initially constant, the larger will be L_M and M and the smaller will be L_A and Q, i.e. production and labor allocation will shift in favor of M and against Q. The marginal product of labor in agriculture will rise and the marginal product of land will fall. What will be the effect on the incentive to adjust the size of the army as a result of the rise in the relative price of manufactures?

If dN/dT is small or negligible the effect will be to reduce the size of the army, since $\partial Q/\partial T$, the value of each additional acre won by the army, is now smaller. It pays instead to deploy some of the former warriors in manufacturing, and thus to sacrifice some territory. If dN/dT is large, however, it pays to expand the army *not* in order to get more territory for its own sake, since land is now less valuable as an input, but in order to absorb more labor from subject populations into the workforce of the empire.

It is interesting to note in this connection that, in the fierce wars waged by the Burmese kings against Thailand from the sixteenth to the eighteenth centuries, the objective was not to take and hold territory but to bring back large numbers of the Thai population, particularly skilled craftsmen. Slave raiding for domestic use was also widespread in Africa and of course in the ancient world of Greece and Rome, especially the latter.

Very similar results will follow from an increase in the supply of capital. Combining these results, we can say that the more important the manufacturing sector is in the economic system, the less incentive will the empire have to expand its army and its territorial extent. An exception to this would be when labor is scarce within the existing borders of the empire but plentiful outside it, and there is furthermore a strong comparative advantage of military force relative to the 'barbarians' beyond the borders.

A more important exception, however, would be the inclusion of manufactured output as an input, along with the army, in the conquest of sphere of influence function, so that instead of simply *r(A)* in Equations (4.3) and (4.4), we have instead

$$T = \alpha\pi r\left(A, M_A\right)^2 \qquad (4.3')$$

where M_A is manufacturing input, such as arms, that is complementary to the army A. The partial derivative of r with respect to M_A would be positive and the second derivative negative, analogous to the conditions regarding the relationship between r and A in Equation (4.4). The cross partials of A and M_A are positive.

Introducing a 'military-industrial complex' in this way clearly opens up many interesting and relevant considerations. Technical progress and capital accumulation in manufacturing now not only raise the opportunity cost of soldiers but potentially increase their marginal product as well. Thus, on balance, it would be possible to have manufacturing progress lead to an *extension* of conquest and aggression as a result of enhanced military effectiveness, particularly if the improvement is confined, at least initially, to the empire itself. Such temporary but nevertheless long sustained monopolies of bronze or iron weapons, chariots, or firearms have been major factors in the annals of conquest and the rise of empires.

Reaction Functions and the Balance of Power

The model has so far dealt with the opponents beyond the borders of the empire as an undifferentiated mass, without any conscious strategy of their own in response to that of the empire. In many historical cases, however, we have the clash of two or even more empires, each with a unified strategy relative to its opponents. Even with such examples as the Germanic tribes beyond the Roman frontiers, or the steppe nomads in the case of China, the 'barbarians' frequently banded together to coordinate their offensive and defensive measures.

To analyze this problem let us consider the following highly stylized extension of our basic model. Suppose that the entire space with which the model is concerned is now finite, a circle with unit radius centered on the home base of our original tribe. The tribe strives to capture and hold a circular area centered on this point, with the fraction of the unit radius under its control determined by the relative sizes of its own army and that of its opponent. For any given disposition of the two forces, the original tribe holds the inner of the two concentric circles, while the opponent retains the complementary area of the outer circle.

Let us call the area held by the tribe the Heartland and that held by its opponents the Rimland, in the evocative terminology of the great geopolitical theorist Sir Halford Mackinder, as depicted in Figure 4.2. Denoting the fraction of the unit radius held by the Heartland as λ, and A_H and A_R as the sizes of the two opposing forces, we postulate that

$$\lambda = \lambda(A_H, A_R) \tag{4.13}$$
$$\partial\lambda / \partial A_H > 0, \quad \partial\lambda / \partial A_R < 0$$

with negative second derivatives in each case.

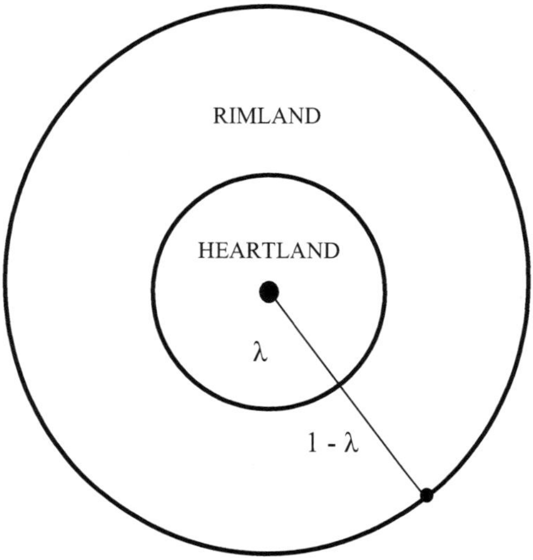

Figure 4.2 The Heartland and the Rimland

Thus given A_R, we see that $\lambda(A_H)$ behaves exactly like our earlier function $r(A)$ in the basic model. An increase in A_R will reduce $\lambda(A_H)$ for any given value of A_H. Similar relations will hold for A_R, given A_H. With technology and resource endowments specified for each side, we can determine the optimum A_H for a given A_R and vice versa. This enables us to derive the 'reaction functions' HH' and RR'. These functions can be negatively sloped as shown in Figure 4.3. (Although other configurations of the reaction functions are also possible, we do not examine them here.) If HH' is steeper than RR', the intersection of the two curves yields a stable equilibrium or 'balance of power' with A_H^* and A_R^* as the optimal force sizes of the two opponents and T_H^* and T_R^* as the corresponding areas of the territories that they control.

What determines the fraction of the radius and hence the relative size of the territory that each side controls in this balance of power? It is clearly not just the relative military efficiency but the entire structure of the two economic systems and 'ways of life'. One obvious application of the model is to think of the Heartland as China, the Central Kingdom as it has been known to its inhabitants for millennia, and the Rimland as the domain of the pastoral nomads. The ratio of territory could be

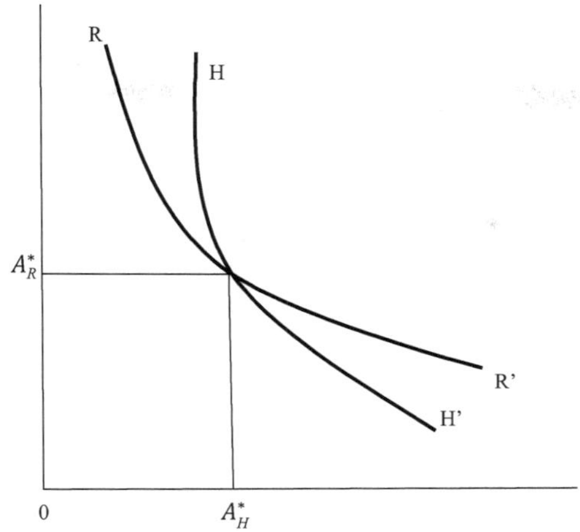

Figure 4.3 Reaction functions

very much in favor of the latter, even though the compact central core might be much wealthier and more sophisticated with a flourishing industry that makes land, and therefore an army, not so essential except for strictly defensive purposes. Chinese culture has traditionally found military activities distasteful, reflecting this fact. For the nomads, on the other hand, with mobility as a way of life that makes them take readily to war, it may be natural to acquire and hold a wide swathe of territory.

An alternative interpretation of the model, however, would be to think of the Rimland as the more 'developed' and 'sophisticated' region, say because the outer land circle is surrounded by water, making transport around the rim and contact with the foreign lands across the sea much easier and therefore leading to an increase in wealth. The Heartland could then be the more pastoral and agricultural of the two regions, giving an incentive for a large army and pushing the Rimland back to a thin corridor around the boundary. It is natural to think here of Europe, with land-based kingdoms such as Prussia and Austria-Hungary in the central core and maritime Rimland nations like Portugal, Holland, England and Italy drawing their wealth from industry and overseas trade rather than from land and agriculture.

Comments on the Literature

While economic factors are explicitly alluded to only incidentally in his stimulating book *A History of Warfare*, the military historian John Keegan (1993) gives considerable attention to a concept developed by the sociologist Stanislaw Andreski (1968) called the military participation ratio (MPR), or the fraction of a population engaged in military activities. It is interesting to note that our model, instead of simply taking this MPR as given by some innate propensity for aggression, *derives* it from more basic structural parameters of resources and technology, though preferences could no doubt be made to play an additional role as well. Thus the fact that many of the great empires were established by nomadic peoples can be accounted for in terms of our model as reflecting what Douglass North (1981) calls a 'comparative advantage in violence', arising from a low opportunity cost of peaceful activities because of a paucity of resources, combined with the externalities for military effectiveness generally by riding, hunting and other such practices that are a natural part of nomadic life. Manufacturing and other peaceful arts, as we have seen, tend to raise the opportunity cost of maintaining armies and hence lower the MPR, though they can also enhance military efficiency through improving the technology or warfare.

Our model does also allow, however, for such cultural or social factors stressed by Andreski and Keegan as cohesion or solidarity of the conquering tribe or nation, what the great Arab historian Ibn Khaldun called *assabiya*. This factor is particularly important in the case of multiple equilibria analyzed earlier. Whether this fact is operative or not could determine whether the 'high' rather than the 'low' equilibrium is determined. The more normal low state could occasionally be punctuated by great unifications and conquests brought about by charismatic leaders. After some time, however, as Ibn Khaldun points out, the bonds of *assabiya* tend to dissolve and the empire fragments or the dynasty loses the 'mandate of heaven', as the Chinese saw it.[3]

[3] On Ibn Khaldun see the selections from his major work translated and arranged, with a valuable introduction, by Issawi (1950).

Our analysis of reaction functions and the resulting balance of power is akin to the well-known mathematical model of 'arms races' associated with the names of Lanchester (1916) and Richardson (1960). The difference, however, is that we link the military sectors to the economic systems through the opportunity costs of allocating resources for war. Our model thus links the arms race itself into the wider context of the economy and society as a whole.

In an extensive comparative study of theories of empire, Michael Doyle (1986) offers threefold classification into metrocentric, pericentric, and systemic, depending on whether the primary stress is laid on tendencies emanating from the center or metropolis in the first case, the dependent periphery in the second, or the relationship between both in some wider contextual space in the third. An example of the first would be the Hobson-Lenin theory of imperialism as the attempt by developed capitalist countries to offset a declining rate of profit at home with investment in colonies. The approach of our original model of expansion by a centralized entity against the resistance of 'barbarians' would also fit this category, while our later analysis of competing empires through reaction functions establishing a balance of power would be an example of a systemic theory.

The sociologist Michael Mann (1986) in a very ambitious and interesting work, subtitled *A History of Power from the Beginning to AD 1760*, makes a distinction between empires of domination, which exact tribute and exercise indirect control, and territorial empires, which conquer and administer directly. While our model is obviously entirely consistent with the second, it can also apply to the first, since the exaction of tribute and the exercise of control also require the allocation of resources to predatory rather than directly productive activities.

Both Doyle and Mann, not surprisingly, devote considerable space to the Roman Empire and its characterization. On this subject our model is entirely consistent with the view of the most eminent recent authority, William Harris (1979). Contrary to many earlier ancient historians, Harris considered the root of the Roman expansion to be the desire to accumulate land, slaves and plunder, with the greatest political and economic rewards going to those members of the Roman upper classes most successful in waging war.[4] The emphasis on a rational, even though implicit, calculus of costs and benefits in extending the limits of the empire is also present in a subtle and penetrating study of the *Frontiers of the Roman Empire* by C. R. Whittaker (1994, p. 86), who points out that 'Roman emperors had some awareness, however crude, of what we would call the marginal costs of imperialism.'

In a central chapter on 'Why Did the Frontiers Stop Where They Did?' Whittaker rejects the idea of 'natural frontiers' such as mountain ranges and rivers like the Rhine, Danube and Euphrates. Despite the authority of Tacitus and numerous subsequent authorities down to the present day, he argues that these were not impenetrable barriers or clear demarcation lines between Roman and barbarian. Rather, he adopts the view of the great student of the interaction between China and the steppe nomads of Inner Asia, Owen Lattimore (1960), p. 40) says 'a major imperial boundary … is not merely a line dividing geographical regions and human societies. It also represents the *optimal limit of growth* of one particular society.' He defines the optimum limit as the point at which 'centripetal gain, accordingly, was converted into centrifugal loss' (Lattimore 1960, p. 242), which I find to be an elegant verbal equivalent to my more cumbersome mathematical first-order conditions.

What Paul Kennedy (1987) in his influential book calls 'imperial overstretch', the tendency of empires to press beyond these rational limits, can also be illustrated in our model as a desire to hold territory as a point of honor or dynastic piety, rather than rationally cutting back consistently with resource availabilities. The many examples include the Habsburgs blindly persisting in wasting the riches of their overseas possessions in trying to hold Flanders and their other European patrimonies.

It would be easy to apply the model to various other historical examples and episodes, but I hope to have convinced the reader already about the relevance of this analysis to the fascinating questions posed in the opening quotation from Mark Elvin. Before closing, however, I would like to point to the strong formal resemblance between this model and those of the division of labor between 'soldiers' and 'workers' among 'social insects' such as ants and wasps, studied by means of very sophisticated

[4] See also Rich and Shipley (1993), for an extended discussion of the Harris thesis.

optimizing techniques in the classic work of George Oster and Edward Wilson (1978). Here we have another striking example of the convergence of biological and economic theory.

References

Andreski, Stanislav. (1968). *Military organization and society*. Berkeley: University of California Press.

Barfield, Thomas J. (1989). *The perilous frontier*. Cambridge, MA: Blackwell.

Boulding, Kenneth E. (1963). *Conflict and defense: A general theory*. New York: Harper.

Bush, Winston C., & Mayer, Lawrence S. (1974). Some implications of anarchy for the distribution of property. *Journal of Economic Theory, 8*, 401–412.

Creel, Herrlee G. (1970). The role of the horse in Chinese history. In *What is Taoism? and other studies in Chinese history*. Chicago: University of Chicago Press.

Crone, Patricia. (1987). *Meccan trade and the rise of Islam*. Princeton: Princeton University Press.

Doyle, Michael W. (1986). *Empires*. Ithaca: Cornell University Press.

Elvin, Mark. (1973). *The pattern of the Chinese past*. Stanford: Stanford University Press.

Friedman, David D. (1977). A theory of the size and shape of nations. *Journal of Political Economy, 85*, 59–87.

Gluckman, Max. (1940). The kingdom of the Zulu of South Africa. In Meyer Fortes & E. E. Evans-Pritchard (Eds.), *African political systems*. London: Oxford University Press.

Harris, William V. (1979). *War and imperialism in Republican Rome 327–70 BC*. Oxford: Oxford University Press.

Hirshleifer, Jack. (1987). *Economic behavior in adversity*. Chicago: University of Chicago Press.

Hirshleifer, Jack. (1991). The technology of conflict as an economic activity. *American Economic Review: Papers and Proceedings, 81*, 130–134.

Issawi, Charles. (1950). *An Arab philosophy of history*. London: John Murray.

Jones, Ronald W. (1971). A three-factor model in theory, trade and history. In Jagdish N. Bhagwati et al. (Eds.), *Trade, balance of payments and growth*. Amsterdam: North-Holland.

Keegan, John. (1993). *A history of warfare*. New York: Knopf.

Kennedy, Paul. (1987). *The rise and fall of the great powers*. New York: Random House.

Lanchester, Frederick William. (1916). *Aircraft in warfare: The dawn of the fourth arm*. London: Constable.

Lattimore, Owen. (1960). *Inner Asian frontiers of China*. New York: Beacon Press.

Mann, Michael. (1986). *The sources of social power* (Vol. 1). Cambridge: Cambridge University Press.

Morris, Donald R. (1969). *The washing of the spears*. New York: Simon & Schuster.

North, Douglass C. (1981). *Structure and change in economic history*. New York: Norton.

Oster, George F., & Wilson, Edward O. (1978). *Caste and ecology in the social insects*. Princeton: Princeton University Press.

Ratchnevsky, Paul. (1991). *Ghengis Khan*. Cambridge, MA: Blackwell.

Rich, John, & Shipley, Graham (Eds.). (1993). *War and society in the Roman world*. London: Routledge.

Richardson, Lewis Fry. (1960). *Arms and insecurity*. Pittsburgh: Boxwood Press.

Samuelson, Paul A. (1971). Ohlin was right. *Swedish Journal of Economics, 73*, 365–384.

Skaperdas, Stergios. (1992). Cooperation, conflict and power in the absence of property rights. *American Economic Review, 82*, 720–739.

Thompson, Earl A., & Faith, Roger L. (1981). A pure theory of strategic behavior and social institutions. *American Economic Review, 71*, 366–380.

Usher, Dan. (1989). The dynastic cycle and the stationary state. *American Economic Review, 79*, 1031–1044.

Whittaker, C. R. (1994). *The frontiers of the Roman Empire*. Baltimore: Johns Hopkins University Press.

Wittman, Donald. (1991). Nations and states, mergers and acquisitions, dissolutions and divorce. *American Economic Review: Papers and Proceedings, 81*, 126–129.

Wolfson, Murray. (1994). *A note on growth, politics and war*. Irvine: Mimeo/University of California.

5

Demographic Shocks and the Factor Proportions Model: From the Plague of Justinian to the Black Death

For all of his professional life, Eli Heckscher was concerned with the methodology of economics and economic history. Straddling both disciplines it was essential for him to come to grips with the problem of what one discipline could learn from the other and vice versa (Findlay 1998; Findlay and Lundahl 2002; Henriksson and Lundahl 2003). Gradually he also introduced the use of statistical time series in his works, notably his four-volume *magnum opus* about the economic history of Sweden from the time of Gustav Vasa (1523–1560) to 'the present', which in practice meant the early nineteenth century. As he moved from the sixteenth to the eighteenth century the availability of quantitative material increased, and Heckscher made use of it. However, he steadfastly refused to be bound by the strict limits imposed by 'hard' facts when it came to the interpretation of a certain epoch. He certainly took great care to weed out hypotheses not grounded in fact, but he was no stranger to

---

Revised from 'Demographic Shocks and the Factor Proportions Model: From the Plague of Justinian to the Black Death' by Ronald Findlay and Mats Lundahl, in Ronald Findlay, Rolf G. H. Henriksson, Håkan Lindgren and Mats Lundahl (eds), *Eli Heckscher, International Trade, and Economic History*, 2006, The MIT Press, pp. 157–198. With kind permission of The MIT Press.

R. Findlay, M. Lundahl, *The Economics of the Frontier*,
DOI 10.1057/978-1-137-60237-4_5

hypothetical reasoning either. Such reasoning was needed for arriving at a historical synthesis, and the refusal to go beyond just what the sources, after thorough critical scrutiny, would reveal was for him to stop short of attempting a synthesis.

The present chapter should be seen as the effort of two economists to provide a building block for a historical synthesis. We would like to combine Heckscher's plea for economic theory in economic history with his insistence on historical synthesis into a plea for economic theory in historical synthesis. The roots of the chapter are found in economic theory, which we employ very much in the fashion that Heckscher used it in his historical works: as a device for explaining the equilibrating processes in economic history during a determined period. We also share with Heckscher the conviction that it is difficult to use economic theory to explain transitions from one historical epoch or era to another. Here factors exogenous from the point of view of economics must be invoked, and we begin and end our story with two such events: the so-called Plague of Justinian in the mid-sixth century AD and the Black Death eight hundred years later.

What our analysis deals with is precisely the period between these two events, and the synthesis that concerns us is one based on a marriage between the historical facts, as provided by the professional historians, and an economic theory that may serve as reading glasses when it comes to the interpretation of the events. Our aim is to provide a reading of some of the fundamentals of eight centuries of the history of Western Europe, eastern Europe and Islam that is consistent with the interplay of the probable basic economic mechanisms at work; that is, we want to put history on a sound theoretical footing, to heed Heckscher's (1929) plea for the use of theory in economic history, and simultaneously to allow economic history to influence theorizing. Heckscher made it clear that theory was useful when it came to organizing the questions to be put to the historical material, and we agree, but it won't do to use any old theory. In order to be efficient, our theory must spring out of the historical material itself. Its categories must be chosen in a way that properly reflects the characteristics of the period we have chosen to deal with. It is only through the interaction between the given historical material and the specific tools we need to construct to reveal its hidden secrets that we can arrive at a better understanding of the underlying processes that made economic history take a particular turn at a given moment in time.

The Plague of Justinian and Its Aftermath

The waves of bubonic plague that swept the world of Late Antiquity and the Early Middle Ages have taken their name from the Emperor Justinian I, ruler of the eastern Roman Empire from 527 to 565. It was during his reign that the first outbreak occurred in Constantinople in 542, killing hundreds of thousands of people according to the historian Procopius, secretary to Justinian's general Belisarius. Procopius, who was an eyewitness, has provided us with the first incontestable description of bubonic plague in history (quoted by Bray 2000, pp. 22–23):

> During these times there was a pestilence, by which the whole human race came near to being annihilated … it did not come in a part of the world, nor upset certain men, nor did it confine itself to any season of the year … but it embraced the whole of the world, and blighted the lives of all men, though differing one from another in the most marked degree, respecting neither sex nor age …
>
> […] with the majority it came about that they were seized by the disease without becoming aware of what was coming. They had a certain fever … The body showed no change from its previous colour, nor was it hot … nor did any inflammation set in … But on the same day, in some cases, in others on the following day, and in the rest not many days after, a bubonic swelling developed; and this took place not only in the particular part of the body which is called the 'boubon', that is below the abdomen, but also inside the armpit, and in some cases also beside the ears and at different points on the thigh … For there ensued with some a deep coma, with others a violent delirium … for neither physicians nor other persons were found to contract this malady through contact with the sick or with the dead, for many were constantly engaged in burying or attending those in no way connected with them … With some the body broke out in black pustules about as large as a lentil and these did not survive even one day, but all succumbed immediately. With many

> also a vomiting of blood ensued without visible cause and straightaway brought death … In some cases when the swelling rose to an unusual size and discharge of pus had set in, it came about that they escaped from the disease and survived.

The emperor himself was infected, but survived. The first wave of the 540s–550s was followed by several others of varying intensity, persisting intermittently until the middle of the eighth century (Biraben and LeGoff 1969). While there is wide disagreement as to the extent of the impact (cf. e.g. Harrison 1999, pp. 141–53, for a critical view), there is little doubt that it was a demographic catastrophe on a scale not exceeded till the Black Death of the fourteenth century. Russell (1968, p. 180) estimates a 20–25 percent loss for the first epidemic of 541–544 and a total loss of 40–50 percent of the pre-plague population over the period 540–700.

The plague is believed to have entered the Mediterranean world at the Egyptian port of Pelusium through Ethiopia and the Red Sea, before spreading both east and west. The populations of Egypt, Syria and Palestine, then all under the sway of the Byzantine Empire, were severely affected. What happened further east is not clear (Bray 2000, p. 27):

> Its distribution to the east of Syria is something of a puzzle. It would seem that the Arabs did not bring the plague back to the Hejaz … Equally it would seem that the Arabs did not bring the plague to Afghanistan, the Indus, Ferghana and Transcaucasia and thus into the Indian subcontinent and China, as all observers have the plague ceasing at about the present western border of Iran and at the Caucasus. Whether it penetrated Africa south of Egypt is anyone's guess.

The Middle East as well was hit by successive outbreaks of the plague. Dols (1974) lists six 'major' epidemics between 627 and 717. The westward spread to Italy, Gaul and Spain was through the seaports of Genoa, Marseilles and Narbonne, proceeding inland along the rivers and trade routes. The impact on the northern lands seems to have been far less severe, though not necessarily negligible. The arrival of the plague at

Marseilles in 588 was vividly described as follows by the contemporary Gallo-Roman historian Gregory of Tours (1974, pp. 510–11):

> ... a ship from Spain put into port with the usual kind of cargo, unfortunately also bringing with it the source of the infection. Quite a few of the townsfolk purchased objects from the cargo and in less than no time a house in which eight people lived was left completely deserted, all the inhabitants having caught the disease. The infection did not spread through the residential quarter immediately. Some time passed, and then, like a cornfield set alight, the entire town was suddenly set ablaze with the pestilence ... at the end of two months the plague burned itself out. The population returned to Marseilles, thinking themselves safe. Then the disease started again and all who had come back died. On several occasions later on Marseilles suffered from an epidemic of this sort.

Before the plague struck, the eastern Roman Empire under Justinian was at the height of its power, with plentiful resources of manpower and revenue. Not only was he able to secure the eastern frontier against the Persians but also to stabilize and push back the frontiers against the Avars, Lombards, Berbers and others, while soundly defeating the Vandals in North Africa in 534–535. The great scheme of once again unifying the eastern and western halves of the empire was not impossible, though of course extremely difficult. The devastating effects of the plague on both manpower and revenue, however, rendered it impossible. Nevertheless, although his plans for expansion failed he was still able to retain most of the eastern territories of the empire.

As often noted, the nomads of the Arabian Peninsula escaped the ravages that the plague wrought on the more settled Byzantine and Sassanid Empires. After the unification of the tribes under the Prophet and his early successors, the 'rightly guided' caliphs, at the beginning of the seventh century, the Arabs rapidly captured Syria, Palestine, Egypt, North Africa and western Mesopotamia from the Byzantines. Sassanid Iran was conquered later by the Arabs under the Umayyad Caliphate. The Byzantine emperor Heraclius (610–641) and his successors could not match the élan of the Arab onslaught with the depleted resources at their command. They retreated to the Anatolian Plateau behind the security of the Taurus mountain range and then successfully resisted successive Arab attacks on Constantinople from the sea.

The empire was to survive for a further 800 years but it had lost the bulk of its territory, population and revenue to the Arabs. In the west the empire's hold on Italy was rendered extremely tenuous, and the Lombard invasion of the peninsula, beginning in 568, could not be checked before most of it had been occupied. Gaul was left to the Merovingian Franks. Spain, under Visigothic rulers, was invaded in 711 by the Muslims, who established the powerful Emirate of Córdoba that occupied most of the Iberian Peninsula. The popes in Rome ceased to look to Constantinople and eventually allied themselves with the rising dynasty of the Frankish warlord Charles Martel, who checked the Arab advance at Poitiers in 732 or 733.[1] Around the same time, say 718 or 722 (Collins 1995, p. 182), after a Christian victory over Muslim forces at Covadonga in Asturias, the Spanish *Reconquista* began.

By the second half of the eighth century the territory of the Roman Empire at its height had come to be divided between three great powers: the Greek Orthodox Byzantine Empire under the vigorous new Isaurian Dynasty, with its capital at Constantinople; the Muslim Abbasid Empire, with its capital at Baghdad; and the Latin Catholic Carolingian Empire with its capital at Aachen. Beyond the frontiers of these empires were Anglo-Saxon England in the west, the pagan Scandinavian and Saxon tribes in the north, and in the east the Slavs and Bulgars in the Balkans.

Population figures for such early periods in history are notoriously unreliable and can only be taken as the best guesses made by scholars on the basis of extremely scanty evidence. Issawi (1981) citing Russell (1968) gives figures of 16.6 million in 350 for the eastern Roman Empire, falling to 10 million by 600, indicating the devastating effect of the early waves of the Plague of Justinian; Treadgold (1997, p. 278) gives a figure of as many as 26 million for the empire under Justinian in 540, before the plague, falling to 17 million in 610 before the Arab invasions and collapsing to 7 million in 780 after that disaster, rising

[1] The traditional date is October 732, but it could also be October 733 (Fouracre 2000, p. 87).

back to 12 million by 1025. Issawi cites 15 million at least for 1000, or about 25 percent higher than Treadgold. The general qualitative picture, however, is similar, with a heavy loss of population due to plague, more loss due to the Arab invasions, and then recovery within the restricted territory.

Issawi's main contribution is an estimate of the area and population of the Arab Empire at its height in 750. He puts the population at between 28 and 36.5 million over the vast arc stretching from Spain to India. The breakdown is 10–13 million in the former Byzantine territories of Egypt, Syria and North Africa; 5–6 million in Spain; 1.5–2 million in the Arabian Peninsula; 5–6 million in Iraq; 3–4 million in Iran; and 3.5–5.5 million in Central Asia, Afghanistan and India. The gross area he puts at 9.8 million square kilometers and the inhabited area at 2.1 million, only slightly more than one-fifth, indicating the highly arid inhospitable nature of much of the terrain.

For the tenth to eleventh centuries Issawi estimates only a very modest rise of the population to 35–40 million, or about 25 percent over three centuries. The Abbasid Empire was about twice as big in both population and inhabited area as the contemporary Byzantine Empire. The only comparable source of population history for the world as a whole is McEvedy and Jones (1980). We have checked Issawi's figures against the comparable estimates that they provide. While their figures are generally lower they are not too far below the bottom range of Issawi. The figures based on their estimates of individual countries are 21 million for 700, 26 million for 1000 and 22 million for 1300. Thus the trend of population for the Islamic world is a modest 25 percent over three centuries for both Issawi and McEvedy and Jones. The fall from 26 million in 1000 to 22 million in 1300 is attributable to the ravages of the Mongol invasion in Iran and Iraq in the east and the Bedouin raids in North Africa in the west.

For Europe, excluding Russia, McEvedy and Jones report a peak of 33 million in 200, falling to a trough of 23 million in 600, rising back to 32 million by 1000 and then accelerating upwards to the huge figure of 70 million in 1300 on the eve of the Black Death.[2] This gives annual growth rates of less than 0.1 percent per annum for the earlier period and 0.25–0.3 percent after the turn of the millennium. David Grigg (1980, p. 53) reports some figures for individual countries: 0.43 percent per annum for England and Wales from 1086 to 1340; 0.49 percent for France from 1100 to 1328; less than 0.2 percent for Italy from 950 to 1300 and for Denmark from 1000 to 1300; 0.46 percent for the Moselle valley between 1000 and 1237; and an average rate of increase for Europe between 1000 and 1340 of 0.26 percent.

While these figures are notoriously uncertain, representing a tendency only, the beginnings of the higher demographic growth that was to last for three centuries can be dated. 'It was 930–50 in Sabina and Lombardy, 940–90 in Catalonia, 980–1010 in Languedoc, Provence, Poitou and the Auvergne, 1010–30 in Flanders and Picardy, Bavaria and Franconia, Burgundy and Normandy, 1050–80 in England and the Rhineland, after 1100 in central Germany' (Fossier 1999, p. 62). If we are to believe the McEvedy-Jones estimates, the increase from the trough in 600 to the peak in 1300 is a remarkable threefold or 200 percent over the seven centuries. For comparison, China increased from the AD 200 peak of 63 million before falling and then rising back to 66 million by 1000, rising further to a peak of 115 million in 1200, before falling to 85 million in 1300 as a result of the Mongol invasions of the country. This approximate doubling took place under the Sung Dynasty, generally regarded as the 'golden age' of imperial China. Yet it does not come close to the European achievement.

Why did the Western Europe of the so-called Dark Ages perform so spectacularly well, relative to what were at that time the far more advanced Byzantine, Islamic and Sung Chinese civilizations? Clearly, the foregoing leads us to suspect that the demographic change caused by the plague had something to do with it.[3] As it seems, the economic trend of Late Antiquity was a downward one in the Mediterranean area. In

[2] Livi-Bacci (2001, p. 27), quoting Biraben (1979, p. 16), has similar figures: 200: 44 million, 600: 22 million, and 1340: 74 million.

[3] The plague may not have been the only disease to gain a strong foothold in Late Antiquity. As McCormick (2001, pp. 38–41) has pointed out, both malaria and leprosy appear to have been on the rise in the Roman world at about the same time as the Plague of Justinian struck.

his monumental work on the 'dark' centuries of the European economy, Michael McCormick (2001, p. 41) concludes his chapter on the end of the ancient world thus:

> Settlement patterns suggest that ill-understood processes of demographic stagnation and decline moved slowly across the old Roman space. They finally reached the east in the sixth or early seventh century. Around the same time, the history of disease marks a new configuration in the health experience of the population. The new pathocoenosis [the array of diseases characteristic of a society] could not by itself have been the leading cause of wide-reaching economic change, for change had started earlier in most of the Mediterranean world. But it surely must have reinforced some aspects of that change, if only by debilitating or destroying part of the work force. Both settlement patterns and disease encourage us to believe that the overall trend of the late Roman world was downward between c. 200 and 700.

The next section of this chapter will develop a model of demographic-economic-ecological interaction that could perhaps provide some clues to the fundamental problem of the unequal patterns of decline and, later, rebirth.

The Model

The model presented in this section draws on our previous work (Findlay 1993; Findlay and Lundahl 2002) combining the Malthusian demographic specification with the concept of an endogenous land frontier, while stripping away the other features of those models.

The Production Function

The economy is considered as producing a single output, denoted Y, with land, A and labor, L, as inputs, according to the production function

$$Y = Y(A, L) \tag{5.1}$$

which is taken to have the usual neoclassical properties of constant returns to scale, positive first and negative second derivatives with respect to each input and complementarity between the inputs. Constancy of returns to scale enables us to write

$$y = y(a) \tag{5.2}$$

where y and a denote Y and A divided by L, respectively. We can also write the rent per hectare and the real wage as

$$r = y'(a) \tag{5.3}$$

$$w = y(a) - y'(a)a \tag{5.4}$$

The Malthusian Mechanism

The fertility and mortality rates of the population are specified as positive and negative functions, respectively, of the per capita consumption, c, of the population (Figure 5.1)

$$\mathrm{f} = \mathrm{f}(c), \mathrm{f}'(c) > 0 \tag{5.5}$$

$$\mathrm{m} = \mathrm{m}(c), \mathrm{m}'(c) < 0 \tag{5.6}$$

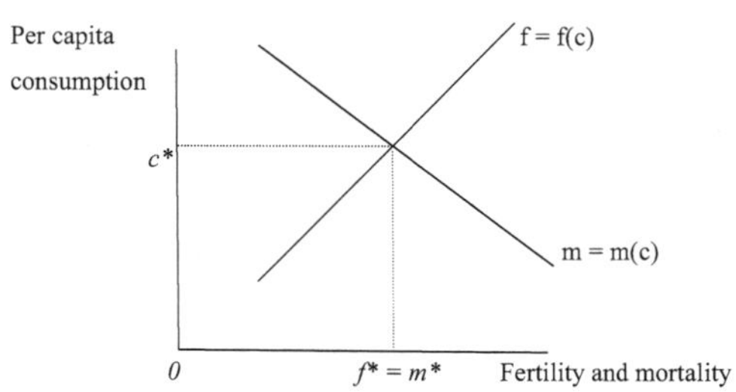

Figure 5.1 The Malthusian mechanism

Labor Productivity and Per Capita Consumption

Labor productivity, as defined above, is

$$y = Y / L \tag{5.7}$$

Suppose that we are in a 'stationary state' with zero net investment. Total consumption will then be equal to total output and the per capita consumption of the population as a whole will be

$$c = Y / P \tag{5.8}$$

where P denotes the entire population.

Suppose that the labor force is proportional to the population so that

$$L = \alpha P \tag{5.9}$$

where α is some fraction. In the pre-industrial economic conditions that we are considering, the non-working population will consist of warriors, priests and people involved in other 'unproductive' occupations as well as those too old or too young to work. Taking a more 'physiocratic' view, we could even include in the $(1-\alpha)P$ artisans, traders and so on who are 'supported' by the surplus generated by agriculture, the only truly 'productive' sector from this standpoint. From Equations (5.7), (5.8), and (5.9) it follows that

$$y^* = c^* / \alpha \tag{5.10}$$

so that y^* is the level of labor productivity that will maintain output, population and the labor force of the 'stationary state' levels compatible with the Malthusian equilibrium level of per capita consumption, c^*.

From (5.2) we can obtain the value a^* of the land-labor ratio that defines y^* as

$$y^* = y(a^*) \tag{5.11}$$

We have therefore determined the long-run stationary values of the intensive magnitudes c^*, y^* and a^*, but we have yet to determine the absolute levels of Y, C, A and P.

Land and the Frontier

The marginal productivity of land and hence the rent per hectare is determined in the stationary state as

$$r^* = y'(a^*) \tag{5.12}$$

We assume that a hectare of land deteriorates in fertility at a rate of μ unless it is maintained. Suppose that the constant rate of time preference in the economy, and hence the rate of interest, is equal to δ.

Then by the usual asset-pricing formula, the price of a hectare of land would be

$$p^* = y'(a^*)/(\delta + \mu) \tag{5.13}$$

Figure 5.2 depicts the determination of p^* by the intersection of the demand and supply curves for the stock of land in the stationary state.

The downward-sloping curve *p(a)* in Figure 5.2 shows the demand price for a hectare of land as a function of the land-labor ratio. Since

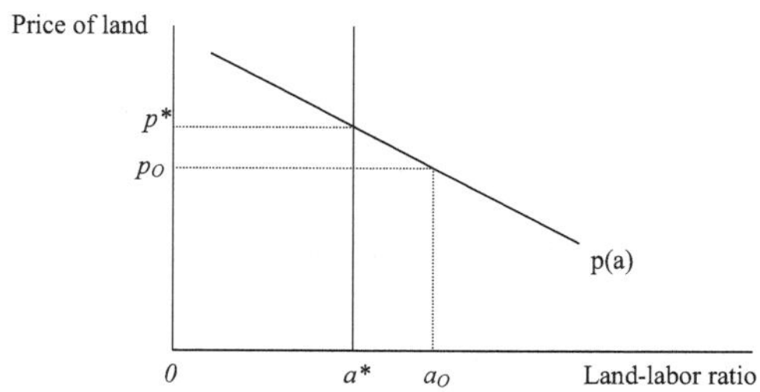

Figure 5.2 Stock equilibrium in the land market

$$y''(a) < 0$$

by the 'diminishing returns' property of the production function (5.2), the value of $y'(a)$ capitalized by the reciprocal of $(\delta + \mu)$ is the negatively shaped curve $p(a)$ in Figure 5.2. The intersection with the vertical supply curve of land per unit of labor a^* in the stationary state yields p^* as in (5.13).

We now turn to the determination of the actual size of the land area A^* of the economy in the stationary state. Once this is determined, of course, the levels of L^*, Y^*, P^* and C^* can all be obtained as well, since we know the equilibrium intensive magnitudes a^*, y^* and c^*.

The area of arable land A^* ultimately available in an economic system depends upon climatic or geographical factors, on the one hand, and on the technology of land clearance and maintenance, on the other. Population, and hence the labor force, is endogenously determined within a Malthusian framework by the same factors and hence is not an independent variable in its own right.

In Figure 5.3 we consider the arable land available, A, as a function of the labor L_a, that is needed to 'establish the frontier', i.e. to ensure that A hectares are available to the economy. To express it differently, L_a is the *cumulative* amount of labor that has gone into the clearance of the A hectares of land currently available in the economy. We postulate that

$$L_a = L_a(A),\ L_a'(\mathrm{A}) > 0,\ \mathrm{L}_\mathrm{a}'' > 0 \tag{5.14}$$

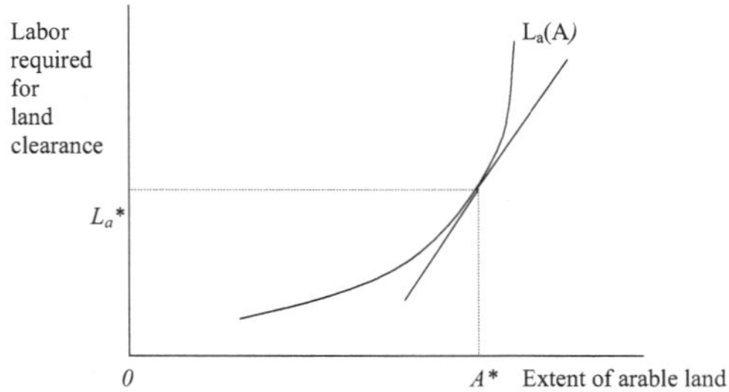

Figure 5.3 Determination of the land frontier

where $L_a'(A)$ is the marginal labor cost of clearing an additional hectare, which increases with the amount of land already cleared, as indicated by the second derivative being positive as well. This formulation illustrates the Ricardian idea that extending the margin of cultivation is an increasingly costly enterprise. The convex function (5.14) is plotted as the convex graph of $L_a(A)$ in Figure 5.3.

In the long-run stationary equilibrium it will be true that

$$w^* L_a'(A) = p^* \tag{5.15}$$

i.e. that the real marginal cost of clearing an additional hectare, the left-hand side of (5.15), must be equal to the equilibrium price per hectare p^*. Note that w^* and p^* in (5.15) have already been obtained by (5.4) and (5.13) alone. This enables us to solve (5.15) for the unique value A^* of A that satisfies this equation. This solution is depicted graphically in Figure 5.3 where the slope of the convex function $L_a(A)$ at A^* is the value of $L_a'(A)$ that satisfies (5.15), given w^* and p^* as determined already.

It is instructive to substitute for p^* from (5.13) into (5.15) to obtain the relation

$$w^* = y'(a)\left[1/L_a'(A)\right]\left[1/(\delta+\mu)\right] \tag{5.16}$$

The right-hand side of (5.16) can be interpreted as the 'indirect' marginal productivity of labor in clearing additional land, the marginal productivity $y'(a)$ of which is capitalized by the 'gross' discount factor, the reciprocal of $(\delta + \mu)$. Since w^* is also equal to its direct marginal product by (5.4) we have the 'efficiency condition' for labor allocation that it requires its direct and indirect marginal productivities to be equal.

Having now determined the absolute magnitude A^* of arable land and knowing already the equilibrium values a^*, y^* and c^* of the intensive magnitudes, we can easily obtain the absolute values L^*, Y^*, P^* and C^* of the labor force, total output, population and consumption. We have thus fully determined the equilibrium values of all the variables in the model.

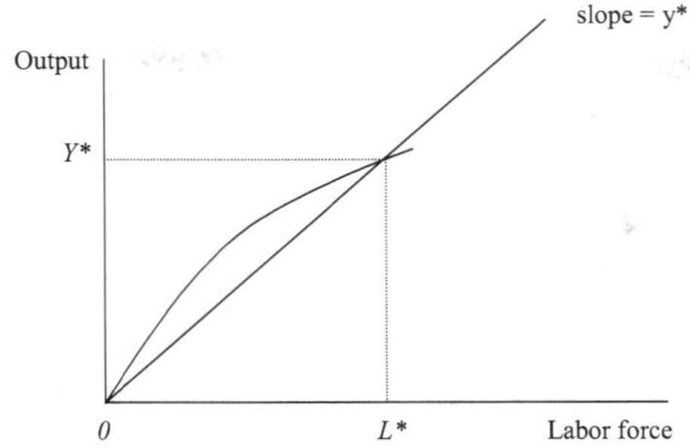

Figure 5.4 Determination of total output

The relation between Y, A and L is depicted in Figure 5.4. Given A^* the concave function shows the relation between Y and L determined by the production function (5.1). The ray from the origin has a slope equal to y^*, so that the intersection with the concave function determines L^* and Y^*.

Employment in Land Clearance

We have established the cumulative labor effort needed to provide the economy with an arable land area of A^*. However, since land is assumed to 'depreciate' at the rate μ, for example through reforestation or soil erosion, it must continuously be replenished by the clearance of *new* land for the stationary state to be maintained. The amount of new land cleared will be an increasing function of the price of land and a decreasing function of the real wage, equal to p^* and w^*, respectively, in the stationary state. Letting N denote the amount of new land cleared (as opposed to the cumulative total, A), and L_n the amount of current labor required for this task, in the stationary state we must have

$$N\left(L_n\right) = \mu A^* \tag{5.17}$$

and

$$L_n^* = L_a(A^*) - L_a[(1-\mu)A^*] \tag{5.18}$$

Assuming land clearance to be an explicit economic activity, 'profits' equal to $p^*N - w^*L_n$ must be maximized, which requires that

$$p^*(\partial N / \partial L_n) = w^* \tag{5.19}$$

which is precisely the condition (5.15) obtained earlier to determine A^* by equating the price p^* to the marginal cost of land clearance $w^* L_a'(A)$. (At the margin it does not matter whether we use A or N.)

Where does L_n^* come from? The number of production workers L is equal to αP by assumption, so the L_n^* workers required for the land clearance come out of the remaining pool of $(1-\alpha)P$. Thus the labor force is the sum of the production workers and the members of the 'land-clearing brigade', and if we add the 'unproductive' members of society we get the total population.

What happens outside of the steady state? Corresponding to any point (A, L) in the input space the production function determines $r(a)$ and $w(a)$ by the marginal productivities of each input. Capitalizing $r(a)$ by the reciprocal of $(\delta + \mu)$ and ignoring expected capital gains and losses we can always obtain $p(a)$ for every $r(a)$. Taking $p(a)$ and $w(a)$ as given, the land-clearing sector maximizes profits in determining the amount of land cleared $N(p, w)$ as an increasing function of p and a decreasing function of w as indicated by

$$N = N(p, w),\ \partial N / \partial p > 0,\ \partial N / \partial w < 0 \tag{5.20}$$

Since the point (A, L) is arbitrary it is clear that $N(p, w)$ may exceed, equal or fall short of μA, allowing A to rise or fall over time depending upon the direction of the inequality.

Dynamic Stability

From a dynamic perspective the model can be represented by the following two-dimensional system of differential equations

$$\dot{L} = \dot{L}(L,A) \tag{5.21}$$

$$\dot{A} = \dot{A}(L,A) \tag{5.22}$$

where the dots indicate the time derivatives dL / dt and dA / dt respectively.

The equilibrium state of this system is reached when the values of L and A are such that (5.21) and (5.22) are both equal to zero. These values are precisely the L^* and A^* that we have obtained above for the long-run stationary state. What is investigated here is whether the system will move towards the point (L^*, A^*) when $L(t)$ and $A(t)$, the state variables of the system, are not equal to these equilibrium values.

The system will be dynamically stable, i.e. $L(t)$ and $A(t)$ will approach (L^*, A^*), when the Jacobian matrix of the partial derivatives of (5.22) and (5.23)

$$\mathrm{J} \equiv \begin{vmatrix} \partial\dot{L} / \partial L & \partial\dot{L} / \partial A \\ \partial\dot{A} / \partial L & \partial\dot{A} / \partial A \end{vmatrix}$$

evaluated at the equilibrium point (L^*, A^*), satisfies

$$\partial\dot{L} / \partial L + \partial\dot{A} / \partial A < 0 \tag{5.23}$$

$$\left(\partial\dot{L} / \partial L\right)\left(\partial\dot{A} / \partial A\right) - \left(\partial\dot{A} / \partial L\right)\left(\partial\dot{L} / \partial A\right) > 0 \tag{5.24}$$

The first of these is called the 'trace' and the second the 'determinant' condition. Together they ensure that the characteristic roots of the matrix are negative, and have negative real parts, as required for dynamic stability.

We may now evaluate each of the four partial derivatives to obtain their signs. The rate of change of population, and hence the labor force, is given by the difference between fertility and mortality rates:

$$\dot{L} = \left[f(c) - m(c)\right]L \tag{5.25}$$

from Equations (5.5) and (5.6) above. Noting that per capita consumption c is proportional to per capita output y as given by (5.10) we obtain the sign of the partial derivative

$$\partial \dot{L} / \partial L = \left[f'(c) - m'(c)\right]\alpha\left(\partial y / \partial L\right) < 0 \tag{5.26}$$

Since $f'(c)$ is positive and $m'(c)$ is negative the expression within parenthesis is positive. But

$$\partial y / \partial L = y'(a)\left(-A / L^2\right) < 0 \tag{5.27}$$

since average productivity per worker falls when L is increased with A constant, ensuring (5.26).

Partially differentiating (5.25) with respect to A we obtain

$$\partial \dot{L} / \partial A = \left[f'(c) - m'(c)\right]\alpha y'(a) > 0 \tag{5.28}$$

From the previous section we have seen that

$$\dot{A} = N(p, w) - \mu A \tag{5.29}$$

Both p and w are functions of A and L, so we have

$$\partial \dot{A} / \partial A = \left(\partial N / \partial p\right)\left(\partial p / \partial A\right) + \left(\partial N / \partial w\right)\left(\partial w / \partial A\right) - \mu < 0 \tag{5.30}$$

since

$$\partial N / \partial p > 0, \quad \partial p / \partial A < 0, \quad \partial N / \partial w < 0, \quad \partial w / \partial A > 0$$

and

$$\partial \dot{A} / \partial L = (\partial N / \partial p)(\partial p / \partial L) + (\partial N / \partial w)(\partial w / \partial A) > 0 \quad (5.31)$$

since

$$\partial p / \partial L > 0, \quad \partial w / \partial L < 0$$

The 'trace' condition (5.23) is clearly satisfied, since both diagonal elements of the matrix *J* have been shown to be negative.

Figure 5.5 is the 'phase diagram' of the dynamic system (5.21 and 5.22). It shows combinations of the state variables *A* and *L* that leave $dL / dt = 0$ and $dA / dt = 0$ along each of the respective functions, with the equilibrium point being *(A*, L*)* where these two functions intersect. It is easy to see that the 'determinant' condition (5.24) is satisfied if the slope of the $dL / dt = 0$ function is steeper than the slope of the $dA / dt = 0$ function, i.e.

$$(\partial \dot{L} / \partial L) / (\partial \dot{L} / \partial A) > (\partial \dot{A} / \partial L) / (\partial \dot{A} / \partial L)$$

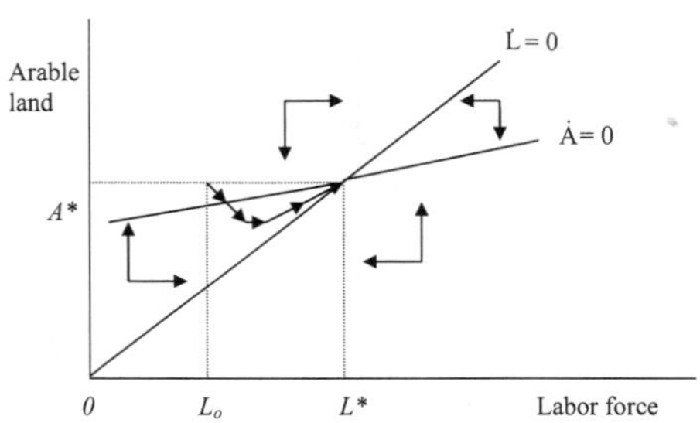

Figure 5.5 The dynamic stability of the model

The $dL/dt = 0$ function is a ray through the origin with a slope equal to a^*, the land-labor ratio that equates the fertility and mortality rates to maintain the Malthusian equilibrium. For any given value of A points to the left of the $dL/dt = 0$ ray have a greater than a^* and hence c greater than c^*, so population, and hence the labor force, must increase. By the same reasoning L must increase for a given A from any point to the right of the $dL/dt = 0$ ray. Similarly, for any given L an amount of A above the $dA/dt = 0$ line will result in A falling vertically to it or rising toward it from any value of A below that line. The $dA/dt = 0$ locus has a flatter slope than the $dL/dt = 0$, as required by the 'determinant' condition for stability. The state variables will move according to the pattern of the arrows in each of the four regions of the input space.

Demographic Shock

An immediate exercise is the impact of a demographic shock such as the bubonic plague. If we start from the equilibrium point (A^*, L^*) in Figure 5.5, the population and hence the labor force as well collapse instantly from L^* to L_O, while A^* is initially fixed. The real wage rises above w^* while the rent per hectare falls below r^*. Hence, the land price also falls below p^*. In terms of Figure 5.2 the land-labor ratio moves to the right, to a_O, so that p falls from p^* along the demand curve to the point corresponding to $p_O(a_O)$. The fall in p and rise in w make the amount of new land cleared fall below μA^* and so the area of land cultivated contracts. The rise in per capita output and consumption stimulates the recovery of population and the labor force so the state variables move down and to the right along the path indicated in Figure 5.5. Once the $dA/dt = 0$ line is crossed from above, the rising price of land and the falling real wage result in the new land cleared exceeding the 'depreciation' μA, and so the area cultivated rises along with the labor force back to the equilibrium point (L^*, A^*).

Comparative Steady States

Suppose that there is Hicks-neutral technological progress in the production function (5.1). At the original land-labor ratio this will raise productivity and hence consumption per capita, so as to increase population growth. To keep $dL / dt = 0$ it is clear that the land-labor ratio a^* has to fall. This implies a rotation to the right of the $dL / dt = 0$ ray as in Figure 5.6. The $dA / dt = 0$ line remains unchanged and so the new equilibrium point (A^{**}, L^{**}) involves an increase in both the labor force and the area of cultivation, with a lower land-labor ratio. Initially A remains fixed at A^* since both p^* and w^* rise in the same proportion. But the increase in labor lowers the real wage rate and raises the rent and the price of land, and thus induces an expansion in the area cultivated as well.

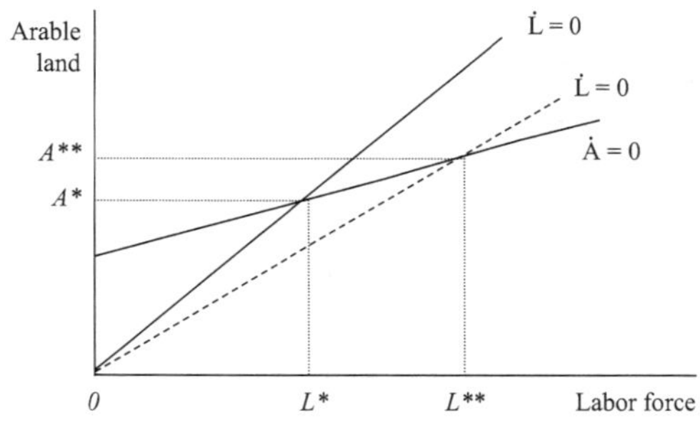

Figure 5.6 Technological progress

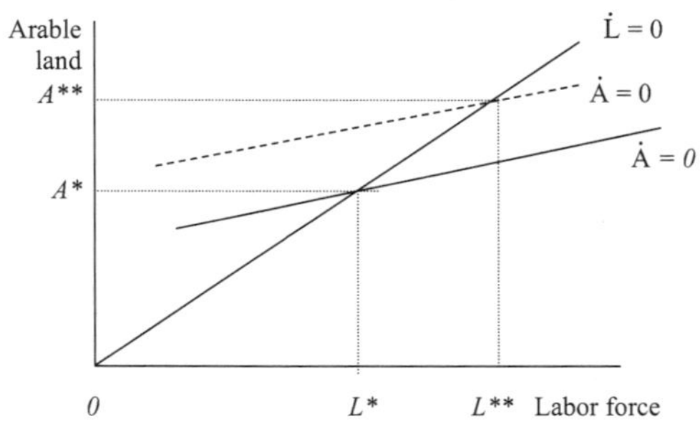

Figure 5.7 A reduction of the cost of land clearance

A reduction in the cost of land clearance, due either to better technology or climatic conditions, will shift the $L_a(A)$ function in Figure 5.3 downwards for each value of A, and also reduce the slope $L_a'(A)$. Thus, for each value of L on the $dA / dt = 0$ line, the area cultivated, A, will have to rise until $p(a)$ has fallen and $w(a)$ has risen sufficiently to equate the price to the marginal cost of land clearance. As we can see from Figure 5.7 this will result in A^{**} and L^{**} both being higher than the previous values A^* and L^*.

From (5.13) it also follows that a reduction in the rate of time preference δ or the 'depreciation' rate μ of land will raise the value of the marginal hectare and hence require an increase in A to leave dA / dt still equal to zero for each value of L, while leaving the $dL / dt = 0$ function unchanged. The result is therefore the same as in Figure 5.7.

As a final exercise a leftward shift in the fertility function $f(c)$ will raise y^* and c^*. The result is to rotate the $dL / dt = 0$ locus to the left, which results in a new equilibrium with A^{**} less than A^* and L^{**} less than L^*, as in Figure 5.8. As can be seen in Figure 5.8 the ratio of the cultivated area A^{**} to the labor force L^{**} rises, implying an increase in per capita output y^{**} over y^*, and per capita consumption c^{**} over c^*. The reduction in fertility thus results in a smaller economy in terms of both cultivated area and population, but one with a higher standard of living.

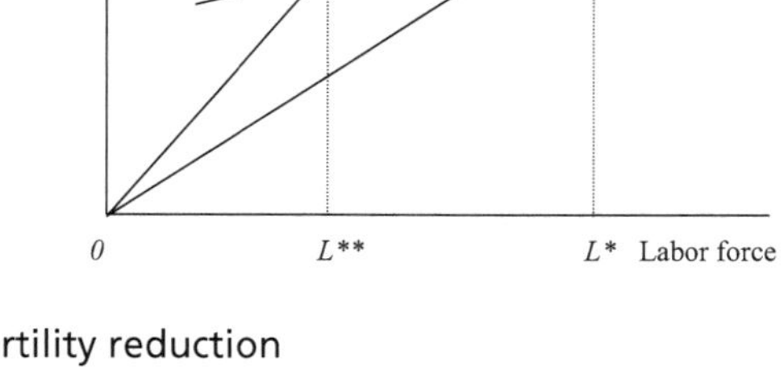

Figure 5.8 A fertility reduction

Performance: The Byzantine Empire

In the next three sections we will briefly examine the respective economic performance of the three systems, mainly with respect to population, labor force, cultivated area and output but also looking at other factors such as urbanization and monetization as indicators of these developments. The intention is to see whether we can relate these outcomes to the implications of the model and what we know of the exogenous shocks that occurred in each case.

As we have noted, the Byzantine Empire before the plague struck in 542 was at its peak in terms of territory and population, put at about 26 million by Treadgold (1997) on the basis of estimates by McEvedy and Jones (1980). It is easy to imagine, with Cyril Mango (1994, pp. 68–69), what must have happened to the economy:

> … all normal occupations were interrupted, prices of goods trebled and quadrupled, starvation set in, fields were deserted and the remaining farmers were burdened with additional taxes on the non-productive land of their deceased neighbours.
>
> There can be little doubt that the plagues of the sixth century, combined with an unprecedented sequence of natural disasters were a factor, perhaps the determining factor in the collapse of urban life. For it is a fact (though some historians still refuse to recognize it) that all round the Mediterranean, the cities, as they had existed in Antiquity, contracted and then practically disappeared.

By 610, as a result of the plague, the Byzantine population had fallen to 17 million, and it continued to fall to a mere 7 million by 780 after the loss of Egypt, Syria, Palestine and North Africa to the Arabs, and further outbreaks of the plague. The population of Constantinople, which was at least 300,000 at the time of Justinian, fell to a mere 40,000 by the middle of the eighth century, after another disastrous outbreak of the plague in 747, 'probably … the lowest point in the medieval history of Constantinople' (Mango 1994, p.78). Antioch and Alexandria, the next largest cities after Constantinople, were lost to the Arabs in the seventh century. Thessalonica was the only other remaining city of any size. Several of the cities of Asia Minor declined to mere *kastra,* citadels surrounded by small civilian settlements (Mango 1994, Chap. 3; Cameron 1993, Chaps. 7–8). That this development should not have been related to the appearance of the plague is difficult to believe. Even an author as cautious as Averil Cameron (1993, p. 164) is quite emphatic:

> The effects are certainly hard to quantify … but it is hard not to think that plague must have been a factor in undermining the generally thriving state of cities in the Near East in the early part of the sixth century … Historians vary sharply in the amount of weight that they are willing to attach to the sixth- and seventh-century plague. Yet the fact remains that this seems to have been the first appearance of bubonic plague in Europe; its impact must therefore have been far greater than that of the regular diseases which ravaged ancient cities as a matter of course.

The period 641–780 is described by Treadgold (2002) as the 'Struggle for Survival', against the twin enemies of the Arabs and the plague. Byzantium may have escaped total collapse by a slim margin. State revenue fell drastically as people died (Treadgold 2001, p. 67):

> The evident explanation for this decline in state spending is the same as that for most of Justinian's failures: the effects of the plague after 541. These were so different from most historical events in magnitude and kind that they were inevitably underestimated by most Byzantine observers, as indeed they have been by most modern historians. Not even the return of the plague in the thirteenth century wreaked such havoc, because it recurred less often and reduced a denser population. If the first outbreak had killed Justinian, as it almost did, it might well have brought on the fiscal and military collapse of the empire that he barely averted.

It was bad enough as it was.

While revenue and population shrank, the size of the army did not fall in the same proportion, so a greater share of resources was devoted to the military, and a reorganization of society along military lines, in so-called *themata* (military districts, each with its own army), took place. As our model predicts, however, per capita income appears to have been on the rise and income disparities were being reduced. Treadgold (2002, p. 150) states that '[in] comparison with earlier Byzantine times the rich appear to have been poorer and the poor richer', which is consistent with the rise in the land-labor ratio lowering rents and raising wages, in terms of our model. He also observes that peasants benefited from the greater availability of land. With labor having become a scarce factor, it became difficult to tie them to the soil. Their freedom of movement increased and they had 'complete and unlimited legal disposal over … [their] land. The Byzantine sources show quite clearly that peasant land was handed down from generation to generation by inheritance and that it could be freely alienated by the possessor just as he chose—by sale, by gift, or limited lease' (Ostrogorsky 1966, p. 210). The Byzantine Empire had uncultivated land at its disposal, in its very heartland, Asia Minor, where the military holdings granted out in return for military service could not obtain labor without bringing in foreigners, mostly of Slavonic origin. The rise in per capita income that all this seems to indicate could also explain how a greater than proportionate military burden was borne, relative to the pre-plague years. In relation to our model the situation would be ripe for the rise in per capita consumption to induce a recovery of population and an associated increase in the area under cultivation.

While the empire had survived, its prospects around the year 800 did not look too good in the ongoing tripartite struggle for power against its two great rivals, the Carolingian Empire of the West and the Abbasid Empire of Haroun al-Rashid in Baghdad. Byzantium had to contend not only with the Arabs but with formidable barbarian peoples on its frontiers, such as the Bulgars and the Pechenegs. In the west the aggressive Normans intruded successfully into Byzantine possessions in southern Italy and the Balkans, after taking Sicily from the Arabs (Norwich 1991, 1997).

Population, and with it manpower and revenue, began to revive from 7 million in 780 to 12 million in 1025 on the death of the Macedonian emperor Basil II, who crushed the Bulgars and stabilized the Balkan frontiers. Also significant, particularly for the future, were the conversion to Christianity of the Kievan Rus' ruler Vladimir and his marriage to a Byzantine princess to cement a mutually beneficial alliance. Meanwhile the Carolingian Empire was fragmented in the succession struggles between Charlemagne's heirs and the power of the Sunni Abbasid caliphs was challenged by the Shia Fatimid Caliphate in Cairo, while Byzantium preserved its political and religious unity.

As the population recovered, the man-land ratio increased, and the relative bargaining power shifted in favor of the larger landholders, who proceeded to buy up peasant property. Efforts on the part of the rulers to protect the peasants proved to be of little avail (Ostrogorsky 1966, pp. 221–22):

> … after the death of Basil II [in 1025] the long series of these laws came to an end … For, as even the government regulations of the tenth century, in spite of their extreme severity, had been unable to suppress the buying-up of peasant and military lands, now the passively benevolent attitude of the government meant that the great landowners' capacity for expansion could develop to the full. The destruction of the small freehold properties continued unrestricted; the great landowners absorbed the land of the peasants and soldiers and made the owners their serfs.
>
> […] Certainly there were free peasants in the late Byzantine period; but whereas in the middle Byzantine period, from the seventh to the beginning of the eleventh century, the free and moving peasantry is the chief factor in agrarian development and the backbone of Byzantine agriculture, from the eleventh century onward, just as in the early period, the great landlord dominates the scene. The agrarian history of the late Byzantine period is that of great landowners and their dependants.

Just when it seemed that the empire could continue its revival, a fateful new challenge arose with the emergence of the Seljuk Turks. They took over much of the interior of the Anatolian Plateau after defeating the Byzantines at Manzikert in 1071. This shifted the center of gravity of the empire from the interior of Asia Minor to the coastal regions of the Balkans and the Black Sea. The rising commercial and naval power of Venice, Pisa, Genoa and the other Italian cities was accommodated by the Byzantines with increasing diplomatic concessions, such as exemptions from customs duties and 'extraterritorial' rights in Constantinople (Nicol 1988). The relative expansion of the West was strikingly displayed in the Crusades, which liberated Jerusalem and Antioch and established new kingdoms in the Holy Land (Runciman 1951; Riley-Smith 1987).

These Christian allies did not accept the authority of Byzantium, and the Fourth Crusade of 1204 that sacked Constantinople and established the so-called Latin Empire that lasted until 1261 was a fatal wound from which the empire never recovered before its fall at the hands of the Ottoman Turks in1453 (Queller and Madden 1997).

Despite the economic expansion from the tenth century onwards, part of which has been well documented by Harvey (1989), it is difficult to resist the impression that the economic history of the Byzantine Empire was one of protracted demographic collapse, as a result of plague and the Arab invasions, from about 550 to 780, followed by a long recovery during which power systematically shifted in favor of the large landowners, until the recovery was set back by the intrusions of the Fourth Crusade and the Turks. Something akin to a new demographic-economic equilibrium was being restored, within the restricted post-plague area imposed by the Muslim advances, as would be implied by our model. This restoration is symbolized by the fact that Constantinople seems to have had the same population, about 300,000, at the time of Justinian and the onset of the plague, as it had when it was sacked by the Crusaders in 1204, after having fallen to as low as 40,000 in the middle of the eighth century. This was also about as many inhabitants as it had on the fateful day of 29 May 1453.

There does not appear to have been any notable technological progress or other economic innovation in the entire history of the empire (Kazhdan and Epstein 1985, p. 27):

> In general, Byzantine technology was extremely conservative. Byzantine agricultural implements remained virtually unchanged from Roman times. The peasant continued to use the light plow dragged by a pair of oxen. It was made of wood and had a removable iron plowshare; it did not have wheels, so the plow bit rather than cut the soil. The scythe was not in use in Byzantium, and the image of Death with its scythe in hand, so popular in the West, would have left the Byzantines unmoved.

The large estates remained partly uncultivated, very much as a result, it seems, of faulty techniques (Ostrogorsky 1966, p. 211):

> The difficulty of making proper use of the larger estates was partly due to the primitive conditions of economic technique; for in this respect the

> Byzantine Empire, so far ahead in culture, was in many ways far behind the West. Thus Byzantium to the end of its days continued to employ an extremely uneconomic and antiquated harness for draught animals, while by the tenth century the West had evolved a greatly improved method of harnessing …

Byzantium maintained and adopted the administrative, military and economic institutions that it had inherited from antiquity, but did not make any significant new breakthrough, as far as one can gather, other than 'Greek fire', the lighted naphtha that was used successfully in naval battles against the Arabs in an early form of chemical warfare, and the importation of the silkworm from China in the sixth century in an early example of commercial espionage. Characteristically, this led to a significant but 'luxury' industry, which was also imitated and supplanted in due course by both of the empire's great rivals, the Muslims and the Latins. The critical 'frontier', in the case of Byzantium, was always a political and military one, not one of settlement and cultivation. As Harvey (1989) points out, there was considerable land reclamation accompanying the population growth from 900 to 1200 but this is not likely to have constituted any net addition to the cultivated area in the same regions before the onset of the plague. None of this should be taken as denigrating the great resilience and adaptability that the empire displayed in dealing with an almost uninterrupted succession of military and political challenges and the crucial role in world history that it played in relation to the Russians and the other Slavic peoples of eastern Europe.

The Islamic World

The extent and rapidity of the Arab conquests of the seventh and eighth centuries comprise one of the most remarkable features of world history. 'The speed, magnitude, extent and permanence of these conquests excite our wonder and almost affront our reason, but the historian who seeks to explain them is impeded by the deficiency of the evidence at his disposal', writes J.J. Saunders (1965, p. 39). The first conquests, however, can perhaps be partly explained with the aid of the Findlay (1996) model of the extension of empires, or simply by interpreting the extension of the land frontier in the present model as a military operation. Justinian's attempt to reconquer the territories lost by Rome to the barbarians had turned the Byzantine frontier into a triple war frontier: Italy, Africa and the east, and the eastern frontier was weakened by the necessity to maintain troops in the two other theaters of war.

The eastern war led to nothing and the plague outbreaks in the sixth and seventh centuries in the eastern Mediterranean and the western part of the Sassanid Empire left the two contending empires militarily weakened, with little power of resistance, whereas the Arabs had escaped the deadly disease and could take advantage of the population vacuum. Damascus, Jerusalem and Alexandria fell to Islam in rapid succession between 635 and 642, and further east the Arabs simultaneously penetrated Sassanid territory.

Islam, and Arabic, the language in which the Qur'ān was written, imposed a cultural unity over a vast extent of diverse peoples and physical environments, stretching from the shores of the Atlantic to the oases of Central Asia and the mountains of Afghanistan. This vast territory was never a single politically and administratively unified empire but it did maintain a unique identity as the *Dar al-Islam,* or Abode of Islam, as opposed to the *Dar al-Harb,* or Abode of War, i.e. the infidel. Thus most of the welter of dynastic changes and power shifts that form so great a part of medieval Islamic history can be ignored for the purposes of this essay since they mostly took place within the same system. It was only on the frontiers of Spain and in the Mediterranean islands, before the Crusades, that land and people moved in or out of the Islamic world itself as a result of political conflict. In Central Asia much of the conversion of the nomadic Turkish and later Mongol tribes and states took place peacefully. The Crusader kingdoms in Syria and Palestine were exceptions, but only temporarily, since they were eventually returned to the Islamic fold by Saladin and the Mamelukes.

In the case of Islam, the extension of the frontier of cultivation was a military operation rather than a peaceful land clearance affair (Hitti 1970, p. 144):

> Islam did provide a new battle-cry, a convenient rallying-point and a party watchword. It undoubtedly acted as a cohesive and cementing agency for the heterogeneous masses never before united and furnished a large part of the driving force. But it is hardly in itself enough to explain the conquests. Not fanaticism but economic necessity drove the Bedouin hordes, and most of the armies of conquest were recruited from the Bedouins, beyond the confines of their arid abode to the fair lands of the north. The passion to go to heaven in the next life may have been operative with some, but the desire for the comforts and luxuries of the civilized regions of the Fertile Crescent was just as strong in the case of many.

Fertile soil was available in abundance in the conquered territories, in the valleys of the Guadalquivir, Nile, Euphrates, Tigris, Oxus and Jaxartes rivers, with the Indo-Gangetic plain being added by the Delhi Sultanate early in the thirteenth century. The string of oases from North Africa to Central Asia also yielded high returns. On the whole, however, the Abode of Islam was situated in one of the most arid zones of the civilized world and 'the struggle between the desert and the sown' has been a persistent theme of its existence.

To quote the eminent French geographer Xavier de Planhol (1959, p. 102):

> ... the heart of Islam remains that desert zone which, slanting across the globe from the Atlantic Ocean to Central Asia, includes the whole of the ancient world between, on the one side, the humid zones of intertropical Africa and monsoon-moistened Asia and on the other side the wet and temperate climate of Europe.

In this zone, according to de Planhol (1959, p. 124), the towns, linked to each other along the trade routes, dominate their rural agrarian environs, which, despite their density, are often no more than 'a farming or truck-gardening suburb'. Reflecting its origins in Mecca and Medina, Islam in this view is essentially a religion of traders and city-dwellers. It has always had difficulty penetrating mountainous and forested areas. Pastoral nomadism is well adapted to the environmental conditions of the Islamic zone and Bedouin Arab, Berber and Turkish nomadic tribes have all interacted positively and negatively with the sedentary cultivators and townsfolk over the centuries, providing the fourteenth-century Tunisian sage Ibn Khaldun (1958) with the theme of his great work. Interestingly, Khaldun says (1958, Vol.1, p. 302), 'Arabs can only conquer flat territories' and also that (1958, Vol.1, p. 308) 'desert tribes and groups are always dominated by the urban population'.

Jared Diamond (1997) has popularized the idea that agricultural innovations can be diffused more readily across the same latitudes, since climatic conditions are similar, rather than on a north-south axis. With its largely 'horizontal' extent around the globe, within a relatively narrow band, the early Islamic world provides an excellent example of this thesis. As Andrew Watson (1983) has demonstrated convincingly in a seminal work, the first three or four centuries of Islam were marked by a remarkable agricultural revolution that saw a very wide variety of new crops diffused from its eastern margins in India all the way to Morocco and Spain. These included such major crops as cotton and sugarcane, as well as rice, hard wheat, sorghum, citrus fruits, coconuts, bananas, artichoke, spinach and eggplant. The introduction of these crops required complementary efforts in irrigation, the construction of canals and the opening up of new lands. The agents of such change were not only farmers and landowners but also rulers and officials who provided the necessary institutional infrastructure.

The following quotation (Watson 1983, p. 129) describes a process that corresponds exactly to the implications of our model:

> … the agricultural revolution was bound up with an ill-documented but none the less real demographic revolution which seems to have touched most parts of the Islamic world from roughly the beginning of the eighth to the tenth century. Rising population levels and increasing levels of output of foodstuffs must continuously have interacted: though both were affected by other factors, at times demographic growth must have been the result of agricultural progress, at times its efficient cause.

Watson cites many instances of this agricultural expansion from all over the Islamic world, and the reader is referred to his book and the many sources cited therein for the evidence. Unfortunately, there appear to be no numbers. Perhaps the strongest evidence for the agricultural revolution of the early Islamic world is the extent and scale of its urbanization. Eric Wolf (1966, p. 13) has defined the peasantry 'in terms of its subordinate relationships to a group of controlling outsiders', and, conversely, urban areas are dependent on the surrounding countryside for their growth.

Watson (1983, p. 132) challenges many published estimates of city size as biased downward, by sheer 'Orientalist' prejudice or 'on the grounds that it is more responsible to underestimate than to overestimate'. Baghdad, and also Samarra, the two capitals of the Abbasid dynasty, could have had populations of close to a million, although half a million would be more plausible and impressive enough, since Constantinople at the time would not have exceeded 300,000. Basra seems to have had at least 200,000. Watson (1983, p. 131) colorfully remarks that 'along the Tigris settlement was continuous, so that before dawn crowing cocks answered one another from housetop to housetop all the way from Basra to Baghdad'. On the eve of the Black Death the twin city of Fustat-Cairo also had a population of the order of half a million, and Nishapur in the ninth century is put at between 100,000 and five times that number. In the west Fez and Qairawan had several hundred thousand each but Córdoba at its peak was comparable to Baghdad at its height, estimated to be between a half and one million. Córdoba surpassed the one million mark. According to a census taken towards the end of the tenth century, the city had 1,600 mosques, 213,077 houses occupied by the lower and middle classes, another 60,300 inhabited by the higher bureaucracy and the aristocracy, and 80,455 stores (Ocaña Jiménez 1975, p. 47). The Islamic world also had very many cities of lesser rank, far outstripping Byzantium and Western Europe.

Agriculture clearly had to be very productive to support urban settlements on such a scale, (as well as the Arab cultural advance in general). The relationship was not confined simply to food supply. Major processing industries such as sugar refining and textile manufactures relied on the supply of raw materials from the agricultural sector. In addition to cotton, raw silk and hemp for linen were important inputs to urban textile industries. Many of these manufactures were exported to other parts of the Islamic world, and also to Europe. In addition to these high value-added manufactured exports, the Islamic world, through the Red

Sea and to the Persian Gulf, was also the *entrepôt* for the precious spices from India and Southeast Asia to be distributed to Europe.

Looking at the admittedly unsatisfactory data provided by McEvedy and Jones we see that the population of the Islamic world seems to have grown from about 21 million to about 27 million from 700 to 1000, say about 30 percent over three centuries. Issawi (1981) gives 28–36 million for 750 and 35–40 million for 1000. Taking the 28 million low estimate for 750 and the 40 million high estimate for 1000 we get what would be a maximum increase of 43 percent over two and a half centuries, as compared with 30 percent over three. While noticeably better than the performance of Byzantium at about 25 percent over three centuries, even the 43 percent over 250 years can hardly be called a 'demographic revolution'. Thus, while fully agreeing with Watson's picture of complementary agricultural and demographic expansions in the early Islamic world, we should not exaggerate the magnitude of either.

There is little doubt that what hindered the further progress of early Islamic agriculture was the unfavorable nature of the physical environment and climatic conditions under which it operated. Once the power of conquest was gone, the character of the frontier changed from one of war to one of land clearance. In the 'struggle between the desert and the sown' the sown had three good centuries, from 700 to 1000, but then the desert seems to have begun its counter-attack. Islam was thus hemmed in by its unfortunate geographical circumstances. As Watson says, there is the possibility that the earlier expansion may have become overextended, with excessive reliance on irrigation leading to soil erosion. Settlement was not continuous in many areas, raising costs of communication.

Warfare and the breakdown of central authority, and the raids of the ever-present nomads, also shrank the margin of cultivation. Neither were the social institutions of the *waqf*, donation of land for religious or charitable purposes, or the *iqta*, a revocable military fief, conducive to sustaining agricultural productivity. The McEvedy-Jones population estimates decline from about 27 million in 1000 to about 23 million in 1300, reflecting the loss of cultivable area and the cessation of innovation. The impacts of the Mongol invasion (Findlay and Lundahl 2006), the sacking of Baghdad in 1258 by Hülegü and the annihilation of the Abbasid Caliphate were also of course additional major factors in this regard.

Western Europe

Western Europe at the outset of our period had a Latin Christian core, soon to be flanked by a Muslim Spain in the southwest, with a pagan fringe in the Scandinavian north and in the east, with the Frisians, Saxons, Balts and Slavs inhabiting the shores of the North Sea and the Baltic and the fertile plains beyond the Elbe, the Oder and the Vistula. By the end of the period the pagan fringe had long since been almost entirely converted and the Muslims in the Iberian Peninsula had been pushed back all the way south to the narrow confines of the kingdom of Granada, and driven out of Sicily, Crete and other Mediterranean islands that they had temporarily occupied.

What were the factors behind this extraordinary advance, which the Roman Empire at its height was not able even to attempt, much less to achieve? Lynn White (1962, 1978) had a deceptively simple answer, that could be colloquially phrased as 'it was the stirrup and the plow, stupid', which led to his being roundly condemned by Sawyer and Hilton (1963) for the intellectual crime of 'technical determinism'.

The plow in question was the heavy wheeled plow with an iron coulter and plowshare, drawn by a team of horses or oxen, that cut deep into heavy soil in long straight furrows, turning the soil over with a moldboard. Though apparently known in antiquity it was not employed, being unsuitable for Mediterranean conditions, where the much lighter so-called 'scratch plow' prevailed. The plains of northern Europe, however, were ideally suited to the heavier instrument. Horses also proved to be more efficient draft animals than oxen, after the invention of the horse collar multiplied the load that they could pull by up to a factor of five. The wear of the heavy loads on the horses' hooves required the complementary invention of the nailed horseshoe.

Another innovation, the three-field rotation in place of the more traditional two-field, raised productivity per worker by 50 percent, if additional land were available, clearly providing a stimulus to land reclamation on a vast scale. In the two-field system, half the acreage was sown with winter crops, while the other half was left fallow. This made sense in the Mediterranean area where rainfall was concentrated in the winter, but in northern Europe, where sowing in the spring could bring another crop, one-third of the area was sown in the fall (wheat or rye), another third in the spring (barley, oats or legumes) and the last third was left fallow. The following year the second field was sown in the fall, and so on, until the cycle recommenced. The three-field system increased both the area under cultivation and the range of crops grown. The new system was introduced in France during the eighth century, but took time to spread, and it was not until after 1250 that the speed of diffusion became rapid. Even so, the two systems coexisted during the thirteenth and fourteenth centuries (Grigg 1980, p. 73).

This new technology required changes in the social organization of the peasant community to adopt a more cooperative basis, in order to take advantage of the economies of scale offered by the more expensive plow and draft animals. The plow is a labor-saving device. It was introduced by a society that had undergone a population decline, but below a certain 'threshold farm size' the introduction of the plow is not profitable, and when the cost of feeding the draft animals is taken into account this size increases (Lundahl 1979, pp. 590–91).[4] The need for oats to feed the horses stimulated greater variety in the mix of crops. These complementarities led to a highly productive system of mixed farming with cereal cultivation and livestock raising becoming the predominant form of agriculture in much of Western Europe.

The stirrup, unknown in antiquity despite its apparent simplicity, led to a revolution in warfare with the armored knight on his powerful warhorse relying on the lance to pulverize opposition. The high cost of horse and armor, and the long period of training required for knightly proficiency, would have been impossible without the surplus for rents and taxes over the peasant's consumption that the heavy plow provided. At a time such as the ninth and tenth centuries, with incessant raids by the Muslims in the south and west, Vikings on the northern coasts and marauding Magyars from the east, the peasant also needed the protection of the knight, so that 'stirrup and plow' together were the effective

[4] Let us assume that the introduction of the plow saves N man-days per hectare, and that the daily wage rate is w. The annual capital cost (the sum of depreciation and interest, which we assume to be given), of plowing S hectares is $c = SNw$, and $S = c / Nw$ defines the lowest ('threshold') farm size that makes it profitable to introduce the plow.

cultural package powering the rise of Western Europe during these centuries (Bloch 1962). Both peasant and warrior needed the consolation and spiritual guidance of the priest, who in turn was supported and protected in his cloister by the peasant and the warrior, together constituting the 'Three Orders' of medieval feudal society as depicted by Georges Duby (1980).

Though the concept of the 'frontier' is usually associated with Frederick Jackson Turner (1986) and the westward expansion of the United States in the nineteenth century, it is if anything even more applicable to early medieval Europe, as many authors have realized and pointed out in the excellent study edited by Bartlett and Mackay (1989). There clearly was an 'internal' economic frontier in already settled areas, between stretches of arable land and the immense forests surrounding them. When reflecting over the data provided by the Domesday Book,[5] M.M. Postan (1966, p. 549) unequivocally concludes that the 'Domesday facts clearly denote dense, and hence ancient settlement, the product of at least six centuries of internal colonization'.

The colonization pattern was generalized in Western Europe (North and Thomas 1973, Chap. 5). Colonization took on different shapes. Trees and bushes were cleared in the neighborhood of villages or in the waste further away, contributing to the scattering of fields. New settlements were established in the forests between villages. Coastal areas were reclaimed by the construction of embankments, and marshes were drained. Most important was the advance into forests. During the first centuries after the plague, 'the forest seems to have held sway over the whole natural landscape' of Western Europe, as Duby (1974, p. 5) writes. Lowland forest was being cleared in the eleventh and twelfth centuries both in England and France, and at the end of the twelfth century the process continued into upland areas as well, in Brittany, above the Moselle, in the Vosges, the Alps and the Pyrenees (Grigg 1980, pp. 71–72).

There was also an 'external' military frontier, which required armed force to push back Muslim warriors in Spain during the entire *Reconquista,*

---

[5] The Domesday Book was put together some time between 1108 and 1109 or between 1111 and 1113 (Poole 1955, p. 1, note).

or Saxon and Slav pagan tribes east of the Elbe, particularly after 1150, settling and cultivating the lands thus won and converting, expelling or killing the previous occupants. With land abundant and labor scarce, particularly on the eastern frontier, once the Saxons or Slavs accepted German rule, Jesus Christ as the 'Deus Teutonicus' and the German heavy plow in place of their less efficient wooden one, they were valued and protected subjects of the German princes and bishops. After a few generations the population became culturally 'German' despite the abundant and perhaps even dominant presence of Slavic genes. On the other hand Polish and other Christian Slavic rulers also welcomed the efficient German peasants as settlers on their own lands. Assimilation was more difficult in Spain, where *cristianos nuevos* were regarded with considerable suspicion, and even in Ireland where there was tension between the native Celts and the Anglo-Norman feudal lords who were granted estates soon after the conquest.

The complementarity between the stirrup and the plow and the three orders on both the eastern and western frontiers is revealed in the vital role played by the military orders in both cases, the Teutonic Knights in the east and the Orders of Calatrava and Santiago in Spain. The *Reconquista* in Spain, with Santiago Matamoros and El Cid as its foremost symbols, and the wars against the Balts and Slavs, merged into the crusading mentality that swept Christendom, and also saw the excursions against the Albigensian heretics in Provence and into Syria and Palestine against the Muslims under the banner of the cross. Not surprisingly, the movement had permanent effects within the contiguous frontiers on the mainland of Europe but proved ephemeral in the Holy Land.

The role of Christianity in the extension of the frontier was not confined by any means to the inspiration of Crusaders. As the greatest landowner in Europe the Church took an active part in promoting land clearance and improving agricultural productivity in other ways. It has also been pointed out, by both Lynn White and Georges Duby, that Christianity induced a more instrumental and exploitative view of nature as something purely for the service of man, rather than as being imbued with a spirit of its own that had to be respected and propitiated. The great forests of beech and oak that were cut down to clear land for pasture and tillage were the abode of spirits that the animistic pagans worshipped.

This cultural shift was thus no less important than the heavy plow or the three-field rotation in making the agricultural revolution possible, so the charge of 'technical determinism' by White's critics is not entirely fair. Indeed most of their objections are on matters of the speed and scope of the technical changes and not on their ultimate significance. Sawyer and Hilton (1963) say that rather than the causal sequence from plow and three-field rotation to food supply to population it might be the other way around, from exogenous increase in population to the need for more food and hence to the changes in agricultural technique, anticipating a thesis advanced by Ester Boserup (1965).

One advantage of the modeling approach adopted in this chapter is that it enables us to escape from being trapped in 'chicken-and-egg' arguments of this type. In our model both food supply and population are endogenous variables, depending upon the state of technical knowledge, geographic and climatic conditions and the biological and behavioral determinants of fertility and mortality rates. The heavy plow may have been known to antiquity, and for that matter to the Islamic world, but there was no incentive to adopt it under Mediterranean environmental and social conditions, as White himself clearly says.

The results in terms of population growth in any case were spectacular, as seen from the figures already cited. The McEvedy-Jones numbers further indicate that growth was particularly rapid in the areas of modern Germany and Poland, where it trebled over the period from 1000 to 1340 and also in the areas of modern France and Great Britain. Italy doubled from 5 to 10 million over the same period but even this was below the average for Europe as a whole. These patterns of population growth in the 'old' and 'new' areas of Europe are consistent with the 'frontier thesis' adopted in this chapter.

Hand in hand with the increase in area cultivated and population went an increase in the growth of towns and trade. While in 1000 there were only 100 or so places in Europe that could be called towns, and half of those were in Italy, 300 years later the figure had increased to between 4,000 and 5,000 (Grigg 1980, p. 77). Western European cities, however, were far smaller than their Islamic counterparts. In 1292 Paris had a population of no more than 59,000 people, and as of 1328 the figure had possibly increased to 80,000. Toulouse, an example of a large provincial town, had around the same time no more than 24,000 inhabitants. In Italy, where the largest cities were found, Milan had 52,000 in the thirteenth century, Padua 41,000 in 1320, Naples 27,000 in 1278, Venice 78,000 in 1363, Bologna 32,000 in 1371, Florence 55,000 in 1381. Before the middle of the fourteenth century only Milan, Venice, Naples and Florence, possibly also Palermo, exceeded 50,000 inhabitants. Some of these cities may have approached the 100,000 mark. In the Low Countries, Ghent had some 56,000–60,000 inhabitants in 1356, and Bruges 25,000–35,000 in 1340. Antwerp was a small town of 18,000 in 1374. In England, London dominated completely, with 35,000–45,000 in 1377, followed by the far smaller York and Bristol, with figures somewhere between 10,000 and 14,000. In Spain, Barcelona, Córdoba and Seville (plus Granada in the Moorish zone) were the only cities with more than 40,000 inhabitants. Only Cologne in Germany was close to the 40,000 mark, while Metz, Strasbourg, Nuremberg, Augsburg, Vienna, Prague, Lübeck, and Magdeburg had populations around 20,000 (Russell 1958, Tables 63–65, van Werveke 1963, pp. 38–39). Even with a generous allowance for the influence of the Black Death on the later figures the European cities were thus extremely small, relative to Constantinople and the Islamic world.

Trade took place not only within Europe but with the Byzantine and Islamic worlds as well, leading to the well-known identification by Robert Lopez (1976) of a 'commercial revolution' of the thirteenth century that was also augmented by the growing trade with Asia both by sea and overland as a result of the Pax Mongolica. As is well known, a Genoese ship from the Black Sea port of Kaffa which was engaged in this lucrative trade returned to the Mediterranean in 1347 and opened another act in the drama of 'Rats, Lice and History' (Zinsser 1935).

Even before the onset of the Black Death, however, the preceding century had been marked by what Archibald Lewis (1958) termed 'The Closing of the Medieval Frontier 1250–1350'. The internal frontier was reaching its natural limits within the prevailing technology and there is the possibility that the climate may have started to become less favorable. Tillage competed with pasture to the detriment of the proper balance between the two. Population continued to grow while the supply of land was not keeping pace, lowering wages and peasant incomes while raising rents (North and Thomas 1973, p. 48), leading to growing inequality and social conflicts in both the countryside and the towns. The external frontiers of Europe also ceased to expand, with the Muslims recovering the Holy Land and the Byzantines Constantinople in 1261.

The second decade of the fourteenth century saw the outbreak of what William Jordan (1996) has called the 'Great Famine' of 1315–1322. A population of Europe in excess of 70 million, under the prevailing technology, was getting to be unsustainable within its geographical confines. A Malthusian crisis of major proportions was clearly looming. Population densities in certain rural areas in 1300 had increased to the point where they were comparable with those of the early nineteenth century, when the farming technology was vastly superior (Grigg 1980, Chap. 7). David Grigg (1980, p. 82) summarizes:

> For perhaps two centuries the expansion of the cultivated area and the adoption of new techniques was sufficient to keep production up with population growth. But by the middle of the thirteenth century the supply of agricultural land was running out; it was in this century that there are most signs of attempts to intensify production by growing legumes and reducing the fallow but they seem to have been insufficient. The primary blockage to improving yields was the lack of livestock manure, and in the densely populated arable areas of south-eastern England and northern France this reflected the lack of grazing, as population growth led to the ploughing of grazing land.

Western European agriculture was getting into a situation typical of a number of today's developing countries, where the pressure of population leads to increasingly intensive cultivation, with diminishing returns to labor and falling productivity per hectare, tantamount to a reduction of the effective land area, in a sequence that easily feeds itself (Lundahl 1979, Chap. 5). The Genoese ship from Kaffa was in the nature of a historically necessary accident waiting to happen.

Conclusions

In the middle of the sixth century AD the Mediterranean world was struck by the so-called Plague of Justinian, an epidemic that would recur in further successive waves until the mid-eighth century. No good estimates exist with respect to death tolls, but there is not the slightest doubt that in the areas where it hit, the consequences were extremely severe. The diffusion in space was limited, however. Northern and northwestern Europe apparently escaped and so did the areas that a century later would constitute the core areas of the new world religion: Islam.

As a result of the plague the population of the eastern Roman Empire hit a trough some time around the late eighth century and then began to rise until the advent of the Black Death in the mid-fourteenth century. Simultaneously, the Islamic population rose, until the Mongol invasions in the mid-thirteenth century. Europe, in turn, saw a population decline in the wake of the plague, followed by a rise that accelerated after 1000 until the early fourteenth century, when famine was followed by another outbreak of the plague. Thus, all three geographical territories display a common demographic pattern: a decline in the size of the population, followed by a rise, continuing on beyond the previous peak.

As our chapter demonstrates, this pattern can be made subject to analytical representation in the form of a simple Malthusian model where birth and death rates are functions of per capita consumption, production is a function of labor and land, and the extent of the arable area is determined by the existence of an agrarian or military frontier that can be extended at a rising cost in terms of labor.

This simple model can be used to investigate the impact of a demographic shock. The shock leads to an instantaneous rise in the land-labor ratio as a result of the collapse of population, higher wages and lower rents, and a gradual reduction of the area under cultivation. Per capita consumption, among the survivors, increases and stimulates population growth. Due to the Malthusian characteristics of the model, however, this increase cannot continue, so the land-labor ratio must fall. The price of land increases and induces land clearance at the frontier and an expansion of the area under cultivation until the original levels of both land and labor are restored.

The model can also be used to investigate the effects of a discrete technological change. This raises labor productivity and consumption per capita and so makes the population grow. Population growth, however, cannot go on indefinitely, and in order to make it cease the land-labor ratio must fall. The larger population raises rents and the price of land, inducing an increase of the area under cultivation but less than proportionately to the increase in population, thus bringing about the fall in the land-labor ratio required to restore the Malthusian equilibrium. The extent of the resulting increases in population and the supply of land depends upon the magnitude of the technical change and the elasticity of the endogenous land frontier with respect to the rise in the price of land that it induces.

A reduction of the cost of land clearance, as a result of technological progress or more favorable climatic conditions, reduces the amount of labor necessary to sustain a given land area as well as the labor needed to clear a hectare of new land. The area under cultivation has to increase until the land price has fallen enough and the wage rate risen enough to equate the land price and the marginal cost of land clearance. This, in turn, increases the population and the labor force, in the same proportion as the increase in the supply of land, to preserve the Malthusian equilibrium.

Analogously, decreases in the rate of time preference or the exogenous rate of land destruction increase the price of land at the margin and hence also the area under cultivation and the labor force in the same proportion.

Finally, an autonomous fertility reduction leads to higher per capita consumption and production in the Malthusian equilibrium. The labor force shrinks, and with it also the area under cultivation, but less than in the same proportion, permitting the economy to enjoy a permanently higher standard of living as a result of the greater relative land-abundance induced by the exogenous reduction in fertility.

The model thus makes some explicit predictions, notably with respect to the demographic shock and the effects of technological change. These predictions can be checked against the historical performance of our three geographical areas: Byzantium, the Islamic world and Western Europe.

In Byzantium the plague (and the subsequent invasions by the Arabs) led to a contraction of the economy. The area under cultivation was reduced and as a result urban life also underwent a decline. Per capita income, however, increased as the land-labor ratio rose, making it possible to shoulder a higher military burden per capita. The increase in per capita income induced population growth from some time between the late eighth century and the early eleventh, a process that also received some aid from the more peaceful conditions prevailing on the political frontier. As predicted by our model, when the population began to grow back, bargaining power in the labor and land markets shifted in favor of the landowners, and this resulted in harsher contractual conditions for the peasantry. Land rents increased at the expense of wages. At the same time, political conditions deteriorated, with the military frontier being pushed in by the Seljuk Turks and the Fourth Crusade. This opened the door for the eventual collapse of the empire with the fall of Constantinople in 1453. Nowhere in this process does technological progress appear to have been present, so that the Byzantine story was simply one of population change and military operations within a shrinking territory and a concomitant loss of population to superior military force.

The core territory of what would later become the Abode of Islam escaped the ravages of the plague. The cycle began by territorial expansion. The military frontier between the Byzantine and Sassanid Empires was weakened by the loss of population resulting from the plague, and into this population vacuum the Arabs could move relatively easily, pushing both north and west, into Byzantine territory in northern Africa, and also east into Iran all the way to the region of Sind in the west of India. The area of arable land was extended not by clearance but by conquest. Territorial expansion was, however, accompanied by remarkable technological progress in agriculture. New crops stimulated the use of irrigation and land clearance, industrial processing of agricultural products, and also demographic growth and urban development. The population of the Islamic world would grow from some time between 700 and 750 to 1000 at a rate that was superior to that of Byzantium, but not sufficiently to be called a 'demographic revolution'. Such a revolution was not possible under the unfavorable conditions of the physical environment. The largely desert-like conditions in much of the territory of Islam could not support a higher population. To this can be added the unfortunate impact of certain social institutions and the devastating blow dealt to Islam by the Mongols.

The last of our three cases, Western Europe, emerges by a wide margin as the 'winner' in our imaginary 'population race'. Of course, we can only speculate about the reasons for this, in the light of our model. One factor was technological change: the improvement of the plow, the substitution of the horse for the ox, the horse collar, the horseshoe, the three-field system of crop rotation and the change in the crop mix, as well as the concomitant changes in the social system. More important, however, was what took place at the frontier of cultivation. In different ways the frontier was spectacularly extended. The dense forests had to yield to the sown. While in the case of the Islamic world the desert increasingly encroached on the sown, in Western Europe population growth induced by technical progress ensured the retreat of the wilderness. The Germans advanced towards the east across the Elbe in an early *Drang nach Osten*, and the Spaniards pushed back the Moors, in an effort that would carry over to overseas conquests beginning in 1492, the very year that the military frontier was closed in the Iberian Peninsula itself. The results of all these frontier movements were spectacular, far above the achievements by Byzantium and Islam. Cities grew, albeit not to the size of those of Byzantium and Islam, but grow they did, both in size and in numbers. Western Europe experienced the same cycle as the other two regions, first a downswing, then an upturn in population. The upturn was nothing short of spectacular in the Malthusian age that we are dealing with, to the point where at the end of the period symptoms of serious overpopulation began to appear. The advent of the Black Death drastically raised the land-labor ratio back to a far more favorable level. In a perverse sense it came as a deliverer, triggering a new demographic-economic cycle that would last all the way up to the Industrial Revolution (Findlay and Lundahl 2002).

References

Bartlett, Robert, & Mackay, Angus. (1989). *Medieval frontier societies.* Oxford: The Clarendon Press.

Biraben, Jean-Noël. (1979). Essai sur l'évolution du nombre des hommes. *Population, 34*, 13–25.

Biraben, Jean-Noël, & LeGoff, Jacques. (1969). La peste dans la haute moyen âge. *Annales: Économie, Société, Civilisations, 24*, 1484–1510.

Bloch, Marc. (1962). *Feudal society* (2nd ed.). London: Routledge/Kegan Paul.

Boserup, Ester. (1965). *The conditions of agricultural growth: The economics of agrarian change under population pressure.* London: George Allen and Unwin.

Bray, R. S. (2000). *Armies of pestilence: The impact of disease on history.* New York: Barnes and Noble.

Cameron, Averil. (1993). *The Mediterranean world in late antiquity.* London/New York: Routledge.

Collins, Roger. (1995). *Early medieval Spain: Unity in diversity 400–1000.* Houndmills/London: Macmillan.

Diamond, Jared. (1997). *Guns, germs and steel: The fates of human societies.* New York: Norton.

Dols, Michael W. (1974). Plague in early Islamic history. *Journal of the American Orientalist Society, 94*, 371–383.

Duby, Georges. (1974). *The early growth of the European economy: Warriors and peasants from the seventh to the twelfth century.* London: Weidenfeld and Nicolson.

Duby, Georges. (1980). *The three orders.* Chicago: University of Chicago Press.

Findlay, Ronald. (1993). International trade and factor mobility with an endogenous land frontier: The general equilibrium consequences of Christopher Columbus. In Wilfred J. Ethier et al. (Eds.), *Theory, policy and dynamics in international trade.* Cambridge: Cambridge University Press.

Findlay, Ronald. (1996). Towards a model of territorial expansion and the limits of empire. In Michelle R. Garfinkel & Stergios Skaperdas (Eds.), *The political economy of conflict and cooperation.* Cambridge: Cambridge University Press.

Findlay, Ronald. (1998). A plea for trade theory in economic history. *Economic and Social Review, 29*, 313–321.

Findlay, Ronald, & Lundahl, Mats. (2002). Toward a factor proportions approach to economic history: Population, precious metals, and prices from the black death to the price revolution. In Ronald Findlay, Lars Jonung, &

Mats Lundahl (Eds.), *Bertil Ohlin: A centennial celebration* (pp. 1899–1999). Cambridge, MA/London: MIT Press.

Findlay, Ronald, & Lundahl, Mats. (2006). The first globalization episode: The creation of the Mongol Empire, or the economics of Chinggis Khan. In Göran Therborn & Habibul Haque Khondker (Eds.), *Asia and Europe in globalization: Continents, regions, and nations*. Leiden: E. J. Brill.

Fossier, Robert. (1999). Rural economy and country life. In Timothy Reuter (Ed.), *The New Cambridge medieval history. Volume III c. 900-c.1024*. Cambridge: Cambridge University Press.

Fouracre, Paul. (2000). *The age of Charles Martel*. Harlow: Longman.

Gregory of Tours. (1974). *The history of the Franks*. Trans. with an Introduction by L. Thorpe. Harmondsworth: Penguin.

Grigg, David B. (1980). *Population growth and agrarian change: An historical perspective*. Cambridge: Cambridge University Press.

Harrison, Dick. (1999). *Krigarnas och helgonens tid: Västeuropas historia 400–800 e Kr*. Stockholm: Prisma.

Harvey, Alan. (1989). *Economic expansion in the Byzantine Empire 900–1200*. Cambridge: Cambridge University Press.

Heckscher, Eli F. (1929). A plea for theory in economic history. *Economic History (supplement to Economic Journal), 1*, 525–534.

Henriksson, Rolf G. H., & Lundahl, Mats (2003). Eli Heckscher, ekonomisk teori och ekonomisk historia. In *Janusansiktet Eli Heckscher: Nationalekonom och ekonomisk historiker*. Texter i urval av Rolf G. H. Henriksson och Mats Lundahl. Stockholm: Timbro.

Hitti, Philip K. (1970). *History of the Arabs: From the earliest times to the present* (10th ed.). London: Macmillan.

Issawi, Charles. (1981). The area and population of the Arab Empire: An essay in speculation. In A. L. Udovitch (Ed.), *The Islamic Middle East* 700–1900. Princeton: Darwin Press.

Jordan, William C. (1996). *The great famine: Northern Europe in the early fourteenth century*. Princeton: Princeton University Press.

Kazhdan, Aleksandr Petrovich, & Epstein, Ann Wharton. (1985). *Change in Byzantine culture in the eleventh and twelfth centuries*. Berkeley: University of California Press.

Khaldun, Ibn. (1958). *The Muqaddimah: An introduction to history*, 3 volumes, trans. F. Rosenthal. New York: Pantheon Books.

Lewis, Archibald R. (1958). The closing of the medieval frontier 1250–1350. *Speculum, 33*, 475–483.

Livi-Bacci, Massimo. (2001). *A concise history of world population* (3rd ed.). Malden/Oxford: Blackwell.

Lopez, Robert S. (1976). *The commercial revolution of the Middle Ages, 950–1350*. Cambridge: Cambridge University Press.

Lundahl, Mats. (1979). *Peasants and poverty: A study of Haiti*. London: Croom Helm.

Mango, Cyril. (1994). *Byzantium: The empire of the New Rome*. London: Phoenix.

McCormick, Michael. (2001). *Origins of the European economy: Communications and commerce, A.D. 300–900*. Cambridge: Cambridge University Press.

McEvedy, Colin, & Jones, Richard. (1980). *Atlas of world population history*. Harmondsworth: Penguin.

Nicol, Donald M. (1988). *Byzantium and Venice: A study in diplomatic and cultural relations*. Cambridge: Cambridge University Press.

North, Douglass C., & Thomas, Robert Paul. (1973). *The rise of the Western world: A new economic history*. Cambridge: Cambridge University Press.

Norwich, John Julius. (1991). *The Normans in Sicily*. Harmondsworth: Penguin.

Norwich, John Julius. (1997). *Byzantium: The decline and fall*. New York: Knopf.

Ocaña Jiménez, Manuel. (1975). Córdoba musulmana. In Juan Bernier Luque et al. (Eds.), *Córdoba: colonia romana, corte de los califas, luz de occidente*. Madrid: Editorial Everest.

Ostrogorsky, Georg. (1966). Agrarian conditions in the Byzantine Empire in the Middle Ages. In M. M. Postan (Ed.), *The Cambridge economic history of Europe. Volume I: The agrarian life of the Middle Ages* (2nd ed.). Cambridge: Cambridge University Press.

Planhol, Xavier de. (1959). *The world of Islam*. Ithaca: Cornell University Press.

Poole, Austin Lane. (1955). *From Domesday Book to Magna Carta 1087–1216*. Oxford: Clarendon.

Postan, M. M. (1966). Medieval agrarian society in its prime. In M. M. Postan (Ed.), *The Cambridge economic history of Europe. Volume I: The agrarian life of the Middle Ages* (2nd ed.). Cambridge: Cambridge University Press.

Queller, Donald E., & Madden, Thomas F. (1997). *The Fourth Crusade: The conquest of Constantinople* (2nd ed.). Philadelphia: University of Pennsylvania Press.

Riley-Smith, Jonathan. (1987). *The Crusades: A short history*. New Haven/London: Yale University Press.

Runciman, Steven. (1951). *A history of the Crusades* (Vol. 3). Cambridge: Cambridge University Press.

Russell, Josiah Cox. (1958). Late ancient and medieval population. *Transactions of the American Philosophical Society, 48*, 3–152.

Russell, Josiah Cox. (1968). That earlier plague. *Demography, 5*, 174–184.

Saunders, J. J. (1965). *A history of Medieval Islam*. London: Routledge and Kegan Paul.

Sawyer, P. H., & Hilton, R. (1963). Technical determinism: The stirrup and the plough. *Past and Present, 24*, 90–100.

Treadgold, Warren. (1997). *A history of the Byzantine state and society*. Stanford: Stanford University Press.

Treadgold, Warren. (2001). *A concise history of Byzantium*. Basingstoke: Palgrave.

Treadgold, Warren. (2002). The struggle for survival (641–780). In Cyril Mango (Ed.), *The Oxford history of Byzantium*. Oxford: Oxford University Press.

Turner, Frederick Jackson. (1986). *The frontier in American history*. Tucson/London: University of Arizona Press.

van Werveke, Hans. (1963). The rise of towns. In M. M. Postan, E. E. Rich, & Edward Miller (Eds.), *The Cambridge economic history of Europe, volume III: Economic organization and policies in the Middle Ages*. Cambridge: Cambridge University Press

Watson, Andrew M. (1983). *Agricultural innovation in the early Islamic world*. Cambridge: Cambridge University Press.

White, Lynn, Jr. (1962). *Medieval technology and social change*. Oxford: Oxford University Press.

White, Lynn, Jr. (1978). *Medieval religion and technology: Collected essays*. Berkeley: University of California Press.

Wolf, Eric. (1966). *Peasants*. Englewood Cliffs: Prentice-Hall.

Zinsser, Hans. (1935). *Rats, lice and history*. London: Routledge and Sons.

6

The First Globalization Episode: The Creation of the Mongol Empire, or the Economics of Chinggis Khan

When the communist system fell in the Soviet Union in 1989, the Mongolian economy and society in general received a tremendous shock. All of a sudden Soviet foreign aid disappeared completely and foreign trade virtually collapsed. GDP fell by more than 20 percent in a mere four years, and in spite of a gradual improvement thereafter, the 1989 level has so far not been reached anew. Mongolia was thrown abruptly into a rapidly globalizing world without being prepared for it. The fall of communism, a system that had been in place for approximately 65 years,

Draft versions of this essay were presented at the conference 'Asia, Europe, and Global Processes: Economic, Cultural, and Normative Dimensions', at the National University of Singapore, 14–16 March 2001, in two seminars at the National University of Mongolia, Ulaanbaatar, at the Faculty of Social Sciences and the School of Economic Studies, 14 March 2002, and at the First SSAPS (Swedish School of Advanced Asia Pacific Studies) Asia-Pacific Annual Conference in Gothenburg, 26–28 September 2002. We are grateful for the constructive comments received on all four occasions, and to Stanley Engerman, for the same reason. The research has been funded by a SAREC (Swedish Agency for Research Cooperation with Developing Countries) grant, which is gratefully acknowledged.

Revised from 'The First Globalization Episode: The Creation of the Mongol Empire or the Economics of Chinggis Khan' by Ronald Findlay and Mats Lundahl, in Göran Therborn and Habibul Haque Khondker (eds), *Asia and Europe in Globalization: Continents, Regions and Nations*, 2006, E. J. Brill, pp. 13–54. With kind permission of Koninklijke Brill NV.

R. Findlay, M. Lundahl, *The Economics of the Frontier*,
DOI 10.1057/978-1-137-60237-4_6

forced globalization on Mongolia in a dramatic way, with little to cushion its immediate impact. The country became, as it were, a 'victim' of globalization.

The fact that Mongolia was victimized by globalization stands out as a bitter irony of history once we begin to extend the perspective backwards in time. In the present age of information technology, increased international trade and factor mobility, it is easily forgotten that globalization is not a latter-day phenomenon (Findlay and Lundahl 2000). On the contrary, such a view implicitly views globalization not as a process but as a *state*: an impossible perspective, given the label. The only sensible way of approaching globalization is by taking the term literally, as the story of how the world became global, and then the roots have to be sought considerably further back in time. We will not attempt to provide a clear-cut answer to the question of when and how globalization 'began'. That would be both out of place and futile. Even the most cursory inspection of the rapidly accumulating literature on this subject indicates that there appear to be about as many answers to the question as there are authors who have posed it.

A definite answer is hardly needed for our present purposes. It is more than sufficient to note that if we go back eight centuries, what was up to that point the strongest wave of or effort at globalization in history emanated from the Mongols. They were the main agents of the process; they 'pushed' globalization, as it were. Needless to say, from the Mongol point of view, the early globalization episode has virtually nothing in common with the present one. On the contrary, the contrast between the two could not be more evident. They should be viewed as opposite endpoints on a scale. At one extreme we find the Mongols in the thirteenth century, as the active agents of the process, in virtually complete control of it, and with more or less total power to decide the distribution of the benefits and costs that arose in the course of the episode. At the other end of the scale, in the current situation, we find them as passive recipients, or even victims, as suggested above, with no power whatsoever to influence the course of events and their effects.

The present essay deals exclusively with the first of these globalization episodes. The Mongols have had a notoriously bad press throughout history:

Now we are gonna ravage,
drink and fight and swear,
burn red cottages,
hit little children
and say dirty words

The quotation comes from a Swedish student play and is not altogether serious.[1] Still, it captures some of the spirit that pervades especially older accounts of the Mongols and even today many people tend to think of them as a bloodthirsty disorganized horde, intent on killing and plunder. There was, however, a great deal more than that to the Mongol explosion in the thirteenth and fourteenth centuries. The Mongol conquests are truly remarkable—in at least two ways. The first is of course the sheer size of the undertaking (Adshead 1993, p. 5):

> The Mongolian explosion was the first real global event. It deeply affected China, Persia, Russia and eastern Europe. Indirectly, and at one remove, it affected India and Southeast Asia. Negatively, it affected Japan, Egypt and Western Europe, by not conquering them, and giving them their chance, so to speak, in their respective cultural areas. More remotely, it entered the causal network which led to Christian expansion in America, Moslem expansion in Africa and Southeast Asia.

The Mongol Empire is the largest continuous empire the world has ever seen. At the time of its peak, after Khubilai Khan's final conquest of southern China, in 1279, it extended from the coasts of southern Siberia, Manchuria, Korea and China down to Amman in the east all the way into Hungary, Poland and Belarus in the west, and from the northern borders of Indochina, Burma and India, the shores of the Persian Gulf, the southern border of Iraq across Syria and the southern coast of Turkey

[1] Lundaspexet *Djingis Khan*, 1954, free translation.

in the south up to a latitude of approximately 60° N in Russia and Siberia (Bold 2001, p. xi).

The second remarkable quality of the Mongol conquests is their unlikelihood. In the twelfth century the Mongols 'were not a linguistic or an ethnological group but simply the dominant tribe of one of the tribal confederations that inhabited the Mongolian steppes' (Fletcher 1986, p. 13). The Mongols gave their name to the Mongol confederation as well, but neither the tribe nor the confederation is likely to have consisted simply of ethnic or linguistic Mongols. The same applied to the Tatars, the Naimans and the Kereits, the three other main confederations in Mongolia. All of them contained ethnic or linguistic Turks too. Altogether, the population of the Mongolian steppes is likely to have numbered no more than around a million people or so in the twelfth century (Fletcher 1986, p. 22), and perhaps only half that number (de Hartog 1989, p. 53), an incredibly small number for a people who just after the turn of the century would embark on a territorial expansion that would not end until the largest continuous empire that the world has yet seen had been created.

In the following we will present a model which combines the main features of the approaches set forth in Findlay and Wilson (1987), McGuire and Olson (1996), Olson (1962) and Findlay (1996) in order to explain why the Mongols could be unified in spite of a tremendous free rider problem, how the unification took place and why they were able to create their continuous empire.

The Unification of the Mongols: The Installation of a 'Stationary Bandit'

Before the epic conquest could be launched, the Mongols had to be united. This in itself stood out as an almost impossible task. The logical point of departure for an analysis of the unification of the Mongols is the observation by Joseph Fletcher (1986) that their steppe habitat determined not only their mode of production but also the form of their society (cf. also Lattimore 1951, pp. 53–83). The ecology of the Central

Asian steppe would in general not sustain sedentary activities, in particular not much agriculture (Fairbank and Reischauer 1979, p. 154):

> The aridity of the Inner Asian steppe, from which no rivers flow out to the sea, has made extensive agriculture impossible. Lacking adequate water resources, the high uplands of Tibet and the grasslands of Mongolia have had a very sparse population. The 'barbarians' lived in areas roughly twice the size of China, but had perhaps no more than one-fortieth of the population.

As Owen Lattimore (1951, p. 63) has observed, when Chinese agriculture moved from the Yellow River bend towards the steppe it encountered diminishing returns. Hunting and herding became the two main productive pursuits. Both required a nomadic lifestyle. The harsh climatic conditions of the steppe forced not only the herders but the entire population to migrate periodically in search of grass and water. Migration was imperative for the 'livestock of a camping group, most of the animal wealth of a tribe, even most of the herds of an entire confederation, could be lost virtually overnight to disease or starvation' (Fletcher 1986, p. 13). The survival algorithm (Lipton 1968) of the Central Asian steppe—the strategy that minimized the risk of ending up below the subsistence level—was periodic mobility, usually, but not always, along fixed and proven routes. 'The nomad's migration was not an aimless wandering but occurred on a seasonal basis, usually to move his flocks and herds from summer pasture on the open plain to winter pasture in some more sheltered area such as a mountain valley, and back again' (Fairbank and Reischauer 1979, p. 155). The hunting pattern, in turn, was determined entirely by the movements of the game animals. All that the hunters could do was to follow them.

The ecology of the Central Asian steppe thus gave rise to a highly mobile population. This population was also dispersed since the meagre vegetation could not sustain large concentrations of people (Lattimore 1951, p. 54; Fletcher 1986, pp. 13–14). A nomadic population poses worse problems of large-scale organization than a sedentary one. We may think of the starting point as resembling the Hobbesian state of nature (Hobbes 1985, Chapter 13), where no laws exist. There are no accepted rules safeguarding human lives and no property rights. The individuals can prey on each other without fear of any retaliation other than what may occasionally be forthcoming from the disorganized prey. 'In such a society, life was simple, selfish and precarious' (Chambers 1999, p. 5), and presumably also, 'nasty, brutish, and short' (Hobbes 1985, p. 186).

It is then quite obvious that there were gains to be made by entering into some kind of binding contract which regulated life on the steppe. Before the rise of Chinggis Khan, the Mongol people 'longed for unity and for a state of order in which human life and property would be secure', claims Paul Ratchnevsky (1991, p. 14). The various tribes were either at war or in some 'state of suspended enmity' with each other (Ratchnevsky 1991, p. 12). Law and order comprise a collective benefit for all the parties concerned. Without a strong supratribal ruler the road lies open to casual plunder, i.e. the various tribes and tribal groups must count on being raided periodically, by marauders who will presumably take as much as they possibly can, since they cannot be sure of when the next suitable occasion for plunder will present itself.

Should these marauding raids turn out to be a recurrent phenomenon, those raided will eventually find that they have an incentive to install a 'stationary bandit' instead (Findlay and Wilson 1987; McGuire and Olson 1996; Olson 2000, pp. 6–12). This bandit can be invited to 'tax' the group regularly, a solution that is likely to be cheaper in the long run than unorganized raids. To see how this works, let us introduce our model.

Let us assume that the maximum production of a nomadic tribe amounts to Y, and that actual production is I. The maximum output is a function of the inputs of labor (L), land (T) and law and order: a public good created by a bureaucracy (G). The maximum production function is taken to be linearly homogeneous, with diminishing returns to all three factors and positive cross-derivatives. The bureaucracy has no other use than as an input in private production. It has to be paid for out of tax money. Hence, there is always a risk that incentives will be distorted by taxation so that actual production (*I*) will fall short of *Y*. *I* will hence depend negatively on the proportional tax rate *t*:

$$I \equiv r(t)Y(L,T,G), \quad r' < 0, r(0) = 1 \tag{6.1}$$

The labor force (*N*), which for the time being is assumed to be given, is divided between labor in production and the bureaucracy:

$$L + G = N \tag{6.2}$$

The stationary bandit maximizes his net tax revenue:

$$R = tr(t)Y(L,T,G) - (1-t)wG \tag{6.3}$$

where

$$w = r(t)Y^L \tag{6.4}$$

i.e. he obtains all the tax revenue that is left once he has paid his bureaucracy. The gross wage obtained by the bureaucrats is equal to the marginal product of labor used directly in production. Since taxation is strictly proportional, the bureaucrats pay the same share *t* of their income as everybody else, i.e. the net wage paid by the ruler amounts to $(1 - t)w$.

In order to maximize his net tax revenue, the stationary bandit has to find the optimal tax rate and the optimal size of the bureaucracy, i.e. he has to maximize (6.3) subject to the labor restriction (6.2). In the case of tax revenue, the restriction does not bind so taking the derivative of the net revenue with respect to the tax rate gives the first-order condition:

$$rY + rY^L G - (1-t^*)r'Y^L G = -t^* r'Y \tag{6.5}$$

The marginal gain of gross tax revenue from a higher tax rate plus the marginal saving on the wage bill when the net wage falls as the tax rate increases must be equal to the marginal loss of gross tax revenue as the amount of distortion increases when the tax rate increases. Thus, the stationary bandit has an incentive to stop taxation when the increase in tax revenue resulting from a higher tax rate equals the loss resulting from falling production. Since taxation is distorting, the share $1-r(t)$ of the maximum production Y is lost (an efficiency or 'deadweight' loss) and a share equal to t^* of this loss accrues to the bandit himself. Thus, when at the margin the bandit's share of the deadweight loss due to distorting taxation exactly offsets what he gets by increasing the tax rate, he will not increase the rate of taxation further. Maximizing his net tax revenue the bandit gets the share t^* of the total output value.

We also need the optimal amount of the public good, which may be calculated by taking the derivatives of the net tax revenue with respect to G and L, respectively. This yields:

$$t^* rY^L - (1-t^*)rY^{LL}G = t^* rY^G - (1-t^*)\mathrm{r}\left(Y^{LG}G + Y^L\right) \tag{6.6}$$

The bandit should increase the creation of peaceful and orderly conditions until the net marginal contribution of the use of labor directly for production to his tax revenue (including the marginal gain on his wage bill as diminishing returns to direct labor drive down the gross wage rate) equals the marginal contribution by the bureaucracy (net of the marginal cost of increasing the number of bureaucrats due to the higher marginal product of direct labor, and hence higher gross wage rate, as more bureaucrats are added, as well as directly to their higher number). With shorter notation:

$$\mathrm{NMRPL} = \mathrm{NMRPG} \tag{6.7}$$

where NMRPL denotes the net marginal tax revenue product of labor in direct production and NMRPG the net marginal tax revenue product of the bureaucracy (law and order).

To conclude, so far, the stationary bandit has an incentive to stop taxation before the 100 percent rate is reached and, in addition, an incentive to provide public goods to the community, since both measures increase his tax revenue. This Leviathan is both productive and predatory.

Law and Order in the Steppe

The problem, however, is whether any binding contracts that will lead to the installation of a stationary bandit will ever see the light of day. Law and order is a public good, i.e. all citizens in the community benefit from it and nobody can be excluded. By the same token, however, it may be difficult to find someone who is willing to organize the community and make certain that the necessary contracts are concluded. The installation of the stationary bandit is fraught with the free rider problem. This point becomes easier to appreciate if we apply Mancur Olson's (1962, 1982) logic of collective action to the problem of state foundation. If we continue to represent the degree of law and order in the steppe with G, the number of bureaucrats, the cost in terms of time, effort, money, and so forth that is required to create the bureaucracy may be assumed to be an increasing function of its size:

$$C = C(G), \quad C' > 0, C'' > 0 \tag{6.8}$$

Without effort, there is no order. Turning to the benefit side, the benefit for the group or community as a whole can also be thought of as a function of the degree of law and order:

$$B_c = L_c G \tag{6.9}$$

where lower-case c indicates community and L_c is an indicator of the 'size' of the community, e.g. in terms of the total herd of grazing animals it disposes of, animals which are completely crucial for survival in a harsh environment. The bureaucracy G is a collective benefit, i.e. its utility to one individual is not diminished by the fact that it extends to other individuals as well, and no member of the community can be excluded from it. Thus, not the entire benefit accruing to the community accrues to the individual. The value of his share F_i must obviously be lower than the total value to the group:

$$B_i = F_i L_c G \tag{6.10}$$

where $F_i < 1$ is assumed to be constant.

Will activities creating law and order be organized at all, and if they are, to what extent? To find the optimum value of G for the group we maximize the difference between community benefits and costs:

$$L_c + G(dL_c / dG) = dC / dG \tag{6.11}$$

The marginal benefits in terms of law and order and herd size must balance the marginal cost of the effort. Likewise, for the individual, we find that

$$F_i\left[L_c + G(dL_c / dG)\right] = dC / dG \tag{6.12}$$

These findings may be put into the simple diagram in Figure 6.1. The community benefit curve B_c rises, but we should not expect it to rise

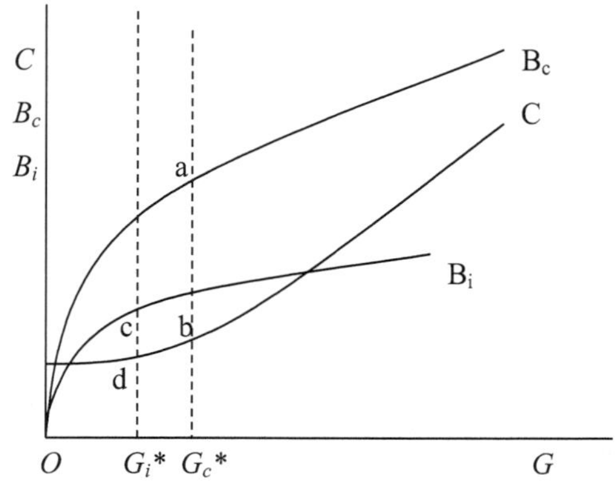

Figure 6.1 The problem of collective organization

indefinitely. Efforts to install order should be subject to diminishing returns. The cost curve *C*, on the other hand, rises monotonically, since the marginal cost should be increasing. The optimal level of *G* for the community is G_c^*, where the marginal benefit equals the marginal cost for the group (where the slopes of the two curves coincide, points a and b). The individual benefit curve, in turn, lies below the community curve, since $F_i < 1$. As shown in the diagram, this means that the optimal level of *G* is smaller for the individual than for the community. The slope of the individual benefit curve equals that of the cost curve at a lower level of *G* (points d and c).

This is Olson's famous finding that a sub-optimal quantity of the collective goods will be produced. In a group where individuals differ widely with respect to the intensity of their interest in creating the collective benefit, and all individuals by definition are less interested than the community as a whole in the benefit in question, it will be very difficult to ensure that somebody undertakes the organizing activities. Furthermore (assuming L_c to remain constant), the larger the number of individuals in the community the more severe will the sub-optimization be, for this will lower the average F_i, i.e. it will rotate the individual benefit curve downwards and hence lower the optimal *G* level for the individual.

The problem does not end here, however. We must also ask ourselves whether any efforts whatsoever will be made to secure peaceful conditions on the steppe. This is far from certain. The pastoral economy characteristic of the Central Asian steppes worked if anything in the opposite direction: clan warfare and recurrent disputes over grazing lands and animals (Jackson and Morgan 1990, p. 8). If the cost curve lies completely above the benefit curve it will never be worthwhile to attempt pacification. This could be the case if the number of individuals in the community is high, so that the individual benefits are low, but the level of costs also plays an important role here. The cost curve in Figure 6.1 is also drawn on the assumption of a fixed number of individuals. Should this number increase, however, the vertical intercept of the cost curve will shift upwards, and with that the entire curve.

Let us assume that the community contains *n* individuals who must be made to agree on efforts to create law and order. All these individuals in principle have to agree with $n - 1$ other individuals not to bother them, i.e. the number of bilateral treaties that must be concluded amounts to

$$K = \sum_{n-1}^{m=1} (n-m) \tag{6.13}$$

and if n increases to $n + 1$, the number of treaties will increase with n. The intercept of the cost curve shifts upwards (Possibly the curve at the same time rotates, also upwards, i.e. the marginal cost of increasing the probability of law and order (C) increases and enhances the sub-optimization problem even further). Thus, unless special incentives for organization can be created, what is in everybody's interest may never happen.

Thus, to conclude, if no coordination mechanisms are available, a large community size will militate against the implementation of peaceful conditions on both the benefit and the cost sides. It is difficult to think of a better illustration of the free rider problem in economics than the literally free Mongolian mounted archers and herders roaming across the Central Asian steppe—difficult to reach in a vast geographical area with a dispersed population. The Mongols had no administrative system or any formal devices for organizing services before Chinggis Khan (Ratchnevsky 1991, p. 44). The best prediction then would be that only relatively small organized and coherent communities would be organized.

The Designation of Chiefs

This prediction receives further support once we look into the Mongol institutions for designating tribal chiefs, i.e. for concluding treaties. Borrowing a Celtic term, Joseph Fletcher (1979–80, p. 239, 1986, p. 17) has called the governing principle 'tanistry': the tribe should be led by the best qualified member of the chiefly house. Two mutually contradictory principles, however, existed: patrilineal succession from father to son on the one hand, and lateral succession from older to younger brother until the current generation had been exhausted and the eldest chief's sons would carry on. In this situation, succession would become subject to bargaining and active choice by the leading members of the tribe and any choice that the leading members of the tribe would make could be justified. In the tribal context the leaders usually managed to settle matters without creating too much resentment, but once the issue was the formation of a larger group, faction frequently stood against faction (Fletcher 1986, pp. 17–18):

> ... in a large tribe, rival candidates for the chieftaincy, each closely backed by his own retinue of personal supporters ... [*nököd*], might occasionally split the tribe, either temporarily or permanently. In a succession struggle, the rival candidates and their ... [*nököd*] competed for the support of the tribe's leading men and formed factions that could either compromise or fight. Nor were the rivals limited to the backing of members of their own tribe. If a tribe were part of a confederation, a given candidate might win the backing of the confederate ruler or other powerful elements within the confederation. Tribes or leading tribal families also commonly had special relationships with tribal (or even non-tribal) elements outside the confederation and sometimes even beyond the edges of the steppe. These too could be called upon for support or for asylum in the event that a given candidate met defeat.

There was nothing in the ecological situation of the Mongols that required organization on a level above that of the tribe. 'Any would-be supratribal ruler had to bring to heel a highly mobile population, who could simply decamp and ignore his claims to authority' (Fletcher 1986, p. 14). The situation very much resembled that in what Samuel Huntington (1968, p. 194) has called praetorian societies, where 'no corps of professional political leaders are recognized or accepted as the legitimate intermediaries to moderate group conflict' (Huntington 1968, p. 196). In these societies, all social forces are politicized: armies, clergies, universities, bureaucracies, labor unions, corporations and so forth. Political life lacks autonomy. Mongol society is a case in point. Before Chinggis Khan came to power, it was characterized by conflict and lack of unity (Ratchnevsky 1991, p. 12), and in principle (Fletcher 1979–80, pp. 240–41):

> … nomadic succession struggles tended to involve everybody. There were no 'non-political' governmental functionaries to hold the realm together while military or other specialized elites determined the succession. Everybody was a warrior. Everybody was involved. Tribal chiefs had to decide which candidate to support, but everybody stood to win by his tribe's making the right choice or to lose by its making the wrong one. Most important was predicting the outcome of the succession struggle and attaching one's tribe to the winning candidate. A tribal chief who backed a losing candidate could forfeit his position or his life, but his whole tribe would suffer, so a chief could not fail to be influenced by his tribesmen's opinions …
>
> Because the khan might fall sick and die or be killed at any time, the political status quo, being suspended from his person, was inherently ready to collapse. So the nomads had always to be sniffing the political breezes and to be ready to choose, form coalitions, and, at every level of society, to act … Nomadic society was therefore more politicized at a deeper social level than the societies of the great agrarian empires northwest and south of the Eurasian steppe.

In praetorian societies, power is fragmented, easily gained and easily lost and allegiances are easily transferred from one group to another. The Central Asian steppe was no exception (Kahn 1984, p. xx):

> Everything was mobile, and as a result families could move not only from region to region as climate and season required, but also from camp to camp, as the fortunes of a clan would wax and wane. A charismatic or fortunate leader would attract a large camp in a short period of time. Conversely, when a leader died or times got bad due to disease, bad weather, or war, a camp could easily break up.

The traditional way of solving this problem among the steppe nomads was via the institution of subordinate tribes, i.e. tribes collectively under the protection of a stronger tribe, but simultaneously exploited by it. Not all of these were conquered. Some submitted voluntarily for the sake of obtaining protection by stronger units (Lattimore 1963a, p. 59):

> Maintenance of the integrity of the subordinate tribe helped to block defection. Its members collectively and its headman individually could be made responsible for mutual loyalty. The conditions of life, however, sometimes made this safeguard ineffective. In fluid, rapidly moving nomadic warfare there were times when the subordinates could tip the scale by abandoning a detested lord and going over to an admired new leader.

The story of the early life of Temüjin (Chinggis Khan) bears ample testimony to the problems of organization. At the time of his birth (possibly in 1162 or 1167) (Grousset 1966, p. 36; Ratchnevsky 1991, pp. 18–19) no central power existed in Mongolia. Temüjin's father, Yesugei, had (Brent 1976, p. 12):

> … gathered a following of his own, a heterogeneous collection of riders … [that] were all of one stock, that of the Borjigin clan. He was one leader in a world from which unity had flown, in which enemies outnumbered friends and in which strength alone could hope to find alliance. The weak fell away, their men left them, their followers found other leaders, the tents in their camps grew fewer, the grazing for their beasts sparser. In the end such groupings were absorbed in the train of another chief, or disappeared under a sudden flight of arrows, to the swift throbbing of hoofbeats and screams of anguish that fell abruptly into silence.

Yesugei, however, was not important enough politically to earn the title of khan. His position was that of a minor chieftain (Morgan 1986, p. 57). Thus, young Temüjin at a very early age got drawn into the rivalry between the Mongols and the other confederations in Mongolia. As a member of one of the most notable Mongol families, his whole life from about the age of ten to his election as khan some time in the 1190s is a chronicle of head-on confrontation with the enemy, desperate struggle for survival, forging and breaking of alliances, attacks and pursuits, flights and retirements (Prawdin 1940, Chapters 2–3; Saunders 1971, pp. 47–49; Brent 1976, Chapter 1; Ratchnevsky 1991, pp. 19–41). Organization could not be achieved without considerable bloodshed.

Peace and self-defense did not provide incentives strong enough to overcome the organization problem in a durable fashion temporary alliances being sufficient. The creation of wealth was a different matter. The nomad (Fairbank and Reischauer 1979, p. 155):

> … remained precariously dependent upon nature, for a severe winter could destroy his flocks. The seminomads, who lived on the fringes of sedentary agricultural societies, shared this constant economic instability. Their lack of accumulated resources gave both types of nomads a periodic incentive not only for increased trade but for military expansion. The nomads were the have-nots of antiquity, always poor in comparison with peoples in more thickly populated farming regions.

The productive base of the steppe was too meagre to allow substantial fortunes to be amassed, and preying on other nomads would yield precisely the same type of goods as those produced by the Mongols themselves. It was mainly when the number of animals dropped below the minimum required for survival that plundering other nomads was attempted. The risk of reprisals was always there and the spoils could not be stored, but the animals had to be put to pasture, which of course put additional demands on the tribe's manpower.

This did not mean that wealth was not sought. On the contrary, there were strong incentives to do so. William Baumol (1990) has made a distinction between productive, unproductive and destructive entrepreneurship. Entrepreneurs are motivated by profit opportunities, but it is not at all necessary that their efforts are concentrated on productive activities. What they will do depends on the incentives they are facing. When signals indicate that rent seeking and lobbying are more rewarding than productive efforts, entrepreneurship turns unproductive. It concentrates on the redistribution of a given cake. Should it, furthermore, be the case that war or piracy yields the highest returns, activities will turn increasingly destructive.

The first alternative for the herding nomad of course was trade. 'His pastoral economy had little need of agriculture so long as it could maintain a minimal trade with settled areas in order to secure grain and also textiles, tea and other "luxuries," and "metals to make weapons"' (Fairbank and Reischauer 1979, p. 154). Conversely, no artisan activities could be developed on a large scale in nomadic society, since that would have required a sedentary life-style (Lattimore 1951, p. 70). The nomads needed trade, but with that exception, the Mongols had no alternatives for the creation of non-nomadic wealth to preying on sedentary agriculturalists, and trade could never yield such huge benefits as plunder. This, however, was not something that isolated bands or tribes could carry out on their own. It required organization on a larger scale. At the same time, it provided an incentive for such organization because it boosted the benefits to the community. Organization offered not only internal peace but also the opportunity of enrichment at the expense of outside groups.

The main target was China (Fletcher 1986, pp. 15–16):

> It was in the case of China, where the steppe-sown dichotomy was sharper than anywhere else in the Eurasian steppe, and where the agrarian government usually monopolized or greatly restricted external trade, that the tribes' desire to extort was strongest.
>
> Three alternative policies were available to the steppe nomads for the continuing acquisition of China's agrarian wealth: invasion, threat of invasion, and outright dependence. A fourth policy, commonly practiced by the desert nomads of Central Asia and the Middle East, namely conquest and dominion, was impractical for the nomads of the steppe because of the geographical separation of the steppe from the world of the sown.

According to Fletcher (1986, p. 16) the main purpose of the supratribal polity was precisely that of extorting wealth from agrarian societies, a very plausible conclusion in the light of the present approach. Given the formidable free rider problem of the steppe it was only to be expected that it would take extraordinary benefits to overcome it (Fletcher 1979–80, p. 237):

> Pasture scheduling could be managed at the tribal level, and raiding could also be carried out under the leadership of the tribal chiefs without help from a supra-tribal ruler. Being nomadic, and consequently mobile, individual tribal groups could move away on their own. The grand khan could not subject his tribes to discipline without offering them a benefit great enough to win their voluntary compliance. Essentially his benefit boiled down to booty, the spoils of war—war which the tribes could not wage on a worthwhile scale without a supra-tribal leader. Social organization above the tribal level therefore came to be predicated on warfare.

Not even the prospects of profitable plunder always provide sufficient incentive for large-scale organization, however. The basic communities remained small and their degree of cohesion was low (Fletcher 1986, pp. 20, 21):

> Given the mobility of nomadic life, the inessential character of supratribal social organization, and the fissiparousness of steppe politics, supratribal polities—being based on segmentary opposition—were unstable and frequently dissolved altogether. So there could be long periods when the largest effective unit was the tribe … Supratribal society slipped back and forth between a supratribal anarchy (a 'nation' of purely imaginary existence) and supratribal polity, which in turn fluctuated between loose confederacy and more rarely) tight autocracy.
>
> Steppe empires came into existence only through the efforts of individual aspirants for the office of supratribal ruler, who, so to speak, conquered the tribes of the supratribal society and then, to keep them united, had no choice but to keep them busy with lucrative wars.

Given the contradictory principles that governed the choice of chiefs among the Mongols it was never self-evident who the supratribal ruler would be. Coalitions were formed and backers were sought in a process with an uncertain outcome—a process that was furthermore completely centered on the person seeking office. The Mongols were ruled by (Fletcher 1979–80, p. 236):

> … the grand khan—the supra-tribal nomad emperor whose authority entailed kingship over a multi-tribal nomadic people, combined with a highly personal command over that people's collective military forces. Under the grand khan's rule, all authority was concentrated in him—not in his office or in any government of officials who acted in his name, but in his person. When he died, the bonds of authority were dissolved, and his realm fell apart.

All allegiances were thus strictly personal. As Fletcher (1986, p. 22) has pointed out, in the Mongol case downplaying the historical role of individuals would be to commit a serious mistake. The system furthered the individual and it was the individual who had to forge his platform and, if he succeeded, make all the decisions (Fletcher 1979–80, p. 241):

> The grand khan … was not just the occupant of an ongoing institution like the thrones of the agrarian empires. He could not delegate his military function to officers of an army separable from society at large. The ruler's physical being provided the monarchy with its very existence. An active, personal, military leader was essential to the cohesion of his people. His person—indeed his personality—was the linchpin of society.

Political structures were volatile and fragile and often collapsed completely. The steppe empire was the creation of its emperor, not the other way around, and when he died, his successor would have to create his own structures and allegiances—again on a completely personal basis.

One of Those Singular Figures of History

The unification of the Mongols was undertaken by Temüjin (later Chinggis Khan). This was no peaceful affair but was bound to involve civil warfare. Temüjin understood that the road to power went precisely through unification of the steppe nomads. Only after having accomplished this, would it be possible to conquer the settled civilizations. Simultaneously, however, he had to hold out the prospects of plunder to achieve the unification. The two could not be separated. Mongol society was a herder and hunter society, but it was also a predatory society. Fletcher (1986, p. 15) argues that it was impossible to forge any durable alliances without allowing plunder. From the point of view of those who entered the alliance this was easy to understand. To be ruled by a stationary bandit was better than being subjected to periodic one-shot smash-and-grab raids. As we have demonstrated in the foregoing, a stationary bandit has an incentive to limit the extent of taxation, not killing the goose that lays the golden eggs. Even better, however, is when the tax is paid by someone else, i.e. if the stationary bandit can use his own community to raid others. Disregarding possible deaths during the raids, this alternative is Pareto sanctioned from the point of view of the community and its ruler.

Chinggis Khan 'must have been a leader of extraordinary talent, capable of iron discipline and the ability to inspire loyalty, and superior in these respects to other steppe leaders of his time' (Fletcher 1986, p. 34). However, his organization of the Mongol nation also rested on a number of principles. 'It was by maneuvering in and out between the conventions and oppositions of the tribal system that Temüjin was able to make himself the supreme chief, strong enough to destroy the tribal system and create something new' (Lattimore 1963a, p. 62). This may not have been as difficult as one might think, because, as David Morgan (1986, p. 37) has pointed out, in a sense the 'tribe' was a relatively open institution where membership was determined as much by political interests as by blood relations. Thus, there was an established precedent to fall back on for Temüjin, when he started to manipulate the structure. What is undeniable, however, is that the scale of manipulation by far outdistanced any of the attempts by his predecessors.

To obtain religious sanction Temüjin pointed to his divine mission, having been sent by the Mongol god Tenggeri. During the *khuriltai* (assembly) that elected him supreme khan of the Mongols in 1206, he had the shaman Teb-Tenggeri proclaim that the Eternal Heaven had appointed him (Grousset 1970, p. 217). Yet, when the shaman became a threat to his power, Temüjin had him killed (Ratchnevsky 1991, pp. 96–101). The Mongols in general assumed a very practical attitude towards religion, and Chinggis Khan used it to realize his own aims. He allowed complete freedom of worship, 'a religious tolerance that makes the Christian Europe of his day seem barbarous by comparison' (Brent 1976, p. 43). This practice was not dictated simply by conviction but also because it could be used to manipulate rivalries between Muslims, Buddhists and Christians in the conquered territories (Onon 1993, p. xiii) and extract from each creed what best served the interests of the khan (Foltz 1999, Chap. 6).

Chinggis Khan, however, also worked by breaking down a number of traditional power structures that militated against large-scale organization, substituting new ones that facilitated the creation of a feudal society. When he began his rise to power, nomad society in Mongolia was organized in a patrilineal kinship system of blood relations, supported by marriages and oaths. This system, however, suffered from the inherent weakness that it 'also supplied the occasions for blood feuds that sharpened the mettle of the nomad warriors' (Lattimore 1963a, p. 57). This weakness was manipulated by the stationary Chinese who—like the Romans—used barbarians to control other barbarians, employing steppe tribes to defend them against other steppe tribes, dividing, and thus conquering, the nomads.

Temüjin was therefore forced to destroy and replace a number of tribal institutions (Lattimore 1963a, p. 58). Instead of forging alliances through the *anda*, whereby two warriors swore allegiance to one another, 'as if they were descended from a common ancestor', but which by its very egalitarian nature presented problems when it came to determining leadership and pecking order, he chose to rely on another—more feudal—institution, the *nökör*, which at the time 'meant a warrior who freely declared himself "the man" of a chosen leader, even to the repudiation of his own tribe or origin'. The *nököd* that Temüjin had assembled when he had become Chinggis Khan became his generals and governors, and his trust in them was almost without limits (Lattimore 1963a, p. 59).

In the process of uniting the Mongols under his own undisputed command, Temüjin had had to destroy the traditional 'double tribe': the Borjigid line, to which he himself belonged, and the rival Taijut line that had attempted to monopolize power on the death of Temüjin's father (Lattimore 1963a, pp. 60, 62; de Hartog 1989, p. 5). He did so by defeating the Taijut completely.

Temüjin pursued his own version of the divide and conquer method. The purpose was always to create loyalties to himself personally, loyalties that were independent of traditional tribal structures (Lattimore 1963a, pp. 62–64):

> At first he was dealing with men whose outlook was completely tribal. To induce them to transfer to him personally their hereditary tribal loyalties, he took care always to be able to justify each move 'morally,' by the standards of the very system he was going to destroy and supplant.

> He would not turn against a former ally, therefore, just because the opportunity looked good. He would first let the situation develop, and if possible help it to develop, in such a way that the other man could be accused of disloyalty in act or intent, and if there remained any shadow on his own loyalty, he would make out a case that what he did was 'for the common good'. The politically valuable victories were those that enabled him to divide defeated enemies by winning some of them over to his own side.

Chinggis Khan was completely loyal to those who served him, his friendship was absolute, but so was his vengeance against those whom he considered to have broken their obligations to him. Significantly, not a single one of his generals ever betrayed him. To ensure that those conquered did not defect or attempt any uprisings, Chinggis Khan resorted to the time-honored system of treating them as subordinate tribes (Lattimore 1963a, pp. 59–60). This institution had a given place in the feudal hierarchy that he built (Lattimore 1963a, p. 64):

> To reduce even further the risk that the conquered tribes would turn against him he also broke them up, distributing their members as vassals to his trusted subordinates. Conversely, the latter received 'appanages'.
>
> These were regions, plainly in the feudal mold, in which the descendants of the first appanage-holder were to be hereditary rulers, bound to furnish military contingents to the successors of Chingis Khan. The new standard of discipline required a man to be obedient to the local ruler, who was usually not of his own tribal blood and pay his tribute within a geographically defined region from which he was not allowed to move.

Law and order was strictly upheld under Chinggis Khan. The extent of crimes diminished, and so did the rivalry between different groups in Mongol society. Raids upon neighbors became a thing of the past and banditry was wiped out. Grazing land was allocated once and for all among the different tribes. This removed one of the main sources of disputes. A police force saw to it that highways were made safe and returned stolen animals to their rightful owners, sanctioning theft of beasts with capital punishment (Brent 1976, pp. 45–46).

The basic organizational rules were explicitly codified in the Great Yasa (Vernadsky 1938; Ratchnevsky 1991, pp. 187–96), the imperial code, supposedly promulgated in 1206[2] and further developed right until Chinggis Khan's death in 1227; the code helped to overcome the centrifugal forces inherent in nomadic society and provided a permanent basis for his rule. It bound not only the people but also the ruler. Functions and duties were regulated. Religious freedom was explicitly spelt out.

Chinggis Khan was also careful to learn and borrow from other people whatever he thought could be applied to his own political construction, frequently taking foreigners as advisers and administrators (Lattimore 1963a, p. 64):

> He needed and employed a few Chinese, but he kept a careful balance. An adviser who had great influence on him was Yeh-lü Ch'u-ts'ai, a Khitan who knew the Chinese culture thoroughly but who, as a Khitan, was felt to be a tribal kinsman … [Chinggis] Khan also employed many Uighur Turks from the oases of Sinkiang and Önggüd Turks from the fringe of Inner Mongolia.

Information was gathered on a regular basis from travelers and prisoners-of-war, and a spy network provided information from foreign countries (Brent 1976, p. 46). In the information network, Muslims (Turks, Iranians, Arabs) played a special role. Most of them were merchants who carried their merchandise across a relatively large territory, from the Near East to China. These people accordingly saw and learned a lot during the course of their travels and Chinggis Khan understood how to make use of their knowledge (Lattimore 1963a, p. 66):

> It was through them that … [Chinggis] Khan learned about the power of the Turkish nomads far to the west of Mongolia. This intelligence probably was influential in shaping his conviction that he must establish complete domination over all the nomad peoples, Turks as well as Mongols, before getting involved too deeply in invasion of the great agricultural and urban

[2] This has been questioned by David Morgan, who argues that it may never have existed, and that what is usually referred to as the *Yasa* may have been nothing but 'an evolving body of custom, beginning long before … [Chinggis'] time and being added to long after' (Morgan 1986, p. 99).

> civilizations. He used these merchants first as intelligence agents, then as go-betweens and finally as more formal ambassadors. As his power increased he appointed some of them governors and administrators [...] In the Moslem world at this time wealthy merchants were more often well-traveled, well-educated men of the world than they were in China, where the merchants were despised by the landowners. Certainly the use of these men as administrators helped the Mongols to win over many of the Upper class in western Central Asia and northern Iran.

Temüjin was elected khan some time in the 1190s, after having forged a number of political alliances during the course of the previous fights and skirmishes. The fact that he had been elected khan did not mean, however, that he ruled all of Mongolia. This was not the case even during the first years after the turn of the century (Ratchnevsky 1991, p. 82). For that more was required. Above all the new ruler must demonstrate his military prowess, i.e. his ability to defeat his rivals in battle and secure booty for his followers. To this end Temüjin reorganized the Mongol army. After his defeat of the ruler of the Kereit confederation in 1203, his men were divided according to a metric or decimal system (Brent 1976, p. 31)[3]:

> He divided his men into ... units of a thousand [*mingghan*]. These were then metrically subdivided into ten companies [*jaghun*], each of ten platoons [*arban*]. Later, when his army grew, he would form ten ... [*mingghans*] into that division of ten thousand men called a ... [*tümen*]. These became the basic groupings that, in various combinations, made up his armies. He divided his horsemen into heavy and light cavalry, the former relying largely on their lances, the latter, who were perhaps twice as numerous, on their mobility and their skill with the bow.

The use of the decimal system was current among the steppe nomads (Morgan 1986, p. 49). Different clans were mixed, however, as another way of neutralizing the traditional power structures. Ninety-five elite commanders—*orloks*—were appointed to lead the thousands—always

---

[3] Brent calls the 1,000-man unit *guran*. We have, however, inserted the commonly used names within brackets.

on the basis of merit only—a creation that resembled a modern general staff (Onon 1993, p. xiv). Two of Chinggis Khan's greatest generals, Jebe and Subedei, had risen to their high position before reaching the age of twenty-five, and were given command over far older officers (Liddell Hart 1967, p. 8). Chinggis Khan also required that commanders and subordinates serve each other with absolute loyalty and obedience. The transfer from one unit of the army to another was prohibited on penalty of death (de Hartog 1989, p. 2).

By the time that Chinggis Khan became the ruler of all Mongols, in 1206, his army probably numbered 105,000 soldiers, and by the year of his death, the size had increased to 129,000 (Morgan 1986, p. 87), not an exceedingly large figure in, for example, Chinese eyes, but considerably larger than anything the Mongols had been able to muster hitherto under a unified chain of command (Fairbank and Reischauer 1979, p. 163), and definitely very large in comparison with the European armies of the day (Morgan 1986, p. 88).

Temüjin had also created his own imperial guard, originally eighty night guards and seventy day guards (*Secret History* 1982, p. 119), a military elite whose privates ranked above regular army officers. This guard built on a 'double' principle: on the one hand, it professed professional, personal allegiance to Temüjin instead of traditional tribal patterns, and on the other, it used a hostage system, with the sons of army generals serving in the guard (Lattimore 1963a, p. 64). The imperial guard would in the end, after the *khuriltai* of 1206, number 10,000 (Fairbank and Reischauer 1979, p. 163).

The new organization of the army was not simply a novel way of increasing discipline or a tactical military device. It also helped the new ruler to increase his political power. Although it did not replace the tribes, it made it possible for the khan to bypass the tribal system in military matters, i.e. it gave him direct and complete control over the machinery of violence. It also made it easier for him to incorporate outside forces (Fletcher 1986, p. 30). The new instrument was put to work, defeating the rival tribes and groupings that still stood between the khan and absolute supremacy over Mongolia. This took less than three years. His authority was confirmed in the year of the tiger, 1206, in a *khuriltai* at the source of the river Onon, one of the three largest rivers flowing through

Mongolia. Then he received the name by which he would henceforth be known: Chinggis Khan (Ratchnevsky 1991, pp. 89–96)—believed to mean either the 'hard' or 'fierce' khan or the 'oceanic' (presumably meaning 'universal') khan (Ratchnevsky 1991, pp. 89–90; Jackson 2000, p. 195).[4]

Based on the organization of the military, his tactical moves among the tribes and his successful military engagements, Chinggis Khan had advanced to the point where he was the autocratic ruler of the Mongols, but only for the time being. For power to endure more was required. '[I]f the tribes were to remain under the discipline of a steppe autocrat, he must raid and invade. The price of autocracy was that the autocrat could not stop. He must continue to enrich and engage his subject by continuing war' (Fletcher 1986, p. 32). Before setting out on his expedition against the Tatars in 1202, Chinggis Khan abolished the age-old custom that allowed plunder whenever the opportunity presented itself. 'From now on all plunder belonged to … [Temüjin]. He would be responsible for distributing it, and no man was to pause for plunder until the order had been given' (Chambers 1999, p. 39). The great conquests were about to begin.

To what extent Chinggis Khan was driven by material factors is difficult to know. A passage originally deriving from the Persian historian Rashid al-Din, who had entered Mongol service towards the end of the thirteenth century, quotes him as saying that the supreme joy was 'to cut my enemies to pieces, drive them before me, seize their possessions, witness the tears of those dear to them, and embrace their wives and daughters' (quoted by Grousset 1970, p. 249). However, as Lattimore (1963a, p. 62) remarks, this 'is the conventional "ideology", to use a modern word, of the barbarian warrior'. Instead, he argues, all 'his moves were politically calculated, and the calculation, from early in his career, was directed toward the building of a structure of power that would be capable of extension in both time and space'. He did not display any 'greed for booty or lust for women' in the process.

[4] Morgan (1986, p. 60) has argued that the naming took place earlier (cf. *Secret History*, 1982, pp. 54–55).

One possible interpretation of Lattimore's argument is that Chinggis Khan may have been seeking power for its own sake, but this is far from certain. A modern Mongol scholar, Bira Shagdar, ventures the hypothesis that Chinggis Khan never intended to build a world empire, only to ensure his supremacy over the steppe nomad peoples of Central Asia (Shagdar 2000, p. 129)[5]:

> It is unlikely that … [Chinggis] Khan had devised a clearly formulated war strategy, it is more probable that he just preferred to carry out his intentions immediately. If his wide-ranging conquests are judged by their real outcome, it becomes clear that he did not really intend to build a world empire in the true sense of the word. His main aim was to subdue all his rivals so that all the nomadic peoples existing throughout Central Asia became his subjects. The most suitable pasture lands which were occupied by the nomadic peoples were in the east–west directions from Mongolia, but not from north to south.

The Mongol Conquests

Leaving the motivation problem aside, the process of conquest itself must now be analyzed in order to shed some light on the question of why the Mongol Empire reached the size it did. This can be done by incorporating the central features of a model by Findlay (1996) into the framework developed above. Findlay (1996, p. 42) conceives of the total population 'as concentrated at a single point on a "featureless plain"' (a good approximation to some of the Mongolian landscape): its 'home base'. In the Mongol economy, we may now conceive of two types of activity. In addition to the production of animal goods with the aid of direct labor and the bureaucracy that provides law and order, the labor force can be used for warfare. Thus the total labor force N must now be divided among three instead of between two pursuits:

$$L + G + A = N \tag{6.14}$$

[5] Cf. also Ratchnevsky (1991, pp. 169–70).

where L workers are busy directly producing, G work in the bureaucracy and A are extending the frontiers of the Mongol Empire. Both the bureaucrats and the army have to be paid by state tax money.

The amount of land available is a function of the size of the army and the military technology (m) (including strategic and tactical skills):

$$T = T(A, m) \tag{6.15}$$

Conquest, however, implies not only that the physical territory is enlarged. In addition, the population that can be used for production and warfare increases, i.e.

$$N = N\left[T(A, m)\right] \tag{6.16}$$

Given the military technology, we can now derive the optimal size of the Mongol Empire from the point of view of the ruler simply by maximizing his net tax revenue:

$$R = t^* r(t) Y(L, T, G) - (1 - t^*) r(t) Y^L (G + A) \tag{6.17}$$

with respect to L, G and A, subject to the labor restriction

$$L + G + A = N\left[T(A)\right] \tag{6.18}$$

This yields the first-order condition

$$\text{NMRPL} = \text{NMRPG} = \text{NMRPA} \tag{6.19}$$

where

$$\text{NMRPL} = t^* rY^L - (1 - t^*) rY^{LL} (G + A) \tag{6.20}$$

$$\text{NMRPG} = t^* rY^G - (1-t^*)r\left[Y^{LG}(G+A)+Y^L\right] \tag{6.21}$$

in direct analogy with (6.6) and (6.7) above, and

$$\text{NMRPA} = \left[t^* rY^T + \text{NMRPL}(dN/dT)\right](dT/dA) - (1-t^*)r\left[Y^{LA}(G+A)+Y^L\right] \tag{6.22}$$

The net marginal tax revenue product of labor must be equal in productive pursuits, in the creation of law and order and in the army. The latter marginal product consists of three components. Conquests extend the area that can be used for production, and the addition is valued at a (shadow) price equal to the net marginal tax revenue product of land. They also increase the population along with the territory, and the addition to the labor force is valued at a (shadow) price equal to the net marginal tax revenue product of labor in direct production. Finally we have the wage bill increase resulting from an increased army size.

Given the harsh conditions prevailing on the steppe, the marginal productivity of labor in production should not have been very high, even when supported by a bureaucracy creating law and order, i.e. employing manpower in the army may well have been a superior strategy, since this would increase the supply of both land and manpower, and with that the base for wealth expropriation (Brent 1976, p. 27):

> The winters were hard, the cold shrivelling all life and comfort; only the Antarctic is colder than north-eastern Siberia, the plains and uplands of which lie to the north of the Mongol territories. Long seasons of snow and darkness stretched down from these near-polar fastnesses—and they were getting longer and harder. This was the thirteenth century, when the globe's ice-caps reached towards the temperate zones and once-fertile fields disappeared under glaciers or hardened into permafrost …
>
> In summer, however, the vast Eurasian landmass heats swiftly, now and then, and, where there are no rivers the soil dries and crumbles, all vegetation wilts. This was no land for agriculturalists to develop their skills. To the north, where rivers hiss through the valleys and ravines, forests of larch, birch, fir and aspen welcome the hunter, not the farmer. Between forest

> and desert lies the grass-ocean of the steppe, gleaming under snow in winter, flickering into a brightness of flowers in the spring, then slowly burning into the dun, khaki, yellow and pale-brown shades of the late summer. Across the plains and woodlands, through the whiplash winds of the deserts, the travelling peoples of these lands made their constant way …

In this setting the nomads were entirely at the mercy of nature. A severe winter could easily destroy the herds upon which they were dependent (Lattimore 1962a, p. 32):

> All through Central Asia winter pasture has always been the determining factor for the size of the herds. Travelers and officials—the old Chinese and Manchu officials and the old Tsarist Russian officials—usually traveled through the pastures in summer, and they often wondered why the flocks and herds were not even larger. The reason was that there were not nearly enough good winter pastures.

The inland climate of Mongolia is one of extremes since there is no moderating sea that serves to cushion the swings. Between October and April the regular temperature is below zero degrees Celsius in present-day Ulaanbaatar, dropping frequently to minus 30 in January and February. In the Gobi Desert, the temperature easily rises to 40 degrees in the summer, to plummet to minus 30 degrees or more during the winter. The steppe has an average temperature of no more than 10 degrees in July, and in the winter minimum values of minus 50 are not infrequent. The spring, in May and June, is windy, with frequent dust storms. The short rainy season extends from mid-July to September (Greenway et al. 1997, p. 21).

The model assumes that the contribution of the army to the territorial extension of the empire is a concave function of army size, i.e. the marginal productivity of the army should decline with army size. This is the conventional assumption of neoclassical economics, and it makes marginal additions of territory possible. There is, however, also the possibility that the function is first convex and only later turns concave. This situation is depicted in Figure 6.2.

The smooth curve indicates that the marginal cost of increasing the size of the army (in terms of output forgone) is increasing. The S-shaped

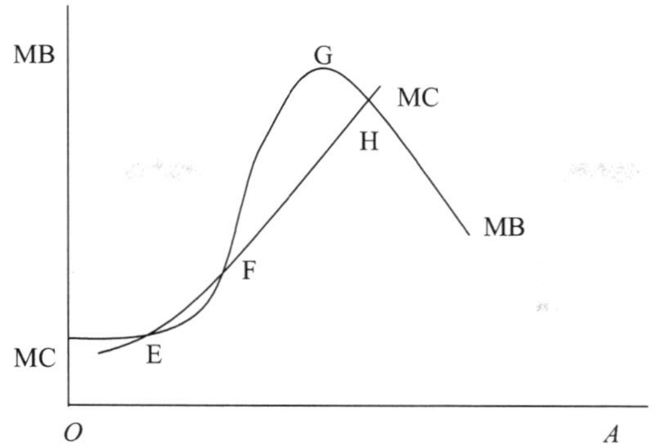

Figure 6.2 The Mongol explosion

curve, in turn, shows the marginal benefit in terms of increased production through the addition of land and labor. This curve first rises and falls only after point G has been reached. The two curves intersect three times. To the left of point E it pays to increase army size, since the benefits of this exceed the costs. To the right of this point it does not, since here the cost curve lies above the benefit curve—*unless* the addition to the army is non-marginal so that point F can be reached. Point E is therefore a stable equilibrium point. Point F is not, however, since moving further to the right entails an excess of benefits over costs at the margin, all the way until a new stable equilibrium is reached in point H.

What this means is that the size of the territory may be kept down by a failure to organize a large enough army. E is not a global maximum point, but it is not possible to move beyond it unless special circumstances are at hand. This seems to have been the situation in the Mongol case, as we have already indicated in our discussion of the problem of organization. We also know that in the Mongol case the 'special circumstances' translate into a single man: Chinggis Khan. Before the advent of Chinggis Khan, the Mongols had no clear sense of their identity as a people. Chinggis Khan became the 'great organizer and unifier of the Mongols' (Fairbank and Reischauer 1979, p. 163). By organizing the tribes on a scale that was large enough, he was able to trigger a cumulative process that did not end until his successors had created the largest continuous empire in the world, possibly even stopping short of point H, the point which gives the maximum return of benefits over costs. We will return to this possibility below.

The War Machine

So far we have said nothing about military technology or tactics, represented in our model by m in (6.15). It is, however, obvious that Chinggis Khan was an innovator in this area as well (Juvaini 1997, pp. 29–30):

> With regard to the organization of their army, from the time of Adam down to the present day, when the greater part of the climes are at the disposition and command of the seed of … [Chinggis] Khan, it can be read in no history and is recorded in no book that any of the kings that were lords of the nations ever attained an army like the army of the Tartars […] What army in the whole world can equal the Mongol army?

wrote Ata-Malik Juvaini, a Persian physician in the service of the Mongols, in 1260. Juvaini may be suspected of less than impartial judgment, but evidently he is not too far from the truth. Owen Lattimore (1963a, p. 66) maintains that as 'a military genius, able to take over new techniques and improve on them, Chinggis stands above Alexander the Great, Hannibal, Caesar, Attila and Napoleon'. It is evident that he was a great strategist who avoided many of the 'classical' mistakes of earlier steppe warriors, notably that of exposing his back and his core territory to competitors while he was away on campaigns (Lattimore 1963b). In his book *The Devil's Horsemen*, James Chambers (1979) offers a description of Mongol battle tactics as they had evolved by the time the Mongols were getting ready to embark on the invasion of Europe some time in the 1230s. His conclusions are extremely clear (Chambers 1979, p. 51):

> In the thirteenth century, the Mongol army was the best army in the world. Its organization and training, its tactical principles and its structure of command would not have been unfamiliar to a soldier of the twentieth century. By contrast, the feudal armies of Russia and Europe were raised and run on the same lines as they had been for several hundred years and their tactics would have seemed unimaginative to the soldiers of the Roman Empire.

Mongol tactical principles were completely modern. The secret of their success in battle was the combination of fire power, mobility and endurance. Although their armies did contain artillery (light and heavy catapults and *ballistae* capable of launching heavy arrows), the most lethal weapon of the Mongols was the bow, small enough to be used from the saddle, easily the best construction in the world at the time (Chambers 1979, pp. 56–57):

> The medieval English longbow had a pull of seventy-five pounds and a range of up to two hundred and fifty yards, but the smaller reflex composite bows used by the Mongols had a pull of between a hundred and a hundred and sixty pounds and a range of over three hundred and fifty yards.[6]

The Mongol bow, made from layers of sinew and horn on a wooden frame, would be superior also to the handgun for a long time to come (Morgan 1986, p. 91). The Mongol archer carried a wide array of arrows, for all kinds of situations: short and long range, armor-piercing, whistling for signaling and targeting, incendiary, and even arrows tipped with little grenades. His skills with the bow were hard to beat (Chambers 1979, p. 57):

> He could bend and string his bow in the saddle by placing one end between his foot and the stirrup and he could shoot in any direction at full gallop, carefully timing his release to come between the paces of his horse, so that his aim would not be deflected as the hooves pounded the ground.

Each man carried two bows, one for the long and one for the short range, and at least two quivers with a minimum of sixty arrows, plus, in the case of the light cavalry, a small sword and two or three javelins. The bowstring was pulled by using a stone ring on the thumb, which allowed a faster and more powerful release than using the fingers and the stirrup provided a firm base for the firing. The heavy cavalry relied on a twelve-foot lance with a hook below the blade, and a scimitar, a battle-axe or a mace.

[6] Saunders (1971, p. 64) gives a range of between 200 and 300 yards. Lattimore (1962a, p. 22) reports that 'an inscription on a stone, a little older than the *Secret History* [*of the Mongols*] and also of the 13th century, records an arrow shot of 335 "spans", which has been estimated as about 500 meters'.

The entire army (with the exception of the siege artillery) consisted of cavalry, which gave it a tremendous advantage in terms of mobility (Liddell Hart 1967, p. 32):

> The prime feature of the Mongol army was … its simplicity, due to the use of a single arm, in contrast to the inevitably complex organization of a combination of several arms which has always characterised European armies. In this way the Mongols solved the ever-difficult problem of co-operation between arms which have radically different qualities and limitations.

Endurance was ensured by the system of remounts (Lattimore 1962a, p. 41):

> The small Mongolian horse, grazing entirely on the open range with no bans and no supplementary grain feed, is amazingly tough. It can carry a man more than a hundred miles in a day—but not the next day; it must have a few days to graze and rest. … [Chinggis] Khan handled this problem by gearing his army to the average horse. His cavalry were accompanied by herds of remounts, which were treated like the standardized, interchangeable parts of a machine. There was no great difference between today's horse and tomorrow's horse: both were called on only for average performance.

Chinggis Khan never resorted to bigger horses that required hay, grain and shelter in the winter because this would have slowed him down and limited the mobility of his army. 'He drew the essence of his power from archers riding tough little range-bred horses, with plenty of remounts' (Lattimore 1963a, p. 68), frequently as many as five (Morgan 1986, p. 86).

The drill was meticulous in the Mongol army. Training lasted several months and skills were thereafter kept up by continual practice. Campaigns were carefully planned (de Hartog 1989, pp. 49–50):

> Before undertaking a campaign … [Chinggis] Khan tried to gather as much information as possible about the political and military situation of the enemy country, chiefly by means of spies. We must assume that obser-

> vation and sense of direction were unusually highly developed in the Mongols, otherwise it is not possible to account for their movements over enormous distances without maps. Special officers had the task of leading the movements of the army and of fixing the position of camps. Cavalry forces of the size used by the Mongols could not be moved at short notice. It seems certain that careful planning preceded each of the major military campaigns.

The Mongol officers constituted a permanent, professional corps, which it had not been before Chinggis Khan (Lamb 1928, p. 80). The Mongol armies also possessed a well-developed signaling system, using black and white flags, and communication behind the lines relied on a system, called *Yam*, of staging posts, inherited from the Khitan, but extended across the entire empire by the Mongols, connecting with a system of riders resembling the American Pony Express—except that it was faster. Urgent messages could be sent at a speed of over 200 miles per day (Morgan 1986, pp. 103–07).

We mentioned above that the size of the Mongol army was comparatively large for its day. However, as Basil Liddell Hart (1967, p. 7) has stressed, it was *quality*, not quantity that made it irresistible: 'Alone of all the armies of their time had they grasped the essentials of strategy, while their tactical *mechanism* was so perfect that the higher conceptions of tactics were unnecessary.' Friar Giovanni di Plano Carpini (1996, p. 91) remarks that 'indeed the Tartars [Mongols] fight more by trickery than by strength'. Mongol battle tactics centered on the use of the light cavalry, which was used for engaging the enemy forces and showering them with arrows before the heavy cavalry moved in to strike the decisive blow (Chambers 1979, p. 63):

> … whenever possible the favourite tactic[7] was to use the *mangudai*. This was a light cavalry corps of 'suicide troops', [8] but their name was more of an honourable tribute to their courage than an exact description of their duty. Ahead of the army the *mangudai* would charge the enemy alone, break ranks and then flee in the hope that the enemy would give chase. The

[7] See Liddell Hart (1967, pp. 9–10, 28, 31–32) for a more detailed discussion of Mongol tactics.

[8] The 'God-belonging' squadron (Lamb 1928, p. 131).

> larger the *mangudai*, the more convincing the flight and sometimes, when good open ground afforded an opportunity to regroup, it was made up of half the army. If the enemy did give chase, his ranks would already be spread out by the time they reached the waiting archers and when the quivers were empty and the heavy cavalry made their charge … the result was devastating. The charge of the heavy cavalry was always the end of a Mongol battle plan. They advanced at the trot and in silence. Only at the last possible moment was the order to gallop sounded on the great *naccara*, a huge kettle drum carried by a camel, and by the time they had let out one hideous scream their lances were among the enemy.

The Mongol armies regularly could move 700 kilometers in two weeks, if necessary cover 300 kilometers in three days (de Hartog 1989, p. 49), and they moved at least twice as fast in battle as their enemies, a feature the significance of which would not be fully appreciated until several centuries later (Chambers 1979, pp. 66–67):

> … it was not until after the advent of mechanized war that the real Mongol genius came to be appreciated and the tactical principles of the Mongol army, based on the combination of fire power and mobility, were seen to be as basic and as constant as the principles of geometry. It was in the armies of … [Chinggis] Khan that 'fire and movement' first effectively became 'fire in movement'. In 1927 Basil Liddell Hart (1967, p. 33) wrote that the tank and the aeroplane were the natural heirs and successors to the Mongol horsemen. At the same time surveys of the Mongol organization and tactics were being published in Germany, and British tank officers were recommended to study the Mongol campaigns. In the world war that would follow, two of the leading exponents of mechanized combat, Rommel and Patton, were both students and admirers of Subedei.
>
> Against the Mongols the European soldiers of the thirteenth century were as courageously helpless as the Polish lancers were against the German *panzers*. The Mongol army was a 'modern' army and the differences between it and the armies in the twentieth century can all be accounted for by progress in science and in technology, but not in the art of war.

The Mongols also picked up military technology from the Chinese (Hucker 1975, p. 280), notably siege warfare, an art that they had not needed to get acquainted with before the invasions of China (Lattimore 1963a, pp. 66–67):

> … when … [Chinggis] Khan set out to campaign in … [Turkestan] and [Khwarazm] … he was able to co-ordinate the use of his cavalry with elaborate siege weapons—powerful catapults, battering-rams and sappers who tunneled under walls and blew them up with gunpowder—against strongly fortified cities.
>
> He certainly recruited his first engineers in northern and perhaps north-western China, where the originally 'barbarian' military power of the Jurchid, or Chin, state and the … [Tangut], or Hsia, state had acquired Chinese techniques. When he took these men westward with him, he brought about a cross-stimulation of Chinese and Iranian engineering and technology. This in turn almost certainly had something to do with the development of the cannon from the use of gunpowder in sapping operations. Unfortunately we do not know the step-by-step details. At any rate the use of cannon both as siege weapons and as field weapons followed very quickly the Mongol conquest.

The Mongols were 'modern' warriors in yet another sense. War was total. On the one hand, this entailed the organization of all of society along military lines (Fletcher 1979–80, pp. 237–38):

> The nomadic social cycle began and ended with tribes in disunity, diffusing their military energies in internecine skirmishes. But once integrated into the grand khan's regime, the tribesmen became cogs in a military machine, soldiers in an all-pervasive army—an army of everybody, for there were no civilians. Tribal autonomy withered, and society itself became an army, a unitary host that directed its military energies outward to the defeat and despoliation of external victims.

All male Mongols below the age of sixty were eligible for military service. 'There was no such thing as a civilian … The Mongol rulers therefore had available to them a cavalry force which could be speedily mobilised, was highly trained, and consisted in theory—and even to some extent in practice—of the entire adult male population' (Morgan 1986, p. 85).

But war also involved the adversary, and here as well, it was total. Battle tactics were supplemented by terror measures directed against the civilian populations. '[Chinggis'] principle seems to have been much the same as President Truman's over Hiroshima and Nagasaki', remarks David Morgan (1986, p. 93). During his Chinese campaigns he began to gather innocent civilians who were forced to march ahead of the troops when these were advancing on fortified cities. On such occasions only the inhabitants of cities that surrendered immediately were spared—and far from always. Those that resisted were ruthlessly killed. This was the case, for example, during the campaigns of 1220 to 1222 against Jalal ad-Din, the son of the ruler of the Khwarazmian Empire, that extended from the Tigris to the Syr-Darya. The army that Jalal ad-Din was leading consisted to a large part of urban Persian civilians. In this campaign Chinggis Khan set out to exterminate the enemy population (Adshead 1993, p. 58):

> It was prosecuted now by calculated horror, an attempt to blot out urban life, extermination rather than simple depopulation. This was the treatment meted out to Balkh, Bamiyan, Herat, Merv and Nishapur … If not immediately massacred, as at Merv and Nishapur, the civilian population of one city was driven on to become a human battering ram against the next … it was warfare of unprecedented ferocity for the middle ages.

At Merv, 'the jewel of the sands, the pleasure city of the Shahs' (Lamb 1928, p. 163), the city of the *Thousand and One Nights* (de Hartog 1989, p. 111), the entire population—men, women and children—was put to death. The job was distributed among the soldiers who each had to execute 300 or 400 people (Adshead 1993, p. 61). Fletcher (1986, pp. 43, 42) has argued that the cruelty demonstrated by the Mongols during their military campaigns resulted from their attitudes against sedentary populations:

> Their havoc proceeded logically from the legacy of the steppe wisdom about how nomads could best obtain what they wanted from the agrarian world … when the steppe pastoralist did invade the settled world, he looted and destroyed as much as his heart desired so as to remind the agrarians of the wisdom of rendering peacefully the wealth that he wanted

> … With the steppe extortion pattern in mind, the Mongols did violence with a will and used terror … to induce their victims to surrender peaceably.

This, from the military point of view, lowered the cost of conquest, but there may have been a second reason too behind the massacres: the numerical inferiority of the Mongols. They constantly had to fear an attack from the rear (de Hartog 1989, p. 49):

> Before … [Chinggis] Khan attacked the Kereit, he destroyed the Taijut and the Tartars, so that they could not stab him in the back. Later in China and in the Khwarazm sultanate, being so far from his own base, he could not risk the survival of forces among the defeated peoples sufficient to rise against him.

Thus, the atrocities regularly committed by the Mongols were not the result of any 'inherent' cruelty. They were calculated and what cruelty there was, was purely instrumental.

Summing up, several factors coincided in shaping the giant Mongol Empire. Production conditions on the steppe made the accumulation of substantial wealth impossible, while deployment of military force displayed a high marginal productivity in terms of both land and people. Conquest became the preferred strategy. Before the rise of Chinggis Khan, organizational problems had precluded the Mongols from putting together an army that was large enough to allow for an extension of Mongol territory. It was only his political and military skills that made it possible to overcome the free rider problem of the steppe. Finally, the Mongols were innovators in the field of warfare. The army consisted almost exclusively of cavalry which combined fire power and mobility in a way that was completely superior to anything that could be mustered by their adversaries. The Mongol conception of warfare was eminently 'modern', also in the sense that it was 'total', i.e. it did not spare the civilian population. On the contrary, the Mongols made a point of instilling as much terror as possible into the civilians, as a deliberate part of their warfare. The lesson was clear. 'What … [Chinggis] Khan wanted to teach his enemies was that resistance was hopeless, that the attempt to mount it would be punished with the utmost cruelty. Only swift and willing surrender would elicit magnanimity—survival hung on instant submission' (Brent 1976, p. 63).

Before leaving the military theme, let us, however, sound a note of caution. As Ratchnevsky has reminded us, the solution of 'the problem of how it was possible for a small, poor, backward nation of hunters and animal-breeders to conquer the most powerful and civilised states of Asia, states which disposed of inexhaustible reserves of people' (Ratchnevsky 1991, p. 170) should not be sought exclusively in the military context, but in two other factors as well. The first of these was the organization of the army, which ensured its elite character, already dealt with above. The second factor was Chinggis Khan's diplomatic and political skill (Ratchnevsky 1991, p. 172): '... his exposure and subsequent exploitation of the internal weaknesses of the enemy determined in advance the outcome of the wars. Genghis showed great skill in exploiting to his advantage the national, social and religious rifts in the enemy camps.' Thus, it was a unique combination of military, organizational, diplomatic and political skill, united in the person of Chinggis Khan that ensured the Mongol conquests.

Once subjugation had been obtained, the time had come to deliver. Chinggis Khan was a man who kept his promises of booty and wealth for his people. For the conquered, it meant paying taxes (Morgan 1986, pp. 100–03; Schurmann 1956; Smith 1970; Ratchnevsky 1991, pp. 175–86). The stationary bandit preyed on the defeated, exactly as we would have expected him to do (Morgan 1986, p. 102; cf. Kwanten 1979, p. 209):

> The purpose of the taxes imposed on the conquered populations was quite simply the maximum conceivable degree of exploitation. There was little pretence that in Mongol eyes their subjects had a justification for their existence except as producers of revenue. As a rule exploitation was limited only by the consideration that it was sensible to leave the peasants sufficient to permit their survival till the next year, so that a further year's taxes could be levied. In the early days of excessive zeal the Mongols did in fact not stop even at that point. Mongol taxation was more a pragmatic series of exactions as seemed appropriate and profitable than any kind of fixed system.

To judge from the experience of the Islamic lands that fell under Mongol rule, the burden of taxation was probably appreciably higher than it had been even under such unenlightened rulers as the … [Khwarazm shahs].

Apogee and Fall of the Mongol Empire

When the time came for the Mongols to turn eastwards, China was no longer united under a single emperor. At the beginning of the tenth century, Khitan nomads had invaded and conquered the north, including the city of Zhongdu. They were, in turn, ousted by Jurchen horsemen from Manchuria early in the eleventh century who established the Ching Empire with Zhongdu as their capital. Somewhat earlier, at the end of the tenth century, Tanguts had invaded northwestern China and founded the Hsi Hsia kingdom. This left only China south of the Wei and Huai rivers for the Sung. (The dynasty was known as the Southern Sung from 1127) (Fairbank and Reischauer 1979, pp. 157–60).

Between 1205 and 1209, Chinggis Khan conquered the Hsi Hsia kingdom. Thereafter he turned against the Chin Empire further east (1211–15), sacking and burning Beijing and leaving more than ninety towns 'in rubble' (Hucker 1975, p. 283). For this it was not enough with just Mongol forces, so whenever possible Chinese troops that chose to defect were welcomed into the ranks of the khan's armies (Morgan 1986, pp. 66–67). Between 1219 and 1225, he conducted a campaign in the west, against the Khwarazm Empire, located in present-day Turkestan, which was subjugated, gaining control in the process over such cities as Samarkand and Bokhara. By the time of his death, the area under Mongol control extended from the Caspian Sea across Central Asia and northern China to the Yellow Sea and the Sea of Japan, and from the forests of Siberia to the Hindu Kush (Brent 1976, Chapter 3). Demetrius Boulger (1900, p. 55) provides the following summary judgment:

Even the Chinese said that he led his armies like a god. The manner in which he moved large bodies of men over vast distances without any apparent effort, the judgment he showed in the conduct of several wars in countries far apart from each other, his strategy in unknown regions, always on

> the alert yet never allowing hesitation or overcaution to interfere with his enterprises, the sieges he brought to a successful termination, his brilliant victories, a succession of 'suns of Austerlitz,' all combined, make up the picture of a career to which Europe can offer nothing that will surpass, if indeed she has anything to bear comparison with it …

At Chinggis Khan's death his empire was divided among the four sons of his first and principal wife (or their descendants). Eventually this division was to crystallize into (1) the khanate of the Great Khan, mainly China, ruled by Ögödei, Chinggis' third son, 1229–1241, Möngke, his grandson, 1251–1259, and Khubilai, also his grandson, 1260–1294; (2) the khanate of Chaghatai, Chinggis' second son, 1227–1242, in Turkestan, the western part of which would be incorporated into the empire of Timur Lenk (Tamerlane) after 1370; (3) the Ilkhanate of Persia, built up by Chinggis' grandson Hülegü, and dissolved after 1335; and, finally, (4) the Kipchak Khanate (the Golden Horde), built up by Chinggis' grandson Batu, 1227–1255?, which dominated Russia and was taken over by Timur Lenk, and was finally broken up in the fifteenth century (Fairbank and Reischauer 1979, p. 165).

The conquest of the Chin Empire of northern China was completed in 1241, by Ögödei, who had a capital built at Kharakhorum, and Korea came under Mongol rule in 1258. Ögödei also turned against the Sung Empire of southern China, the conquest of which would, however, not be finished until Khubilai had become khan. When Möngke died in 1259, Khubilai had to interrupt his campaign against the Southern Sung and for four years deal with his brother Arigh Böke who had challenged him for the position as khan. In 1264 Khubilai moved the capital from Kharakhorum to Beijing and in 1271 he adopted the dynastic name of Yüan, although it would be a further eight years before full control was achieved over southern China. Mongol control over China was to last until 1368.

Before that, however, the Mongols had once more turned westwards. Already during the Khwarazmian wars, in 1221, an army under Subedei had taken the route south of the Caspian Sea through Georgia and annihilated a Russian army on the Kalka river, north of the Sea of Azov, in 1223. Less than fifteen years later, the Mongols returned to the west. Moscow was burned, Kiev was taken, and in 1241 Poland, Bohemia, Hungary and the Danube valley were invaded (Chambers 1979). The Mongols finally penetrated as far as the Adriatic Sea. The European adventure came to an abrupt end, however, since in March 1242, Batu received the notice that Ögödei had died in December, and had to return back home to elect a new khan. As it seems, the Mongol invasion of Europe thus stopped short of what was possible to achieve—short of point H in Figure 6.2. The superior Mongol war machine had not given the Europeans much of a chance, and the likelihood that a further westward penetration could have been successfully resisted by stationary armies unaccustomed to the mobile warfare of the Mongols is not very high (Morgan 1986, p. 1; Jackson 1999, p. 706). In this sense, the Mongol Empire was too small. It did not reach its optimum extension. Europe was saved by the bell, as it were, a bell that tolled for the supreme Mongol leader, and subsequent plans of reassuming the conquests in the west were effectively checked on the one hand by the death of Möngke in 1259 and the civil wars that followed (Jackson 1978; Morgan 1986, pp. 156–57). An ecological factor also intervened, however. In May 1260, Hülegü withdrew most of his forces from Syria, for lack of grazing facilities, and the smaller contingent left behind suffered a defeat at the hands of the Mamelukes at Ayn Jalut, in Galilee, on 3 September 1260. The Mamelukes had a thorough understanding of Mongol warfare and cleverly used their weaknesses to their own advantage. Subsequent efforts in Syria foundered on the same problem: pastoral limitations and inadequate water supply (Smith 1984).

In the south and the east, climatic and geographical factors were responsible for putting a 'natural' end to the extension of the empire. India proved too hot for conquest. It escaped with occasional raids of plunder (Saunders 1971, pp. 61, 248, note). The Mongols attempted to invade Japan on two occasions, in 1274 and in 1281 (Rossabi 1988, pp. 99–103, 207–12). On the first occasion, they were forced to withdraw by a violent storm, and on the second occasion a typhoon, interpreted by the Japanese as a *kamikaze* (heavenly wind), wiped out the invasion forces. The Mongols were also checked in Vietnam. The efforts made by Khubilai Khan to conquer Annam in the north and Champa in the south between 1281 and 1287 forced the Mongol troops into a guerilla war in hot and disease-infested forests and mountains: the kind of warfare for which they were least suited (Rossabi 1988, pp. 215–18).

In another sense, the empire was far too large. Yelui Ch'u ts'ai, Chinggis Khan's trusted adviser, is reputed to have said: 'The Mongol Empire has been won from the saddle—it cannot be ruled from the saddle' (Brent 1976, p. 60). He was right, and as it seems, the Mongol rulers understood it (Shagdar 2000, p. 129). Chinggis Khan did not make any effort to occupy the land he had conquered on any permanent basis. For that, his forces were insufficient. But permanent occupation was hardly necessary as long as a sufficient part of the output value produced could be skimmed off by means of taxation. To this end he left behind a number of military governors who could simultaneously act as tax collectors and as representatives of the khan's power, providing a credible threat to those who refused to comply. Failure in thus respect would lead to sporadic punitive raids. In this he may simply, as Bira Shagdar (2000, p. 129) suggests, have been following 'the traditional form of submission typical of all steppe empires'. According to this tradition (Shagdar 2000, p. 129):

> ... it was more important to master the peoples as appanage (*ulus*) rather than to govern the territories of the conquered countries. With regard to sedentary societies ... [Chinggis] preferred to ensure the economic exploitation of those countries by establishing a system of tax collection and of receiving tributes. Keeping this in mind, he distributed the conquered peoples among his four sons. The empire of ... [Chinggis] Khan was more a nomadic confederation than a world empire which ruled, in the real sense, the countries of sedentary civilizations.

Chinggis Khan did not divide his troops between garrisons in the conquered territories across his wide empire. Instead he stationed smaller contingents, known as *tamma*, on the borderlands between the steppe and the settled populations (Morgan 1986, pp. 93–94). He preferred to keep his main forces as a mobile reserve in the steppes of Mongolia, southern Russia and Turkestan. From there they could easily be deployed wherever the political and military circumstances called for it. But of course, in the end, a more settled governance and life-style was inevitable (Lattimore 1963a, p. 68). In the end the *tamma* became the nuclei of the permanent military forces in the subsidiary khanates (Morgan 1986,

p. 95). The very size of the empire required a large-scale sedentary administration—but this also sealed its fate. Significantly, the part of the empire that lasted longest—until 1502—was the Golden Horde (Kwanten 1979, p. 252; cf. Morgan 1986, p. 174):

> The Golden Horde settled in the nomadic zone and incorporated the nomadic population into its state structure; and from the nomadic zone it controlled the conquered sedentary areas, primarily Russia. The Horde preferred to follow the steppe tradition of acting as distant overlords rather than directly. It contented itself with collecting taxes and tribute, which was gathered for it by the subjected population, appointing princes, and acting as arbiters in disputes. This policy meant that the Horde rarely became embroiled in local politics and it never identified its interests with those of its Russian subjects.

The other parts of the empire that Chinggis Khan built had already fallen when the end came to the Golden Horde. The Chaghatai Khanate was a loosely structured coalition between a handful of peoples. It had no formal capital and it was located in nomadic territory. However, it failed to control the nomadic population and was subject to constant intervention by the other three parts of the Mongol Empire. As a consequence, the Chagatai Khanate never stabilized. It had no fewer than nineteen rulers between 1227, the year of its creation, and 1338, when it was split into two parts. The Mongols ended up being absorbed by the Turks (Kwanten 1979, pp. 250–52). In the Ilkhanate, the Mongols converted to Islam and began to intermarry with the Persians and, even more, with the Turkish speakers. In fact, they were never driven out but had simply been absorbed by the time of the death of the last Ilkhan in 1335 (Morgan 1986, p. 170). China, in turn, had an almost proverbial ability to absorb foreign elements into its own immense population, and the descendants of Chinggis Khan constituted no exception in this respect (Lattimore 1963a, p. 68):

> It was when his successors—notably … [Khubilai] Khan in China—turned their backs on the steppe and began to concern themselves with civilization that the old nemesis of civilization began to erode the empire of the great barbarian genius, as it had the empires of many similar but lesser barbarian conquerors.

The logic of collective action defeated the Mongols. Keeping together the largest continuous empire the world has ever seen called for extraordinary administrative measures, and a large mobile administration is a contradiction in terms (Dardess 1972–73; Morgan 1982). As Lattimore (1962b, p. 257), has observed, 'it is the poor nomad who is the pure nomad'. The mobile nomads reached their maximum control over wealth when they conquered China, but by the same token, their mobility was undermined. They became dependent on 'the swarming bureaucracy needed to collect revenue and to allot patronage' (Lattimore 1951, p. 77). Once the Mongols had reached the point where their enormous conquests had made their rulers and nobles dependent on trade and taxation of agriculturalists and urban dwellers, i.e. on 'non-nomad sources of privileged income', the capacity of their leaders for initiating collective action vanished. Their lust for further conquests was dulled. Once they started to settle, the conquerors were conquered by the conquered and the impossible empire crumbled.

References

Adshead, Samuel Adrian M. (1993). *Central Asia in world history*. New York: St Martin's Press.

Baumol, William J. (1990). Entrepreneurship: Productive, unproductive, and destructive. *Journal of Political Economy, 98*, 893–921.

Bold, Bat-Ochir. (2001). *Mongolian nomadic society: A reconstruction of the 'medieval' history of Mongolia*. Richmond, Surrey: Curzon Press.

Boulger, Demetrius Charles. (1900). *A short history of China: An account for the general reader of an ancient empire and people* (New ed.). London: Gibbings & Co.

Brent, Peter. (1976). *The Mongol empire: Genghis Khan: His triumph and his legacy*. London: Weidenfeld and Nicolson.

Chambers, James. (1979). *The devil's horsemen: The Mongol invasion of Europe*. London: Weidenfeld and Nicolson.

Chambers, James. (1999). *Genghis Khan*. Phoenix Mill, Stroud, Gloucestershire: Sutton Publishing.

Dardess, John W. (1972–73). From Mongol empire to Yüan dynasty: Changing forms of imperial rule in Mongolia and Central Asia. *Monumenta Serica, 30*, 117–165.

de Hartog, Leo. (1989). *Genghis Khan: Conqueror of the world.* London/New York: I.B. Tauris.

Fairbank, John K, & Reischauer, Edwin O. (1979). *China: Tradition and transformation.* Sydney: Allen and Unwin.

Findlay, Ronald. (1996). Towards a model of territorial expansion and the limits of empire. In Michelle R. Garfinkel & Stergios Skaperdas (Eds.), *The political economy of conflict and cooperation.* Cambridge: Cambridge University Press.

Findlay, Ronald., & Lundahl, Mats. (2000). *Globalization, economics and history.* Mimeo. Stockholm: Stockholm School of Economics.

Findlay, Ronald, & Wilson, John D. (1987). The political economy of Leviathan. In Assaf Razin & Efraim Sadka (Eds.), *Economic policy in theory and practice.* London: Macmillan.

Fletcher, Joseph. (1979–80). Turco-Mongolian Monarchic tradition in the Ottoman empire. In Ilhor Ševčenko & Frank E. Sysyn (Eds.), *Eucharisterion: Essays presented to Omeljan Pritsak. Harvard Ukrainian Studies, 3–4,* 236–251.

Fletcher, Joseph. (1986). The Mongols: Ecological and social perspectives. *Harvard Journal of Asiatic Studies, 46,* 11–50.

Foltz, Richard C. (1999). *Religions of the Silk Road: Overland trade and cultural exchange from antiquity to the fifteenth century.* Basingstoke/London: Macmillan.

Greenway, Paul, Storey, Robert, & Lafitte, Gabriel. (1997). *Mongolia* (2nd ed.). London: Lonely Planet Publications.

Grousset, René. (1966). *Conqueror of the world: The life of Chingis-Khan.* New York: Viking.

Grousset, René. (1970). *The empire of the steppes: A history of Central Asia.* New Brunswick: Rutgers University Press.

Hobbes, Thomas. (1985). Ed. C. B. Macpherson. *Leviathan.* London: Penguin Books.

Hucker, Charles O. (1975). *China's imperial past: An introduction to Chinese history and culture.* Stanford: Stanford University Press.

Huntington, Samuel P. (1968). *Political order in changing societies.* New Haven/London: Yale University Press.

Jackson, Peter. (1978). The dissolution of the Mongol empire. *Central Asiatic Journal, 22,* 186–244.

Jackson, Peter. (1999). The Mongols and Europe. In David Abulafia (Ed.), *The New Cambridge medieval history, Volume V c. 1198–c.1300.* Cambridge: Cambridge University Press.

Jackson, Peter. (2000). The state of research: The Mongol empire, 1986–1999. *Journal of Medieval History, 26*, 189–210.

Jackson, Peter, & Morgan, David. (1990). 'Introduction' to *The mission of Friar William of Rubruck: His journey to the court of the Great Khan Möngke 1253–1255*. London: The Hakluyt Society.

Juvaini, Ata-Malik. (1997). *Genghis Khan: The history of the world conqueror.* Trans. and Ed. J. A. Boyle. Manchester: Manchester University Press.

Kahn, Paul. (1984). Introduction to *The secret history of the Mongols: The origins of Chingis Khan*. San Francisco: North Point Press.

Kwanten, Luc. (1979). *Imperial nomads: A history of Central Asia 500–1500*. Philadelphia: University of Pennsylvania Press.

Lamb, Harold. (1928). *Genghis Khan: Emperor of all men*. London: Thornton Butterworth.

Lattimore, Owen. (1951). *Inner Asian frontiers of China* (2nd ed.). New York: American Geographical Society of New York.

Lattimore, Owen. (1962a). *Nomads and commissars: Mongolia revisited.* New York: Oxford University Press.

Lattimore, Owen. (1962b). *Studies in frontier history: Collected papers 1928–1958*. London: Oxford University Press.

Lattimore, Owen. (1963a). Chingis Khan and the Monol conquests. *Scientific American, 209*(2), 54–69.

Lattimore, Owen. (1963b). The geography of Chingis Khan. *Geographical Journal, 129*, 1–7.

Liddell Hart, Basil H. (1967). *Great captains unveiled.* New York: Books for Libraries Press.

Lipton, Michael. (1968). The theory of the optimising peasant. *Journal of Development Studies, 4*, 327–351.

McGuire, Martin C, & Olson, Mancur, Jr. (1996). The economics of autocracy and majority rule: The invisible hand and the use of force. *Journal of Economic Literature, 34*, 72–96.

Morgan, David O. (1982). Who ran the Mongol empire? *Journal of the Royal Asiatic Society, 14*, 124–136.

Morgan, David. (1986). *The Mongols*. Cambridge, MA/Oxford: Blackwell.

Olson, Mancur. (1962). *The logic of collective action: Public goods and the theory of groups*. Cambridge, MA: Harvard University Press.

Olson, Mancur. (1982). *The rise and decline of nations: Economic growth, stagflation, and social rigidities*. New Haven: Yale University Press.

Olson, Mancur. (2000). *Power and prosperity: Outgrowing communist and capitalist dictatorships*. New York: Basic Books.

Onon, Urunge. (1993). 'Introduction' to *Chinggis Khan: The golden history of the Mongols*. London: The Folio Society.

Plano Carpini, Giovanni di. (1996). *The story of the Mongols whom we call the Tartars*. Trans. with an introduction by Erik Hildinger. Boston: Branden Publishing Company.

Prawdin, Michael. (1940). *The Mongol empire: Its rise and legacy*. London: Allen and Unwin.

Ratchnevsky, Paul. (1991). *Genghis Khan: His life and legacy*. Oxford/Cambridge, MA: Blackwell.

Rossabi, Morris. (1988). *Khubilai Khan: His life and times*. Berkeley: University of California Press.

Saunders, J. J. (1971). *The history of the Mongol conquests*. New York: Barnes and Noble.

Schurmann, H. F. (1956). Mongolian tributary practices of the thirteenth century. *Harvard Journal of Asiatic Studies, 19*, 304–389.

Shagdar, Bira. (2000). The Mongol empire in the thirteenth and fourteenth centuries: East–west relations. In Vadime Eliseeff (Ed.), *The Silk Roads: Highways of culture and commerce*. New York/Oxford: Berghahn Books.

Smith, John Masson, Jr. (1970). Mongol and nomadic taxation. *Harvard Journal of Asiatic Studies, 30*, 46–85.

Smith, John Masson, Jr. (1984). ᶜAyn Jālūt: Mamluk success or Mongol failure? *Harvard Journal of Asiatic Studies, 44*, 307–345.

The Secret History of the Mongols (1982), Trans. and Ed. Francis Woodman Cleaves. Cambridge, MA/London: Harvard University Press.

Vernadsky, George. (1938). The scope and contents of Chingis' Khan's Yasa. *Harvard Journal of Asiatic Studies, 3*, 337–360.

7

Towards a Factor Proportions Approach to Economic History: Population, Precious Metals and Prices from the Black Death to the Price Revolution

In the history of economic doctrine the name of Bertil Ohlin is inseparable from that of Eli Heckscher. The origin of the famous Heckscher-Ohlin theorem is the seminal article by Heckscher (1919) in the special 1919 David Davidson *Festschrift* issue of *Ekonomisk Tidskrift*, later developed by Ohlin in his doctoral dissertation *Handelns teori* (1924) and his monumental *Interregional and International Trade* (1933). Together, these three works established the factor proportions approach to international trade.

We are indebted to Rolf Henriksson for letting us dip into his immense knowledge of Eli Heckscher's ideas and to André Burgstaller, Stan Engerman, Duncan Foley, Paul Krugman, David Laidler, Lars Magnusson and Alan Taylor for constructive comments. Carin Blomkvist and Lilian Öberg typed the manuscript. The essay has been financed by a SAREC research grant which is gratefully acknowledged.

Revised from 'Towards a Factor Proportions Approach to Economic History: Population, Precious Metals, and Prices from the Black Death to the Price Revolution' by Ronald Findlay and Mats Lundahl, in Ronald Findlay, Lars Jonung and Mats Lundahl (eds), *Bertil Ohlin: A Centennial Celebration 1899–1999*, 2002, The MIT Press, pp. 495–528. With kind permission of The MIT Press.

R. Findlay, M. Lundahl, *The Economics of the Frontier*,
DOI 10.1057/978-1-137-60237-4_7

Heckscher, History and Theory

When it came to economic history, Ohlin and Heckscher differed completely. There are historical examples in both *Handelns teori* and *Interregional and International Trade,* but Ohlin was mainly concerned with theory and contemporary economic problems in his work. Heckscher was different. In spite of his original contributions to trade theory and his numerous pieces on the empirical economic problems of his day he was first and foremost an economic historian—'the sole creator of economic history in Sweden as an institutionalized field' (Henriksson 1991, p. 142)—with such works as *Mercantilism* (1931a) and a four-volume (uncompleted) economic history of Sweden from the early sixteenth century to 1815 (1935–1949) to his credit. It was the writing of the latter that he conceived of as his 'real task' (Henriksson 1991, p. 148).

Even so, it would be unfair not to conclude that Heckscher had one foot in history and another in economic theory. What is more, he was a pioneer when it came to linking the two. Heckscher dealt with the principles of connection between economic theory and economic history on at least nine occasions: 1904, 1920, 1922, 1929, 1930 (1933, 1936), 1937 (1944), 1942, 1947 and 1951. The main credo was laid down in the very first of these (1904), when the inductive method was rejected and the use of deductive economic theory was (implicitly) held out as the method to be applied in the gathering and interpretation of historical facts. This part of Heckscher's research program was to stay with him for the rest of his life. Both the early 1904 article and his subsequent publications on method foreshadow the development of the modern analytical approach by the New Economic History movement that began in the late 1950s. This is true not least of his 1920 article and 1922 book chapter (which overlap to some extent). The latter headed a volume intended to demonstrate the connection between the study of economics and of history, the importance of knowledge of general economic relations and of insight into the historical development for understanding economic relations (Heckscher 1922, p. 9).

For Heckscher, the most important characteristic of economics was that it deals with problems of scarcity, and since scarcity is a feature that has accompanied mankind since the beginning of history, 'the economic problem must be *fundamentally* the same in all ages' (Heckscher 1929, p. 527). It then follows that economic theory should have some contribution to make not only when we deal with recent times but also to the study of more remote historical periods (Heckscher 1922, p. 29, 1929, p. 526). Already in 1904, quoting the dedication to Gustav Schmoller of a book of essays by William J. Ashley (1900, p. v), he wrote that for the economic historian it was 'an imperative duty' to 'be an economist without ceasing to be an historian' (Heckscher 1904, p. 198). To be sure, Heckscher never argued that all of history could be explained by economic factors (Heckscher 1944) and he was also quite adamant that the use of economic theory had its limitations. Theory was useful in the analysis of events during a given period or epoch with more or less given characteristics, but when it came to questions such as how one epoch evolved into another he argued that economic theory had little to offer (Heckscher 1920, p. 20). The causes had to be sought elsewhere, 'since the changes in the conditions of economic life have sprung mainly from other areas of society and hence must be considered as inaccessible for economic theory' (Heckscher 1951, p. 54; cf. Henriksson 1991, p. 165).

Heckscher was also cautious to point out that in the historical perspective the institutional framework matters (Heckscher 1922, pp. 24–25):

> … it is very dangerous to regard economic history only from the point of view of material for comparison with the theories that aim to explain present-day economic relations, since to a large extent, the kind of theory required to explain the circumstances of earlier times must be one that *differs* from the one valid for today. The economic theory that has been developed above all during the last century and a half takes as its point of departure a host of assumptions both with respect to the organization of society—rule of law, regular transportation possibilities, market organization, etc.—and with respect to the state of mind—the ability to calculate, procure information, take care of one's interests, etc. which in no way have always been present in previous times or, for that matter, today.

Still, he argued that 'for most periods of known Economic History the changes necessary in the usual theory are not fundamental, however' (Heckscher 1929, p. 528). Furthermore (Heckscher 1922, p. 29),

> ... nothing could bear more witness of less insight into the ways of science than believing that a theory would be completely useless because something, no matter what, in the surrounding reality has changed ... Sometimes, it seems the reasoning criticized here more or less explicitly takes as its point of departure the notion that it is impossible to apply modern economic theory to times when it did not exist. The absurd character of such an idea, however, immediately stands out.

What was fundamental for Heckscher was that when it came to the '*choice* of facts and the *explanation* of them' (Heckscher 1929, p. 529; cf. 1951, pp. 45–54) the use of economic theory was indispensable, since 'only when the pure theory of economic relations has been made clear has a heuristic principle been found, and insight obtained about the questions to be posed in the area of economic history' (Heckscher 1936, pp. 10). At the end of the day, the 'plea for theory' had to be made, 'since central parts of the course of economic history cannot be studied successfully without access to or, rather, familiarity with the body of ideas of the economic science' (Heckscher 1951, p. 45).

Strangely enough, however, in his empirical historical work Heckscher does not appear to have made much use of the basic theoretical construct he himself originated: the factor proportions approach. His 1919 paper receives a passing mention in a footnote in *Mercantilism* (Heckscher 1931a, Vol. 2, p. 110), and in the discussion of labor as a factor of production in the mercantilist system he notes that the policy of keeping labor costs down would lead to increased exports of labor-intensive goods (Heckscher 1931a, Vol. 2, p. 135). No use of the approach is made either in his work on the history of industrialism (Heckscher 1931b), or in his two major surveys of Swedish economic history (Heckscher 1935–49, 1942).

What was it then that inspired Heckscher to produce his 1919 theoretical breakthrough? If we are to believe the introduction of Flam and Flanders (1991) to their translations of Heckscher's 1919 article and

Ohlin's 1924 dissertation, it was his desire to defend free trade from the charge by Knut Wicksell, that it might induce extensive emigration, as happened in Sweden at the end of the nineteenth century under the stimulus of cheap grain imports from across the Atlantic. If it was possible, even if not empirically likely, that trade alone could equalize factor prices, then it would not be necessary for any adjustment through factor movements to occur at all.

In this chapter we will attempt to demonstrate the power of the factor proportions approach not just as a pure theoretical construct but as a tool of economic history. To some extent the point has already been made by the literature that emanated from the 'sector-specific' version of the factor proportions model of Ronald Jones (1971). The connection of this theoretical contribution with the explicitly historical concerns of Habakkuk (1967), Temin (1966, 1971) and Fogel (1967) is examined in Findlay (1998).

A major historical episode, to which the factor proportions approach must be applicable if indeed it is applicable at all, is the Black Death, the catastrophic plague epidemic that reduced the population of Europe in the middle of the fourteenth century by a third, possibly even more. We will propose in what follows a suitably extended factor proportions model that can account for the most important facts of this momentous event.

An Extended Factor Proportions Model

The model that we are going to sketch is an extended version of the Jones model with sector-specific inputs. One sector produces 'goods', considered as a generalized commodity à la Solow, with a specific factor 'capital' that is a stock of the same 'stuff' as the output that it produces together with labor. The only other sector of the economy produces a commodity, 'silver', with inputs of a specific stock of natural resources (which we can think of as an essentially limitless deposit of silver), obtainable with the input of labor but with diminishing returns at the margin. Thus far the model has exactly the same structure as the original Jones (1971) article.

The relevant equations are

$$G = G(L_g, K) \tag{7.1}$$

$$S = S(L_s, \bar{N}) \tag{7.2}$$

$$L_g + L_s = L \tag{7.3}$$

where G and S are the flow outputs of goods and silver, L_g and L_s the labor allocated to each sector, K the specific input to G and N the specific input to S. The labor allocations to each sector add up to the total labor force L available. Both production functions have constant returns to scale and positive but diminishing marginal products for all the inputs. Of the three inputs only natural resources, the specific input N to the silver sector, is fixed as in the original Jones model.

The supply of labor is determined endogenously by a Malthusian mechanism of the type proposed by the economic demographer Ronald Lee (1973). Denoting the real wage in terms of goods as w we have fertility f and mortality m as increasing and decreasing functions respectively of the real wage, as stated in Equations (7.4) and (7.5) and Figure 7.1.

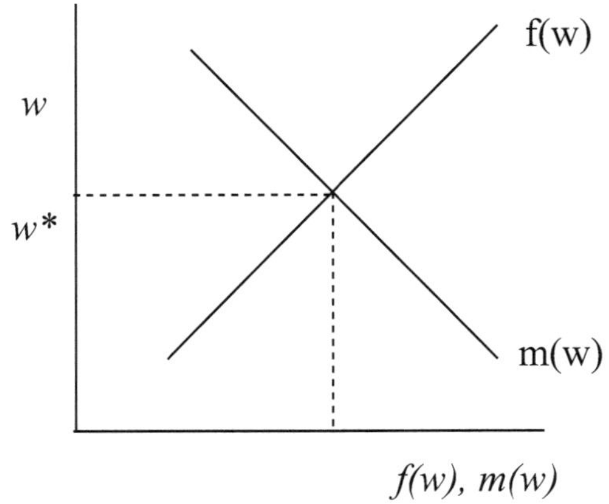

Figure 7.1 The Malthusian mechanism

$$f = f(w),\ f'(w) > 0 \tag{7.4}$$

$$m = m(w),\ m'(w) < 0 \tag{7.5}$$

Population is stationary at a real wage w^* in terms of goods where

$$f(w^*) = m(w^*) \tag{7.6}$$

The *size* of the population and labor force at this equilibrium real wage w^* will depend upon the endowment of capital and natural resources that the economy has. Assuming, for the moment, that the capital stock K and the relative price of goods and silver is given, the equilibrium level of employment in goods and silver, and thus the size of the total labor force, will be given by

$$\partial S / \partial L_s (\bar{N} / L_s) = pw^* = p(\partial G / \partial L_g)(K / L_g) \tag{7.7}$$

where $p = P_g / P_s$ is the price of a unit of goods in terms of silver. The equilibrium allocations L_s and L_g are determined from the values specified for p and K by equating the marginal value products of labor in the two sectors.

Suppose now that the Black Death occurs, carrying off a third of the labor force. With fixed stocks of natural resources and capital, and holding the relative prices constant, the effect will be a substantial rise in the real wage, a fall in the outputs of both sectors and reduced total incomes of the specific factors. This follows directly from Jones (1971).

With higher real wages and per capita incomes the Malthusian mechanism will lead to a fall in natural mortality after the 'one-shot' decline in population resulting from the plague and a rise in fertility. Population and the labor force will therefore slowly recover, driving down real wages and per capita income until the economy gradually returns to its initial position with the equilibrium values of all variables unchanged. This initial drop in population, and the sharp rise in real wages, followed by a population recovery and a long slow fall in real wages is broadly consistent with European experience over the century and a half after the Black Death.

We now turn to the full extension of the model endogenizing the relative price of goods in terms of silver and the capital stock. If we take silver as the unit of account, so that one 'ducat' has a silver content of one ounce in a system of commodity money such as we are going to specify, the national income in the model can be expressed as

$$Y = pG + S \tag{7.8}$$

Since p is defined as P_g/P_s, where P_g and P_s are the 'nominal' prices of goods and silver in terms of 'ducats', it can be thought of not only as the relative price of goods in terms of silver but also as the price level of goods in terms of silver. With silver and goods transformable into one another at increasing marginal cost, a price level of, say, five 'ducats' per unit of goods will also be equal to a relative price and a marginal rate of transformation of five ounces of silver for one unit of goods.

The flow supplies of goods and silver are functions of p so that we have

$$G = G(p),\ G'(p) > 0 \tag{7.9}$$

$$S = S(p),\ S'(p) < 0 \tag{7.10}$$

As the reader can readily verify we also have

$$Y'(p) > 0,\ Y'(1/p) < 0 \tag{7.11}$$

The national income in terms of silver is an increasing function of the relative price of goods in terms of silver, and a decreasing function of its reciprocal, the relative price of silver in terms of goods.

For any given values of the capital stock K, the natural resource N and the total labor force L the production possibility frontier showing the trade-off between the flow supplies of goods and silver will be determined as depicted in Figure 7.2. Changing the slope of the tangent to the production

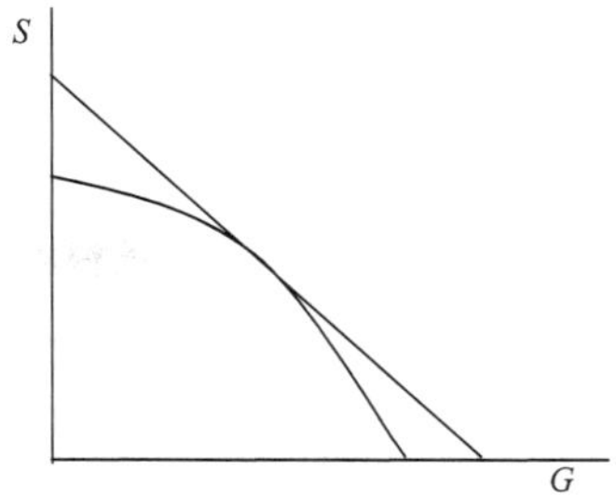

Figure 7.2 The production possibility frontier

possibility frontier, i.e. the relative price of the two goods, depicts the effects on national income Y of these changes in terms of the vertical intercept, the axis for silver in Figure 7.2.

It also follows from the familiar properties of the specific factor model that the real wage w and the real return to capital r in the goods sector are determined as

$$w = w(p),\ w'(p) < 0 \tag{7.12}$$

$$r = r(p),\ r'(p) > 0 \tag{7.13}$$

Raising the relative price of goods in terms of silver increases employment in the goods sector with K unchanged and so reduces the marginal physical product of labor in this sector and hence also the 'real wage' w in terms of goods, while raising the marginal physical product of capital and hence the real return on capital r in terms of goods. In the silver sector, the marginal product of labor increases and the marginal product of the natural resource decreases. The wage in terms of goods and the wage in terms of silver thus move in opposite directions in response to a relative price change, the familiar 'neoclassical ambiguity' in the specific factor model, as opposed to the Stolper-Samuelson or Heckscher-Ohlin-Samuelson model where the real wage changes in the same direction in both sectors when there is a shift in relative product prices.

We now turn to the monetary side of the model. Paper or 'fiat' money has become universal only since the twentieth century. In the medieval and early modern periods of Western history, and for the

Middle East and Asia until quite recently, movements of precious metals and their impact on price levels have been of utmost significance. While commodity money is mostly ignored in current modern works on monetary theory it was the focus of detailed attention by the early writers on the subject, from Hume and Ricardo to Wicksell, Marshall and Irving Fisher. It is an indispensable feature of the story we wish to tell here.[1]

The money supply in our model consists, at any moment, of a stock of coins with a given silver content. For convenience we maintain the convention that each coin has a 'face value' of one ducat and a silver content of one ounce, i.e. we do not consider debasement and other related issues although these could be analyzed as comparative static exercises within the context of the model. The commodity silver can be costlessly minted into coins. The coins in circulation 'depreciate' at a given rate due to 'wear and tear', so that we assume that a fraction μ of the coins simply disappears per unit of time.

The demand for money in our model for transactions purposes is given by the familiar Fisher quantity theory in its Marshallian or 'Cambridge' version:

$$M_d = \alpha Y(1/p, K, L) \tag{7.14}$$

where α, the Cambridge 'k', is the reciprocal of the income-velocity of circulation of money. Thus M_d is a 'stock' demand, related to the flow of national income, Y, through the desired ratio, α.

Denoting the supply of money at any moment by M, and requiring demand and supply to be balanced at every moment, we obtain the 'momentary' equilibrium condition

$$M = \alpha Y(1/p, K, L) \tag{7.15}$$

[1] We are grateful to David Laidler for drawing our attention to the exposition by Marshall in a volume of his early writings edited by Whitaker (1975), in which the money commodity is the shells of an extinct fish that can be dredged for at increasing marginal cost in terms of goods.

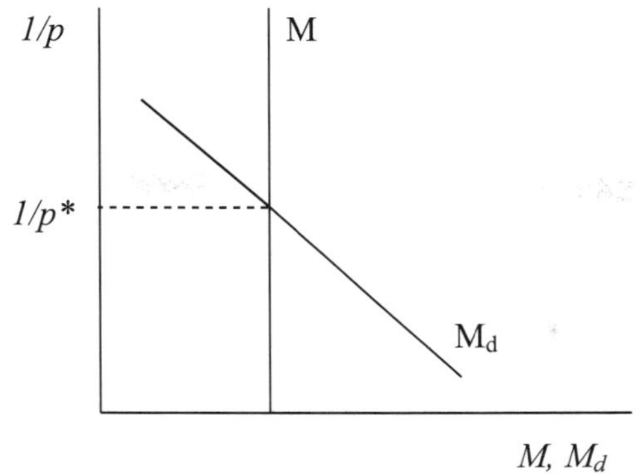

Figure 7.3 Money market equilibrium

Taking K and L, together with M, as state variables initially given by history, (7.15) is one equation in one unknown, the reciprocal of the price level of goods in terms of silver $1/p$. Figure 7.3 depicts the momentary equilibrium specified in (7.15) by showing how the value of $1/p$ that prevails will equate M to M_d when M, K and L are given. The demand for money curve is negatively sloped because Y varies inversely with $1/p$, as specified in (7.11), and M is vertical because it is determined by past history at any given point in time.

With the relative price of goods and silver determined at any instant by equating the stock demand for money to the given stock of money in circulation, the relative price $1/p$ thus emerges as an 'asset price' instead of in its more familiar role as equating the flow demands to flow supplies in standard Walrasian general equilibrium fashion of which the specific factor model is a particular case. What we therefore have is an instance of what André Burgstaller (1994) calls the 'asset market approach to the theory of value'.

The relative price p determined by (7.15) determines the flow supplies of goods and silver as specified in (7.9) and (7.10). These flow supplies have now to be reconciled with flow demands, which will be specified below.

The consumer budget constraint is given by the national income Y, which is determined at any moment by the historically determined values of M, K and L, which also determine p through (7.15). With this income consumers can either purchase domestically produced goods or what we will term 'Eastern luxuries', such as spices, silk, porcelain and other exotic wares that were not produced within Europe at all. We assume, with historical justification, that all these goods had to be paid for in silver. We also assume that the prices of all these goods are fixed in terms of silver, irrespective of the level of Western demand. Thus, by suitable choice of units, we can set the price of a 'bundle' of these Eastern luxuries at one unit of silver so that p, the relative price of a unit of goods in terms of silver, is also the relative price of a unit of goods in terms of Eastern luxuries, and its reciprocal is the relative price of Eastern luxuries in terms of goods.

Additional flow demands for silver and goods will be the 'depreciation' of the stock of silver coins, equal to μM, and the depreciation of the capital stock, δK, where δ is also a constant.

The budget constraint can be written as

$$Y = pG + S = p\left(G_c + \delta K\right) + \left(E + \mu M\right) \tag{7.16}$$

where

$$G_c = G_c\left(p, Y\right),\ \partial G_c / \partial p < 0,\ \partial G_c / \partial Y > 0 \tag{7.17}$$

and

$$E = E\left(1/p, Y\right),\ \partial E / \partial\left(1/p\right) < 0,\ \partial E / \partial Y > 0 \tag{7.18}$$

are the consumption demands for goods and Eastern luxuries, respectively. The total flow demands for goods and silver are obtained by adding the depreciation of the capital stock δK and of the money supply μM to the respective consumption demands. There is no guarantee that flow demand will equal flow supply since

$$G_d \equiv G_c + \delta K \gtrless G \tag{7.19}$$

$$S_d \equiv E + \mu M \gtreqless S \tag{7.20}$$

Walras' law and Equation (7.16), however, imply that

$$(S_d - S) \equiv p(G - G_d) \tag{7.21}$$

i.e. the excess flow demand for silver equals the value of the excess flow supply of goods. Our model implies that the excess flow demand (supply) reduces (increases) the corresponding stock of either money or goods, so that we have

$$\dot{K} = (G - G_d) \tag{7.22}$$

$$\dot{M} = (S - S_d) \tag{7.23}$$

From (7.21) it follows that $\dot{K}$ and $\dot{M}$ are either both equal to zero, when flow demands equal flow supplies, or of opposite sign. For the economy to be in a long-run steady state equilibrium it is of course necessary for all the state variables, L, K and M, to be constant, that is:

$$\dot{L} = \dot{K} = \dot{M} = 0 \tag{7.24}$$

We now turn to the determination of this long-run steady state equilibrium of the model. For population and the labor force to be stationary we know from (7.6) that the real wage in the goods sector must be equal to w^*. From (7.7) this determines uniquely the ratio of capital K to employment L_g in the goods sector that makes the marginal physical product of labor in this sector equal to w^*. Also from (7.7) it follows that for each value of p there is a unique employment level L_s in the silver sector that equates the marginal physical product of labor in that sector to pw^*, the wage in terms of silver. The lower is p, the higher is $1/p$, the greater is L_s and hence the output of silver $S(1/p)$, that equates the marginal physical product of labor in the silver sector to the lower wage in terms of that commodity. Thus, given the size of the stock of natural resource deposits N, Equation (7.7) determines the long-run steady state flow supply curve of silver

$$S = S\left(1/p, w^*, \bar{N}\right) \qquad (7.25)$$

which is depicted in Figure 7.4 as the positively sloped curve SS'. The long-run flow demand for silver, S_d in Figure 7.4, at each price $1/p$ will depend only on K, since L_s is determined by $1/p$. L_g is proportional to K, as determined by w^*, and so the labor force L and national income Y are determined for each value of K. By (7.14) the stock demand for money M_d is determined by $1/p$ and Y, and so the money supply M and its 'depreciation' μM are determined as well. The expenditure on Eastern luxuries E is also determined by $1/p$ and Y from (7.18). The total flow demand for silver, equal to E plus μM, is thus an increasing function of Y, and hence K, for each value of $1/p$. By (7.20) we can therefore find the unique value of K, and hence L, Y and M, that equates the flow demand S_d for silver to the flow supply $S(1/p)$ for each value of $1/p$, as illustrated in Figure 7.4. It also follows that steady state L, K and M are all increasing functions of $1/p$.

We therefore see that there is a continuum of steady state equilibria (L, K, M), each corresponding to a particular value of $1/p$ and varying positively with changes in this relative price.

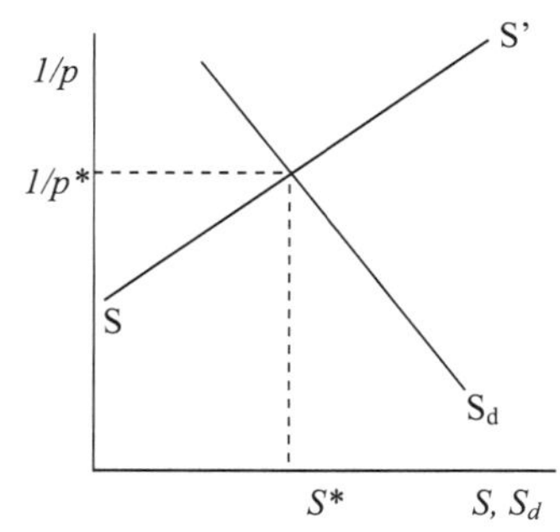

Figure 7.4 Flow equilibrium in the silver market

To determine a unique steady state we now introduce the final behavioral equation of the model. This is a long-run 'portfolio balance' equation that makes the desired ratio of physical capital *K* to the money supply *M* an increasing function of the relative rate of return to holding capital instead of commodity money as an asset, so that we have

$$K / M = h(\rho),\ \ h'(\rho) > 0 \tag{7.26}$$

where

$$\rho \equiv (r - \delta) + \mu \tag{7.27}$$

The higher the net rate of return $(r - \delta)$ on capital itself, the more attractive it clearly is to hold capital. Commodity money 'depreciates' at the rate μ, so that holding capital instead of commodity money as an asset brings an additional return of μ, as stated in (7.27).

In every steady state the real wage must be equal to w^*, and hence the marginal product of capital must be equal to $r(w^*)$ by the 'factor-price frontier' in the goods sector. Whatever the price level p may be in the steady state, its future values are stationary at that level so that there is no Fisherian 'capital gain' component to add to the relative rate of return ρ as defined in (7.27). Thus ρ is uniquely determined by w^* and so the *ratio* of *K* to *M* in all steady states is a ray through the origin *OR* as in Figure 7.5.

The other curve *BB′* in Figure 7.5 shows the *values* of *K* and *M* corresponding to each other in a segment of the continuum of steady states (*L*, *K*, *M*), one value for each value of *1/p*, as determined above. We assume that 'diminishing returns' in the natural resource-based silver sector are so strong that the curve *BB′* cuts *OR* from below, i.e. that capital accumulation proceeds faster than the increase of the money stock as *1/p* increases. The intersection of *BB′* and *OR* determines K^* and M^*, and consequently L^* and $1/p^*$, as the unique long-run steady state equilibrium of the model.

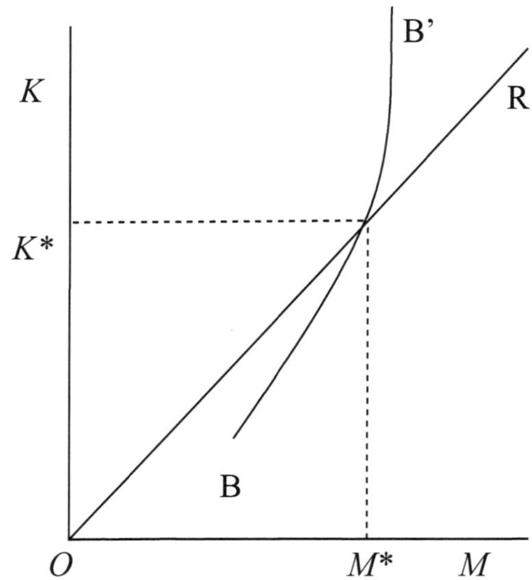

Figure 7.5 The portfolio balance

Economic Consequences of the Black Death

To model the impact and consequences of the Black Death we assume that the European economy of the mid-fourteenth century was initially in the long-run demographic, monetary and economic equilibrium corresponding to the steady state depicted in the last section. The Black Death itself is conceived of as a one-time, instantaneous shock that reduces population and the labor force substantially. (The exact proportion does not matter since our analysis will be qualitative rather than using or providing numerical estimates.) We begin by deducing the consequences from the model in the first section below. The second section briefly examines the historical record to check whether the analytical consequences derived from the model broadly conform to the facts established in the voluminous historical literature on this demographic catastrophe.

Model Analysis

The instantaneous decline of the labor force has some obvious immediate consequences. Wage rates rise in terms of both goods and silver, and the output of both commodities falls. Silver deposits and the capital stock (at first) are unchanged but the decline in the labor force means that the production possibility frontier shifts inwards. The outputs of both sectors decline, if relative prices are held constant, because each sector will employ less labor due to the rise in the real wage.

The relative price of goods and silver, as we have seen, is determined in the asset market, i.e. it depends upon what happens to the stock demand for money since the stock of silver coins is at its initial level. The stock demand for money falls, since national income declines because of the reduction in the labor force. The result is an instantaneous fall in the relative price of silver in terms of goods, i.e. a jump in the price level of goods in terms of silver. All of this follows from quantity theory reasoning. In terms of the famous Fisher equation, MV is constant and Q falls, so p must rise.

This shift in relative prices implies that the fall in the output of silver induced by the reduction of the labor force is accentuated by the fact that goods production is now relatively more attractive. The flow supply curve of silver has shifted to the left, so production falls at constant relative prices, and the fall in the relative price induces a movement down the supply curve as well. In the goods sector, on the other hand, the rise in relative prices moves production up the supply curve, mitigating the reduction in output caused by the decline in the labor force.

Real wealth and income per capita of the surviving population are both considerably higher than before the catastrophe. The demand for Eastern luxuries, in particular, will then rise. The combination of the reduction of the population and the shift in relative prices that this creates on impact thus produces an excess demand for silver and an excess supply of goods. The stock of silver coins in circulation therefore starts to shrink, while the capital stock increases. The rise in the real wage makes fertility exceed mortality, so population begins to increase slowly from its level in the immediate aftermath of the Black Death. With labor and capital both increasing, the production possibility frontier begins to expand, making it possible for production in both sectors to recover. The increase in national income means that the stock demand for money also starts shifting back towards its original level. Together with the ongoing decline in the money supply (silver in circulation) due to depreciation and purchases of Eastern luxuries this makes the relative price of silver rise again, i.e. the jump in the price level of goods that was the consequence of the negative population shock begins to be reversed. This encourages the recovery in the production of silver relative to that of goods.

The picture we have of the post-catastrophe scenario is that population and production are expanding from the depressed levels in the immediate aftermath of the arrival of the plague, while the price level and real wages decline from their initially inflated levels. Real wages fall as population recovers, although they remain well above their pre-plague level for a long time. The price level of goods in terms of silver continues to fall since production is recovering while the stock of silver is shrinking, because the output of silver is insufficient to cover 'depreciation' and the expenditure on Eastern luxuries induced by the rise in per capita wealth and income.

However, the deflation of the price level itself stimulates the output of silver. Together with falling real wealth and per capita income resulting from the rise in population, it also reduces the demand for Eastern luxuries while at the same time the 'depreciation' component of the flow demand for silver itself shrinks, because its base is reduced. Eventually, the excess demand for silver must therefore reverse itself into an excess supply, and the amount of silver in circulation begins to rise again. The mirror image of the excess demand for silver, the excess supply of goods, must also be reversed and the capital stock, which is above its pre-plague level, is reduced.

The relative price of silver l/p must continue to rise as long as the money supply is contracting, since the stock demand for money must be rising because of the increasing labor force and capital stock. If the money supply continues to fall when the price of silver rises to its initial pre-plague level $1/p$ will 'overshoot' its initial level, i.e. the price of goods in terms of silver must fall below the pre-plague level. Eventually, however, the excess flow demand for silver that is contracting the money supply must be reversed and the money supply will begin to increase again. The relative price of silver *1/p* will continue to rise if the demand for money rises faster than the supply. The long deflation of the price level must, however, eventually be reversed to an inflation as the labor force and the capital stock converge back towards their initial levels. The initial pre-plague price level is returned to from below rather than from above. The price level of goods in terms of silver will thus display an initial upward spike on the impact of the plague, followed by a long deflationary phase that takes the price level below its initial value (i.e. 'overshooting'), followed by a gradual inflation as the supply of money increases faster than demand, converging asymptotically back to the pre-plague level when the full adjustment is completed and the values of all variables have returned to their initial levels.

It is conceivable, however, that the money supply will begin to expand before the rise in the relative price of silver *1/p* has reached its initial pre-plague level. At this turning point, the demand for money always increases faster than the rising supply. Otherwise *1/p* would fall and the system would not get back to the initial equilibrium. Then the possibility arises that *1/p* continues to rise until the initial level is attained and the labor force and capital stock will converge to their long-run steady state values, without any 'overshooting' of the price level. The initial inflationary spike is followed by slow deflation back to the original pre-plague level. It is, however, also possible for *1/p* to rise above the initial level before the long-run equilibrium is attained, i.e. there is 'overshooting'. In this case, again, the deflation of the price level must eventually be reversed and followed by an inflationary phase as the initial pre-plague price level is approached from below rather than above.

Thus, 'overshooting' will not occur in one of the three cases considered. However, the two cases in which it does occur both appear to be more consistent with the historical record, as we shall argue below.

The process that we have described is depicted graphically in Figure 7.6. The initial position is that of point a, with money supply $M(0)$, money demand $M_d(0)$ and the price of silver in terms of goods at $1/p^*$. The Black Death instantaneously shifts the money demand function downwards on the vertical supply curve $M(0)$ to point b, producing a fall in the relative price of silver in terms of goods $1/p$. In quantity theory terms MV is constant while Q falls, so p must rise, i.e. $1/p$ must fall. For the reasons that

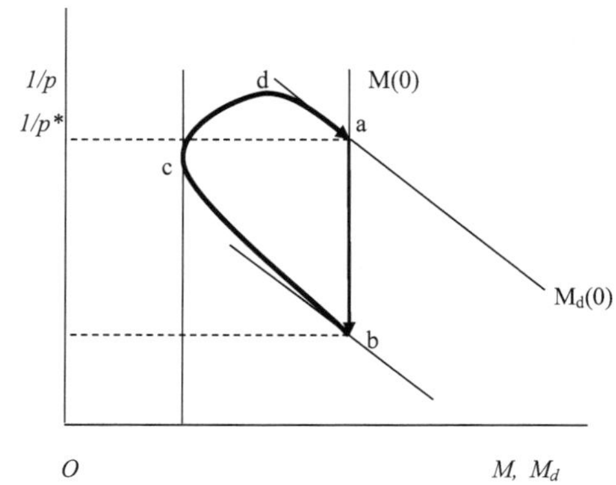

Figure 7.6 The long swing in the price level due to the Black Death

we have explained above, there is now an excess flow demand for silver, which means that the money supply shrinks, shifting the vertical supply curve of the money stock leftwards. The recovery of population and the labor force, and the increase of the capital stock due to the excess flow supply of goods, means that the stock demand curve for money starts to shift back upwards again. The relative price of silver *1/p* therefore starts to rise above the level to which it initially fell at point b, since the demand for the money stock of silver is rising while the supply is falling.

Eventually, however, the excess flow demand for silver that is draining the stock must be reversed as the rising price of silver and the falling real wage in terms of goods increase the flow supply while the demand for Eastern luxuries is reduced and the 'depreciation' component μM is also falling as M itself declines. At point c in Figure 7.6 the money supply stops contracting and begins to increase back towards its initial level (As noted above, point c could be above point a, without affecting the essentials of the process described here).

The stock demand for money continues to rise because of the increasing labor force. Despite the beginnings of the increase of the money supply, the increase in the demand for money keeps on raising *1/p*, the relative price of silver. The rise in *1/p* can 'overshoot' the original level of *1/p*, corresponding to point a, if the increase in the stock demand for money at that price is larger than the increase in the amount of silver in circulation. The price of silver *1/p* then rises to point d in Figure 7.6, after

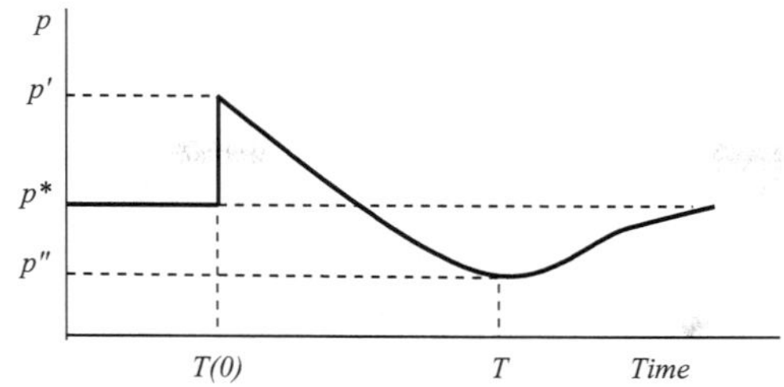

Figure 7.7 The price-level pattern following the Black Death

which the increase in money demand, which is being dampened as the original size of the labor force and capital stock are being approached, falls short of the increase in money supply, causing *1/p* to fall thereafter towards the original level at point a. At this point the recovery from the effects of the Black Death is complete. With all parameters, technology and behavioral relations unchanged, the system returns to the original position.

The time path of the price level p over the entire sequence is depicted in Figure 7.7, which is drawn for the 'overshooting' case. At the onset of the Black Death, at time *T(0)*, the price level jumps instantaneously from p^* to p', and then descends slowly from that level, falling below p^* itself and reaching a floor at p'' at time *T*, after which it rises back towards the original equilibrium level p^*, with all other variables unchanged as well.

The next section examines the historical record to assess the extent to which the predictions of the model are consistent with historical facts and interpretations.

History

The bubonic plague, *Yersinia pestis*, that struck Europe in 1347 was, ironically, a consequence of the increased trade and commercial activity between East and West stimulated by the unification of the Eurasian continent under the Pax Mongolica. According to McNeill (1977) the plague bacillus was transmitted to Central Asia by Mongol troops who were infected by it on a punitive expedition to the Burma-Yunnan border in 1253. It crossed Central Asia to the port of Kaffa on the Black

Sea, a major Genoese trading station. From there it was apparently carried by Genoese vessels to Messina in Sicily and eventually to the whole of Europe. The death rate during the initial outbreak was devastating. Carlo Cipolla (1964, p. 131) gives an estimate of 25 million killed out of a total population of approximately 80 million between 1348 and 1351. The plague recurred in several waves of diminishing average intensity, before disappearing from Europe by the end of the seventeenth century. There has been a prolonged debate on the extent of the mortality but no disagreement on the fact that it was substantial.

The way we have modeled this demographic disaster, as an instantaneous one-shot catastrophe, is thus not strictly accurate but it corresponds quite well to the estimates of Cipolla for the 1348–1351 period. Our treatment of the plague as an exogenous shock is also supported by demographic evidence. Massimo Livi-Bacci (1997, p. 53) says: 'The plague constitutes a population check largely exogenous, or external, to the sociodemographic system.' He also notes the tendency of endogenous economic and social forces to reduce mortality and increase fertility, just as in the present model. A reduction in the age of females at marriage is an important adjustment stressed by many demographers and historians, which can plausibly be explained by the better economic circumstances of the surviving population. Under the influence of the induced effects on fertility and mortality the population of Europe seems to have regained its pre-plague level by the end of the sixteenth century. It took over two centuries for the shock that we give to our model to peter out and long-run Malthusian equilibrium to be restored.

There is also considerable scattered evidence on the consequent rise in real wages. England provides the best data, partly because of the famous index of real wages calculated for a period of seven centuries by Phelps-Brown and Hopkins (1956). This index is effectively combined by John Hatcher (1977, p. 71, Fig. 2) with estimates of population from 1250 to 1750. Population falls from a peak of close to 6 million around 1300 to about 3 million in 1350, continuing to decline to barely 2 million around 1450. It then slowly climbs back to reach the 1300 level of 6 million only as late as 1750. The real wage index (of building craftsmen) rises from a level of 60 in 1300 to 105 in 1450, i.e. 75 percent. The 1450–1460 decade sees the trough of the population curve coinciding with the peak of the real wage index. Real wages decline after the 1450 peak to a trough with the index at 40 in the first half of the seventeenth century. It then rises slowly back to the 1300 level of 60 only as late as 1750. In other words, real wages were unchanged at the beginning and end of half a millennium! The 1460 peak of 105 was not attained until the second half of the *nineteenth* century. The swing in real wages that our model predicts is thus dramatically borne out by the English data. Goldthwaite (1980, p. 334) presents evidence on the construction industry in Florence, showing that real wages were about 50 percent higher than the 1360 level in the period from 1420 to 1470, after which they fall back to pre-plague levels by 1600.

Economic historians have conducted an intense debate about whether the two centuries after the Black Death, which coincide with the conventional periodization of the Renaissance, could be characterized as a boom or a depression. Robert Lopez (1953) tries to account for the paradox of cultural efflorescence during an economic contraction by arguing that 'hard times' with low rates of return on investment induce rational businessmen and bankers such as the Medici to 'invest in culture' instead. Cipolla (1964) criticizes this and a related paper by Lopez and Miskimin (1962), pointing to evidence of prosperity. The controversy can be reconciled by distinguishing between total and per capita magnitudes. Total production and trade would fall in response to the decline in numbers but much less than proportionately, so that per capita wealth and incomes would go up. The point is made with a macabre sense of humor by A. R. Bridbury (1962, p. 91) when he remarks that the Black Death corresponded to a 'sort of Marshall Plan on a stupendous scale'.

From simple two-sector general equilibrium reasoning we can expect that labor-intensive goods would decline in production while land-intensive or capital-intensive goods would expand, if relative product prices are held constant (the Rybczynski (1955) theorem). Furthermore, since per capita income is now higher, the relative prices of labor-intensive goods would rise and the prices of land or capital-intensive goods would fall. There is considerable evidence of this sort of shift in the composition of total production, with livestock-raising and viticulture expanding relative to food crops, for example. Luxury consumption of all kinds would also rise because of the higher per capita incomes. Examples abound. Indeed the primacy of Italy during the Renaissance can partly be explained by her comparative advantage within Europe in luxury products, such as silk-weaving and other high quality textiles, expensive arms and armor and especially the Venetian and Genoese grip on the supply of Eastern spices and other goods.

One sector of production to which we have paid particular attention in our theoretical analysis is the mining of precious metals, 'silver' as we have called it. A strong prediction was that this sector would be particularly hard hit, since it would suffer not only from the general labor shortage and rise in wages but also because the sharp fall in the demand for money would lower the price of silver relative to goods in general. This prediction is strongly confirmed in the historical record. John Nef (1987, p. 721) states that in the aftermath of the Black Death 'the production of gold and silver in Europe as a whole actually declined', and he also speaks (Nef 1987, p. 722) of a 'long slump which lasted for several generations'. Recovery only came with the revival of population and total real incomes.

Combining this reduction in the supply of silver with the rise in demand for Eastern luxuries, also amply documented in the historical record, makes for an excess demand for silver that must result in a contraction of the stock of silver coins in circulation. This is exactly what happened, for so long and to such an extent that it led the monetary historian John Day to speak of 'The Great Bullion Famine of the Fifteenth Century' (Day 1987, Chap. 1). The shortage of silver and precious metals generally in Europe in the century or so after the Black Death is well attested and analyzed in this work and other authoritative treatments, such as Miskimin (1975) and Spufford (1988, Chaps. 14–16).

Our model predicts first a rise in the relative price of goods in terms of silver, when real income drops and the money supply is constant, followed by a fall in this relative price as the demand for money begins to rise back to its initial position and the money supply contracts. The scanty data on industrial and agricultural prices expressed in terms of silver exhibit exactly this pattern. John Day (1987, p. 100) presents two industrial price indices rising from 100 to 125 and 100 to 133–200 from 1330 to 1370, and falling from 125 to 72 in 1410 and 43 in 1470, and from 133–200 in 1370 to 83–100 in 1410 and 104–125 in 1470. Indices of agricultural prices in Northern France go from 100 for the 1331–1340 decade to 107 in 1361–1370, then fall to 78 in 1401–1410 and 42 in 1461–1470. In England the pattern for the same periods is from 100 to 127, then falling to 102 and 69. Some other evidence and discussion is also provided in the book on price history by Fischer (1996).

The demand for Eastern luxuries, to which we have assigned major weight in connection with the reduction in silver output as the cause of 'the great bullion famine', is extensively documented, although numerical estimates are relatively scarce. We should first note that 'Eastern' does not necessarily mean 'Southern', the familiar exotic products of the Islamic world, the East Indies and China. Russia, Finland and the eastern shores of the Baltic also provided a major luxury import for Western Europe, namely the rich furs of ermine, sable and marten, so familiar to us from the Renaissance portraits not only of the nobility but also of the merchant princes of the age. Harry Miskimin (1975, p. 138) reports that 450,000 furs were shipped from Riga to Bruges in one year, 1405, alone, and Riga was not the sole outlet for the fur supply. This fur trade particularly enriched the merchants of the Hanseatic League. Wax for candles was also a luxury import of a rather morbid kind, since the main source of demand was the lighting of candles at masses for the dead.

More than matching the drain of silver to the northeast through the Baltic for furs, wax and amber was the drain to the southeast through Italy, especially Venice and Genoa, and then to Egypt, where the spices and silks of Asia were acquired by European merchants. A particularly fascinating account of the drain of silver eastwards in exchange for luxuries is given in an article by Lopez et al. (1970). The article has three sections, one by each author. The first, by Miskimin, tells how silver was drained out of England and France to Italy, in exchange for luxuries of various kinds. The next section, by Lopez on Italy, explains how all this northern silver did not stay in Italy but was transferred to Cairo and Alexandria by Venetian and Genoese merchants in exchange for spices, silks and other Eastern luxuries. The third section, by Abraham Udovich on Egypt, explains how all this Italian silver did not remain in Egypt but was drained eastwards to the region of the Caspian Sea in exchange for slaves and furs and through the Red Sea to India and the East Indies for spices and silks. All three regions meanwhile were devastated about equally by the plague. The authors report that they were looking for expert co-authors on India and China to explain what finally happened to the silver but could not find anyone suitable in time for the conference at which they had to present the paper.

Our model predicts that this persistent drain of silver was destined to end and be reversed. This again is exactly what happened. From about 1460 the stock of silver in circulation appears to start rising again, the excess (flow) demand for silver now being converted into an excess supply. On the demand side the 'depreciation' as a constant fraction of a declining stock was becoming a smaller proportion of a rising flow supply in response to the rising relative prices of silver in terms of goods. Per capita wealth and income were shrinking as population rose, reducing the demand for Eastern luxuries. The rising relative price of silver encouraged the re-opening of old mines, stimulated the search for new ones and also the search for better methods of extracting metal from the ore. Nef (1987, p. 735) speaks of a 'boom in mining and metallurgy' from 1460 to 1530, reporting that: '[b]etween 1460 and 1530 the annual output of silver in Central Europe increased several times over, perhaps more than fivefold', reaching a maximum during the 1526–1535 decade.

It is vitally important to note that all the events that we are describing have nothing to do as yet with the voyages of discovery in the last decade of the fifteenth century. As we will see in the next section, the fact that prices in terms of silver were rising in Europe *before* the great influx of silver from the New World in the middle of the sixteenth century has been taken in some quarters to refute the monetary view of the Price Revolution of the sixteenth century, and even the quantity theory itself.

American Silver and the Price Revolution

Few ideas have been more famous or controversial in economic history than the celebrated thesis of Earl Hamilton (1934) about the impact of the influx of silver from the New World on European prices in the sixteenth century and its implications for the future course of economic development. Despite an enormous outpouring of theoretical, statistical and historical research the subject does not appear to have found a resolution, more than sixty-five years later. While a full discussion of even the most basic of the issues involved will require more space than is available for the present essay, it may be useful to put the model presented here through the paces of another exercise. As we shall see, the results could be illuminating, particularly if taken in conjunction with those of our analysis of the consequences of the Black Death. For other interesting approaches to this problem of American silver and the Price Revolution the reader is referred to Niehans (1993) and Flynn (1996).

As in the previous exercise we assume that the system begins in full long-run equilibrium with population, money supply and capital stock all stationary. The 'discovery of America', for purposes of the model, will simply be an exogenous increase in the stock of silver deposits available. The initial effect is therefore to shift out the production possibility frontier on the silver axis. The rise in real income that this represents shifts the demand for money function to the right, with the initial supply of money (stock of silver coins in circulation) remaining constant. The immediate impact of the discovery is therefore to raise the relative price of silver in terms of goods, i.e. there is a *deflationary* spike in the price level of goods in terms of silver at the moment of the discovery. The flow supply curve shifts to the right so the flow output will increase because the relative price of silver in terms of goods has risen as well. Although the demand for Eastern luxuries will rise because of the higher real income, this increased expenditure will be less than the increase in the flow supply of silver so that there is an excess supply of silver leading to an increase in the stock of silver coins in circulation. Thus the fabled influx of 'American treasure' into Europe begins.

The rise in real income and the increase in silver output pull labor out of the goods sector, raising the real wage in terms of goods. This, under the demographic regime that we have postulated, leads to an increase in population and the labor force. That in turn shifts out the production possibility frontier even further for both commodities and implies increasing real income, shifting the demand for money outwards as well. On the basis of the historical evidence it is clear, however, that the increase in the net supply of new silver, added to the money stock, must have exceeded the increase in the demand for money due to the higher real income. The discovery of American silver led to huge additions to world silver stocks, about 50 percent during the sixteenth century and 85 percent during the seventeenth. Out of these additions 74 and 71 percent respectively reached Europe, and 40 percent was passed on to Asia. Production in the Americas amounted to 74 percent of world output from 1493 to 1600 and 85 percent from 1601 to 1700 (Barrett 1990). When the addition to the money stock exceeds the increase in the transactions demand for money the price of silver in terms of goods will fall, i.e. there will be inflation of the price level of goods in terms of silver. It is this outcome and its continuation that constitutes the celebrated 'Price Revolution of the Sixteenth Century'.

The falling relative price of silver in terms of goods will tend increasingly to reduce the flow supply of silver, despite the increases in the labor force induced by a real wage above the Malthusian equilibrium level. The 'depreciation' component of the flow demand will rise steadily, proportionately to the increasing base of the total stock of silver in circulation. The expansion of real incomes also means that the expenditure on Eastern luxuries is rising. Thus, eventually, the rate of growth of the money supply will slow down, below the rate of expansion of the demand for money, caused by increasing real incomes, and the relative price of silver $1/p$ will begin to rise. Deflation will follow inflation, creating another 'long wave' in the price level. In the end, the excess flow supply of silver must turn into an excess flow demand, so that the stock of silver in circulation within the extended European economy will start to shrink. The falling real wage will also eventually lead to a stationary population.

The final long-run equilibrium will therefore have the same real wage that preceded the discovery of the silver deposits of the New World that set the whole 'long wave' in motion. Population will be stationary, but at a higher level than previously, because of the augmented stock of silver deposits. The capital stock first declines because there must be an excess demand for goods corresponding to the excess flow supply of silver during the inflationary phase of the 'long wave'. It begins to increase when the money supply starts to shrink, because of the logic of the model. The final capital stock will be larger, supporting the increased population and augmented natural resources created by the discovery. This, in turn, means that the price level must 'overshoot'. To the increase of the capital stock through the excess supply of goods corresponds an excess flow demand for silver and a reduction of the monetary stock. Deflation must follow inflation and lower the price level of goods in terms of silver back towards its initial value.

The final long-run steady state to which the system tends can now be briefly described. The three state variables, the labor force L, the capital stock K and the supply of money M, will all increase in proportion to the increase in the stock of natural resource deposits N due to the 'discovery of America'. The real wage w^* and price level p^* will remain constant at their original levels. Thus the stock demand and supply of money in Figure 7.3 will both shift proportionately to the right leaving the relative prices of silver, $1/p^*$, and hence the price level, p^*, unchanged. In Figure 7.4 the flow supply and demand for silver will also be shifted to the right at unchanged $1/p^*$, in proportion to the increase in N. In Figure 7.5 the desired proportion of capital stock to money stock remains unchanged, since $r(w^*)$ is unaffected by the increase in natural resource deposits. The BB' curve shifts to the right as a result of the increase in N, leading to an increase in the same proportion of K and M at the point where the new BB' curve intersects the ray OR from the origin.

We begin in Figure 7.8 at the initial steady state equilibrium at point a. The discovery of the additional natural resource deposits shifts out the production possibility frontier and raises real income and the stock demand for money. With the initial money supply given this implies a jump in the relative price of silver $1/p$ from point a to point e. The additional resource deposits and the higher relative price stimulate the output of silver, leading to an excess flow supply and hence an expansion of the money supply. The demand curve for money shifts steadily to the right,

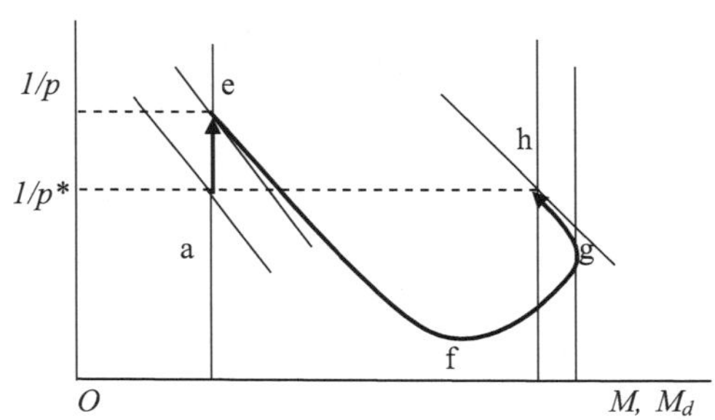

Figure 7.8 The long swing in the price level due to the American silver

because the higher real wage induced by the expansion in silver production stimulates the growth of population and the labor force. The rate of expansion of the money supply exceeds the growth of money demand, leading to a falling relative price of silver *1/p* or an inflation of the price level of goods in terms of silver.

The fall in *1/p* continues to point f, falling below the initial relative price $1/p^*$. The growth of the money supply begins to slow down and is exceeded by the expansion of money demand, leading to a rising relative price *1/p* from point f to point g. At point g the excess flow supply of silver finally becomes zero, after which it turns negative, i.e. the money supply starts to contract while the relative price *1/p* continues to rise in response to the continuing rise in money demand. Equilibrium is finally restored at point h, where *1/p* returns to the original level $1/p^*$, the real wage falls back to w^*, and the capital stock, labor force and the money supply all have increased in the same proportion as the increase in the natural resource deposits. Since the money supply is contracting from g to h, the capital stock now rises, recovering its losses in the transition from e to g and increasing in proportion to the money supply and the labor force.

Figure 7.9 plots the time path of the price level p that is a reciprocal of the movement of *1/p* in Figure 7.8. At *T(0)* there is an initial deflationary spike from p^* to p', after which there is a long inflationary phase from *T(0)* to a peak of p'' at T, followed by an asymptotic decline of the price level back towards p^*.

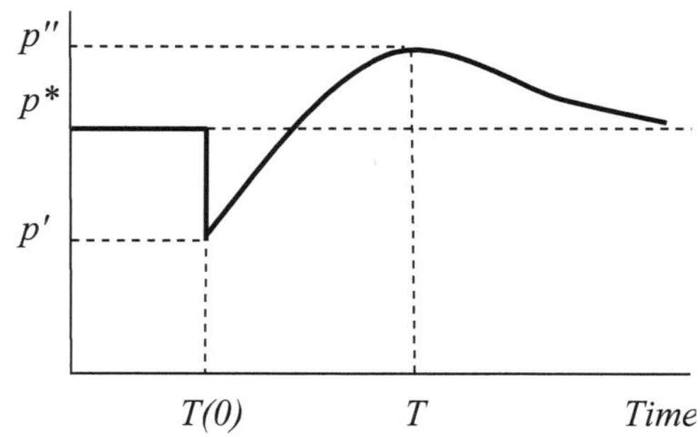

Figure 7.9 The price-level pattern following the silver discoveries

To confront the implications of our model with the actual historical experience is a task that we will not attempt here. There is no doubt that the price level of goods throughout Europe rose in terms of silver throughout the sixteenth century, although there is much disagreement about the extent and pattern of the rise. The causes, however, continue to be fiercely debated. Hamilton's quantity theory explanation was criticized by historians on many grounds. Some are mutually contradictory, such as the assertion that the Fisher formula is 'only a truism' and that it is 'based on unrealistic assumptions'. Stronger than these criticisms of the internal logic of the 'monetarist' explanation was the contention, pointedly made in an influential article by Ingrid Hammarström (1957), that prices had been rising well before the influx of American silver ever reached the shores of Europe.

This is where our consideration of the long-run adjustment to the shock of the Black Death can be useful. That shock was deflationary for a long time, during the 'bullion famine' of the fifteenth century, but was eventually self-correcting since the rise in the relative price of silver would stimulate an expansion of silver output. This rise in European silver output has been well established by the work of Nef (1987) on the 1460–1530 mining boom. The two 'thought experiments' that we conduct for our model, on the Black Death and the discovery of New World silver, are not fully separated in historical time. The *Niña*, *Pinta* and *Santa María* sailed before the full adjustment to the Black Death, a century and a half earlier, had been worked out. The American silver started to arrive at Seville before the inflationary final phase of the Black Death 'long wave' had ended. Thus it is no valid criticism of Hamilton's thesis to say that inflation was already occurring in Europe. The inflation was undoubtedly greatly amplified and prolonged by the American silver.

In their disillusionment with 'monetary' explanations several historians have looked for 'real' explanations, with population changes as the most favored among these. Much of the underlying logic of these arguments appears spurious and exasperating to economists. The pressure of population on scarce land making food more expensive and thereby causing 'inflation' is only one of the more egregious examples. Nevertheless, the controversies between 'Monetarists' and 'Malthusians' among economic historians—see, for instance, the exchange between Robinson (1959) and Postan (1959)—have the merit of trying to do justice to what are undoubtedly two fundamental factors involved in all these episodes, factors that economists have for the most part kept in separate compartments. Our model, however, embraces both population and commodity money as endogenous variables along with production in a general equilibrium framework. In this model the price level of goods in terms of silver is a *relative* price of goods and silver and so the distinction between 'real' and 'monetary' factors loses its relevance.

The model requires the Price Revolution to recede and be followed by a deflationary phase. Here again it conforms to reality. While the sixteenth century was a booming inflationary period with an initial rise in real wages and expanding population under the stimulus of the discoveries, the seventeenth century was a century of stagnation and falling prices, as emphasized in a famous article by Eric Hobsbawm (1954) on the 'seventeenth-century crisis', which is still the subject of a debate that shows no signs of ending. In that century real wages had fallen towards the Malthusian equilibrium level, making population stagnate, while the drain of silver to the East through the activities of the Dutch and English East India Companies lowered the price level. The model thus has the merit of pointing to a necessary connection between two historical episodes that have been considered as quite distinct. The explanation for the 'seventeenth-century crisis' has been sought in such exogenous factors as, for example, climatic change, when a good part of the story can be traced to the consequences of the preceding epoch.

Concluding Observations

We began this essay by invoking Heckscher on the relation between theory and history. Our intention was to respond to his 'plea for theory' in the practice of economic history. In 1929 his plea was a cry in the wilderness, not heeded until about a generation later, by the emergence of the New Economic History school. The main emphasis of that school, however, was on the application of econometric techniques to historical data and less on theory *per se*. Almost as a by-product of this work a number of contributions emerged that specifically applied or developed appropriate economic models to investigate historical problems. Whenever possible it is sufficient to simply take a well-known model or conceptual tool 'off the shelf', as it were, and apply it directly to economic history. Frequently, however, the historical circumstances are such that no standard model applies directly. One then needs to be sufficiently resourceful and opportunistic to 'do it yourself'. What we have presented here is just such a do-it-yourself model.

The core of our model is the Ronald Jones (1971) specific factors construct, which was itself inspired by the historical problem of Anglo-American productivity differences in the nineteenth century. What we have added is the endogenization of the labor supply by appending a neo-Malthusian demographic regime, combined with a model of commodity money, requiring stock-flow adjustments through the application of the asset market approach. The best modern treatment of commodity money is Robert Barro (1979). His paper also uses the stock-flow adjustment mechanism but takes real national income and the flow supply curve of 'gold' as exogenously given. In our system real national income and the flow supply of silver are both endogenously determined along with the supplies of labor, capital and money in a full general equilibrium framework. What we have done therefore is to start with one of the standard variants of the 'factor proportions' approach, endogenizing the supplies of factors and money, in the spirit of the Findlay (1995) Ohlin Lectures. It is interesting to note that Heckscher himself briefly considered the implications of making factor supplies respond positively to increases in their own real rewards in his 1919 article.

The application of this analytical apparatus to history takes the form of 'thought experiments', investigating the effect on the long-run equilibrium of the model and the transition to that state of some 'shock' that corresponds to a significant historical event. The two experiments that we have conducted are the Black Death, in which one-third of the population and labor force disappears overnight, and the effect of the discovering of rich silver deposits in the New World. The first is a demographic shock that has subtle and complex monetary consequences since we show that the phenomena associated with the great bullion famine of the fifteenth century can be derived as consequences of the demographic disaster of the previous century. The other is a monetary shock that has demographic consequences. Together, the two experiments show that it would be misguided to take an exclusively 'Malthusian' or 'Monetarist' view of history, since the demographic and monetary regimes are both embedded in a wider system of general interdependence.

We also saw that despite his plea for the application of theory to the analysis of historical epochs Heckscher did not consider it applicable to shifts from one epoch to another, since the determinants of such shifts generally lie outside the realm of economics. The plague outbreak in Europe in the mid-fourteenth century and the discovery of silver mines in the New World are both examples of Heckscher's point. Each of these events had momentous economic consequences but was largely, though not entirely, brought about by circumstances independent of economic conditions.

The spirit of our model is entirely 'classical'. What we call long-run equilibrium is nothing but the 'stationary state' of Malthus, Ricardo and Mill. Why else did Paul Samuelson (1971) talk about the Ricardo-Viner model? The system returns to its original state, as in the case of the adjustment to the Black Death. But can it really be that the Europe of, say, 1547, was the same as the Europe of 1347 even if population, real wages, money supply and so on were all the same? Not really. What is missing is 'hysteresis', the alteration to the underlying parameters of the system when it is subjected to a shock, so that it does not return to the original starting point but to some other position determined by the changes during the transition.

This is the idea underlying the brilliant little book by the late Harvard medievalist David Herlihy (1997) entitled *The Black Death and the Transformation of the West*. Herlihy argues persuasively that the experience of affluence in the aftermath of the Black Death fundamentally altered cultural and social values in a direction conducive to material advancement and economic growth. To take but one example, the age at marriage of females could have increased, shifting the fertility curve of our Figure 7.1 to the left, resulting in a higher equilibrium wage and per capita income, with a smaller equilibrium population. Such changes could ultimately have led to the Industrial Revolution, in which the 'Unbound Prometheus' of technological change altered the world forever and made our 'pre-industrial' classical model no longer applicable.

References

Ashley, William J. (1900). *Surveys historic and economic*. London: Longmans & Co.

Barrett, Ward. (1990). World bullion flows, 1450–1800. In James D. Tracy (Ed.), *The rise of the merchant empires. Long-distance trade in the early modern world, 1350–1750*. Cambridge: Cambridge University Press.

Barro, Robert J. (1979). Money and the price level under the gold standard. *Economic Journal, 89*, 13–33.

Bridbury, A. R. (1962). *Economic growth: England in the later Middle Ages*. London: George Allen & Unwin.

Burgstaller, André. (1994). *Property and prices*. Cambridge: Cambridge University Press.

Cipolla, Carlo M. (1964). Economic depression of the Renaissance? *Economic History Review, 16*, 519–524.

Day, John. (1987). *The medieval market economy*. Oxford: Basil Blackwell.

Findlay, Ronald. (1995). *Factor proportions, trade, and growth*. Cambridge, MA/London: MIT Press.

Findlay, Ronald. (1998). A plea for trade theory in economic history. *Economic and Social Review, 29*, 313–321.

Fischer, David Hackett. (1996). *The great wave: Price revolutions and the rhythm of history*. Oxford: Oxford University Press.

Flam, Harry, & Flanders, June M. (1991). Introduction. In Harry Flam & June M. Flanders (Eds.), *Heckscher-Ohlin trade theory*. Cambridge, MA/London: MIT Press.

Flynn, Dennis O. (1996). *World silver and monetary history in the 16th and 17th centuries*. Aldershot: Variorum Collected Series, Ashgate.

Fogel, Robert. (1967). The specification problem in economic history. *Journal of Economic History, 27*, 283–308.

Goldthwaite, Richard A. (1980). *The building of Renaissance Florence*. Baltimore: Johns Hopkins University Press.

Habakkuk, H. J. (1967). *American and British technology in the nineteenth century*. Cambridge: Cambridge University Press.

Hamilton, Earl J. (1934). *American treasure and the price revolution in Spain*. Cambridge, MA: Harvard University Press.

Hammarström, Ingrid. (1957). The price revolution of the sixteenth century: Some Swedish evidence. *Scandinavian Economic History Review, 5*, 118–154.

Hatcher, John. (1977). *Plague, population and the English economy 1348–1530*. London: Macmillan.

Heckscher, Eli F. (1904). Ekonomisk historia: några antydningar. *Historisk Tidskrift, 24*, 167–198.

Heckscher, Eli F. (1919). Utrikeshandelns verkan på inkomstfördelningen. *Ekonomisk Tidskrift, 21*, 1–32.

Heckscher, Eli F. (1920). Historia och nationalekonomi. *Historisk Tidskrift, 40*, 1–22.

Heckscher, Eli F. (1922). *Ekonomi och historia*. Stockholm: Albert Bonniers förlag.

Heckscher, Eli F. (1929). A plea for theory in economic history. *Economic History* (A supplement to the *Economic Journal*), *1*, 525–534.

Heckscher, Eli F. (1930). Den ekonomiska historiens aspekter. *Historisk Tidskrift, 50*, 1–85.

Heckscher, Eli F. (1931a). *Merkantilismen: ett led i den ekonomiska politikens historia* (Vol. 2). Stockholm: P. A. Nordstedt och Söner.

Heckscher, Eli F. (1931b). *Industrialismen: Den ekonomiska utvecklingen 1750–1914*. Stockholm: P. A. Nordstedt och Söner.

Heckscher, Eli F. (1933). The aspects of economic history. In *Economic essays in honour of Gustav Cassel*. London: George Allen & Unwin.

Heckscher, Eli F. (1935–49). *Sveriges ekonomiska historia från Gustav Vasa* (Vol. 4). Stockholm: Albert Bonniers förlag.

Heckscher, Eli F. (1936). Den ekonomiska historiens aspekter. In *Ekonomisk-historiska studier*. Stockholm: Albert Bonniers förlag.

Heckscher, Eli F. (1937). Materialistisk och annan historieuppfattning. *Svensk Tidskrift, 27*, 109–120.

Heckscher, Eli F. (1942). *Svenskt arbete och liv: från medeltiden till nutiden*. Stockholm: Albert Bonniers förlag.

Heckscher, Eli F. (1944). Materialistisk och annan historieuppfattning. In *Historieuppfattning: materialistisk och annan*. Stockholm: Albert Bonniers förlag.

Heckscher, Eli F. (1947). Ekonomisk historia och dess gränsvetenskaper. *Historisk Tidskrift, 67*, 1–17.

Heckscher, Eli F. (1951). *Studium och undervisning i ekonomisk historia*. Lund: C.W.K. Gleerups förlag.

Henriksson, Rolf G. H. (1991). Eli F. Heckscher: The economic historian as economist. In Bo Sandelin (Ed.), *The history of Swedish economic thought*. London/New York: Routledge.

Herlihy, David. (1997). *The Black Death and the transformation of the West.* Cambridge, MA: Harvard University Press.

Hobsbawm, Eric J. (1954). 'The crisis of the seventeenth century', *Past and Present,* no. 5–6, reprinted in Trevor Aston (Ed.) (1967). *Crisis in Europe 1560–1660.* New York: Doubleday Anchor Books.

Jones, Ronald W. (1971). A three-factor model in theory, trade and history. In Jagdish N. Bhagwati et al. (Eds.), *Trade, balance of payments and growth: Papers in international economics in honor of Charles P. Kindleberger.* Amsterdam: North Holland.

Lee, Ronald. (1973). Population in pre-industrial England: An econometric analysis. *Quarterly Journal of Economics, 87,* 581–607.

Livi-Bacci, Massimo. (1997). *A concise history of world population* (2nd ed.). Oxford: Basil Blackwell.

Lopez, Robert S. (1953). Hard times and investment in culture. In Wallace K. Ferguson et al. (Eds.), *The Renaissance: Six essays.* New York: Harper Torchbooks.

Lopez, Robert S, & Miskimin, Harry A. (1962). The economic depression of the Renaissance. *Economic History Review, 14,* 408–426.

Lopez, Robert S, Miskimin, Harry A., & Udovich, Abraham L. (1970). England to Egypt, 1350–1500: Long-term trends and long-distance trade. In Michael A. Cook (Ed.), *Studies in the economic history of the Middle East.* London: School of Oriental and African Studies.

McNeill, William H. (1977). *Plagues and peoples.* New York: Anchor Books.

Miskimin, Harry A. (1975). *The economy of early Renaissance Europe, 1300–1460.* Cambridge: Cambridge University Press.

Nef, John U. (1987). Mining and metallurgy in medieval civilisation. In M. M. Postan & Edward Miller (Eds.), *Cambridge economic history of Europe, vol. 2. Trade and industry in the Middle Ages* (2nd ed.). Cambridge: Cambridge University Press.

Niehans, Jurg. (1993). A reassessment of scholastic monetary theory. *Journal of the History of Economic Thought, 15,* 229–248.

Ohlin, Bertil. (1924). *Handelns teori.* Stockholm: A.B. Nordiska Bokhandeln.

Ohlin, Bertil. (1933). *Interregional and international trade.* Cambridge, MA: Harvard University Press.

Phelps-Brown, E. H., & Hopkins, Sheila V. (1956). Seven centuries of the prices of consumables, compared with builders' wage rates. *Economica,* N.S., *23,* 296–314.

Postan, M. M. (1959). Note. *Economic History Review, 12,* 77–82.

Robinson, W. C. (1959). Money, population and economic change in late medieval Europe. *Economic History Review, 12*, 63–76.

Rybczynski, T. M. (1955). Factor endowment and relative commodity prices. *Economica*. N.S., *22*, 336–341.

Samuelson, Paul A. (1971). Ohlin was right. *Swedish Journal of Economics, 73*, 365–384.

Spufford, Peter. (1988). *Money and its use in medieval Europe*. Cambridge: Cambridge University Press.

Temin, Peter. (1966). Labor scarcity and the problem of American industrial efficiency in the 1850s. *Journal of Economic History, 26*, 361–379.

Temin, Peter. (1971). Labor scarcity in America. *Journal of Interdisciplinary History, 1*, 251–264.

Whitaker, J. K. (Ed.). (1975). *The early economic writings of Alfred Marshall, 1867–1890* (Vol. 1). London: Macmillan.

8

International Trade and Factor Mobility with an Endogenous Land Frontier: Some General Equilibrium Implications of Christopher Columbus

Adam Smith devoted no fewer than fifty-six pages of his great treatise to the subject of 'The Advantages which Europe has derived from the Discovery of America', considering Columbus' voyages, and the almost contemporaneous journey to India around the Cape of Good Hope by Vasco da Gama, to have been 'the two greatest and most important events recorded in the history of mankind' (Smith 1976, Vol. 2, p. 141). While the theme of the emergence and expansion of 'the Atlantic economy' has been one of the staple topics of economic historians, it is surprising that it does not appear to have made much of an impression in the theoretical

I am indebted to Richard Baldwin, André Burgstaller, Richard Clarida, Max Corden, Stanley Engerman, Michael Gavin, Knick Harley, Kevin O'Rourke and Alwyn Young for very helpful comments.

Revised from 'International Trade and Factor Mobility with an Endogenous Land Frontier: Some General Equilibrium Consequences of Christopher Columbus' by Ronald Findlay, in Wilfred J. Ethier, Elhanan Helpman and J. Peter Neary (eds), *Theory, Policy and Dynamics in International Trade: Essays in Honor of Ronald W. Jones*, 1993, Cambridge University Press, pp. 38–54. With kind permission of Cambridge University Press.

R. Findlay, M. Lundahl, *The Economics of the Frontier*,
DOI 10.1057/978-1-137-60237-4_8

literature of international trade, perhaps because of the long Ricardian tradition of *defining* a 'country' as a fixed bundle of resources existing independently of trade rather than as emerging in response to the opportunities opened up by trade itself.[1]

An important feature of the Discoveries was that they should not be considered as having made available at an instant a large additional supply of land and other natural resources. Rather they opened up a new 'frontier' where land could be extended indefinitely but only at a rising marginal cost in terms of other real resource. Wilderness had to be cleared before crops could be grown, harvested and gathered. The westward movement of this frontier provided the historian Frederick Jackson Turner (1861–1932) with his famous thesis that it was the influence of this factor that was the key to the experience of American history, accounting for such features as 'rugged individualism', democratic values and entrepreneurial vigor. Turner's thesis was refined and expanded by the Texas historian Walter Prescott Webb (1888–1963) into the concept of a 'Great Frontier' for the core society of Western Europe that comprised not only the Americas but also Australasia, Oceania and Southern Africa. Yet another distinguished American historian, William H. McNeill, has integrated these considerations together with the eastern expansion of Russia into the steppes of Central Asia and Siberia into a global version of the original frontier thesis (Turner 1920; Webb 1986; McNeill 1983).[2]

Webb saw the Discoveries as a gigantic resource windfall for Western Europe. He estimated the population of that region to be about 100 million in 1500, with a land area of 3.75 million square miles. To this was added a vast potential of about 20 million square miles overseas as the direct result of the voyages, raising the available hectares per capita from about 24 to 148, a sixfold increase. It was not until 1900 that the original per capita ratio was once again attained, after an enormous increase in population (Webb 1986, p. 18). The role of this factor in European development is also stressed in the stimulating work of Eric Jones (1981).

---

[1] See Williams (1929) for a classic critique of the Ricardian model in this regard.

[2] Turner's thesis was first advanced in an essay of 1893. Webb's thesis is perceptively discussed in Chapter 3, 'The New Frontier', by Elliott (1969).

The overseas areas identified by Webb correspond to what the League of Nations statisticians used to refer to as 'Regions of Recent Settlement'. The aboriginal populations of these areas were decimated by contact with the early European settlers, through warfare but mostly by disease. Initially the New World resources were used for the cultivation and export of tropical products such as sugar, tobacco and cotton. The labor force that produced these crops consisted of African slaves, while European workers were for the most part indentured servants. It is estimated that nearly 8 million Africans were taken to the New World as slaves before 1820, while the corresponding figure for Europeans who arrived free or indentured was less than 2 million (McNeill 1983, p. 19). This early phase in the history of the Atlantic economy of the 'triangular trade' involving slaves, raw materials and manufactures between Africa, the New World and Europe was succeeded from about the middle of the nineteenth century by an enormous torrent of Europeans going overseas, 46 million between 1846 and 1920.[3] These people produced the wheat, wool, beef and other products of the North American prairies, the Argentine pampas and the Australian outback. Accompanying this vast wave of settlers was the massive export of capital to provide the necessary infrastructure of transportation and housing.

Simultaneously with the opening of the new regions two other changes of great significance were taking place: a massive population upsurge and the technological breakthroughs of the Industrial Revolution. Together these processes fused into the creation of a truly global network of trade and factor flows in the nineteenth century in which manufactures from Europe were exchanged for primary commodities from the 'Great Frontier', with both types of output being produced by European capital and labor either at home or overseas. In the words of Alfred Marshall, 'the splendid markets which the old world has offered to the products of the new, since the growth of steam communication have rendered North America, Australia and parts of Africa and South America, the richest large fields for the employment of capital and labor that there have ever been' (Marshall 1938, pp. 668–69). The details of the extent and timing of these unprecedented flows of goods, capital and people are conveniently

[3] See Findlay (1990) for a model of the earlier phase of the Atlantic economy.

summarized by William Woodruff (1973). A brilliant perspective on the early history of the Atlantic migration is given by Bernard Bailyn (1988).

The purpose of the present chapter is to provide a simple general equilibrium model that attempts to capture the stark outlines of the economic structure that emerged by the late nineteenth century as a consequence of the European discoveries 400 years earlier. In addition to the general historical reflections on the significance of the frontier cited earlier, the specific inspiration was provided by the work of Guido Di Tella (1982) on the Argentine experience. Peter Kenen (1965) is another relevant contribution on the relation between natural resources, capital and trade. The analytical core of the model presented here, however, as of so much else in the trade theory of the last two decades, is the classic work of Ronald Jones (1971) on the role of 'specific' factors in international trade. It is very interesting to note, however, the links between Jones' own work and the 'staples' theory of the Canadian economic historian Harold Adams Innis that inspired the contributions of Chambers and Gordon (1966), Caves (1965, 1971) and Easton and Reed (1980). The relation between the approach taken in the present chapter and the 'staple' theory is provided in Findlay and Lundahl (1994).

The Closed World of Europe

A necessary prelude to our analysis of the impact of the discoveries is to first specify the closed world of 'Europe' that existed prior to that event. There is a fixed endowment of labor and land available to this economy. One of the goods produced, 'food', has labor and land as inputs in a constant returns to scale production function

$$F = F\left(L_F, T\right) \tag{8.1}$$

of the usual neoclassical type, with positive first and negative second derivatives with respect to each argument. The supply of land T is fixed, and used exclusively for food. Essentially therefore we have the output of food as a concave function of the labor input L_F.

Labor is also used to produce manufactures. This good uses two additional inputs, capital K and raw material R. The production function is

$$M = \min\{H(L_M, K), R/\alpha\} \qquad (8.2)$$

where H is α constant returns to scale neoclassical production function with the same qualitative properties as (8.1), while α is a constant. Thus capital and labor are substitutable in the production of the 'final' output of M but there is a fixed proportion between the gross output of M and the intermediate input R.

We assume that capital is in perfectly elastic supply at a constant rate of time preference, equal to the rate of interest, ρ. This is consistent with a long-run view of capital accumulation in which the capital stock eventually adjusts to a level at which its marginal product is equal to the rate of interest or time preference. Capital, as in Ramsey and Solow, is of the same 'stuff' as the output of manufactures, and so its marginal product is a pure number per unit time.

Under perfect competition, which we assume throughout, we will have as a result of profit maximization

$$(1-\alpha p)h'(k_M) = \rho \qquad (8.3)$$

where $h(k_M)$ is the production function H in intensive form, k_M is the ratio of K to L_M and p is the relative price of the raw material in terms of manufactures. The left-hand side of (8.3) is the 'net' marginal product of capital.

Profit maximization under perfect competition also provides us with

$$(1-\alpha p)\{h(k_M) - h'(k_M)k_M\} = w \qquad (8.4)$$

and

$$q(\partial F / \partial L_F) = w \qquad (8.5)$$

where w is the real wage in terms of manufactures and q is the relative price of food in terms of manufactures. Together (8.4) and (8.5) imply that the marginal productivity of labor in food, evaluated in terms of the numeraire good manufactures, will be equal to the net marginal product of labor in manufactures.

With food and manufactures as the only goods produced within the system we also have

$$L_F + L_M = \bar{L} \tag{8.6}$$

where $\bar{L}$ is the fixed endowment of labor.

The supply of the raw material R is assumed to be initially in fixed supply, determined exogenously by a monopolistic source of Mediterranean or Baltic supplies such as Venice or the Hanseatic League. This gives us

$$\alpha M = \bar{R} \tag{8.7}$$

which states that the demand αM for the raw material has to be equal to the supply $\bar{R}$.

We assume that the proceeds $p\bar{R}$ of the sale of the raw material to the manufacturing sector are all paid in terms of the output of manufactures and do not constitute income of Europe itself. It would of course be trivial to make part of this income, the 'rent' accruing to the trading body, be earned by Europe. With the option that we have chosen, national income is

$$Y = (1 - \alpha p)M + qF \tag{8.8}$$

the sum of 'value-added' in manufactures and the value of food output.

We now turn to the demand side of the model. Taking preferences as given, we have the budget constraint

$$Y = M_D + qF_D \tag{8.9}$$

and the demand function for food

$$F_D = F_D(Y, q) \tag{8.10}$$

where F_D and M_D are the demands for the two final goods, which are positively related to income and negatively to 'own' relative prices. By Walras' law we close the model by clearing either one of the two markets. We choose

$$F_D = F \tag{8.11}$$

Equations (8.8) to (8.11) enable us to show that M_D would equal $(1-\alpha p)M$, which is therefore not an independent equation.

We thus have 11 equations in the 11 unknowns p, q, w, L_F , L_M, K, Y, F, M, F_D and M_D, giving us a determinate system.

The determination of equilibrium is depicted in Figure 8.1. The positive relationship between L_F and F is simply the concave production function (8.1) for the food sector. The negative relationship between L_F and F_D depends upon the working of the whole model. To establish this we first derive a positive relationship between L_F and q

$$q = q(L_F), \quad q'(L_F) > 0 \tag{8.12}$$

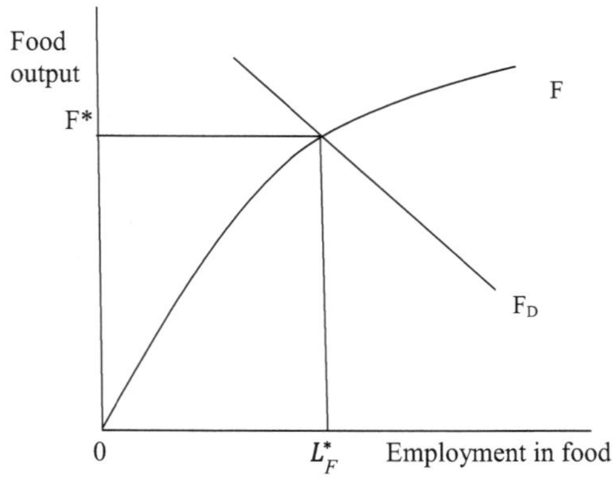

Figure 8.1 The food market

To each value of L_F there corresponds from (8.6), a value of L_M. The fixed amount of $\bar{R}$ determines M by (8.7), and the production function H in (8.2) determines the corresponding value of K for each value of L_M. The ratio k_M of K to L_M is therefore determined and hence the marginal product of capital $h'(k_M)$ as well. From (8.3) this determines the price p of the raw material. Equating the left-hand sides of (8.4) and (8.5) enables us to solve for q since $\partial F / \partial L_F$ also depends only on L_F. Thus we have derived the value of q corresponding to the given value of L_F. Increasing L_F lowers L_M and raises K, so k_M is increased. Raising k_M lowers p by virtue of (8.3). The higher k_M and lower p result in a higher value of w by (8.4). The higher L_F lowers $\partial F / \partial L_F$ and so must raise q by (8.5). This proves that $q'(L_F)$ is positive as required. The negative relationship between q and F_D from the demand function (8.10) finally allows us to obtain the negative relationship between L_F and F_D depicted in Figure 8.1, if income effects are not strong enough to overcome substitution effects, as we will assume here.

The intersection of two functions in Figure 8.1 determines the equilibrium price ratio q^* and labor allocation L_F^* and thus the equilibrium values of all other 9 unknowns as well. Our specification of the closed European economy on the eve of the Discoveries has emphasized the effect of the 'raw material constraint' in determining the limits of its potential. Capital is in perfect elastic supply at a fixed interest rate and so is not a limiting factor while technological improvements in industry cannot achieve much in the face of the bottleneck in raw materials. Easing the raw material constraint by an increase in $\bar{R}$, however, would raise the output of M directly by virtue of (8.7). For any given value of L_F the output of F will of course remain constant, i.e. the positive concave function in Figure 8.1 will be unchanged. Since a given L_F implies the same L_M and M has increased because of the rise in $\bar{R}$, it follows that K must increase and therefore k_M as well. From (8.3) this means that p must fall since $h'(k_M)$ declines with a rise in k_M. At constant q it follows from (8.8) that Y must increase since p falls, M rises and F remains constant. Thus, from the demand function (8.10), the negative relation between L_F and F_D in Figure 8.1 must be shifted upwards for each value of L_F. The new equilibrium must therefore result in higher values of L_F and F. This implies that L_M falls so that K and k_M rise even more than at constant q, and the fall in p is also greater. The fall in p and the rise in k_M imply a higher w in (8.4), which together with the higher L_F implies a rise in q by (8.5).

Thus the easing of the raw material constraint results in increases in the outputs of both final goods and in the capital intensity of production in manufactures, as well as a rise in the relative price of food. With limits on production set by the fixed supply of land and the scarcity of raw materials, production increase in Europe was also limited by the prospect of diminishing returns and declining per capita incomes. The 'animal spirits' of entrepreneurs and the flow of inventions would also be constricted in this closed world, as witnessed by the failure of the Eastern societies to develop in sustained fashion despite promising beginnings.

It is time therefore, following Winston Churchill, to 'call in the New World to redress the balance of the Old'.

The Role of the New World

Our conception of America or the New World as a 'Great Frontier' is that it is initially a vast wilderness from which an economic resource, land, denoted T_A, can be obtained only at an increasing marginal cost in terms of capital. We postulate that

$$K_A = \phi(T_A) \tag{8.13}$$

with

$$\phi' > 0,\ \phi'' > 0,\ \phi(0) = 0$$

In other words, the more the frontier is extended, the higher the marginal cost of an additional hectare. Once the land is cleared it can be used to produce either food F or the raw material R, in conjunction with labor. The production functions for these two goods will be of the usual neoclassical type, with constant returns to scale. The only source of labor in the whole system is the original European stock. The production system for America is therefore summarized by (8.13) and the following four equations

$$F_A = F_A\left(L_A^F, T_A^F\right) \tag{8.14}$$

$$R_A = R_A\left(L_A^R, T_A^R\right) \tag{8.15}$$

$$T_A^F + T_A^R = T_A \tag{8.16}$$

$$\left(L_A^F + L_A^R\right) = L_A = \bar{L} - \left(L_E^F + L_E^M\right) \tag{8.17}$$

where L_E^F and L_E^M indicate European employment in food and manufacturing as described in the previous section. 'Capital' is thus used either to produce manufactures in Europe, according to the production function (8.2), or to clear land in America, as in (8.13). Equation (8.17) for the world economy now replaces Equation (8.6) for Europe in isolation as the constraint on labor. It would of course be trivial to incorporate 'native' American labor into the system but we prefer to emphasize the role of immigration from Europe in the starkest possible manner.

We will also assume that food is land-intensive at any factor price ratio in America, i.e.

$$T_A^F / L_A^F > T_A^R / L_A^R \tag{8.18}$$

for all possible ratios of land rentals to real wages. America therefore has a Heckscher-Ohlin-Samuelson production structure except for the fact that both the endowments of land and labor are endogenous. There is perfect capital and labor mobility in the world economy so that the rate of interest ρ will prevail both in European industry and in clearing land in America, while the real wage will also be equalized on both sides of the Atlantic as well as between sectors in each region.

If we define π as the relative price of food in terms of the raw material, the Stolper-Samuelson theorem immediately determines for us the real wage and rent per hectare in terms of either of those commodities, with the rent per hectare an increasing, and the real wage a decreasing, function of π. In what follows we will vary π as a parameter and then obtain the general equilibrium of the whole system by clearing the world market for food.

Since we have

$$w_F = w_F(\pi),\ w_F'(\pi) < 0 \tag{8.19}$$

from the Stolper-Samuelson theorem, where w_F is the real wage in terms of food in America, we also obtain

$$\partial F_E / \partial L_E^F = w_F(\pi) \tag{8.20}$$

i.e. the marginal product of labor in European production of food must be equal to this same real wage by the hypothesis of perfect international labor mobility. This determines L_E^F and F_E, employment and output in the European food sector, as increasing functions of π.

The Stolper-Samuelson theorem also gives us $w_R(\pi)$, the real wage in terms of the raw material. The real wage in terms of manufactures, w, is equal to $pw_R(\pi)$ where p, as in the previous section, is the price of raw material in terms of manufactures.

Replacing w with $pw_R(\pi)$ in (8.4), Equations (8.3) and (8.4) give us two equations in two unknowns p and k_M for any given value of π and hence $w_R(\pi)$. In Figure 8.2 the negatively sloped curve is the relation between p and k_M given by (8.3) while the positively sloped curve is the relationship between these variables in (8.4), for a given value of π. The intersection of the two curves gives us p and k_M corresponding to the given value of π.

The Stolper-Samuelson theorem also gives us the rental per unit of land in terms of the raw material as a function of π, which will be denoted $g_R(\pi)$. Since we have just determined p as a function of π we have also determined the rental per unit of land in terms of manufactures as a function of π, which we will denote as $r(\pi)$.

The hypothesis of perfect international capital mobility requires

$$\rho = r(\pi) / \phi'(T_A) = pg_R(\pi) / \phi'(T_A) \tag{8.21}$$

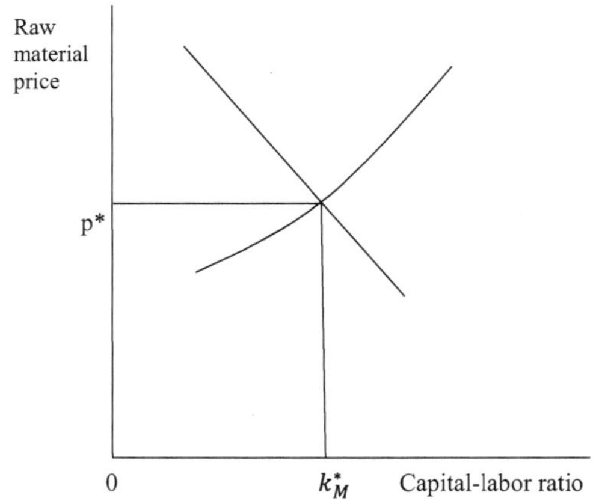

Figure 8.2 Determination of the raw material price and the capital-labor ratio

Thus, to each value of π, there is a unique value of T_A that makes $\phi'(T_A)$ satisfy (8.21).

What remains is to determine employment in manufactures, as well as the capital engaged in that sector, along with the labor force migrating to America and the distribution of employment between the two sectors there and the corresponding output levels.

Suppose all the labor not employed in European agriculture $\left(\bar{L}-L_E^F\right)$ were to be engaged in manufactures. Since $k_M(\pi)$ is known we know what K_E^M, the total stock of capital in manufactures, will be and also the level of output M and the demand for the raw material αM less the original exogenous supply $\bar{R}$. This gives the excess demand for raw material which can only be supplied from America. In the absence of any labor force in the New World, however, this excess demand could not be satisfied since production in America would be zero. Sufficient European labor must therefore migrate to reduce demand for the raw material from European industry and increase its supply from production in America until demand is equal to supply in this market. The necessary equilibrium condition is

$$R_A\left\{\pi, T_A(\pi), L_A\right\}=\alpha h\left[k_M(\pi)\right]\left\{\bar{L}-L_E^F(\pi)-L_A\right\}-\bar{R} \qquad (8.22)$$

It can be seen that this equation depends only on L_A, for any given value of π. The right-hand side of (8.22) gives us the excess demand for R in Europe which is a decreasing function of L_A since the larger is L_A, the smaller is employment in manufactures and hence output, since productivity per worker is determined by the given value of π.

Labor that emigrates to America can produce either food or the raw material. For 'small' amounts of L_A America will be completely specialized in food. Once L_A attains a critical minimum, however, further increase in L_A will raise the output of the raw material and reduce the output of food, by the Rybczynski theorem since the former is more labor-intensive. Given π there is therefore some value of L_A that equates the two sides of (8.22). This value of L_A also determines the output of food in America and the allocation of land and labor in America between food and the raw material.

The given value of π has therefore determined the supply of food in America as well as in Europe. In other words we have a point on the 'world supply curve' for food. We now have to examine how the supply of food in Europe and America will respond to an increase in π.

Since food is land-intensive, an increase in π must result in a fall in the real wage in terms of food in America, by the Stolper-Samuelson theorem, and hence in Europe also by the hypothesis of perfect international labor mobility. Thus employment in European agriculture must rise and hence the food supply F_E as well.

We now examine the effect of the increase in π on Equations (8.3) and (8.4) which we solved to obtain k_M and p corresponding to the given value of π. Equation (8.3) is independent of π so the negatively sloped curve in Figure 8.2 remains unchanged. The rise in π, however reduces w_R in (8.4) because $w_R'(\pi) < 0$ by the Stolper-Samuelson theorem. This reduces the right-hand side of (8.4) for any given value of p and so k_M must fall for (8.4) to continue to hold, i.e. the real wage in terms of manufactures must fall in the same proportion as w_R if p is held constant. Thus the positively sloped curve in Figure 8.2 shifts to the left and so p rises and k_M falls in response to the rise in π.

The rise in π must increase g_R, the rental per unit of land in terms of raw material in America, by the Stolper-Samuelson theorem since food is land-intensive. Because p also rises as a result of the increase in π it follows that $r(\pi)$ must also rise. Thus from (8.21) it follows that T_A must increase to make $\phi'(T_A)$ rise in proportion to $r(\pi)$ to make the ratio continue to equal p, because $\phi''(T_A)$ is positive. This gives us the crucial result that the extent of the frontier in the New World is an increasing function of the relative price of food, the land-intensive good.

Our next task is to determine the effect of the increase in π on the extent of migration to America and hence on the output levels of food and raw material in America and the corresponding output of manufactures in Europe. To consider these questions, suppose initially that L_A in (8.22) is constant while π increases. What will be the effect on the excess demand for raw material from America? It is immediately apparent that the left-hand side of (8.22), the supply of R_A, must fall if π rises and L_A is held constant. The rise in π means a fall in the relative price of the raw material and thus a decline in its supply if T_A is held constant along with L_A. But, as we have just seen, $T_A'(\pi)$ is positive so T_A goes up, which by the Rybczynski theorem means that the supply of R_A must fall even further. Thus we have a reduction in the supply of R_A at a constant value of L_A.

Turning now to the right-hand side of (8.22) we see that productivity per worker in manufactures $h(k_M)$ must fall as a result of the rise in π since $k_M(\pi)$ is negative. Since L_E^F also rises as a result of the rise in π it is clear that the right-hand side of (8.22) must also fall. European demand and American supply of the raw material both fall as a result of the rise in π. We distinguish between two cases below corresponding to whether the American supply falls by more or less than the reduction in European demand.

(a) If American supply falls by more than the European demand, migration to America L_A must increase to restore the equilibrium. The increase in L_A will raise R_A, by the Rybczynski theorem, while it will reduce European output of manufactures, and hence European demand for raw material, even further than what was induced by the rise in π at constant L_A. In America the higher T_A and L_A, combined with a higher π and a lower output of R_A, must result in a rise in the supply of food from America F_A.

(b) Suppose, however, that American supply falls by less than the European demand for raw material. Migration to America L_A must therefore fall to restore equilibrium in the market for raw material. By the Rybczynski theorem this must increase F_A even more than by the rise in π with L_A constant.

Thus, in either case (a) or (b), the supply of food from America F_A must rise in response to the rise in π. Since the supply of the raw material R_A also falls in either case it follows that the output of manufactures in Europe must fall in either case in response to the rise in π and the associated rise in p.

We have defined q as the relative price of food in terms of manufactures. It can be seen that

$$q = (P_R / P_M)(P_F / P_R) = p\pi \tag{8.23}$$

and that since p is an increasing function of π it follows that q is also an increasing function of π.

The world economy as a whole can be considered as producing the final goods—food and manufactures—as a function of the relative price q, with the frontier and migration to the New World determined endogenously along with the output of the raw material. World income Y_w is determined for each value of π, and hence of q, as world output of food and raw material plus value-added in manufactures. This is readily seen to be the same thing as the wage-bill of the total labor force $\bar{L}$ plus the income of landowners in America and Europe and the profits of capital in the manufactures sector pK_E^M. The total rent of land in America is equal to the interest on the capital cost of clearing $\phi'(T_A)\,T_A$, evaluated at the margin.

World demand for food can be specified as before as a positive function of world income Y_W and a negative function of the relative price q. The world supply of food has been shown to be an increasing function of π, and hence q. We close the model by clearing the world market for food by the condition

$$F_W^D\left[Y_W, q(\pi)\right] = F_A\left[q(\pi)\right] + F_E\left[q(\pi)\right] \tag{8.24}$$

The value π^* of π that satisfies (8.24) will also, of course, clear the world market for manufactures, the supply of which has been shown to be negatively related to π and hence to q.

The general equilibrium of the entire world economy has therefore been determined.

Exogenous Shocks

The purpose of the present section is to consider the effects of some exogenous shocks on the variables of the system.

An Increase in the Labor Force

We begin with an increase in the total labor force $\bar{L}$ available to the system. In terms of the way in which we obtained the general equilibrium solution in the previous section we observe that to each parametric value of π the associated values of the factor prices, k_M and p will remain unchanged since all the relevant functional relationships are independent of the magnitude of the labor force. It is Equation (8.22) that depends explicitly on $\bar{L}$. Thus if π and L_A are unchanged the left-hand side of (8.22) will remain unchanged. On the right-hand side, however, k_M and L_F^E remain unchanged because real wages depend only on π but since $\bar{L}$ is increased, employment and output in manufactures will be higher and therefore the demand for raw material from America will also be higher. Therefore L_A has to be increased to increase the supply of the raw material from America and reduce the demand for it in Europe until the two are equal. Thus, at a constant π some of the increment in the labor force will migrate to America while the rest will be engaged on manufactures in Europe. Employment in the food sector in Europe, and hence output, remains unchanged because w_F depends only on π.

In America π and $T_A(\pi)$ are constant but L_A has increased. By the Rybczynski theorem this causes a reduction in the supply of the land-intensive good food in America. Thus at each π and therefore q, since p depends only on π, there is a reduction in the world supply of food, since

European supply is constant while American supply has decreased. World demand for food has, however, increased since real factor prices are constant, the labor force is higher, and the supply of capital engaged in producing manufactures is larger because k_M is unchanged and employment has increased. Thus π must rise to restore equilibrium in the world food market and the system as a whole.

The rise in π will, of course, for reasons already given in the previous section, induce a chain of consequences for the other prices and quantities of the system. First, by the Stolper-Samuelson theorem, there will be a fall in w_F and w_R and a rise in g_R. The fall in w_F will lead to a rise in L_F^E and therefore food output in Europe. The decline in w_R will lead to a rise in p and a fall in k_M. The rise in p and g_R raises the rental on land in America and therefore induces the extension of the frontier and an increase in T_A. The rise in π and p means that q must also rise. The rise in π and the extension of the frontier will both tend to increase the output of food in America.

The increase in population, therefore, despite inducing an extension of the frontier and having the 'safety valve' of emigration to America available, will nevertheless manifest itself in a decline in real wages and labor productivity in both agriculture and industry, where it causes a decline in capital intensity.

For suitable values of the parameters the likely scenario would be for an expansion of output in all four sectors of production, F_E, F_A, R_A and M, and an increase in emigration L_A together with the expansion in T_A. Per capita real income would tend to fall along with real wages on both sides of the Atlantic. The only beneficiaries would be the landowners, à la Ricardo.

An Industrial Revolution in Europe

The main shock that we intend to subject the system to is an 'industrial revolution' in Europe. This is conceived as a Hicks-neutral shift in the production function H for manufactures, with α constant. A parameter λ, initially equal to unity but now increased can now be inserted into all equations involving H or its intensive form h. We now investigate the impact of this shift on the entire system.

As before we hold π constant initially at its original equilibrium value π^*. Consider now Equations (8.3) and (8.4) involving p and k_M, which give the value p^* and k^*M corresponding to π^* before the technical change takes place. Inserting λ as a coefficient in front of $h'(k_M)$ in Equation (8.3) and in front of $\{h(k_M) - h'(k_M)k_M\}$ in Equation (8.4), differentiating totally with respect to λ and holding π^* constant, the reader can verify that both p and k_M must increase in response to the increase in λ. In other words, the Industrial Revolution would raise the capital intensity of production and the relative price of the raw material in terms of manufactures. In terms of Figure 8.2 the downward sloping curve shifts to the right and the upward sloping curve to the left. Since λ is now greater than one and k_M rises, it is clear that output per worker goes up in the industrial sector.

Holding π^* constant implies that w_F is constant also and hence so is employment and output of food in Europe. Turning now to Equation (8.22) we observe that if American endowments T_A^* and L_A^* are held constant along with π^* the output of the raw material in America R_A^* will also be constant whereas the demand for the raw material from Europe will now be increased, since employment in industry is the same as before and productivity per worker has gone up both because of the increase in λ and the induced rise in k_M. The disequilibrium requires L_A to increase, raising R_A and reducing the demand from Europe until Equation (8.22) is satisfied once more, but at a higher value of L_A than the original L_A^*. The increased migration to America raises R_A because that is the labor-intensive good; the output of the land-intensive good food in America must therefore contract at π^* by the Rybczynski effect.

The technical progress in European industry and the associated rise in capital intensity, at a constant value of π, imply an increase in world real income. With homothetic preferences the demand for food at constant relative prices must therefore be higher. As we have shown, however, the supply of food at a constant π is unchanged in Europe and reduced in America. There is consequently a positive world excess demand for food at unchanged relative prices. Equilibrium can only be restored by an increase in π and associated increases in p and q.

From Equation (8.21) we see that the rise in π will raise g_R as well and since p increases also the rental $r(\pi)$ in the numerator goes up. This induces an extension of the frontier T_A to drive up the marginal cost $\phi'(T_A)$ of land clearance appropriately to equate the return to ρ. The rise in π thus not only leads to diverting existing resources to food in America, but induces an extension of the frontier as well. In Europe the rise in π that reduces w_F in America lowers the real wage in European agriculture by the mobility hypothesis and so increases employment and output of food in Europe.

The rise in migration in America that we noted at constant π cannot be reversed even after the full general equilibrium adjustments to π and T_A have been made. This is because the increase in world real income and the fall in the relative price of manufactures implied by the rise in q associated with the rise in π mean that consumption of manufactures must be higher. This means that R_A must be higher. Since π and T_A are both higher, and each has a negative impact on R_A, this implies that L_A must be higher than before for R_A to be higher than originally, because the raw material is the relative labor-intensive good.

The interested reader can work out the effects of other exogenous shocks, such as technical progress in either of the goods produced in America, or in food production in Europe.

The model as it stands confines the production of manufactures to Europe, and thus represents a stage prior to significant industrialization getting under way in America. If America has the identical technology for manufactures available, however, production of this commodity could take place indifferently on either side of the Atlantic, since capital and labor are both 'foot loose' in this model.[4] A historically reasonable hypothesis would be that America is initially less efficient, and that tariffs are necessary to launch industrialization, as was in fact the case. Protection of European agriculture is another problem that could be studied within the present framework.

We hope therefore to have marked the fifth centennial of the voyage of the 'Admiral of the Ocean Sea' by this modest memorial—a small-scale general equilibrium model that attempts to capture the 'stylized facts' of the new Atlantic world that it brought into being.

[4] I am indebted to Alwyn Young for making this important point.

References

Bailyn, Bernard. (1988). *The peopling of British North America: An introduction*. New York: Vintage Books.

Caves, Richard E. (1965). Vent for surplus models of trade and growth. In Robert E. Baldwin et al. (Eds.), *Trade, growth and the balance of payments*. Chicago: Rand McNally.

Caves, Richard E. (1971). Export-led growth and the new economic history. In Jagdish N. Bhagwati et al. (Eds.), *Trade, balance of payments and growth*. Amsterdam: North-Holland.

Chambers, Edward J., & Gordon, Donald F. (1966). Primary products and economic growth: An empirical measurement. *Journal of Political Economy, 74*, 315–332.

Di Tella, Guido. (1982). The economics of the frontier. In Charles P. Kindleberger & Guido Di Tella (Eds.), *Economics in the long view: Essays in honour of W. W. Rostow*. London: Macmillan.

Easton, Steven T., & Reed, Clyde G. (1980). The staple model. Mimeo, Simon Fraser University.

Elliott, J. H. (1969). *The old world and the new—1492–1650*. Cambridge: Cambridge University Press.

Findlay, Ronald. (1990). The triangular trade and the Atlantic economy of the 18th century: A simple general equilibrium model. *Essays in International Finance,* no. 117, International Finance Section, Princeton University.

Findlay, Ronald, & Lundahl, Mats. (1994). Natural resources, vent for surplus and the staple theory. In Gerald M. Meier (Ed.), *From classical economics to development economics. Essays in honor of Hla Myint*. Basingstoke: Macmillan.

Jones, Eric L. (1981). *The European miracle*. Cambridge: Cambridge University Press.

Jones, Ronald W. (1971). A three-factor model in theory, trade and history. In Jagdish N. Bhagwati et al. (Eds.), *Trade, balance of payments and growth*. Amsterdam: North-Holland.

Kenen, Peter B. (1965). Nature, capital and trade. *Journal of Political Economy, 73*, 437–460.

Marshall, Alfred. (1938). *Principles of economics* (8th ed.). London: Macmillan.

McNeill, William H. (1983). *The great frontier*. Princeton: Princeton University Press.

Smith, Adam. (1976). *The wealth of nations*. Chicago: University of Chicago Press.

Turner, Frederick Jackson. (1920). *The frontier in American history*. New York: Henry Holt.

Webb, Walter Prescott. (1986). *The great frontier*. Lincoln: University of Nebraska Press.

Williams, J. H. (1929). The theory of international trade reconsidered. *Economic Journal, 39*, 195–209.

Woodruff, William. (1973). The emergence of an international economy 1700–1914. In Carlo M. Cipolla (Ed.), *The Fontana economic history of Europe* (Vol. 4, Part 2). London: Fontana.

9

Natural Resources, 'Vent-for-Surplus' and the Staples Theory

The 'vent-for-surplus' approach to trade and development, which Hla Myint (1958) derived from the writings of Adam Smith, is a celebrated contribution to economics. The objective of this chapter is to unify the 'vent-for-surplus' approach with what Watkins (1963) has called the 'staples' theory of economic growth and with the factor proportions theory of comparative advantage. The basis for the proposed unification will be the concept of an endogenous land frontier.

The formal theory of international trade and specialization has developed majestically on its Ricardian foundations for almost two centuries, and its logic has been impregnable against the perennial critiques of assorted protectionists. As a tool for historical research on trade patterns in the course of economic development, however, both the original Ricardian model and its Heckscher-Ohlin offshoot have not, on the whole, proved very sharp or effective. Although this may have been due to the fact that capital accumulation and technological change have

Revised from 'Natural Resources, "Vent-for-Surplus" and the Staples Theory' by Ronald Findlay and Mats Lundahl, in Gerald M. Meier (ed.) *From Classical Economics to Development Economics*, 1994, Palgrave Macmillan, pp. 68–93. With kind permission of Palgrave Macmillan.

R. Findlay, M. Lundahl, *The Economics of the Frontier*,
DOI 10.1057/978-1-137-60237-4_9

only recently been incorporated into the theory, the fact remains that economic historians and applied economists have not as yet found it very helpful in their own research.

Since an intellectual vacuum, like any other, cries out to be filled, recourse has had to be found somewhere. One popular candidate, for those of a radical persuasion, has been the 'dependency' theory, with its machinations of a hegemonic center against a helpless periphery. Far more successful, in our view, has been the 'staples' theory of the Canadian economic historian, Harold Adams Innis, in his classic series of works on the role of primary exports in the economic development of his native country (Innis 1930, 1940). Innis' work was highly influential within Canada itself and also inspired the important work of Douglass North (1966). The approach was also applied to Australia (McLean 1989).

In 1958, Hla Myint published his now celebrated article on the 'classical theory of international trade and the underdeveloped countries'. By 'classical' Myint definitely meant Adam Smith and *not* David Ricardo. Partly, this implied a difference of style, the historically based 'realism and relevance' of the former as against the strict deductive reasoning from 'unrealistic' premises of the other. Substantively, however, the main difference, as Myint saw it, was that in Ricardo the gain from trade was associated with a reallocation of given and fully employed resources, whereas in Adam Smith trade provided a 'vent' for labor and natural resources that were in 'surplus' before the opening of trade. Thus the expansion of exports did not have to come at the expense of import-competing production and so the gains from trade would be larger than in the case of initial full employment and utilization.

This 'vent-for-surplus' theory was eagerly adopted by several writers on the development of the 'export economies' of Asia, Africa and Latin America. Richard Caves (1965) examined the 'staples' and the 'vent-for-surplus' approaches as alternatives to the standard trade doctrine in relation to the experience of Canada and other 'regions of recent settlement' and the tropical underdeveloped economies. Caves tended to associate the former cases with surplus land and the latter with surplus labor *à la* Lewis (1954) although Myint had taken the view that both land and labor were in surplus in the case of the tropical economies.

The 'staples' approach was first formalized by Chambers and Gordon (1966). In their model the export staple is produced by fixed land specific to that sector and labor, which is also used to produce an importable good, 'gadgets', together with capital specific to that sector, and a non-traded good, 'haircuts'. Caves (1971) gave an extended critique, extension and application of this model in relation to the wheat boom of the first decade of this century in Canada. Interestingly, 1971 was the same year that Ronald Jones (1971) and Paul Samuelson (1971) both published their now classic papers on the 'specific factors' or Ricardo-Viner model of international trade. As just noted, the essential features of this model were all contained explicitly in Chambers and Gordon, though not developed as fully and elegantly as by Jones and Samuelson. The relationships between these papers and other works on international trade and factor mobility are very thoroughly explored in an inexplicably unpublished paper by Easton and Reed (1980).

The simplest way in which natural resources have been introduced into international trade is the so-called 'availability' theory of Irving Kravis (1956) where it is reduced to a matter of geography. The answer given to the question: 'Why does Kuwait export oil?' is the same as the mountaineer Mallory gave to the question of why he wanted to climb Everest: 'Because it is there.' This, of course, begs the question of the opportunity cost of complementary, non-specific inputs needed to get the oil out of the ground, as is pointed out in Findlay (1970, pp. 76–81), so that there is really no escape from the necessity of the logic of comparative cost.

Myint (1958), however, also wanted to escape from the confines of Ricardian comparative cost by postulating the existence, presumably in equilibrium, of 'surplus' resources, both land and labor. One or the other can of course be accommodated, with the other as the binding constraint, but how can we account for both? Findlay (1970, pp. 70–76) attempts to provide a possible explanation in terms of an endogenous supply of labor, with the initial price of manufactures (produced by a primitive handicraft sector) so high that it restricts the supply of labor, which expands once cheaper manufactures become available through imports, thus initially permitting food exports to expand without any contraction in handicrafts. Over time, however, the latter would be slowly wiped out by competition with cheaper imports.

We now believe, however, that a far more powerful and historically relevant interpretation of the 'vent-for-surplus' approach is in terms of the concept of an endogenous land 'frontier'. Originally introduced in the famous work of the American historian Frederick Jackson Turner (1921), this concept has been used extensively by historians and geographers for a wide variety of times and places but has been neglected by economists. An exception is a highly suggestive paper by Guido di Tella (1982) on the role of natural resources in the development of Argentina, which has been formally developed into a general equilibrium model of the links through trade and factor mobility of a previously settled 'Europe' and an effectively empty 'America' by Findlay (1993).

In the present chapter we will apply a restricted 'small open economy' version of this model to the experience of the export economies of different types. Before we do that, however, we will briefly survey the historical record with respect to some selected cases that are illustrative of the general trends and patterns that were observed.

Case Studies

This section examines some brief case studies of export-oriented growth, concentrating on the period 1870–1914, which was the 'golden age' of the creation of the modern world economy. It will be useful to classify our cases into three groups. First, we have the so-called 'regions of recent settlement'. These are what originally were almost 'empty' lands in the temperate zones of the Americas and Australia, which attracted substantial inflows of capital and labor from Europe to produce and export primary commodities in great abundance in return for manufactured imports. Here we look at the experience of Canada, the United States, Argentina and Australia. Next we will consider a pair of what we might call 'plantation economies'. These are tropical countries in which cash crops were introduced into what were previously mostly subsistence economies by foreign capitalists and entrepreneurs who employed imported as well as indigenous labor on large estates. Our cases will be Malaya in Southeast Asia and Costa Rica in Central America. The third category will be 'peasant export economies', cases where native peasants themselves turned from subsistence to export production of tropical commodities. Our examples here will be the Gold Coast (now Ghana) and Burma.

Regions of Recent Settlement

The studies of Innis and others have told the story of Canadian development in terms of successive discoveries and exploitation of natural resources, such as furs in connection with the Hudson Bay Company, the cod fisheries of Newfoundland and the moving frontier for wheat cultivation on the prairies, all against a background of growing world demand and rising prices for these products. This expansion induced very substantial inflows of capital and labor, particularly around the turn of the century and over the following two decades. Manufacturing production also increased, though not without tariff protection. Linkage effects from the primary export sector to the rest of the economy were substantial, particularly because of the transportation networks required to bind the vast country together. Caves and Holton (1959) give a very detailed analysis of the development of the Canadian economy, explicitly within the framework of the 'staples' theory. It is also interesting to note that Meier (1953) rightly amended the classic analysis of Viner (1924) of capital inflows into Canada to take into account the growth of primary exports and associated linkage, as emphasized in the 'staples' theory.

Given the similarities in the resource base of the Canadian and United States economies, it comes as no surprise that the 'staples' approach illuminates the pattern of United States growth as well. The approach was first applied extensively by North (1966) who emphasized that international demand for export products had been the 'prime mover' of economic development in the United States since early colonial times. In particular, North applies the 'staples' approach to the case of cotton and the *ante-bellum* South. Not only did cotton lead to a spectacular development of the southern 'plantation economy' itself but it also generated strong linkage effects to other regions of the country. The Northeast supplied the South with finance, transportation, insurance and marketing facilities, and most importantly, manufactures. Simultaneously the West was developed to supply the South, highly specialized on cotton, with its grain requirements. Westward migration was induced and the transportation network, first canals and then railroads, had to be provided for the South to be adequately supplied. According to North it was this interlinked process of staple-based growth, involving the inflow of people and capital to extend the agricultural frontier, that generated the prosperity of the United States in the *ante-bellum* period.

The post-Civil War period can, of course, also be described within the framework of the 'staples' theory. The frontier continued to be extended westwards, but now it was wheat, livestock, and minerals that were the staples around which development was generated, along with a surge of industrialization in the East to supply a return flow of manufactures to the western regions. Massive inflows of capital and population from Europe also took place, particularly from about 1890 to 1920.

A particularly interesting case of staple exports was Argentina in the late nineteenth century and up to the Depression in 1929 (Díaz-Alejandro 1984; Cortés Conde 1985). Argentina was a relatively 'empty' country in the mid-nineteenth century. However, the expansion of foreign trade during the latter half of that century provided strong incentives for economic expansion and rising per capita income. A number of staples contributed to this expansion: wool, hides and salted meat in the 1870s, wheat (a leading product in the 1890s), corn and linseed around the turn of the century, and frozen meat a decade later. On the eve of the Depression, staples-led growth had raised real GDP per capita to over two and a half times the corresponding figure in 1880. During this period the land 'frontier' had expanded continuously, though not at zero cost, and in the process the best pampa land had been concentrated in the hands of a powerful landowner class that was to constitute the most important political group during the pre-1929 period. This expansion was complemented by massive immigration from southern Europe, fueled by the interest of the landowners in peopling the 'wilderness' and bringing it to economic use. The step from cattle-raising for hide production to sheep-raising, agriculture and beef production represented a substantial increase in the man-land ratio—one which could not be achieved with the aid of only the domestic population. Also, the country could count on a substantial inflow of capital from Europe, notably Britain, and later also from the United States, which brought foreign investment to a level almost comparable to that prevailing in Canada.

For the growth locomotive to function, a number of linkages had to be established. As it appears, export prices were falling in the 1880s but the fall in transport costs that took place with the construction of the railroad network increased the profitability of staples production even in the face of falling product prices, mainly by opening the road to the fertile lands of the interior. In this process capital raised abroad played a crucial role. Not until the turn of the century was a strong impulse received from overseas demand.

The development of the transport network was instrumental in extending the domestic market as well. The rising incomes were distributed across the national territory and this gave rise to increased domestic trade in consumer goods. Many of the items could be manufactured domestically with the result that demand, or consumption, linkages were quickly established. The share of such items as staple foods and textiles in total imports fell significantly from the 1880s or 1890s until World War I, because local producers were able to take over. Backward and forward linkages were also established. Refrigerated ships, meat packing, marketing and so on, with the aid of foreign technology, machinery and equipment were all necessary, and forward linkages to the processing of agricultural and livestock products developed (Díaz-Alejandro 1970). Still Argentina remained a primary exporter. The reasons for this are easily discernible (Ferns 1969, p. 125):

> In 1896 the terms of trade began to alter in a way favourable to producers of food products, and these terms of trade became progressively and even fantastically favourable to Argentina until 1929, except for a period after World War I in 1920–24. The production of foodstuffs, linseed, and wool was very profitable. Capital naturally flowed into these activities, and commercial and industrial activities were nourished by the agricultural sector. It was so patently economically advantageous to do what Argentina in fact did that it seems a waste of time and a profitless exercise to look for any other explanation of what happened. Argentina became a highly specialized producer because it was profitable to do so, and those who profited most had no motive to seek alternative policies.

The entire Argentine economy revolved around the staple exports, including the infrastructure, notably the transport network. However, in the middle of the *belle époque,* it was seen only as a matter of time before a more balanced structure would prevail in the economy (Ferns 1969, p. 125):

> Looking at the evidence of the 1890s and taking account of the profitability of agriculture and ranching compared with industrial activity at that time, there was no reason to suppose that industry would not develop as it did in Canada or Australia or other states producing primary products.

Unfortunately, things did not turn out this way. The Depression was to mark the end of export-induced prosperity in Argentina. Internationally, the political mood had turned increasingly in favor of protectionism during the 1920s, and in the 1930s Argentine exports were to be hit severely by the efforts of the industrialized countries to protect their own primary producers. As a result of this (and the generally negative effects of the Depression on exports), Argentina decided to follow suit. A period of import substitution that aimed at fostering the growth of the domestic manufacturing sector followed.

Another case of staples-induced expansion combined with an extension of the open range and vast inflows of labor and capital is that of Australia from the 1830s to the 1890s (McLean 1989; also Lougheed 1968). As with Argentina, the expansion of the international economy over this period contributed many of the forces that propelled Australia on a path of rapid growth. From 1860 to 1890 the country experienced a real GDP growth of close to 5 percent per annum.

Again, the expansion process rested on increased employment of land, labor and capital—to a far greater extent than on technological change, which was to assume major importance only later. To what extent favorable price movements were responsible for the expansion process is uncertain. No reliable figures are available for the pre-1870 period, but it nevertheless appears likely that Australia's terms of trade improved from around 1850 to 1870, since world commodity prices rose. However, the 1870s displayed no clear trend and a decline set in from around 1880.

At any rate, the discoveries of gold that began in the 1850s brought a tremendous boom in mineral exploitation, one which was to repeat itself after 1890 (Maddock and McLean 1984, pp. 1047–67). The demand for wool was also high enough to make the land frontier expand, even though sheep ranchers had problems obtaining clear title to their lands during much of the period—opposed as they were by the miners. Wool accounted for no less than 54 percent of Australia's total exports in the 1880s (Díaz-Alejandro 1984, p. 334).

Exports may not have led growth during the entire period. The ratio of exports to GDP declined from 1861 to 1890. However, this may be a bit beside the point. The ratio probably rose during the gold rush days, and even a declining ratio may be compatible with the staples approach (McLean 1989, p. 27):

> All that is required is that activity in the non-export industries expands along with the export expansion and the export ratio (usually measured with annual data) will remain unchanged. In a historical inquiry, the role of exports in growth is more appropriately viewed in a dynamic and general equilibrium context.

The extension of mining and of the land frontier in Australia could not take place without complementary production factors. Again, immigration and capital inflow provided the solution. During the three decades following 1860, the share of immigration in the total population increase and that of foreign capital inflow in total capital formation both exceeded one-third on average (McLean 1989, p. 16).

Plantation Economies

The rubber plant was introduced in Malaya in the late 1870s, during a period of rising European demand and increasing prices, and towards the end of the century large-scale planting was begun. The first exports took place in 1906 and, in just a few years, Malaya became the leading rubber exporter in the world. The period between 1906 and the beginning of the 1920s represented 'a period of expansion with few comparisons in the history of tropical agriculture ...' (Gunnarsson 1979, p. 69).

In this development, the estate sector (holdings of more than 100 acres) took the lead. Coffee plantations already existed in Malaya before the arrival of rubber in the country and when relative prices turned in favor of rubber, after 1896, a switch took place towards the latter crop. The organization of production was similar for the two crops and this facilitated the process. The planters were also given support by the colonial government: loans, land leases at low rents, and assistance with labor immigration. The plantation sector expanded on virgin lands with the aid of European capital and mainly Indian (Tamil) labor (and to a lesser extent Chinese, Malays and Javanese). The necessary political stability was obtained in the 1890s as the British gained control over the Malacca peninsula and exports were greatly facilitated by the transportation network that had been developed when tin production expanded before the turn of the century.

The initial reluctance shown by the European capital markets to invest in Malaya was gradually overcome as prices and dividends increased after 1900. As British merchant firms moved in, a link was created between the London capital market and the planters. This flow of capital was later supplemented by plowback of profits, and it is possible that the latter source was more important than the former during the great expansion period.

Plantation production of rubber required a large labor force and this demand could not be met locally. Beginning in 1907 the colonial government moved to facilitate the immigration of Tamil workers from India. They were cheaper than the Chinese, had a reputation of being excellent workers and easy to handle, and the fact that the migration took place between two British colonies greatly facilitated the process, in particular since it also allowed for a reduction of the labor force in times of stagnation.

With time, the leading 'plantation' segment had to face competition from a 'smallholder' (less than 100 acres) sector. Between 1910 and the outbreak of World War II, the smallholder acreage and output grew at a rate very few people had thought possible. As a matter of fact the expansion was, with very few exceptions, unique in the history of tropical agriculture during the colonial era (Gunnarsson 1979, p. 21). Most of this expansion took place in the 1910s.

The mechanisms behind the growth of the smallholder sector differed considerably from those that fueled plantation expansion. The smallholders hardly received any government support. Rather, smallholder expansion was discouraged by a colonial government intent on fostering 'commercial' agriculture. Also, the sector had no direct access to the European capital markets. In spite of these handicaps, the smallholder sector turned out to be a competitor that very strongly threatened the profitability of the plantation sector.

The expansion of smallholder rubber production took place in a 'vent-for-surplus' situation. The new crop could easily be fitted into the existing agricultural system without detrimental effects on food production. There was plenty of unused suitable land that could be cultivated with the aid of a domestic labor force which had hitherto preferred leisure. Alternatively, cultivation was undertaken by immigrant Chinese who were better connected with the commercially oriented economy than the Malays and who could hardly be classified as 'peasants'. Thus both domestic and foreign migration was involved.

Capital played a subordinate role. The exceedingly simple methods employed only required some initial investment plus credit to carry the farmers over the dead season. The latter was supplied by the European merchant firms, and it is possible to argue that even in this case there probably was an element of capital inflow from abroad. After 1910 seeds were freely available and could be gathered by any prospective grower.

The smallholder expansion was highly successful, so much so that the British authorities saw fit to put into effect a series of restriction schemes during the 1930s' Depression years when rubber prices dropped, which favored the plantations over the smaller holdings.

Our next case, Costa Rica, represents a mixture between small-farm and plantation export production (Cardoso 1977; Bulmer-Thomas 1987). The first staple product, coffee, began to be exported to Chile in 1832, for processing there and re-exportation to Europe, and, more importantly, to Britain in 1843—long before the coffee expansion in the rest of Central America. In 1890, coffee dominated the export trade completely, accounting for no less than 91 percent of Costa Rica's total export value. During the latter half of the nineteenth century, coffee drinking was becoming *à la mode* in Europe, and the rapidly increasing demand was translated into an increasing price trend, with the result that in Costa Rica, coffee was to rise to a leading position in terms not only of exports but of the entire economic life of the country.

The second staple was bananas. Banana cultivation was established much as a result of forward linkage from the coffee industry, when in 1884 construction was begun on a railway from San José to Puerto Limón on the Atlantic coast to facilitate coffee exports. From this was born the well-known story of how Minor Keith, the future founder of the United Fruit Company, began growing bananas along the railroad tracks to pay for some of the construction costs and how this with time would make Costa Rica the world's leading banana exporter with a world market share of 60 percent in 1929.

When coffee production began, Costa Rica was a sparsely populated country. The population in 1840 was a mere 72,000 and 137,000 in 1870 (Woodward 1985, p. 478). The pressure on the available land was low. Only the Meseta Central had any population density to speak of, but even there a considerable number of *terrenos baldíos* (waste lands) existed. These were owned by the state, and when coffee production began, the procedure for acquiring these lands free of charge was simplified considerably, while public lands (*tierras públicas*) were sold at low price. As a result, the period of Costa Rican history between 1832 and the Great Depression following the crisis of 1929 was strongly marked by a 'moving frontier' of internal colonization associated with the vigorous expansion of coffee cultivation (Cardoso 1977, p. 177). Until the 1880s, coffee growing could be extended in the Meseta Central without encroaching on areas planted with other crops, before the land frontier was closed.

In the banana case, the expansion took place in a completely uninhabited part of the national territory—the swamps and jungles of the Atlantic coast that had no alternative use. After the railway construction in 1884, a 'vent-for-surplus' phase was inaugurated that was to last until the 1920s, when banana production too could go on expanding only at the expense of other crops (Bulmer-Thomas 1987, p. 38).

Coffee producers faced a serious labor shortage problem. In relation to the needs of the expanding staple the Meseta population remained scant, and there was no large-scale immigration (Cardoso 1977, p. 179). Only land, not labor, was in abundance in the central highlands. Coffee could expand only at increasing wages as the Meseta Central population moved outwards when the coffee *fincas* did.

The banana case was different. The unhealthy conditions prevailing on the Atlantic jungle coast made the population in the Meseta reluctant to move there. The only solution possible consisted of bringing in black laborers from the West Indies at wages that were comparatively high in the Costa Rican context, while prohibiting the new immigrants by law from moving to the interior.

The early period of coffee production was financed out of capital that had been accumulated during the colonial era and the first years of independence from the cultivation of cocoa and tobacco and from exports of *palo brasil*. Because processing techniques were simple at the time and land cheap (or free), little capital was needed. However, as more sophisticated processing procedures were substituted for the original primitive ones, the demand for finance grew. From the 1840s a pattern was established whereby commercial houses in Britain made advances to Costa Rican exporters against future delivery and the exporters extended credit to the growers.

The banana venture differed from that of coffee insofar as it was dependent on external finance from the outset. Large investments were required to transform the jungle and swamp areas into areas suitable for humans, and housing, schooling and health care added to the sums required. With time, the banana industry became firmly concentrated and vertically integrated in the powerful American-owned United Fruit Company.

The export-led growth of the Costa Rican economy involved the creation of a number of linkages. The most obvious is in processing, which made Costa Rican coffee a high-quality one fetching a comparatively high price in the international market. Transport was another area, with coffee first being exported via the Pacific coast and then, with the inauguration of the Atlantic Railway in 1890, being easily exported from the Atlantic side of Costa Rica. This venture also constituted a forward linkage to banana production. Coffee exports resulted in the creation of banking facilities in the mid-nineteenth century whereas in the case of bananas, dominated by an American company, the demand for banking facilities lay in the United States, not in Costa Rica.

Beyond activities directly connected with the two staples, however, few production linkages were created. The coffee interests did not diversify because the relative price structure did not favor such investment, social infrastructure was lacking, and so was energy. Banks catered almost exclusively to the export sector. The banana sector was in foreign hands that concentrated on the vertical integration of the banana trade itself and furthermore employed mainly import-intensive inputs. As a result, 'developments in manufacturing activity in general in the 1920s were minimal' (Bulmer-Thomas 1987, p. 40).

Moreover, coffee production resulted in delinkage once the land frontier in the highlands had been closed. Food shortages emerged a number of times during the nineteenth century, and competition between export agriculture and domestic use agriculture was gradually intensified as the banana industry was also running out of empty lands.

The demand structure generated out of coffee and banana production was concentrated on imports. This was definitely the case with the American-owned banana industry, but the same was true for coffee, despite the dominance of smallholder family farms in the sector, since there was considerable concentration at the later stages of the commercialization and processing process.

Finally, the Costa Rican government failed to diversify the economy via the tax system. The taxes applied to the export sector were not elastic with respect to the value of production and the domestic market was believed to be too small to sustain any industry (Bulmer-Thomas 1988, pp. 46–47).

Dependence on two main export products lasted a long time in Costa Rica, until the late 1950s, and this dependence made for vulnerability. The failure to diversify the economy meant that when the Great Depression hit in 1929, the subsequent adjustment had to take place directly through a fall in real income and employment in the export sector. Nonetheless, the concentration on the primary sector continued during the next three decades.

Peasant Exporters

Our first example of a staple-exporting peasant economy is the Gold Coast (later Ghana), which became the world's leading exporter of cocoa in 1910 after a brief but remarkably rapid expansion over only two decades. Ghana continued to be the world's leading producer until she lost that position in the late 1970s, mainly as a result of the misconceived monopsonistic policies of its marketing board.

Cocoa is not indigenous to Africa but was introduced there from the New World by the Portuguese. Stimulated by the growing world demand for chocolate in the late nineteenth century, production of this crop was taken up by the Akwapim people of the Gold Coast around 1890. Seeds and the elementary planting techniques were provided by the colonial Department of Agriculture but all subsequent development was a strictly African affair. The Akwapim, who originally inhabited a very infertile hilly region, had displayed remarkable drive and adaptability in their economic pursuits, which ranged from working as porters for the British army during the Ashanti wars to the cultivation of oil palms. When prices for palm oil dropped sharply in the 1880s they took up the cultivation of cocoa on virgin forest lands that they acquired from another tribe. The dramatic story of these developments is well told by Polly Hill (1963). Exports rose from just over 500 tons in 1900 to 5,000 tons by 1904 to over 50,000 tons in 1913, by which time the Gold Coast had become the world's leading producer with over half of the value of its exports accounted for by this commodity (Holmes 1970).

Szereszewski (1965) makes the very Myint-like argument that cocoa cultivation was simply added, by 'interseeding' with food crops, and so there was no switching of activities involved as in the comparative cost doctrine. However, this needs to be modified to take account of the migration of farmers to areas that were better suited for cocoa. Capital requirements were initially modest and provided by the farmers themselves, but once the export trade was well established, European trading houses began to finance the farmers over the harvest cycle. Linkage effects to other sectors, apart from the transportation involved in getting the crop to market, were modest.

Equally remarkable is the story of the rapid expansion of rice exports from the Irrawaddy delta region of lower Burma in the second half of the nineteenth century. The essentials were told in the classic study by J.S. Furnivall (1957) but more recent work by Aye Hlaing (1964) and especially Michael Adas (1974) has rounded out the picture significantly.

In 1852, when the area was occupied by the British after the Second Anglo-Burmese War, it was sparsely populated despite its potential fertility, the Burmese population being concentrated in its original heartland in central Burma, still under the rule of the Burmese dynasty. Production and trade were restricted by the deliberately autarkic and restrictive policy of the dynasty. British rule opened the region to the forces of the expanding world economy, particularly after the Suez Canal was constructed in 1869, which brought European markets for rice as well as cheap imports of manufactures. A stable political and administrative framework was created, along with infrastructure such as roads, railways and canals to supplement the already abundant rivers and creeks.

With these incentives Burmese cultivators rapidly migrated into the region from central and upper Burma in large numbers, supplemented by a substantial inflow of Indian temporary migrant workers to work in the rice mills and docks that processed and shipped the rice to world markets. The steam-powered rice mills were mostly established by European trading houses. There are no estimates of how much capital was brought in, and it is likely that high initial profits from rice milling and exports were the main source of further investment.

The area under rice cultivation rose from a million acres in 1852 to 6 million by the turn of the century and 8 million by 1915, with rice exports having risen from nothing to over 2 million tons by the first decades of the twentieth century when Burma was the leading rice exporter in the world. Substantial exports of teak and minerals, such as petroleum, were additional contributions of the primary sector to the development of the country.

Linkages, however, were largely confined to the milling of rice and the sawing of logs. Manufactured imports, particularly cotton piece goods and household items, displaced local handicrafts. Socially the system created what Furnivall termed a 'plural society' in which the Burmese were the rural labor force that produced the rice, on credit extended over the years by Indian moneylenders, while other Indians processed the paddy in the European-owned rice mills and loaded it on to ships at the main ports, and the British were the administrators and managers of the firms that handled most of the commerce, transport, banking and insurance.

Hlaing (1964, p. 51) estimates that GDP grew between 1901 and 1931, the onset of the Great Depression, at 1.9 percent per annum while population grew by 1.1 percent per annum, so that there was a rate of per capita growth that was quite respectable for that time. Since then the Depression, World War II, and decades of mismanagement by the military rulers of Burma have ruined the prosperity of what was once the world's leading rice exporter.

The Land Frontier

Despite their considerable differences, all three types of export economy that we examined in the previous section display a remarkable uniformity in the character and pattern of their development. In every case the stimulus to development comes from rising prices and expanding markets in the world economy that leads to an extension of the land frontier internally, accompanied by substantial inflows of foreign capital and labor immigration, either from outside the country or another region within the same political borders. The frontier might be on the prairies of North America, the pampas of Argentina or the outback of Australia, in the case of the regions of recent settlement, or on the malarial swamps and jungles in the tropical lands of the plantation and peasant export economies. But in every case it was extended substantially at a significant cost in terms of the resources required to clear the land and provide the necessary physical, social and administrative infrastructure. The new activities associated with the production of the primary export products generated additional demands for capital and labor that were met partly from foreign sources in every case, so that international and interregional factor mobility is always an integral part of the story.

Thus, at least as far as the 'opening up' process in the creation of the modern world economy is concerned, the geographical differences between temperate and tropical zones, the ethnic differences between

European settlers on the one hand and Asian and African peasants and workers on the other, all do not seem to matter. The 'stylized facts' in every case conform remarkably to a simple model that we hope will capture the underlying structural pattern in all these instances, and thereby serve to integrate the vision of both the 'vent-for surplus' and the 'staples' theories.

Although the model we construct is sufficiently flexible to cover all three cases in essentials, it is nevertheless important to respect the differences among them. Accordingly we will present the basic model in two alternative forms. The first, or 'basic' model, intended to apply to the regions of recent settlement, is closer to the 'staples' theory. The second, or 'modified' model, intended to apply to the plantation and peasant economies of the tropics, is closer to the 'vent-for-surplus' theory. The common feature of both, however, will be an endogenous land frontier, which serves to unify the two theories.

The Basic Model

The core of our formalization of these two theories is the so-called Ricardo-Viner 'specific factors' model, which was itself influenced by earlier work on the staples approach, in the case of Ronald Jones (1971).

The basic technology consists of the constant returns to scale production functions for Primary Products, designated A, and Manufactures, designated M, which are

$$A = A(N, L_A) \tag{9.1}$$

$$M = M(K_M, L_M) \tag{9.2}$$

where N is the specific natural resource input or 'land' into A, and K_M is the input of 'capital' specific to M. The total labor force is given and we have

$$L_A + L_M = \bar{L} \tag{9.3}$$

We shall now, however, depart from the Jones formulation in two crucial respects. First, we do not take K_M as exogenously given. Instead we regard it as in perfectly elastic supply in the long run, at an interest rate $\bar{\rho}$ determined by domestic time preference. As in Solow (1956) we can think of the flow output of M as capable of being either consumed or invested, so that K_M consists of an accumulated stock of M. The marginal productivity of M with respect to K_M is therefore a pure number per unit time.

The other crucial difference with the Ricardo-Viner model is that we regard the natural resource input N as determined by an endogenous 'frontier' as in Findlay (1993) instead of being simply given. N can be increased by incurring a rising marginal cost in terms of capital so that we have

$$K_A = \phi(N) \tag{9.4}$$

with

$$\phi'(N) > 0, \phi''(N) > 0$$

where $dK_A / dN = \phi'(N)$ is the marginal cost of 'clearing' a unit of land, which is a 'convex' function of the amount of land that is cleared.

It will be convenient to choose M as the *numéraire,* and so p is the relative price of A and w the real wage, both in terms of M.

If we define output per worker and capital per worker in the M sector as m and k respectively, we can then write the production function for M in intensive form as

$$m = m(k) \tag{9.2'}$$

Profit maximization under perfect competition must then result in

$$m'(k) = \bar{\rho} \tag{9.5}$$

The value $\bar{k}$ of k that satisfies (9.5) also determines the equilibrium real wage as

$$\bar{w} = m(\bar{k}) - m'(\bar{k})\bar{k} \tag{9.6}$$

The given value of the rate of interest $\bar{\rho}$ thus determines $\bar{k}$ and hence $\bar{w}$ because of constant returns to scale in the *M* sector.

Writing *a* and *n* for output per worker and 'land' per worker in the *A* sector, perfect competition and free mobility between sectors for labor result in

$$p\left[a - a'(n)n\right] = \bar{w} \tag{9.7}$$

Thus to each value of *p* there corresponds a unique value of *n*, and hence of the marginal productivity of land $a'(n)$ that satisfies (9.7).

The extent of the frontier, and hence the amount of land *N*, is determined by the condition that the rate of return on clearing land must, in the long run, be equal to the rate of interest so that we have the crucial condition

$$pa'n(p)/\phi'(N) = \bar{\rho} \tag{9.8}$$

in which the numerator is determined by (9.7) and thus the amount of land *N* is determined by the value of the marginal cost of land, equal to the asset price of land, which is the denominator $\phi'(N)$, that satisfies (9.8).

From (9.7) and the fact that

$$a'(n) > 0, a''(n) < 0$$

it follows that a rise in *p* leads to a fall in *n* and therefore to a rise in the numerator of (9.8), since the marginal physical productivity of a unit of land $a'(n)$ rises in response to the rise in *p*. Thus since $\phi''(N) > 0$ there must be a rise in N for (9.8) to continue to hold. Thus we have proved that

$$N = N(p), N'(p) > 0 \tag{9.9}$$

so that the extent of the frontier is an increasing function of p, the relative price of the agricultural commodity in terms of the manufactured good.

Since to each p there corresponds a unique $n(p)$ and $N(p)$, it follows that it also determines a unique L_A and hence A. Since $N'(p)$ is positive and $n'(p)$ is negative, from (9.7) it follows that L_A as well as N is an increasing function of p and thus we obtain

$$A = A(p), A'(p) > 0 \tag{9.10}$$

as the positively sloped supply curve of A.

To each p there corresponds a unique value of L_A, as we have just shown, and therefore by (9.3) a unique value of L_M as well. Since $\bar{k}$ is determined uniquely by (9.5) we know K_M and hence M as well. Since L_M is a decreasing function of p we obtain

$$M = M(1/p), M'(1/p) > 0 \tag{9.11}$$

as the positively sloped supply curve for M as a function of its own relative price, the reciprocal of p.

National income, denoted Y, is also determined as a function of p since

$$Y \equiv \bar{w}(L_A + L_M) + \bar{\rho} K_M + qN \tag{9.12}$$

where

$$q \equiv pa'(n)$$

is the rental per unit of land in terms of the manufactured good.

Assuming that consumers have identical and homothetic indifference curves we can define demand functions

$$A_D = A_D(p,Y) \qquad (9.13)$$
$$\partial A_D / \partial p < 0, \ \partial A_D / \partial Y > 0$$

and

$$M_D = M_D(1/p, Y) \qquad (9.14)$$
$$\partial M_D / \partial(1/p) < 0, \ \partial M_D / \partial Y > 0$$

From (9.10) and (9.13) we obtain the excess supply function for A as

$$E_A(p) = A(p) - A_D(p), \ E_A'(p) > 0 \qquad (9.15)$$

with a positive slope. The value $\bar{p}$ of p that makes

$$E_A(p) = 0 \qquad (9.16)$$

determines the full general equilibrium for the closed economy.

Opening to Trade: Rise in the Relative Price of Primary Products

We now imagine the economy being opened to the rest of the world. The main impact, of course, will come through a rise in the relative price of primary products, so that p rises from $\bar{p}$ to an appreciably higher level p^*, determined by conditions in the world as a whole that the economy is too 'small' to influence.

The effect on all the endogenous variables of the economy is easy to evaluate since we have already obtained each of them as a function of the relative price p. Basically the economy moves up the excess supply function $E_A(p)$ defined in (9.15). A compact summary of the main effects is provided below, with the bar above a variable denoting the closed economy value and an asterisk the free trade equilibrium after the opening to trade. Since p^* is greater than $\bar{p}$, it follows immediately that

$$N^* > \bar{N} \tag{9.17}$$

$$L_A^* > \bar{L}_A \tag{9.18}$$

$$A^* > \bar{A} \tag{9.19}$$

$$q^* > \bar{q} \tag{9.20}$$

$$L_M^* < \bar{L}_M \tag{9.21}$$

$$K_M^* < \bar{K}_M \tag{9.22}$$

$$M^* < \bar{M} \tag{9.23}$$

It is useful to begin by assuming that N and K_M remain initially fixed, as in the standard Ricardo-Viner model. Then A increases and M falls because the rise in p increases L_A and reduces L_M. But the rise in p and L_A raises the rental per unit of land q. This raises the numerator of (9.8) and so the rate of return on the extension of the frontier. To reduce this rate to equality with the interest rate $\bar{\rho}$, N has to increase to raise the marginal cost of a unit of land $\phi'(N)$ relative to the rental. The additional land pulls even more labor out of M and into A. Since the interest rate and wage rate remain constant at $\bar{\rho}$ and $\bar{w}$ the capital-labor ratio in M remains unchanged also at $\bar{k}$. The stock of capital K_M in M must contract proportionally to the decline in L_M caused by the rise in p and the induced rise in N.

Thus the effect of making N and K_M endogenous is to *enhance* the impact of the rise in p on the economy, since both the increase in A and the decline in M are larger than they would be in the pure Ricardo-Viner case.

Opening to the World Capital Market: Fall in the Rate of Interest

The process of opening up the export economies in the nineteenth century was not simply a matter of higher relative prices for primary products. There was also a fall in the real rate of interest, inducing further extension of the frontier, the building of infrastructure, and to some extent an expansion of manufacturing. We accordingly postulate a fall in the real rate of interest, from the $\bar{\rho}$ of the closed economy to $\tilde{\rho}$ in the new equilibrium. We shall ignore the balance of payments effects and the question of ownership (whether foreign or domestic) of the new equilibrium capital stock.

From (9.5) we see immediately that a fall in ρ from $\bar{\rho}$ to $\tilde{\rho}$ will raise the capital-labor ratio in manufactures to a value $\tilde{k}$ greater than $\bar{k}$. From (9.6) the rise in k from $\bar{k}$ to $\tilde{k}$ will raise the real wage from $\bar{w}$ to $\tilde{w}$ in terms of manufactures. Since p remains unchanged at p^*, we note from (9.7) that the rise in the real wage from $\bar{w}$ to $\tilde{w}$ must raise the marginal physical productivity of labor in A, that is, the land-labor ratio must rise in the primary-producing sector.

If N is held constant, the left-hand side of (9.8) will fall in proportion to the numerator q, the rental per unit of land, which declines because of the rise in the land-labor ratio. If q falls less than proportionally to ρ, however, it will be profitable to *extend* the frontier as a result of the decline in ρ, that is, the new equilibrium may require an increase in N to raise $\phi'(N)$ sufficiently for the rate of return on clearing land to equal the lower rate of interest $\tilde{\rho}$.

A plausible case therefore is one in which N is increased as a result of the fall in the rate of interest, but the rise in the land-labor ratio n results in L_A falling and L_M rising. Since the capital-labor ratio $\tilde{k}$ rises above $\bar{k}$ this means that K_M and hence M are both higher as well. Thus the lower rate of interest increases L_M, K_M, and M. The effect on A is ambiguous because even if N increases, the fall in L_A may result in lower output. It is possible, however, that if the increase in N is large and the decline in L_A small, the output of A as well as M will increase because of the decline in the rate of interest. The possibility of general expansion arises because the decline in the rate of interest produces both a deepening of capital, which tends to raise M, and an extension of the frontier, which tends to raise A.

Labor and Immigration

The opening to trade, as we have seen, leads to an increase in L_A and a reduction in L_M. What, however, if the increase in L_A is so large, and the initial L_M so small, that the former exceeds the latter? In this case the demand for labor will exceed the available supply at the wage $\overline{w}$, and so an inflow of foreign labor will be required even if the economy is to be completely specialized on A at the wage $\overline{w}$. Any inflow of labor beyond this, however, will leave the output of primary products unchanged at A^*, and serve only to increase L_M, K_M and M in the same proportion. This situation—a rapid extension of the frontier requiring an influx of labor—was present in most of the historical cases considered.

Since all immigration in excess of L_A^* leads to an expansion only of M^*, the rise in national income must cause a reduction in the export surplus of primary products and hence of imports of manufactures because the supply of A is constant while domestic demand for A increases. Thus, as we would expect, the degree to which the economy is 'open' varies inversely with the size of the labor force.

The reason why immigration does not reduce the real wage, of course, is because that variable is determined by the production function for manufactures and the rate of interest $\overline{\rho}$.

The Modified Model

The main difference between the situation considered in the basic model and that of the tropical economies on the eve of the export expansion process is that labor was mostly engaged in traditional 'subsistence' agriculture in the latter instance, supplemented by handicrafts during the slack periods of the year. Thus there was no specialized manufacturing sector as we have postulated for the basic model, designed to apply to the regions of recent settlement.

Within the subsistence sector, however, we can suppose along with Lewis (1954) and Hansen (1979) that peasants can obtain a real income $\bar{w}$, measured in terms of a composite 'basket' of food and other household necessities. Land suitable for cultivation of food is not a scarce factor. Initially the entire economy consists of this subsistence sector.

Now we introduce international trade and the world market for specialized primary exports in return for imports of manufactures, together with the possibility of borrowing capital at a fixed rate of interest. The primary export commodity, however, such as cocoa or rubber, is best grown on forest land that is abundant but which takes time to clear, during which period the labor has to be provided with the means of subsistence, as in the 'advances to labor' of the Physiocrats and Ricardo. In terms of the notation of the basic model, p^* is the price of cocoa in terms of the subsistence basket, ρ^* is the rate of interest at which the peasant who wishes to enter the market can borrow, and $\phi'(N)$ is the marginal cost of clearing an acre of forest land in terms of the 'wage fund' that has to be borrowed. With this interpretation it is easy to see that a 'rational' peasant will obey Equation (9.7), since the opportunity cost of his labor input into cash crops, at the world price p^*, must be equal at the margin to $\bar{w}$. The value n^* of the land-labor ratio that satisfies (9.7) determines the numerator of Equation (9.8), which together with ρ^* on the right-hand side determines the value N^* of $\phi'(N)$ that satisfies this equation. The extent of the frontier N^* in turn determines the labor engaged in cash crops L_A^*, since the land-labor ratio n^* is already known.

Ostensibly the real income of a cash crop cultivator is greater than that of a peasant who remains in the subsistence sector, since in addition to $\bar{w}$ he enjoys the 'rent' on his holding of the newly cleared land devoted to the cash crop. However, in equilibrium this rent is going to be just equal to the interest cost of the borrowed funds needed to tide him over the period while he was clearing his holding. Thus, in 'net' terms, the two real incomes are equal, as they should be, since the peasants form a homogeneous group initially, and the cash crop frontier is an open one.

Suppose, however, that the cash crop is coffee as in the case of Costa Rica or some other case where it is produced by large-scale foreign estates or plantations, instead of individual peasants. Here the 'technology' of producing the crop and extending the frontier can be left unchanged but now the subsistence farmer simply becomes a full-time worker on the plantation, earning $\bar{w}$, while the 'rents' accrue to the plantation owner, as returns on his original investment in clearing the land on which the cash crop is cultivated.

The situation is perfectly analogous to the question of whether the typical 'firm' in the primary-producing sector in the United States, Canada, Australia and Argentina is a family farm, the famous 'forty acres and a mule', or a huge ranch or *estancia* with hired hands. Although the social consequences of these different arrangements are of course highly significant, they can be fitted into the same framework at the present level of generality.

Conclusion

The objective of this chapter has been to provide a synthesis of the insights derivable from the 'vent-for-surplus' and 'staples' theories with the standard factor proportions formulation of comparative advantage, the key link being the concept of an endogenous land frontier. As we hope to have shown, our models conform in their implications to the main stylized facts of the patterns of resource-based export growth summarized here. In this concluding section we indicate the possibilities for further extensions and applications of the framework that we have attempted to construct.

While, as we have argued, there is an underlying similarity in the 'opening up' phase in the development of all the staple export economies, there has been an enormous diversity in the final 'outcomes' of the process initiated by primary export growth. Within the regions of recent settlement the United States, Canada, and Australia have all followed growth paths that have led them to per capita incomes at the highest levels in the world. Argentina, however, has remained stagnant for decades since World War II. The plantation economies of Malaya (now Malaysia) and Costa Rica have attained the position of middle-income countries, with Malaysia forging ahead rapidly in recent years on the basis of manufactured exports in addition to her traditional primary commodities. At the other end of the scale, the peasant export economies of Burma and Ghana, like Argentina, have been mired for decades in stagnation and even decline, after their highly promising beginnings around the turn of the last century.

Much of the explanation undoubtedly lies in 'political economy' factors that, while partly exogenous, can also be linked to the ownership patterns and income distributions associated with their economic systems. Many important insights, still waiting to be explored, on these questions are contained in a splendid pair of early papers by Robert Baldwin (1956, 1963). More explicit discussion of the role of the state and political economy can be found in Hirschman (1977) and Findlay (1988).

The nature of the industrialization undertaken by the primary exporters is a problem of great interest and significance. Broadly speaking, there have been two main avenues. One is resource-based industrialization (Roemer 1979; Findlay 1985, 1987) in which the primary export itself is processed further within the country. Another is import substitution for final consumer goods. Each has its own set of special problems that have been widely explored in the literature.

An important turning point in all the countries has been the 'closing of the frontier', the challenge confronted by a society when it is no longer capable of 'extensive' development, and this is a key factor in the political economy of attempts by the state, as in Argentina, Burma and Ghana, to squeeze the primary producers by manipulating relative prices against them.

These and many other issues of comparable importance can be discussed within the framework developed here. In purely technical terms the models can be extended and enriched in many ways. Thus multiple primary exports, each with its own associated frontier, can readily be introduced, or more than one primary export can be produced on each type of 'land'. The manufacturing sector can be sub-divided into capital-intensive and labor-intensive components, and non-traded goods and services introduced. Moreover, the productive, as well as predatory, role of government can be accounted for along the lines of Clarida and Findlay (1992).

References

Adas, Michael. (1974). *The Burma delta: Economic development and social change on an Asian rice frontier, 1852–1941*. Madison: University of Wisconsin Press.

Baldwin, Robert E. (1956). Patterns of development in newly settled regions. *Manchester School of Economic and Social Studies, 24*, 161–179.

Baldwin, Robert E. (1963). Export technology and development from a subsistence level. *Economic Journal, 73*, 80–92.

Bulmer-Thomas, Victor. (1987). *The political economy of Central America since 1920*. Cambridge: Cambridge University Press.

Bulmer-Thomas, Victor. (1988). *Studies in the economies of Central America*. London: Macmillan.

Cardoso, Ciro F. S. (1977). The formation of coffee estate in nineteenth century Costa Rica. In Kenneth Duncan and Ian Rutledge with the collaboration of Colin Harding (Eds.), *Land and labor in Latin America*. Cambridge: Cambridge University Press.

Caves, Richard E. (1965). Vent-for surplus models of trade and growth. In Robert E. Baldwin et al. (Eds.), *Trade balance of payments and growth*. Chicago: Rand McNally.

Caves, Richard E. (1971). Export-led growth and the new economic history. In Jagdish N. Bhagwati et al. (Eds.), *Trade, balance of payments and growth. Papers in international economics in honor of Charles P. Kindleberger*. Amsterdam: North-Holland.

Caves, Richard E. & Holton, Richard H. (1959). *The Canadian economy: Prospect and retrospect*. Cambridge: Harvard University Press.

Chambers, Edward J., & Gordon, Donald F. (1966). Primary products and economic growth: An empirical measurement. *Journal of Political Economy, 74*, 315–332.

Clarida, Richard H., & Findlay, Ronald. (1992). Government, trade and comparative advantage. *American Economic Review* (Papers and Proceedings), *82*, 122–127.

Cortés Conde, Roberto. (1985). The export economy of Argentina 1880–1930. In Roberto Cortés Conde & Shane J. Hunt (Eds.), *The Latin American economies: Growth and the export sector 1880–1930*. London/New York: Macmillan.

Díaz-Alejandro, Carlos F. (1970). *Essays in the economic history of the Argentine Republic*. New Haven: Yale University Press.

Díaz-Alejandro, Carlos F. (1984). No less than one hundred years of Argentine economic history. In Gustav Ranis et al. (Eds.), *Comparative development perspectives*. Boulder: Westview.

Di Tella, Guido. (1982). The economics of the frontier. In Charles P. Kindleberger & Guido Di Tella (Eds.), *Economics in the long view: Essays in honour of W. W. Rostow* (Vol. 1). London: Macmillan.

Easton, Stephen T., & Reed, Clyde G. (1980). The staple model. Mimeo. Vancouver: Simon Fraser University.

Ferns, H. S. (1969). *Argentina*. New York: Praeger.

Findlay, Ronald. (1970). *Trade and specialization*. Harmondsworth: Penguin.

Findlay, Ronald. (1985). Primary exports, manufacturing and development. In Mats Lundahl (Ed.), *The primary sector in economic development*. London: Croom Helm.

Findlay, Ronald. (1987). Intermediate goods, export taxation and resource-based industrialization. In Henryk Kierzkowski (Ed.), *Protection and competition in international trade*. Oxford: Oxford University Press.

Findlay, Ronald. (1988). Trade, development and the state. In Gustav Ranis & T. Paul Schultz (Eds.), *The state of development economics*. Oxford: Blackwell.

Findlay, Ronald. (1993). International trade and factor mobility with an endogenous land frontier. In Wilfred Ethier et al. (Eds.), *Theory, policy and dynamics in international trade: Essays in honor of Ronald W. Jones*. Cambridge: Cambridge University Press.

Furnivall, J. S. (1957). *An introduction to the political economy of Burma*. New York: Institute of Pacific Relations.

Gunnarsson, Christer. (1979). Malaysian rubber production: Patterns of growth 1900–1975. Meddelande från Ekonomisk-historiska Institutionen, No. 6, Lund: Lund University.

Hansen, Bent. (1979). Colonial economic development with an unlimited supply of land: A Ricardian case. *Economic Development and Cultural Change, 27*, 611–627.

Hill, Polly. (1963). *The migrant cocoa farmers of Southern Ghana*. Cambridge: Cambridge University Press.

Hirschman, Albert O. (1977). A generalized linkage approach to development, with special reference to staples. *Economic Development and Cultural Change, (Special Supplement), 25*, 67–98.

Hlaing, Aye. (1964). *A study of the economic development of Burma*. Rangoon: University of Rangoon.

Holmes, A. Baron. (1970). The Gold Coast and Nigeria. In W. Arthur Lewis (Ed.), *Tropical development 1880–1913*. London: Allen and Unwin.

Innis, Harold A. (1930). *The fur trade in Canada*. Toronto: University of Toronto Press.

Innis, Harold A. (1940). *The cod fisheries*. Toronto: University of Toronto Press.

Jones, Ronald W. (1971). A three-factor model in theory, trade and history. In Jagdish N. Bhagwati et al. (Eds.), *Trade, balance of payments and growth. Papers in international economics in honor of Charles P. Kindleberger*. Amsterdam: North-Holland.

Kravis, Irving B. (1956). Availability and other influences on the commodity composition of trade. *Journal of Political Economy, 64*, 143–155.

Lewis, W. Arthur. (1954). Economic development with unlimited supplies of labour. *Manchester School of Economic and Social Studies, 22*, 139–191.

Lougheed, A. L. (1968). International trade theory and economic growth. *Australian Economic History Review, 8*, 99–109.

Maddock, R., & McLean, Ian W. (1984). Supply-side shocks: The case of Australian gold. *Journal of Economic History, 44*, 1047–1067.

McLean, Ian W. (1989). Growth in a small open economy: A historical view. In Bruce Chapman (Ed.), *Australian economic growth: Essays in honour of Fred H. Gruen*. Melbourne: Macmillan.

Meier, Gerald M. (1953). Economic development and the transfer mechanism: Canada 1895–1913. *Canadian Journal of Economics and Political Science, 19*, 1–19.

Myint, Hla. (1958). The classical theory of international trade and the underdeveloped countries. *Economic Journal, 68*, 317–337.

North, Douglass C. (1966). *The economic growth of the United States, 1790–1860*. New York: Norton.

Roemer, Michael. (1979). Resource-based industrialization in the developing countries: A survey. *Journal of Development Economics, 6*, 163–202.

Samuelson, Paul A. (1971). Ohlin was right. *Swedish Journal of Economics, 73*, 365–384.

Solow, Robert M. (1956). A contribution to the theory of economic growth. *Quarterly Journal of Economics, 70*, 65–94.

Szereszewski, Robert. (1965). *Structural change in the economy of Ghana 1891–1911*. London: Weidenfeld and Nicolson.

Turner, Frederick Jackson (1921). *The frontier in American history*. New York: Holt.

Viner, Jacob. (1924). *Canada's balance of international indebtedness 1900–1913*. Cambridge: Harvard University Press.

Watkins, Melville H. (1963). A staple theory of economic growth. *Canadian Journal of Economics and Political Science, 29*, 141–158.

Woodward, R. L., Jr. (1985). Central America from independence to c. 1870. In Leslie Bethell (Ed.), *The Cambridge history of Latin America* (Vol. 3). Cambridge: Cambridge University Press.

10

Resource-Led Growth—A Long-Term Perspective: The Relevance of the 1870–1914 Experience for Today's Developing Economies

An apparently paradoxical finding of the empirical literature on economic development in the last thirty years is that resource-abundant countries seem to perform more poorly than less well-endowed ones. Neither does it seem to matter whether the natural resources in question are agricultural or mineral. A number of hypotheses have been put forward to account for this puzzle. Bad growth performance, however, has not always accompanied the efforts of primary producers. On the contrary, during the 'golden age' of resource-led development, from approximately 1870 to the beginning of World War I, a number of primary exporters

Thanks are due to Richard Auty, Mansoob Murshed and Moshe Syrquin for generous and constructive criticism of an earlier version of the present chapter. This study was prepared within the World Institute for Development Economics Research, United Nations University (UNU-WIDER) project on Environmental, Export and Human Development Problems in Natural Resource-Based Growth Models, being directed by Professor Richard M. Auty, UNU-WIDER and Lancaster University, UK. UNU-WIDER gratefully acknowledges the financial contribution to the project by the Government of Sweden (the Swedish International Development Cooperation Agency (Sida)).

Revised from 'Resource-Led Growth – A Long-Term Perspective: The Relevance of the 1870–1914 Experience for Today's Development Economies' by Ronald Findlay and Mats Lundahl, WIDER Working Paper 1999/162. This paper is reproduced by permission of UNU-WIDER, Helsinki, which commissioned the original research and holds copyright thereon.

R. Findlay, M. Lundahl, *The Economics of the Frontier*,
DOI 10.1057/978-1-137-60237-4_10

did exceedingly well. This inevitably raises the question of why performance has differed so radically between countries and historical epochs.

In the present chapter we will attempt to find out whether the 1870–1914 period was in some sense 'unique', i.e. whether the success of the resource-rich economies during these years built on a configuration of factors that is not likely to be replicated in future periods, or whether the episode contains lessons that are applicable a century later. The story of resource-based growth has been told before, but there is no consensus as to the conclusions. On the contrary, there are at least three 'stylized' views—the 'Marxist', the 'Liberal' and the 'Interventionist'—that diverge considerably. We therefore begin with a short sketch in general terms of each one of them.

The second part of this chapter provides an account of the world economy as it evolved during the period under consideration. The nineteenth-century story of resource-led growth is simultaneously a story of technological progress, international trade, factor movements and institutional change. Without a firm grasp of these factors no understanding of the experience of the resource-rich nations in this era is possible. The third part examines the record of fifteen resource-rich economies from approximately 1870 to 1914, in the light of some neoclassical theories of trade, factor movements and growth, to discover to what extent their experiences resemble one another and where they diverge. The final section makes use of the stylized facts and development trends that emerge to discuss the relevance of the historical experience for today's developing economies and in addition examines the three stories in the light of this experience.

Three Stories of Resource-Led Development

The Marxist-Dependency Story

Perhaps the most widely known story of resource-led economic development is the view of more or less total failure propagated by Marxist and *dependencia* theorists (e.g. Prebisch 1950; Singer 1950; Baran 1957; Frank 1969; Furtado 1970; Amin 1974). According to this view, the world may be divided into an industrialized center and a primary-producing periphery which interact through international trade and capital movements from the center to the periphery. The central message is that in this setting it becomes impossible for the periphery to develop. Interaction with the center will simply serve to perpetuate the position of the periphery as a low-income primary producer.

The center, which is the engine of the system, can develop by itself. Growth at the center, however, does not spread to the periphery. The income elasticity of demand for primary products is low, and monopolistic structures in product and factor markets ensure that productivity gains do not translate into lower prices, while such gains in the competitive periphery will simply benefit consumers elsewhere. In the periphery, foreign investment emanating from the center is concentrated on an export sector producing minerals or agricultural produce which has little contact with the rest of the economy. Management and skilled labor come from abroad, profits and salaries are remitted to the center and the demand generated in the export enclave is geared mainly towards imports. The only contact with the local economy is through the market for unskilled labor, where, however, wages are low because of high population growth and because imports of manufactures from the center have wiped out the handicraft sector and reduced the available employment alternatives.

The failure of international trade to increase wage income in the periphery effectively precludes industrialization. The mass market which would make import substitution of manufactured consumer goods possible does not come into existence. The periphery is trapped in a situation where it will go on producing primary products forever, without experiencing any growth of incomes.

The Liberal Story

The second story is almost exactly the opposite of the 'Marxist-Dependency' one. It represents a 'liberal' view (e.g. Viner 1953; Bauer and Yamey 1957; Haberler 1959; Lal 1983). According to this, the Marxists and *dependentistas* are mistaken in stating that specialization according to comparative advantage would be wrong for resource-rich countries and in inferring that international trade would not confer any benefits on primary producers. Squeezing agriculture to promote industry would be wrong, since agricultural incomes provide markets for the manufacturing sector as well as foreign exchange, and in economies with small non-agricultural sectors they would also be the only source of capital formation. Also, international trade should be an integral part of the development strategy of resource-rich nations. The traditional arguments for trade apply, and trade may also have dynamic effects of various kinds. It may be conducive, for example, to capital accumulation and technological progress, and this, in turn, may make it possible to move up the ladder of comparative advantage over time, away from resource-based products, via labor-intensive, skill-intensive and capital-intensive manufactures towards sophisticated products resting on 'created' production factors related to R&D activities. The reasons why some primary producers failed to turn the use of natural resources and the participation in trade into growth have to be sought elsewhere—notably in faulty policies that stunted efficiency.

The problem is one of excessive *dirigisme*. The state did not stick to its basic functions (providing law, order, defense, education, health care and the like) but believed that it could interfere systematically with the market mechanism so as to increase efficiency and growth, and even more to increase equality. The outcome was completely different, however. Government intervention created more inefficiencies than it destroyed, and did not necessarily improve the distribution of income and resources. In particular, there was a tendency to get prices more or less systematically wrong. Instead of improving the functioning of the imperfect markets the interventions made the situation worse.

International trade is a case in point. Interventions took the form of protection of the manufacturing sector, drawing resources away from the sectors where the economy had a comparative advantage based on natural resources. Internal trade is also affected. Private middlemen are not trusted but governments frequently undertake to regulate the marketing of agricultural produce by substituting parastatal marketing boards for them, bureaucratic organizations that are usually both inefficient and corrupt. In this way, producers receive less than the world market price for their goods. Likewise, mineral producers (particularly if they are foreign) are subjected to high taxes which are thereafter spent in a way that does not contribute to increasing the rate of growth. Thus, the failure of resource-rich economies to grow fast is due not to external factors, but to internal, policy-related ones. The remedy is clear: get prices right, remove distortionary interventions and do not discriminate against the export sector. Producers (including producers of primary products) are no fools. They react to incentives, regardless of whether these are 'right' or 'wrong'.

The Interventionist Story

According to the 'interventionist' view (e.g. Ranis 1991; Sachs and Warner 1995; Sachs 1996; Auty 1998), a number of factors operate on resource-rich economies which require specific government intervention if they are not to have negative effects on growth. Such factors are found both outside and inside the domestic economy.

Most importantly, resource-rich economies may be caught in a 'staple trap'. When production expands in the resource-based export sector, this may produce 'Dutch disease' effects which lead to an increased production of non-traded goods while labor and capital are pulled out of a shrinking manufacturing sector. The tradeables sector of the economy becomes overly specialized on primary products. If manufacturing for example has important backward and forward linkages, learning effects or increasing returns to scale, this could be inimical to growth. Should anything happen to the expansion of primary exports, the economy faces the risk of a growth collapse.

The above points to the importance of policy intervention. The resource-rich economy cannot be left to itself, because that may kill an incipient manufacturing sector. Neither should protectionism be allowed to carry the day, but unfortunately, resource-rich economies easily develop factional states, where rent creation looms large, because rents constitute an important building material for political coalitions. Thus, policy reform may be difficult.

It should be obvious from the above that the views of what impact the existence of natural resources in a country will have on economic growth and development differ sharply among the three schools of thought. We will come back to them at the end of the chapter, in order to find out to what extent each of them stands up in the light of the historical experience. Before we do that, however, we must examine the experience itself: that of the 1870–1914 period. We will begin with a sketch of the most important—revolutionary—trends in the international economy.

The Golden Age: 1870–1914

The years between 1870 and 1914 were years of relatively high growth in many countries. From the mid-nineteenth century, strong growth impulses emanated from those countries in Europe, and later North America, where industrialization was taking place. From 1870 to 1913 GDP grew at 2.1 percent per annum in Western Europe and at 3.9 percent in the United States (Maddison 1995, pp. 60, 182), and between 1880 and 1910 industrial output in Britain, France, Germany and the United States expanded at 3.65 percent a year (Lewis 1978, p. 136). While these rates, as Arthur Lewis (1978, p. 136) has pointed out, do not appear as extraordinary from a post-World War II perspective, they were nevertheless sufficiently high to lay the foundations for an international economic boom.

The participants in this boom were not only the 'core' European and North American countries, but economies in both the European and non-European periphery were drawn into it as well. At the root of the expansion was the industrial—i.e. technological—revolution which had started during the latter half of the eighteenth century in Great Britain but which did not spread very much for the next 100 years. By 1850, only France and Belgium had been reached by the new British manufacturing techniques, but as industrialization spread over the next sixty-five years, powerful growth impulses were transmitted from the core to the more peripheral areas.

The mechanism of transmission was the network of international transactions and factor movements that was built up during the latter half of the nineteenth century. Goods began to move in larger quantities and across a wider geographical area than at any time hitherto, and huge quantities of both people and capital began to flow from the core to the periphery. On the highest level of aggregation, the world economy behaved very much in the fashion captured by North-South models of trade and capital flows (e.g. Findlay 1980; Burgstaller and Saavedra-Rivano 1984) where a growing industrial North is linked to and transmits growth impulses to a primary-producing South via the terms of trade and international capital mobility.

The Trade Machine

Between 1870 and 1914 trade was an 'engine' (Robertson 1938) or at least a 'handmaiden' (Kravis 1970) of growth—one which was not confined to the developed part of the world. Manufactured goods were increasingly exchanged for primary products (agricultural goods and minerals) in a process driven by industrial growth. Between 1883 and 1913 the elasticity of world trade of primary products with respect to world manufacturing output was 0.86 (Lewis 1978, p. 175). In value terms, the exports of tropical countries grew at 3.4 percent per annum and in terms of volume the growth rate was slightly higher: 3.6 percent (Stover 1970, p. 46). During the entire period Europe dominated trade on the world level in quantitative terms (Lamartine Yates 1959, pp. 32–33). The pattern, however, involved drawing non-European economies into a very intimate relation with Europe (Kenwood and Lougheed 1992, p. 82):

> … the direction of world trade in the period before 1913 was dominated by Europe's ever-growing demand for foodstuffs and raw materials. Before World War I Europe absorbed more than 80 per cent of the exports of … Argentina, South Africa and New Zealand; 75–80 per cent of those of … Australia; over 60 per cent of those of … the United States; and more than half of Canada's and India's.

There was a movement away from protection, on a most-favored-nation basis, during some but not all of the period. Britain in particular moved towards free trade. The 1880s saw a return to protectionism, in the wake of the invasion of Europe with cheap American and Russian grain, with only Britain, Holland and Denmark adhering to the canon of free trade (O'Rourke and Williamson 1997, Chaps. 2, 5).

Long-distance trade was more consistently facilitated by progress in transport and communications (O'Rourke and Williamson 1997, Chap. 2). Drastically falling transport costs brought countries and continents closer to one another. It became easier both to make use of foreign supplies of inputs and to find markets. The steam-driven railway opened up the interior of vast countries and made possible the transportation of export products to ports. The introduction of iron steamships revolutionized maritime transportation, and the opening of the Suez Canal in 1869 did away with the cumbersome route around the southern tip of Africa, halving the distance between London and Bombay. Between 1873 and 1908 inward ocean freight rates to Britain fell by no less than 73 percent (Cairncross 1953, p. 176), and the cost savings on overland transport as a result of the railways were even more spectacular (Reynolds 1985, p. 33). The development of refrigeration made the transportation of meat and butter across the oceans possible, and the telegraph facilitated long-distance communication enormously. The result of all this was to turn a number of goods into staples, i.e. primary products with a value per unit of weight or volume high enough to make intercontinental transportation of them profitable.

Changes in institutions also played a significant role for the expansion of trade. The development of a large multilateral payments system, after 1870, which reduced the need for bilateral balancing of trade greased the trade machinery, and so did the extension of the gold standard. In 1870, only Britain, of all the major European and North American countries, was on a gold standard, but thereafter the use of the latter gradually spread across the globe.

Factor Movements

The result of the forces just described was a degree of commodity market integration never experienced before in world history. The world between 1870 and 1914 was, however, not a pure Heckscher-Ohlin world, but one fueled by factor movements as well. Both capital and labor became more mobile than during any previous period.

The degree of capital market integration reached before World War I appears to have been as high as it is today (O'Rourke and Williamson 1997, Chap. 11). Gross foreign investment rose from some 6 billion US dollars in 1870 to 43 billion in 1914, with Britain accounting for 43 percent of the total in the latter year, outflows having increased until a stunning 9 percent of national income was reached in 1913 (Kenwood and Lougheed 1992, p. 27, cf. Cairncross 1953; Hall 1968; Edelstein 1982, for details). In the last decade before the war, the share of foreign investment in total net British capital formation reached 53 percent (Landes 1969, p. 331).

Most of this foreign investment went to Europe, but by 1914 the regions of recent settlement had attracted 40 percent of the total (Kenwood and Lougheed 1992, p. 28) and between 1907 and 1913 no less than 92 percent of Britain's overseas investment flowed into non-European areas (Taylor and Williamson 1994, p. 350). About 80 percent of it went to regions with natural resources but little labor, and there it was used mainly for social overhead investment, such as railroads and harbors (O'Rourke and Williamson 1997, Chap. 11).

Not only capital, but people as well, moved out of the European countries. The nineteenth century and the beginning of the twentieth constituted an 'age of mass migration' (Hatton and Williamson 1998), with some 60 million leaving Europe for the New World between 1820 and 1920. The transport revolution in particular made an upward trend possible, with more than 600,000 leaving every year from the mid-1870s, rising to over a million after the turn of the century (Hatton and Williamson 1998, p. 8). The source shifted, with Britain, and to some extent Germany, dominating before the mid-century, the Scandinavian countries joining the movement around that time, Italy, Spain and Portugal rising to prominence in the 1880s and Austria-Hungary, Russia and Poland following suit in the next decade (cf. Hatton and Williamson 1994, for details).

The majority of these flows went to the United States. Between 1851 and 1880 this country received over two-thirds of all international migrants, and for the period between 1881 and 1915 the figure is only slightly lower, barely below 60 percent (Kenwood and Lougheed 1992, p. 47). After the mid-1880s Argentina and Brazil began to attract significant numbers of Europeans and so, after the turn of the century, did Canada. Smaller numbers were moving from Britain to Australia, New Zealand and South Africa. The reasons varied somewhat, but the relative labor scarcity in the regions of recent settlement resulted in a wage gap between the New and Old Worlds. This gap was narrowed over time, as migration took its course, but such factors as high population growth, increasing the share of young adults (with good income expectations if they emigrated) in the domestic labor force, the presence of relatives abroad (chain migration) and the rising mobility of labor as a consequence of industrialization at home more than compensated for this (O'Rourke and Williamson 1997, Chap. 7).

The outflow of Europeans to the regions of recent settlement was not the sole component of the history of migration during the 1870–1914 period. There was also a South-South current of Indians and Chinese, mainly indentured, workers. Thus Indians were shipped to the West Indies, Mauritius, Fiji, East and South Africa and South America. The main receiving regions were in Asia, Burma, Ceylon and Malaya. Altogether close to 16 million left India between 1871 and 1915, around three-fourths eventually returning home. The number of Chinese that emigrated is not known, but in 1880, some 3 million were residing abroad, a figure which in 1922 had increased to 8 million. The vast majority stayed in Asia, notably the Dutch East Indies, Thailand and Malaya (Lewis 1978, p. 185).

Resource-Led Growth

The regions of recent settlement and the countries producing tropical goods all had certain features in common (Findlay and Lundahl 1994). They all participated in the international exchange of commodities, trading their primary staples for manufactures. Staples production everywhere depended on the existence of a land frontier—not necessarily an open range, as in the classic piece by Frederick Jackson Turner (1921) on the westward expansion of the United States; it could as well be a virgin *selva* that needed clearing. This frontier could not be put to productive use unless it was somehow 'developed', commonly by the extension of transportation to the frontier region—a process that required investment. This capital to a notable extent had to be found in the international markets. The exploitation of the frontier also required workers. Both in the regions of recent settlement and in some tropical areas labor scarcity prevailed on the national level, which made international migration necessary. In other cases, scarcity was a regional problem that could be solved by domestic labor flows from surplus regions to the regions where staples were produced.

The mode of functioning of the world economy during the forty-five years preceding World War I produced growth rates of real GDP per capita in the regions of recent settlement and Latin America that exceeded those of Western Europe (1.5 percent per annum against 1.3 percent) (Maddison 1995, pp. 62–63), and by 1913 Australia and New Zealand had reached living standards exceeding those of the European countries, ranking with those of the United States and Britain as the highest in the world, and the figure for a country like Argentina (the richest in Latin America) was not only above that of, for example, Italy but 9 percent above the average for twelve Western European countries (Maddison 1995, pp. 23–24).

No reliable national income figures for tropical countries exist for the 1870–1914 period, but it seems very likely that export-led growth strong enough to raise income per head took place also in this group. Food supply expanded as quickly as the population for the tropics as a whole and exports increased by 3.5–4 percent per annum in terms of real purchasing power, if we are to believe Arthur Lewis, who furthermore adds (1978, p. 216):

> In the tropical countries at the top of the growth list, national income must have been growing as fast or faster than in Britain or France per head of population at this time (1.0 to 1.5 per cent per annum) and faster than in much of Central and South-East Europe. This must have been the case for say Ceylon, Burma, Thailand, Malaya or Gold Coast, and was certainly true of the developing regions of many other countries, such as Colombia or Mexico. Celso Furtado reaches the same conclusions for Brazil, and although this is in dispute for the country as a whole, it cannot be disputed for southern Brazil. Even India as a whole seems to have grown by an

> annual average of about one per cent per head over the fifteen years before the First World War, after a bad patch in the 1890s, and the growth rate was naturally much higher in those regions of the country where the response was concentrated …

Thus, while the response of the tropical economies to the challenge posed by growth at the industrial core of Europe and North America was not uniform, there were some definite success stories that merit exploration. This was even more true for the regions of recent settlement. In the present section we will examine fifteen such stories in more detail. We have chosen to divide our cases into three main groups: regions of recent settlement (Canada, United States, Australia and Argentina), tropical countries, either dominated by plantations (Brazil), peasant family farms (Burma, Siam, Gold Coast), or a mixture of the two (Colombia, Costa Rica, Ceylon, Malaya), and, finally, mineral economies (Bolivia, Chile, South Africa). We begin with the experience of the regions of recent settlement.

The Regions of Recent Settlement: Theory

What Folke Hilgerdt called the 'regions of recent settlement' (League of Nations 1945) are basically offshoots of Europe projected into the 'empty' continents of America and Australia by the export of population and capital. The factor 'land', however, had to be created by a process of investment that extended the 'frontier' further and further but at an increasing marginal cost. The whole process is explained in stylized terms by the 'Christopher Columbus' general equilibrium model (Findlay 1993, 1995, Chap. 5) and the integrated staples and vent-for-surplus model (Findlay and Lundahl 1994).

In the Christopher Columbus model, 'Europe' has a fixed endowment of land and population with which she can produce two goods, food and manufactures. The supply of capital is perfectly elastic at a fixed interest rate in the long run. Manufactures require a raw material (e.g. cotton) that can only be supplied from overseas, say 'America'. Land in 'America' can be obtained at increasing marginal cost by the investment of capital (e.g. railroads to the West). Food and the raw material can be produced with land and labor at different factor intensities, the labor being provided by migration from 'Europe'. In equilibrium, the value of the marginal product of land in food production is equal to the marginal cost (in terms of capital) of clearing land. The model thus has three factors—capital, land and labor—and three goods—food and manufactures which are final consumer goods and the raw material, which is an input into manufactures. Given constant returns to scale technology for the three goods and consumer preferences for food and manufactures the model determines the distribution of population between 'Europe' and 'America', the output of the three goods, the prices of all the goods and factors, the extent of the land frontier and the endogenous supply of capital.

The implications of population growth, technological change in manufactures or an exogenous shift in the cost of frontier extension can all be ascertained by the appropriate comparative statics exercise for the model. The nineteenth-century experience of the United States, Canada, Australia and Argentina can all be accounted for in terms of the predictions of this model.

The Christopher Columbus model does not allow for industrial production in the regions of recent settlement. This feature can, however, be introduced in a model of staples production (Findlay and Lundahl 1994). The (agricultural) staple is produced with the aid of labor and land. The latter has to be developed with the aid of capital before it can be used. Manufactures are in turn produced with the aid of labor and a capital stock consisting of the manufactured good itself. As before, manufactures can be both consumed and invested and capital is in perfectly elastic supply, at a given interest rate.

The given rate of interest determines the marginal product of capital and hence the capital-labor ratio in manufacturing as well as the wage rate. The marginal product of labor in agriculture depends on the land-labor ratio. Using manufactures as the *numéraire*, the wage rate then provides us with a unique ratio for each relative price of agricultural goods and hence also with unique marginal products of labor and land in the sector. Exactly as in the Christopher Columbus model, the value of the marginal product of land in agriculture must be equal to the marginal cost (in terms of capital) of developing land in equilibrium.

When the relative price of agricultural goods increases, labor is pulled into agriculture from manufacturing. The land-labor ratio falls and the marginal product of land increases. If equilibrium is to be preserved the marginal cost of land must then increase, i.e. the price rise must lead to increased development of land (an extension of the frontier). This, in turn, leads to further migration of labor from industry to agriculture.

Trade is opened by an increase in the relative price of the agricultural staple, above the autarky price. Then the agricultural frontier will be extended, labor moves into agriculture from manufacturing and agricultural production increases, whereas in manufacturing the opposite sequence takes place, with a reduction of the capital stock and falling output as labor leaves.

Staples production also entails movements of capital and labor. Assuming that the rate of interest above was the one that prevailed in a closed economy, the opening up of the capital market to international conditions can be expected to make the interest rate fall. The capital intensity of the manufacturing sector will increase and labor will be pulled into that sector from agriculture. Possibly the land frontier will also be extended. This happens if (as a result of the loss of labor) the value of the marginal product of land in agriculture falls proportionally less than the rate of interest, so that the marginal cost of land will have to rise again, to preserve the equality of marginal product value and marginal cost of land. Thus, an inflow of capital will lead to an expansion of industrial production and possibly—if the rate of interest falls enough—also to increased agricultural output, i.e. to a general expansion of the economy.

The opening of staples trade may also be connected with an inflow of labor. As stated above, the initial effect of a rise in the relative price of agricultural goods is that labor will leave manufacturing for agriculture. In sparsely populated countries the manufacturing labor force may be very small, so small that the increased demand emanating from agricultural expansion may empty the sector completely at the given wage rate. This is likely to result in immigration. Labor will then flow into agriculture until output has risen there to the extent required by the relative world market price of agricultural goods. Any inflow in excess of this level will go into manufacturing, where it will trigger a corresponding increase of the capital stock, so as to maintain the factor proportions in that sector that are compatible with the given rate of interest and wage rate. This, in turn, increases the national income and with that the domestic demand for the agricultural staple so that the exportable excess supply of the latter will shrink.

The Empirical Picture

The traditional view of the growth process in the regions of recent settlement is that countries like the United States and Canada managed to extend growth across a wider spectrum of sectors than just the primary export ones, in a manner reminiscent of Walt Rostow's (1960) take-off stage while, for example, Australia and Argentina failed to do so. Beginning with Canada, the economy for which the staples theory of growth was originally developed (Innis 1930, 1940), linkages were created from the numerous staples, notably from wheat production which made the westward extension of railroads across the prairies necessary and furthermore stimulated the manufacture of agricultural inputs. Warehousing, processing, construction, housing and public utilities received strong impulses, staples production provided raw materials for flour mills, saw mills and paper mills, and the incomes generated in the West were spent on manufactures in the East.

The growth rate of the Canadian manufacturing industry was surpassed only by that of the Japanese (Meier 1953, pp. 5–6; Stovel 1959, pp. 123–24; Bertram 1963). Possibly, tariff protection had something to do with this, but it does not seem to have been responsible for the establishment of any of the major branches (Stovel 1959, pp. 96, 102). The impetus from staples production carried over into later periods as well. Not only between 1900 and 1913, but also 1920–1929 and 1946–1956, the Canadian manufacturing sector grew as domestic markets developed around the export raw material base, replacing imports (Watkins 1963, p. 158). Pulp and paper production, as well as mining and natural gas, led to the development of forward linkage and in addition turned out to stimulate each other (Caves and Holton 1959, p. 46).

The United States constitutes an even better example of how trade in staples created extensive linkages across a wide territory (North 1966).

The first impulses were generated in the cotton kingdom of the South before the Civil War. A growing international demand for cotton raised incomes and also created a demand for inputs not produced in the region. The South provided neither the food it needed nor the manufactured consumer goods, so linkages were established both with the wheat-growing West and the industrialized Northeast. The western frontier could not, however, be developed without previous extension of the canal and railroad network, pulling migrants as well as international capital (North 1956) along in the process. Staple-induced growth was at work.

The process continued after the Civil War, however, with slightly different protagonists. Now, wheat itself, together with livestock and minerals, notably coal, was a staple, with migrants pushing the frontier westwards, along with the transportation network, in a movement that would not cease until the West had been settled, around 1890. Simultaneously a widening of the market for northeastern manufactures took place (Perloff et al. 1960, Chaps. 12–14).

To what extent the staples theory applies to the case of Australia has been subject to some controversy. As a minimum, however, it appears to apply to the 1850s, the 1870s, part of the 1880s and the years immediately before World War I (Lougheed 1968). However, even though growth took place in rushes and booms, the entire period beginning in the 1830s and extending up to World War I was characterized by a substantial extension of the resource base. Gold and wool provided the stimulus (McLean 1989), and immigrants (Pope and Withers 1994; Taylor 1994) and capital (Pope 1990) flowed in to help with the extension of the frontier on the outback and with the extraction of the precious metal.

The overwhelming majority of the immigrants were British (Australia maintained a 'whites only' policy). Most of these ended up in urban-based jobs (Pope and Withers 1994, p. 243). A diversified industrial sector was built up, under the natural protection of distance. At certain points this sector came under strain. Thus, the gold rush in the 1850s produced Dutch disease effects for a full decade. It stimulated imports of a number of manufactured consumer goods, to the detriment of domestic producers, but spurred the output of industries related to construction that were producing non-tradeables (Maddock and MacLean 1984, pp. 1059–60). At any rate, between 1860 and 1890 the industrial sector picked up again. In 1891, one out of every three Australians lived in an urban center and less than one-third of the wage earners worked in mining or rural production (Denoon 1983, p. 147). This trend was to continue during the next decade. Although most urban pursuits were related to exports, each of the Australian colonies in 1899 could boast a range of industrial activities as well, and in 1910 almost one-fifth of the labor force was employed in manufacturing (Denoon 1983, p. 153).

It was, however, still the primary sector that was most important economically, being the only exporter. When World War I broke out, the Australian economy continued to be dominated by pastoral, agricultural and mining production, although a diversification had taken place, with mutton, butter, wheat and sugar having been added to wool and gold (and other minerals) on the export list (Denoon 1983, pp. 100–04).

Argentina attracted both capital (Taylor 1992) and large numbers of immigrants (Taylor 1994) who peopled the Pampa (Jefferson 1926) as the agricultural frontier was extended. Between 1890 and 1913 half the population growth of the country was due to immigration (Taylor 1994, p. 97). From the 1860s a number of staples appeared on the scene: hides, wool, salted meat, wheat (notably in the 1890s), corn, linseed and frozen meat. Linkages were not missing. Extending the frontier required railroads (Cuccorese 1969), and exportation required *frigoríficos*, packing facilities and so on. Forward and backward linkages were developed from livestock and agricultural products (Denoon 1983, pp. 157–59), and domestic manufacturers began to compete with imports in the market for consumer goods (Díaz-Alejandro 1970, 1984).

The conventional wisdom in the Argentine case is that by 1913 there was not much industry to speak of in the country and that the industrialization process dates from the 1930s (e.g. Ferrer 1963). This has, however, been questioned by a number of authors (cf. the references in Cortés Conde 1992) who have argued that an import-substitution process was at work even before World War I. High growth rates of manufacturing output were obtained as domestic production of consumer goods replaced imports, in the face of increasing and diversifying demand (Cortés Conde 1985, pp. 349–51) and linkages to primary production were exploited (Denoon 1983, pp. 157–59). While the industrial sector remained small in absolute terms in 1913, a beginning had been made.

Our four examples of regions of recent settlement present a relatively uniform pattern. All of them based their export activities on the existence of an unexploited land frontier, all of them received both capital and labor from abroad and all of them were in the process of industrializing as World War I broke out. Primary exports had provided an impulse that was not confined to the resource-intensive sectors themselves but spread to other sectors as well through linkage effects of various kinds. Thus these four case studies exemplify the benign scenario of the 'liberal' story, with perhaps some further 'interventionist' stimulus.

Tropical Countries: Theory

For our tropical case studies the most useful theoretical framework will be the classical dual economy formulation of Arthur Lewis (1954), but extended and formalized to explicitly account for international trade in primary products and manufactures in Findlay (1973, Chap. 5). The model has a 'peasant hinterland' that plays the role of a source for a perfectly elastic supply of labor at a fixed real wage. The 'modern' sector consists of profit-maximizing entities such as plantations, mines or commercial farms that use capital and labor to produce an output that can be sold on the world market. The economy is too 'small' to affect the relative price of imported manufactured consumer or capital goods but is assumed to be a significant supplier of its primary export (e.g. Brazilian coffee or Malayan rubber). There is thus a world demand curve for the export staple that is assumed to shift over time at some exogenous rate λ. Given the initial capital stock profits are maximized when the marginal value (or revenue) product of labor is equal to the given real wage, profits are the sole source of capital accumulation. Denoting the profit rate by π and the propensity to save out of profits by s, the growth rate of capital, g, will be equal to $s\pi$. The profit rate π is endogenous and depends upon the terms of trade, the relative price of the primary exportable in terms of manufactures.

It is readily demonstrated that if g is greater than λ—i.e. supply of the primary export grows more rapidly than world demand—its relative prices will fall, thus pulling down π and hence g until it is equal to λ. Increasing g through a higher rate of saving or π through technical progress does no good in the long run, since the economy is permanently constrained by the growth of world demand. When this is brisk, as it was for most tropical products in the 1870–1914 period, trade is truly an 'engine of growth'. When it sputters, however, as in the interwar period, the prospects are bleak. This situation then corresponds to the pessimistic 'Marxist' story.

The possibility of labor-intensive manufactured exports has, however, to be introduced. Here any developing country by itself would be 'small', so the growth prospects of an open dual economy are still given by $g = s\pi$ as before but π is now constant (given the technology and the real wage) since the relative price of the labor-intensive exports and capital goods imports is given. Higher rates of saving or technical progress can now *permanently* raise g since they no longer induce declining terms of trade.

If we denote the rate of growth of a 'pure' manufacturing dual economy (i.e. an economy where the modern sector produces only manufactures) by μ, an interesting case to consider is when the economy has both a profitable primary sector and the possibility of manufactured exports. Thus suppose that g is greater than μ which is in turn greater than λ. Primary production may initially be very profitable if demand is very high. These high initial primary sector profits make g greater than μ and so the economy can initially grow even faster than if it were completely specialized on manufactured exports. Even though initially high, however, the world demand for the primary export grows relatively slowly at the rate λ (less than μ). Manufacturing production, however, now starts to become increasingly important and the primary exports, though growing in absolute volume at the rate λ, become less and less important relative to manufactured exports. The limiting growth rate is μ (greater than λ) and so the economy can successfully escape the 'trap' of slowly growing world demand for primary exports.

The foregoing assumes that the staple economy has at least some degree of monopoly power in world trade. If the economy is truly 'small', however, the relative price of the staple would be exogenous and so the growth rate would depend only on supply-side factors such as capital accumulation and the rate at which the frontier can be extended.

Here, the staples model (Findlay and Lundahl 1994) is also of relevance. Tropical staples production in the context of a peasant economy, however, differs from staples production in the regions of recent settlement. In the tropics, there was no specialized manufacturing sector but just subsistence agriculture combined with handicrafts during the dead season. Assuming that the economy has abundant land, we may model this sector simply as one where the peasants can obtain a given wage (real income) along the lines of Bent Hansen (1979) and Arthur Lewis (1954).

When international trade is opened, this economy can export a staple in return for imports of manufactures and also gets access to capital at a given rate of interest. Again, the staple has to be grown on land that must be cleared, and for the latter the peasants have to be fed out of the subsistence sector, i.e. the cost of clearing land is measured in terms of subsistence goods (a wage fund or a kind of circulating capital). The value of the marginal product of labor in staples production must then be equal to the given subsistence wage, and the value of the marginal product of land must equal the marginal cost (in terms of the wage fund that has to be borrowed) of clearing it. This determines the agricultural frontier and, hence also the number of workers producing staples, since once the world market price of staples is known so is the land-labor ratio.

In the peasant setting, the rent created by clearing land for staples production will simply be equal to the interest cost of the wage fund that has to be borrowed in order to make it possible for the peasants to clear the land, since land is in infinitely elastic supply. Thus, the real income of a cash crop cultivator and a subsistence cultivator will be equal. If instead, the farm producing staples is a plantation there is no real difference in the mechanism through which the land is cleared. However, instead of peasants we will have agricultural workers recruited from the subsistence sector earning the fixed wage, and instead of the wage fund we have the plantation owner borrowing the funds necessary for the clearing.

Tropical Countries I: Plantation Economies

The experience of the tropical exporters is less uniform than that of the regimes of recent settlement. This should not come as any surprise, since both the structure of their economies and the export crops differed widely from country to country. We begin with the plantation economies.

In Brazil, coffee exports began to take a rapid upward turn in the 1830s, as coffee drinking spread throughout North American society. In the 1880s the center of production shifted from Rio to São Paulo, and from the beginning of that decade to the outbreak of World War I, export volumes almost tripled, expanding to the point where Brazil could wield considerable monopoly power in the world market, supplying more than half the internationally marketed coffee (Dean 1986, p. 694). The coffee plantations rapidly attracted around 1.5 million immigrants between 1880 and 1913 (Coes 1970, pp. 102–03). Smallholders participated in production, since land was more easily available in São Paulo than in general in a country dominated by large estates. 'The coffee frontier swept forward like a bush fire' (Dean 1986, p. 701), clearing the forest, towards the western part of the state of São Paulo.

The coffee industry received support from the government in various ways. Much of the migration was subsidized by the federal or the state government (Dean 1986, p. 704). The railroad network was expanded from the coastal ports into the coffee-growing areas in the interior, with the aid of foreign capital, but also with considerable government support, and the state also intervened first by devaluing the currency, and later by supporting large-scale price stabilization efforts, when downward price movements threatened incomes (Cardoso de Mello and Tavares 1985, pp. 95–105).

During the 1870–1914 period Brazil also saw the rise and fall of another primary export crop, rubber, which grew wild in the Amazonas and could simply be tapped by collectors who were drawn into the area. Between 1872 and 1900, the population of the Amazonas grew by 5 percent per annum, far faster than in any other region of the country. Once rubber seeds had been smuggled out of Brazil in 1876, it was just a matter of time before prices began to fall precipitously (in 1910) and the rubber boom came to a rapid end (Coes 1970, pp. 117–18).

The coffee boom brought incipient industrialization to Brazil (Dean 1986), notably in the non-tradeables sector (Catão 1992, pp. 36–43). Coffee bags were needed on the plantations and clothes were demanded by the coffee workers (Stein 1957). This made for the beginning of a local textile industry which in 1913 was able to supply over 75 percent of the total Brazilian consumption of cotton textiles. Gradually, markets widened, as a result of export incomes and improved transportation. Coffee growers diversified their assets by investing in manufacturing as well, and the foreign exchange generated by coffee made it possible to import the needed capital goods (Cardoso de Mello and Tavares 1985, pp. 114–17). Chemicals, food preparation and metal working were early starters (Coes 1970, pp. 119–20).

The results of the coffee and rubber booms in terms of growth were uneven. The rate of growth of real GDP per capita appears to have been below 1 percent (Catão 1992, p. 1), with the coffee-producing regions reaching 1.5 percent, and the Amazonas no less than 4 percent—a figure that, however, quickly became mere history (Coes 1970, pp. 123–25).

Tropical Countries II: Mixed Economies

Another coffee-producing country is Costa Rica, the first Central American country to export—as early as in the 1830s. The staple phase of coffee growing, dominated by smallholders, began in the early 1840s, with exports to Britain, and less than fifty years later less than 10 percent of Costa Rican exports did not consist of coffee (Bulmer-Thomas 1987, p. 3). In the meantime, a second (plantation) staple had made its appearance: bananas, which had been grown along the railroad for coffee exports that was being built from Puerto Limón to San José, to contribute to covering the cost of its construction (Gaspar 1979, pp. 21–32).

In the first stages of expansion, until the 1880s, coffee benefited from the fact that Costa Rica was a sparsely populated country, with much waste land (Cardoso 1977). Bananas, in turn, were grown in swamps and jungles that had no alternative commercial use, right up to the 1920s (Bulmer-Thomas 1987, p. 38). Labor was a far worse problem. Coffee could expand only by bidding the wage level up (Cardoso 1977, p. 179), and bananas were grown in such an unhealthy climate that the white population refused to work there. Black workers from the West Indies had to be brought in (Gaspar 1979, pp. 111–24). British commercial houses financed Costa Rican coffee exporters (Cardoso 1986, p. 204) and external finance was completely necessary for the banana venture as well, which had to build an infrastructure from scratch in an uninhabited area (Bulmer-Thomas 1987, p. 7).

Linkages were created, not only from coffee to the Atlantic railroad and from there to bananas, but also to banking (the financial requirements of the banana industry being such that North American banks had to be involved). Against this, however, we must set the fact that the banana industry required mainly import-intensive inputs and tended to form an enclave in the domestic economy, that coffee production drove food production out in the areas where it expanded, and that no industry to speak of had developed by the 1920s (Bulmer-Thomas 1987, p. 40). In the absence of production linkages, the demand generated by incomes from staples production was directed mainly towards imports and was not large enough to make domestic production in a country the size of Costa Rica viable.

Coffee also dominated the exports of Colombia. Production began to surge in the Antioquia province in the 1880s, where it became a smallholder crop which could fit into the already existing pattern of peasant agriculture without problems and without replacing food crops in the process (Harbison 1970, p. 79). The land, which was easily available, in the relative absence of pre-existing large estates, was uniquely suited to its inclusion, and the volume of coffee exports increased eighteenfold between 1878 and 1914 (Harbison 1970, p. 83).

Colombia was not one of the main recipients of European labor in Latin America, but the hands needed for coffee growing could be secured via internal migration, both permanent and seasonal. Some of the capital was foreign but essentially, the coffee industry remained a Colombian undertaking (Deas 1986, p. 655). As late as 1914 foreigners owned a mere 4 percent of the Colombian capital stock. Most of this investment was in the transport sector (Harbison 1970, p. 96). Railroads began to be developed (see Horna 1992, for a fascinating case story), though only on a small scale, mainly to serve coffee exports, and were combined with steamboats for further transportation on the Magdalena river.

Since the Colombian coffee growers were mostly smallholders, the fruits of growth were spread across many hands and this in turn helped to create linkage effects, through increased demand for products 'which could be produced most economically in increasing quantities at home' (Harbison 1970, p. 84), such as textiles. At first, crafts and cottage industries dominated (Ocampo 1991, pp. 216–17), but factories were established in Medellín immediately after the turn of the century (Reynolds 1985, pp. 114). The simple technology employed made for backward linkage in the form of sacks and simple implements that could also be produced locally. Only Medellín, however, managed to develop a significant industrial sector before World War I (Harbison 1970, p. 87). On the national level, manufacturing remained relatively undeveloped.

What the effects of coffee exports were in terms of growth rates is impossible to say, since no GDP estimates are available for the period. Besides, some traditional exports, like tobacco and straw hats, were having problems, so that export trade as a whole may have been in decline until 1902, when the so-called War of the Thousand Days (a civil war, 1899–1902) ended (McGreevey 1985, p. 27). However, the most likely picture resembles the one given by Lloyd Reynolds (1985, p. 115) for 1885–1930:

> It is almost certain that per capita income was rising, though with fluctuations associated with the varying fortunes of exports … It is certain also that growth was uneven regionally, with Antioquia enjoying a rate well above the national average. Further, a considerable part of the population—small subsistence farmers in the interior of the country—was largely left out of the growth process.

Coffee was the staple crop of Ceylon as well from the 1840s to the 1880s, when the industry was ruined by a fungus disease from which it never recovered (Corea 1975, pp. 58–64). The next three decades saw instead the rise of a trio of new staples: tea, coconut products and rubber. Rising per capita consumption, together with a growing preference in Britain for the Ceylonese product over that of its Chinese competitor, provided a stimulus for the extension of the area under tea cultivation, notably after 1884, up to 1906, with continued growth of output up to the outbreak of the Great War (Corea 1975, pp. 71–75). Rubber, benefiting from strongly rising prices, as the automobile industry expanded, joined tea as an important export product in the 1890s and the cultivated area grew rapidly up to 1910, when prices began to drop. Coconut products, finally, had begun their expansion in the 1870s. Together these three crops made for a rapid growth of exports. Between 1880 and 1913 the dollar value of exports rose by an average of 5.4 percent per annum (Craig 1970, p. 221).

Two of the new staples were excellently suited to smallholder production. Capital requirements were low in both rubber and coconut production, and relatively little labor was needed. Tea required both more labor and more capital per unit of land (Craig 1970, p. 228). Capital had to come from abroad and the plantations absorbed large numbers of Indian (Tamil) immigrants who had already begun to come into the country during the days of coffee exports. In the 1880s an estimated 200,000 workers had settled together with their families (Snodgrass 1966, p. 25) and in 1911, their number had increased to 366,000 (Craig 1970, p. 230). The native Sinhalese avoided plantation work, apparently because they had better options remaining in their villages. As elsewhere, the government was active in the extension of railroads, roads, irrigation facilities and port facilities (Reynolds 1985, p. 137; Bruton et al. 1992, p. 21).

The Ceylonese plantation sector has often been pointed to as a classic example of enclave development, importing even the food for its workers. However, as Lloyd Reynolds (1985, pp. 137–38) has emphasized, the export sector as a whole is likely to have had important spread effects, since it made it possible for smallholders to increase their incomes, and it led to the creation of a domestic planter class in the coconut and rubber sectors. This, in turn, may have widened the domestic market, and some industrial development in fact took place, with employment in manufacturing increasing at 2.8 percent per annum between 1881 and 1911, until a figure of 170,000 workers (10 percent of the workforce) was reached (Craig 1970, p. 245). Altogether, GDP per capita may have increased at some 2 percent per annum (Reynolds 1985, p. 137).

Rubber was introduced into another colony in Southeast Asia as well: Malaya. Exports began in 1906, and expanded extremely fast until the beginning of the 1920s (Gunnarsson 1983, p. 6). The initial expansion was fuelled by plantation development. British capital combined with cheap Tamil labor from India to make use of virgin lands, mainly on the west coast where a good infrastructure, in the form of roads, railroads and ports, had already been established to serve tin exports (Bruton et al. 1992, p. 178). With time, Chinese and Indian growers became involved as well, both on plantations and on small farms, where rubber could easily be fitted into the existing growing pattern. After 1910, output in the smallholder segment, which by then also included Malays, grew exceedingly fast (up to World War II) in spite of government measures to the contrary (Gunnarsson 1983, p. 21).

Malaya had a second staple, tin, which had been mined mainly by Chinese entrepreneurs who managed to take advantage of rising demand and a changing technology in the mid-nineteenth century, aided by government railroad construction from 1885. Large numbers of Chinese workers were brought in. In 1911, when Malaya accounted for half the world production, the Chinese composed over 95 percent of the tin-mining community (Bruton et al. 1992, p. 177). After 1912, however, when yet another, capital-using, technological change, which furthermore required skilled workers, took place, the British began to take over. When World War I broke out, the Chinese, however, still accounted for three-fourths of the output (Reynolds 1985, p. 151).

With the exceptions already mentioned, neither rubber production nor tin mining did much to establish linkages. Chinese and Indian workers ate imported rice (which differed from the domestic variety consumed by the Malays) and manufacturing failed to develop. As late as 1947, less than 7 percent of the labor force was employed in 'industry', which actually consisted mainly of handicraft operations and small establishments (Reynolds 1985, p. 152).

Tropical Countries III: Peasant Economies

An agricultural staple does not have to be a product that is introduced from the outside. On the contrary, some of the most successful Asian staple exporters grew by simply expanding the output of their main food crop. Such was the case for example with Burma (Furnivall 1957; Hlaing 1964; Adas 1974). In the mid-nineteenth century, lower Burma was nothing but a sparsely populated, but potentially fertile, area. Things changed, however, as the British occupied the territory in 1852 and even more after the opening of the Suez Canal in 1869. The availability of European manufactures increased. An upward pressure on the price of rice ensued, rice turned into a commercial crop and the British administration began a conscious policy of boosting its cultivation in lower Burma. Cultivators from central and upper Burma were induced to move southwards, and laborers (both permanent and temporary) were imported from southern India (from the 1880s) with the aid of subsidies. Transportation facilities (railroads, canals, and so on) were improved (Hlaing 1964, pp. 32–36).

The expansion process quickly reached the point where it fed on itself without any further need for intervention. Indian Chettyars (money-lenders) and reinvested profits provided the capital for cultivation and European trading houses financed the steam-powered rice mills. The area under rice cultivation grew eightfold between 1852 and 1915 (Hlaing 1964, p. 6) and Burma become the leading rice exporter in the world. With the exception of rice milling and sawing of logs, rice production failed to produce any substantial linkages, however. Handicrafts and cottage industries failed to meet the competition from imported manufactures (Furnivall 1957, pp. 161–62). Still, it has been estimated that during the first three decades of the twentieth century per capita income grew at 0.8 percent per annum (Hlaing 1964, p. 51, Appendix A). To what extent this increase was widely shared is in some doubt, since a process of land concentration was operating (Furnivall 1957, Chapter 6) and real wages may have stagnated or even fallen (Hlaing 1964, Chapter 2).

A second rice-exporting economy was that of Siam. There, exactly as in Burma, around 1850 rice was the main subsistence crop. In 1851 the country saw the ascent of a modernizing king to the throne who four years later signed the so-called Bowring treaty with Britain, followed by similar treaties with other European nations, opening Siam for international trade. The road lay open for a fast increase of rice exports, fifteen-fold from the late 1850s to World War I, after the opening of the Suez Canal and the concomitant cheapening of European manufactures. The main demand for Siamese rice came from Malaya and China and the share of exports in total output rose from about 5 percent in 1850 to 50 percent at the turn of the century (Reynolds 1985, p. 158). Tin and teak wood supplemented rice on the export list, both with upward trends as steep as that for rice exports.

Siam could draw on unused land in the expansion process, first in the central plain and thereafter east of Bangkok. The Crown freed the agrarian population from forced labor services for the nobility and facilitated access to these lands for smallholders, refusing to create a landed aristocracy (Phongpaichit and Baker 1995, pp. 3, 23–25). Canals, mainly for drainage, were dug and railroads constructed, financed by bond issues in London. Migration played a comparatively smaller role in Siam than in Burma. Migrant workers from the northeast were used mainly to meet seasonal peaks, but the main labor input came from a reduction of the leisure of the peasant families themselves (Chinese workers, however, were drawn into urban areas, since the success of rice contributed to keeping wages high). Also, capital requirements were comparatively small, in the main limited to a plow and a bullock, which could usually be financed by a local merchant (Phongpaichit and Baker 1995, p. 32).

The rice-producing economy failed to develop any linkages into manufacturing (Akira 1996, pp. 33–39). On the contrary, hand in hand with the expansion of exports went an expansion of imports of European manufactures. Domestic industries, like sugar refining and cotton weaving, went into decline. European goods proved much cheaper. In 1919, Bangkok could boast a mere seven modern factories. As in the Burmese case, the only offshoots of rice production were saw milling and rice milling. The Siamese economy grew by absorbing the growing population into rice cultivation, not by diversifying into manufacturing (Ingram 1971).

Peasant economies, however, also managed to develop export crops that were not originally part of their agricultural tradition. One of the best examples of this is cocoa in the Gold Coast. Cocoa was introduced there in the 1860s, and when the price of palm oil (the main export product) fell in the 1880s, cocoa production rapidly took off, until in 1913 the Gold Coast had become the world's leading cocoa exporter (Hill 1963). Between 1891 and 1913 the export volume increased from 50 pounds to 50,600 tons (Holmes 1970, p. 151) and real income per head may have grown at 1.8–1.9 percent per annum (Szereszewski 1965, pp. 111,127), driven by cocoa (and to some extent gold, the production of which, however, was very enclave-like) (Holmes 1970, pp. 151–52).

Cocoa was easy to integrate into the already existing agricultural systems. Traditional food crops and the new export products could coexist without problems (Szereszewski 1965). Labor was secured by a migration of the enterprising Akwapim to the southern cocoa-producing region where forest land that could be cleared was plentiful (Hill 1963). In the beginning, little capital was needed, but as the industry expanded, European merchant houses gradually moved in and provided credit for investment and consumption during the months preceding the harvest (Gunnarsson 1978, pp. 51–53). Transportation was no problem, since the production areas remained within about fifty miles from the coast (Holmes 1970, p. 152). By the same token, however, few linkages developed. Railroads did not arrive in the Gold Coast until after 1900 and then only to serve the needs of gold mining (Holmes 1970, pp. 163–65).

The patterns characterizing the tropical producers are not as easy to sum up as those of the regions of recent settlement, because of the greater variety of economic structures. Still, a few common themes emerge. The most salient is the failure to industrialize (with the exception of Brazil). Exportation of tropical crops created fewer and weaker linkages of the type necessary for industrialization. Growth thus tended to be concentrated on the export sectors themselves. Secondly, the character of migration differed. Some countries relied mainly on internal movements and those that did not received Indians and Chinese, not Europeans. Thirdly, crops were often easy to graft on to the existing systems of production and required relatively little capital. Hence, capital movements played a lesser role than for the regions of recent settlement. When larger injections were necessary, however, they came from foreign sources.

Mineral Producers

We now turn to the three mineral exporters. For the most part our models will apply in this instance as well. The 'frontier' now will extend vertically downwards rather than be horizontally extensive as in the case of land and agriculture. With this modification the framework of the staples model (Findlay and Lundahl 1994) can be used here as well.

A country which switched from one mineral to another in the 1870–1914 period was Bolivia. In the late 1840s the silver mining, once so important for the Spanish Empire, was in a state of crisis, employing a mere 9,000 miners (Klein 1986, p. 554). However, in the decades following 1850 a revitalization took place. Cheap steam engines made it possible to reopen old closed and flooded mines, and a lowering of the cost of mercury cheapened silver extraction. Mining expertise was available from Chile and Peru and profits made on grain production in the Cochabamba valley were partly reinvested in silver mining. In the 1870s new mines were producing on the Pacific coast, with the aid of foreign capital. At the end of that decade Bolivia was once more a leading producer of refined silver. From the 1850s to the 1890s output increased almost nine times (Klein 1986, pp. 554–57).

Silver mining created two important backward linkages. One was to agriculture. The Bolivian *haciendas* had been more or less dormant for half a century. The increased demand for foodstuffs that resulted from the expansion of silver mining, however, changed this. Production increased, unfortunately to the point where the large estates began to encroach on the lands of the Indian communities. The second backward linkage consisted in the stimulus offered to the construction of railroads which made exports a great deal easier and which furthermore contributed to the widening of markets, not least for agricultural products (Klein 1986, pp. 557–59).

Railroad construction, in turn, played an important role in developing the second mineral. In the mid-nineteenth century, a number of events took place that made tin exports possible (Hillman 1994). Smelting techniques improved in Britain. The use of tin plate, notably for cans, increased. The expansion of silver mining created skills and knowledge that could easily be transplanted to the tin sector. Above all, the high internal transportation costs (an almost insurmountable obstacle to exports) were gradually lowered by a series of railroad constructions, pursued by successive Bolivian governments (Contreras 1993, pp. 2–3).

When the silver market collapsed (Hillman 1994, p. 414), tin entered an extremely expansive phase, with exports more than doubling between 1900 and 1910 and employment increasing from 3,000 to 15,000 in 1915, backed by the entrance of foreign (British, Chilean and US) capital (Contreras 1993, pp. 32–35). Exports grew at 5.9 percent per annum up to 1919 (Klein 1986, p. 566).

Silver and tin failed to transform the Bolivian economy. Mining as such employed relatively few people, and the harsh working conditions in the high altitude mines in combination with the seasonal demand emanating from agriculture made labor scarce, which in turn fostered mechanization in many places as early as 1912–1915 (Contreras 1993,

p. 4). Also, no industrialization to speak of had taken place as late as the beginning of the 1950s (Klein 1986, pp. 585–86).

Bolivia's neighbor, Chile, experienced a boom in nitrate production between 1880 and 1919 (Mamalakis 1971; Monteón 1982; O'Brien 1982; Cariola and Sunkel 1985). The 'Nitrate Age' began with an exceptional event. No nitrate deposits existed within Chile's borders. They were acquired from Peru and Bolivia through the victory in the War of the Pacific (1879–1883). Hereby Chile obtained a virtual world monopoly of nitrate production which permitted a twelvefold expansion of exports between 1880 and 1913 (Mamalakis 1971, p. 184), with employment in the nitrate industry increasing from 2,800 to 53,200 (Cariola and Sunkel 1985, p. 186). During the war, British interests had started buying into the nitrate industry (with the aid of loans from a Chilean bank) and in 1890 they controlled 70 percent of the industry, a figure which, however, was to fall to 39 percent in 1914 (Blakemore 1974, p. 22; Centner 1942, p. 81).

Nitrate exports generated growth of per capita income, at an estimated rate somewhere between 1 and 2 percent per annum (Mamalakis 1976, pp. 4–6). This growth was the result not least of linkages. In the 1860s and 1870s Chile had been a wheat exporter, but thereafter the extensive grain producers in North and South America, Russia and Australia took over the international market. However, since the nitrate fields were located in the desert areas of the Norte Grande, where agriculture was impossible, a domestic market could be found among the workers and their families who had migrated there (Bauer 1975, Chapter 3). For this, and for the development of nitrate production, extension of the railroad system was necessary. From 1860 to 1887 its total length was expanded ten times (Kirsch 1973, pp. 17–20). The Chilean government, which had become totally dependent on nitrate taxes for revenue, also devoted some of the revenue to the expansion of the educational system. Between 1860 and 1915 the number of students enrolled in the public education system increased from 20,500 in 1860 to 368,000 in 1915 (Cariola and Sunkel 1985, p. 208).

Nitrate mining and agricultural production helped create an industrial sector in Chile. In 1875 a mere 1–1.5 percent of the labor force was employed in manufacturing (García 1989, pp. 146, 150). Between 1880 and 1913, however, the sector began to grow. Agricultural products were processed and processing equipment was manufactured in Chile. Nitrate production, in turn, provided the foreign exchange necessary to bring in industrial inputs and also provided an expanding market for industrial goods (Kirsch 1973, pp. 23–29; Cariola and Sunkel 1985, pp. 165–70). Altogether, industrial output almost doubled in Chile between 1880 and 1913 (Kirsch 1973, p. 49). Henry Kirsch (1973, p. 80) concludes:

> … during the period stretching from 1880 to 1914, judged by the criteria of rate of growth, product diversification, systematic linkages with its own sector, integration to the rest of the economy and technological advance, Chilean industry experienced considerable expansion and progress. The common belief that a real process of industrialization did not exist before the outbreak of World War I may be considered nothing more than an unsubstantiated myth.

South Africa became a mining economy during the last quarter of the nineteenth century, after the discoveries of diamonds in Kimberley in 1867 and gold on the Witwatersrand in 1886. These discoveries, which resulted in a spectacular growth of output and exports, in particular of gold (Houghton 1971, p. 18), were supported by an inflow of both people and capital from abroad. From 1860 to 1920 the white population grew at over 3 percent per annum, on average (Nattrass 1981, p. 130). This was far from enough, however, since 'an almost insatiable demand for labour' (Houghton 1976, p. 12) arose. The mines began to exert pressure on the government to provide Africans at low wages. Thus, through a series of laws, culminating in the 1913 Natives Land Act, the Africans were confined to a mere 7 percent of the South African territory (Bundy 1972, pp. 384–86; Horwitz 1967, p. 134). In addition, various attempts were made by the Chamber of Mines to monopsonize labor recruitment. After various failures these finally succeeded in 1911. Finally, the borders were opened for an inflow of workers from the neighboring territories (Jeeves 1975). The end result was stunning. Wages in gold mining were no higher in 1971 than in 1911 (Lipton 1985, p. 388). Willing hands were not lacking, however. While at the beginning of the 1860s mining employment was virtually nil, in 1912 it had risen to 325,000 (Houghton 1971, p. 19).

Capital came from different sources. High returns to diamond mining made it easy to expand on the basis of reinvested profits during the early years and it was not until the concentration that ended with the creation of a monopoly in 1889 began to take place that foreign loans were resorted to (Nattrass 1981, p. 132–33). Gold was a different matter, with low-grade ore bodies at deep levels. Here, foreign capital entered the picture virtually from the outset (Frankel 1938).

The diamond and gold fields were located in an area without modern communications. From 1860–1869 to 1900–1910 the railroad network was expanded no less than 100 times, with the mining districts as the hub of the system. This was complemented by road construction which furthermore contributed to bringing agricultural districts into closer contact with the mines where 'fantastic prices' were being paid for food (Houghton 1971, pp. 19–20). The huge concentrations of people in the mining districts also provided the demand that was necessary for the beginning of manufacturing. Mining equipment, dynamite and other inputs (like miners' boots) needed for the extraction of the precious metals were soon being produced locally, but since competition from the mines for skilled labor and entrepreneurship was very keen, it was not until World War I forced import substitution on South Africa that the industry began to grow (Houghton 1976, p. 121). Thereafter, however, the pattern would be one of very intimate relations between mining and manufacturing. Jill Nattrass (1981, p. 164) summarizes:

> The foreign exchange earned from the sale of minerals financed the extensive importation of both capital goods and essential intermediate inputs that were needed by the growing industrial sector. The new sector also drew on the pool of skilled labour and the financial and business know-how that had developed as the mining industry expanded. Mining houses started to diversify their activities and moved into the industrial field, both directly and indirectly, allowing capital accumulated in the mining enterprises to be used to expand South African industrial capacity.

The patterns prevailing among the mineral exporters resemble those of the agricultural producers of the regions of recent settlement. In mining the frontier is vertical, not horizontal. The mineral, however, resembles land in the agricultural societies. Both have the character of an intermediate good that has to be produced before it can enter as an input in the production of other goods. Also, transportation costs loomed large in all three cases. A second common characteristic of the three mineral economies was that all of them were large actors in the world market, particularly Chile with its virtual monopoly on nitrates, but also South Africa and Bolivia. Thirdly, internal migration played an important role. Only in the South African case did large numbers of workers come in from abroad. It was only for skilled manpower that the other two countries relied on immigration. Finally, the experience with respect to industrialization differed. Only Chile managed to push ahead before World War I, while Bolivia failed completely. In South Africa the war provided the impetus, but thereafter the minerals sector and manufacturing developed a strong relationship.

Conclusions

The 1870–1914 years comprised a period of high growth rates in resource-rich economies. Through their incorporation in the international economic network these economies were able to make use of not only trade with the industrialized regions of the world but also of flows of capital and labor from abroad. All of them were producing and exporting staples, i.e. resource-based products in high, frequently increasing, demand in international markets.

However, not all resource-rich economies succeeded in spreading the growth impulses emanating from their primary sectors. As we have seen in the foregoing, in a number of instances the staples sector turned out to be an enclave with little contact with the rest of the economy. This fact is not the result of a single configuration of circumstances but may be due to a number of factors. The staples approach to growth and development is 'rich' in the sense that it allows for different outcomes. It points clearly to the interplay between international commodity trade, international factor movements and the existence of a land frontier. This does not, however, mean that a given combination of factors would always result in identical growth effects, even when the commodity produced happens to be the same. The staples theory does not proceed beyond the analysis of how various sectors interact with each other, i.e. like other neoclassically inspired approaches it points out signs and directions, not magnitudes.

If we are to explain magnitudes, like growth rates, empirical examination is necessary. Robert Baldwin (1956), over fifty-five years ago, pointed to the importance of the characteristics of the production function (capital intensity, elasticity of substitution between labor and capital, use of skilled labor, etc.) and its relation to the institutional setting in which the staples sector has to operate. Thus, if we are to arrive at a complete understanding of why some primary exporters managed to industrialize and others not, the formalized general equilibrium staples analysis must be combined with an investigation of how a particular institutional setting shapes the parameters of the economy. The technological characteristics of the production function provide just one example of such parameters. Path-dependence created by the initial conditions prevailing during the period under investigation also looms large here, and so do political considerations. The linkage concept is simply a catch phrase which may contain a very mixed bag of interacting factors, combining to produce identical or diverse results, according to the circumstances. Thus, it is highly doubtful whether one should attempt any far-reaching generalizations on this point.

This has at least not been the intention behind the present chapter. Rather, as we emphasized at the beginning, we have attempted to pinpoint some of the most important characteristics of the world economy during the 1870–1914 period in order to contrast these with the present-day situation. To these contrasts the concluding section will be devoted.

One of the main lessons of the world economic history of the past 200 years is that the road to sustained growth goes via industrialization. The classic works of Allan Fisher (1939) and Colin Clark (1940) pointed out that increasing levels of per capita income go hand in hand with an increasing share of secondary activities in GDP. Their findings were later confirmed by Simon Kuznets (1966) and Hollis Chenery and his associates (e.g. Chenery 1979; Chenery et al. 1986). Structural change is one of the most important features of the development process. The staples theory of growth stresses the development of linkages between the export sector and an incipient manufacturing sector. However, as should be obvious from our fifteen cases, far from all the primary exporters managed to develop a viable industrial sector. By and large, the regions of recent settlement succeeded and the rest failed.

Why was this the case? In one sense they all had the same starting point: their natural resource base. Thereafter, however, their paths diverged. On one level, this result may have been expected. Hollis Chenery (1979, p. 34) summarizes the historical modern growth experience: 'Virtually all countries start to develop by specializing in exports based directly on their natural resources; only later do they develop exportable manufactured goods and services.' Thus, it is possible to argue that in any given time period we should expect the early starters to industrialize before the others. This is very much the position taken by Arthur Lewis (1970, 1978) who argues that a market economy had been created in Europe and North America as a result of canals and railroads a century before modern transportation began to unite the hitherto isolated areas in the tropics. Had it not been for the two World Wars and the Great Depression, 'the leading tropical countries would now [1970] be unrecognizable' (Lewis 1970, p. 44). They were simply not given enough time during the 1870–1914 period.

Clearly the time element was important. The per capita resource endowment of the regions of recent settlement, despite large inflows of migrants, was much higher on average than in the tropical countries, most of which had already fairly dense populations. The necessary internal market for domestic manufacturing was thus available much earlier in the temperate zone than in the tropical primary exporter countries. Real wages did not grow substantially either, in the latter, with cash crops drawing their labor supplies from the peasant sector, on very favorable terms, with Indian and Chinese migration providing a further check on upward wage pressure. Thus, it can be argued that the majority of the tropical countries did not have enough time to develop a domestic market for manufactures before World War I.

What they did manage, however, Lewis argues, was to lay the foundations of future growth: 'to give themselves railways, roads, harbours, water supplies; to build towns, schools, hospitals; to sprout a professional and trading middle class; to improve their economic, legal and political institutions, and to establish new ones' (Lewis 1970, p. 44). Had it not been for the three anomalous events that took place from 1914 to 1945, this would sooner or later have borne fruit (Lewis 1978, pp. 223–24):

> In the thirty years since the Second World War we have become accustomed to seeing some tropical countries growing by 2 to 3 per cent per head, thus matching European and North American performance. This took the world by surprise, and was therefore assumed to be quite new. But it was only the resumption of a phenomenon which had already begun in the 1880s, and had lasted until the outbreak of war in 1914. With that war, the tropics went into hibernation. The terms of trade moved against them in the twenties, the great depression impoverished them, and in the forties they were isolated by the Second World War. Thirty-five years of slow or zero growth is long enough for the world to forget what has happened before, and to take it for granted that nothing has happened before.

It is, however, doubtful that the sequence envisaged by Lewis would have materialized even in the absence of the Wars and the Depression. There are at least two reasons for this.

The first is that some features of the 1870–1914 period were unique, and three of these features are central in the staples theory of growth. This was the case with the 'frontier'. Today, 'frontiers' exist only in mining, in the sense that the level where the mining operations have to take place tends to get deeper over time. It is far more difficult to find an agrarian frontier, with virgin land waiting to be developed. In the regions of recent settlement the latter type of frontier began to be closed towards the end of the nineteenth century or during the first or second decades of the twentieth (O'Rourke and Williamson 1997, Chap. 12). Today, land is no more in 'unlimited' supply.

The second unique feature was that the 1870–1914 years form part of the 'age of mass migration'. Millions of people, the vast majority of whom were unskilled, moved out of Europe, India and China to find jobs. Again, today we are in a completely different situation. Mass migration is no longer possible, other than under very special circumstances, usually some kind of disaster, and definitely not for economic reasons. Borders are open for people possessing scarce skills, not for the rest. The closing of borders is not a feature of the post-World War II period either. On the contrary, this also began during the period under investigation here. After the 1880s, up to 1930, the regions of recent settlement (including southern Brazil) were gradually shut to immigrants (O'Rourke and Williamson 1997, Chap. 10).

The third unique feature of the 1870–1914 period is the drastic reduction of transport costs that followed such innovations as the steamship, the railroad and the building of the Suez Canal (followed by the completion of the Panama Canal in 1914). Even in the era of supersonic intercontinental flights it is difficult to think of any technological advances in the transportation area in the foreseeable future that would have such a large *economic* impact as the changes that took place in the nineteenth century.

International capital flows are a different matter. These dried up in the 1920s and 1930s, and it was not until the 1970s and 1980s that capital flows began to pick up again, from the bottom levels reached in the 1950s and 1960s, without, however, producing quite the same degree of capital market integration as during the pre-World War I period (Taylor 1996; O'Rourke and Williamson 1997, Chap. 11). Still, this proves that the early experience is likely to be replicated and presumably more so in the future. On the other hand, it may be argued that without additional land and additional labor the return to increasing stocks of capital will decrease, but that amounts to limiting the attention to the three 'traditional' production factors. Today's industrial patterns build more on human capital and R&D-related activities which may both boost the return to capital.

A similar argument may be brought to bear on demand. The prime mover of growth between 1870 and 1914 was expansion at the core of the international economy, an expansion that expressed itself among other ways in an increased demand for primary products produced by other regions, and there are of course no principal reasons why this could not happen again. On the other hand, the inputs demanded are likely to be different in today's setting. Most importantly, the production pattern will probably require far less raw material per unit of output. The secular upward shifts in the production functions of most manufactures have changed input-output relationships significantly.

Another limitation may come from the fact that some of the staples of the 1870–1914 period were crops that were new to the areas where they were produced. This was the case with coffee, tea, rubber, cocoa and bananas. Part of the success story consisted in matching crops and climates. This took place during an era when our knowledge of the geography of the Earth was far less complete than it is today, which, in turn, means that the scope for matching was far larger than at present. That does not of course mean that new crops will not be introduced both here and there, but they are hardly likely to be of the staple variety. Also, some of the staple crops were successful because they did not disturb the existing production patterns in the peasant economy but could simply be 'grafted' on to these, non-specialized, patterns. Since then, however, monocultures have spread, especially as far as export crops are concerned. Economies of scale in agricultural production are far more important today than a century ago.

The second reason why the Lewis pattern may be illusory builds on a finding by Hollis Chenery (1979, p. 34): 'Primary specialization can also be characterized as a strategy of deferred industrialization.' Primary producers tend to industrialize and diversify their export patterns accordingly at a higher level of per capita income than resource-poor countries. 'This lag in transforming the export pattern is so common that it may be considered a typical feature of the SP [small primary-oriented country] pattern of development although it can be avoided by suitable policies' (Chenery 1979, pp. 102–03). As long as the change does take place, the lag may be a minor problem, but there is also the possibility that under certain circumstances pursuing a pattern of primary specialization makes it difficult to switch at all.

The period from the Industrial Revolution to World War I can be viewed as the period when the fundamental characteristics of the present international division of labor were cemented. A new era was dawning. The industrial revolution spread. Economic tasks were divided between regions according to comparative advantage. Labor and capital moved from areas of comparatively low to areas of comparatively high returns. An industrial core was created which traded with primary producers in other parts of the world. What has taken place thereafter has only been a modification of the fundamental pattern. Resource-poor economies have been forced to opt for industrialization and some primary producers have managed to do so as well. In the light of the experience of the last couple of decades, however, it seems as if the former have been far more successful (Auty 1998). Natural resources may delay the emergence of labor-intensive manufactured exports, for some of the 'political economy' reasons discussed in Findlay and Wellisz (1993). The rents generated by the natural-resource sectors divert policy-making into competition between interest groups for the spoils, whereas economies such as Hong Kong and Singapore had no alternative but to concentrate on manufactured exports from the beginning.

The question then is whether being a latecomer to the industrial table means that you have to be content with the remains from a party that is over. Hla Myint (1954–55) has suggested that staple economies run the risk of 'fossilization', i.e. they may push the specialization on primary exports beyond the point where their marginal returns begin to fall short of their marginal cost. They fail to transform (Kindleberger 1962, Chap. 7). Seen in a historical perspective, transformation may have been easier for those countries that managed to become successful exporters relatively early during the period before World War I, because comparative advantage in industrial production is not stiffly defined by physical resource endowment. It also has a lot to do with the accumulation of knowledge and human capital, and in a situation where such advantage has not yet become 'entrenched' it is presumably easier to enter, while once the territory has been divided up, as it were, latecomers have to face stiff competition from efficient producers who have been around for some time. We then have a situation which is almost exactly the opposite of the one suggested by Alexander Gerschenkron (1952), where the more 'backward' a country is, the easier it is for it to draw on the knowledge and experience accumulated by other nations. This would explain why the regions of recent settlement made the transformation while the tropical countries had problems—and presumably would have continued to have problems even in the absence of the troublesome years of 1914 to 1945.

It is also possible that industrialization becomes more difficult as the years go by. In our own time per capita income tends to be highest at the top of the ladder of comparative advantage, i.e. when manufacturing is based on 'created' production factors that are heavily research-intensive. Simple assembly operations, on the other hand, near the lower end, characterized by intensive use of unskilled labor, have comparatively little to offer a primary producer who is trying to break the dependence of resource-based products. Markets tend to be of the low income elasticity of demand type: sluggish and stagnant, but they may be the only ones available. Moving up the ladder requires more sophisticated techniques, but R&D activities are unlikely to be profitable in a situation where cheaper, differentiated, imports are available, especially for countries where the existing R&D capacity is low (Bardhan 1993, p. 24). Participation in international trade locks the resource-led country into a situation where the alternatives to fossilization are few and not particularly attractive. Wages tend to be higher in land-abundant countries than in countries with high man-land ratios, but this is true only for unskilled workers and would only serve to increase the capital intensity of their manufacturing sectors, not to push them on to the upper part of the ladder of comparative advantage.

Being earlier starters, notably in the sense that their higher per capita resource endowment made for a larger internal market, the regions of recent settlement developed products with higher skill requirements than the tropical countries. Over time, wage levels were pushed up and the regions of recent settlement attracted European immigrants with a better educational background, and more experience of manufacturing, than the tropics could do, and in addition stimulated the development of the domestic educational system. This advantage is likely to have been reinforced in a cumulative fashion as industrialization ran its course, and that, in turn made recurrent transformation easier. In the tropics both skill requirements and wage levels were lower, so low that European migrants were not interested, just Chinese and Indians who, being less skilled, were prepared to move at lower wage levels in the recipient countries.

Up until now we have taken a critical stance towards the optimistic hypothesis of Arthur Lewis that the tropical countries would have been on a promising development path but for the adverse shocks of the two World Wars punctuated by the Great Depression. If we 'fast forward' to the last thirty years, however, it is possible to defend the Lewis thesis. Two of our tropical countries in Southeast Asia, Siam (now Thailand) and Malaya (now Malaysia), enjoyed impressive growth rates from about 1960 to the early 1990s. They continued to expand traditional primary exports but also diversified their natural resource base to include new crops, such as soybeans and kenaf in the case of Thailand. More importantly, however, they both industrialized substantially, not only for the home market but also for export in labor-intensive areas such as apparel and electronic assembly.

Our two other Southeast Asian countries, Ceylon (now Sri Lanka) and Burma (now Myanmar), have stagnated miserably. In both cases, however, the explanation has to be sought in drastic policy failures and bitter internal ethnic and political conflict. There was no reason why Myanmar could not have followed Thailand or Sri Lanka have followed Malaysia. Hla Myint (1967) long ago pointed out the difference in success between the 'outward-looking' and the 'inward-looking' countries of Southeast Asia. The relevance of policy is brought out further in the extensive comparative study synthesized in Lal and Myint (1996). Ghana also missed the bus by her strangulation of cocoa exports through misguided policies of the marketing board.

The three Latin American tropical countries do not present a common picture. Brazil, the giant of the southern hemisphere, has had a notable and uneven but on the whole highly successful last thirty or forty years. Industrialization has been deep and pervasive despite many inefficiencies and imbalances. The unstable macroeconomic framework has undoubtedly hindered the progress of industrialization and export diversification. Costa Rica has had a high initial level of per capita income but import substitution based on the small Central American Common Market had its inherent limitations, and a rapid expansion of the public sector (in combination with an unfavorable external environment) led to a crisis in the 1980s with the result that growth was held back. Colombia, finally, has suffered from chronic internal violence and instability caused by the drug trade but has still managed a fairly impressive growth performance.

Argentina wasted her early golden years as a result of the distortionary policies of the Perón era and the aftermath of macroeconomic instability. In the 1990s, however, growth has been rapid and sustained in the context of monetary and exchange rate stability. Once again, we see the importance of the right policy choices.

Among the mineral economies Chile has clearly been the biggest success, once again as a consequence of the market-oriented policies undertaken by the military regime and continued by its democratic successors.

Bolivia has had spurts of growth and reform but does not seem to be on a sustained path to stability and prosperity. South Africa has suffered from the tensions of apartheid, sanctions and the transition to majority rule. The future remains uncertain, with strong pressures for redistribution towards the vast poor black majority—a redistribution which can, however, not be carried out unless the economy manages to break out of its present deadlock and raise the growth rate.

Finally, let us return to the three stories with which we started. Despite many disappointments in the performance of resource-abundant countries outside of the 'regions of recent settlement' we believe it is clear that the pessimism of the 'Marxist-Dependency' story is firmly refuted by the historical record that we have outlined. Even if growth is 'dependent', the stable growth of the 'North' has meant that the 'South', at least until recently, had the opportunity to grow as a consequence. The performance of the laggards is clearly due more to internal problems and policy failures than to lack of opportunities in the world market. We therefore feel that the 'liberal' framework, with a dose of interventionism, has on the whole been vindicated. International trade and factor movements were instrumental when it came to raising the rate of growth in resource-abundant economies during the late nineteenth and early twentieth century, albeit under circumstances that may have been almost unique for the period. That some countries performed badly later is a different story. They made the wrong policy choices and either failed to industrialize or industrialized on an inefficient basis, i.e. they failed to make the transition that has been critical for making the best use of trade in the second half of the twentieth century when international exchange of goods and services has indeed been an engine of growth again—perhaps even more than it was during the 'golden age' of 1870–1914 that has been the subject of this chapter.

References

Adas, Michael. (1974). *The Burma delta: Economic development and social change on an Asian Rice Frontier, 1852–1941*. Madison: University of Wisconsin Press.

Akira, Suehiro. (1996). *Capital accumulation in Thailand, 1855–1985*. Bangkok: Silkworm Books.

Amin, Samir. (1974). *Accumulation on a world scale. A critique of the theory of underdevelopment*. New York/London: Monthly Review Press.

Auty, Richard M. (1998). *Resource abundance and economic development. Improving the performance of resource-rich countries* (Research for Action 44). Helsinki: UNU/WIDER.

Baldwin, Robert E. (1956). Patterns of development in newly settled regions. *Manchester School of Economic and Social Studies, 24*, 161–179.

Baran, Paul A. (1957). *The political economy of growth*. New York/London: Monthly Review Press.

Bardhan, Pranab. (1993). The new growth theory, trade and development. In Göte Hansson (Ed.), *Trade, growth and development: The role of politics and institutions*. London/New York: Routledge.

Bauer, Arnold J. (1975). *Chilean rural society from the Spanish conquest to 1930*. Cambridge: Cambridge University Press.

Bauer, Peter T., & Yamey, Basil S. (1957). *The economics of under-developed countries*. Chicago: University of Chicago Press.

Bertram, Gordon W. (1963). Economic growth in Canadian industry, 1870–1915: The staple model and the take-off hypothesis. *Canadian Journal of Economics and Political Science, 29*, 159–184.

Blakemore, Harold. (1974). *British nitrates and Chilean politics, 1886–1896: Balmaceda and North*. London: University of London/Athlone Press.

Bruton, Henry J. (1992) in collaboration with Gamini Abeysekera, Nimal Sanderatne and Zainal Aznam Yusof. *The political economy of poverty, equity, and growth: Sri Lanka and Malaysia*. New York: Oxford University Press.

Bulmer-Thomas, Victor. (1987). *The political economy of Central America since 1920*. Cambridge: Cambridge University Press.

Bundy, Colin. (1972). The emergence and decline of a South African peasantry. *African Affairs, 71*, 369–388.

Burgstaller, André, & Saavedra Rivano, Nicolás. (1984). Capital mobility and growth in a North–South model. *Journal of Development Economics, 15*, 213–237.

Cairncross, Alec K. (1953). *Home and foreign investment 1870–1913*. Cambridge: Cambridge University Press.

Cardoso, Ciro F. S. (1977). The formation of the coffee estate in nineteenth-century Costa Rica. In Kenneth Duncan & Ian Rutledge (Eds.), with the collaboration of Colin Hardin. *Land and labor in Latin America. Essays on the development of agrarian capitalism in the nineteenth and twentieth centuries*. Cambridge: Cambridge University Press.

Cardoso, Ciro F. S. (1986). Central America: The liberal era, c. 1870–1930. In Leslie Bethell (Ed.), *The Cambridge history of Latin America. Volume 5, c. 1870 to 1930*. Cambridge: Cambridge University Press.

Cardoso de Mello, João Manoel, & Tavares, Maria da Conceição. (1985). The capitalist export economy in Brazil, 1884–1930. In Roberto Cortés Conde & Shane J. Hunt (Eds.), *The Latin American economies: Growth and the export sector 1880–1930*. New York/London: Holmes & Meier.

Cariola, Carmen, & Sunkel, Osvaldo. (1985). The growth of the nitrate industry and socioeconomic change in Chile, 1880–1930. In Roberto Cortés Conde & Shane J. Hunt (Eds.), *The Latin American economies: Growth and the export sector 1880–1930*. New York/London: Holmes & Meier.

Catão, Luis. (1992). *The failure of export-led growth in Brazil and Mexico, c. 1870–1930*. Research Paper no. 31. London: University of London, Institute of Latin American Studies.

Caves, Richard E., & Holton, Richard H. (1959). *The Canadian economy: Prospect and retrospect*. Cambridge, MA: Harvard University Press

Centner, Charles William. (1942). Great Britain and Chilean mining 1830–1914. *Economic History Review, 12*, 76–82.

Chenery, Hollis. (1979). *Structural change and development policy*. Washington, DC: The World Bank/Oxford University Press.

Chenery, Hollis, Robinson, Sherman, & Syrquin, Moshe. (1986). *Industrialization and growth: A comparative study*. Washington, DC: The World Bank/Oxford University Press.

Clark, Colin. (1940). *The conditions of economic progress* (3rd ed.). London: Macmillan.

Coes, Donald. (1970). Brazil. In W. Arthur Lewis (Ed.), *Tropical development 1880–1913*. London: George Allen and Unwin.

Contreras, Manuel E. (1993). *The Bolivian tin mining industry in the first half of the twentieth century*. Research Paper no. 32. London: Institute of Latin American Studies.

Corea, Gamani. (1975). *The instability of an export economy*. Colombo: Marga Institute.

Cortés Conde, Roberto. (1985). The export economy of Argentina 1880–1920. In Roberto Cortés Conde & Shane J. Hunt (Eds.), *The Latin American economies: Growth and the export sector 1880–1930*. New York/London: Holmes & Meier.

Cortés Conde, Roberto. (1992). Export-led growth in Latin America: 1870–1930. *Journal of Latin American Studies, 24* (Quincentenary Supplement), 163–179.

Craig, J. Edwin. (1970). Ceylon. In W. Arthur Lewis (Ed.), *Tropical development 1880–1930: Studies in economic progress*. London: George Allen and Unwin.

Cuccorese, Horacio Juan. (1969). *Historia de los ferrocarriles en la Argentina*. Córdoba: Ediciones Macchi.

Dean, Warren. (1986). The Brazilian economy. In Leslie Bethell (Ed.), *The Cambridge history of Latin America. Volume 5, c. 1870 to 1930*. Cambridge: Cambridge University Press.

Deas, Malcolm. (1986). Colombia, Ecuador and Venezuela, c. 1880–1930. In Leslie Bethell (Ed.), *The Cambridge history of Latin America. Volume 5, c. 1870 to 1930*. Cambridge: Cambridge University Press.

Denoon, Donald. (1983). *Settler capitalism: The dynamics of dependent development in the Southern Hemisphere*. Oxford: Clarendon.

Díaz-Alejandro, Carlos F. (1970). *Essays on the economic history of the Argentine Republic*. New Haven/London: Yale University Press.

Díaz-Alejandro, Carlos F. (1984). No less than one hundred years of Argentine economic history plus some comparisons. In Gustav Ranis et al. (Eds.), *Comparative development perspectives: Essays in honor of Lloyd Reynolds*. Boulder: Westview Press.

Edelstein, Michael. (1982). *Overseas investment in the age of high imperialism: The United Kingdom, 1850–1914*. New York: Columbia University Press.

Ferrer, Aldo. (1963). *La economía argentina: Las etapas de su desarrollo y problemas actuales*. México/Buenos Aires: Fondo de Cultura Económica.

Findlay, Ronald. (1973). *International trade and development theory*. New York/London: Columbia University Press.

Findlay, Ronald. (1980). The terms of trade and equilibrium growth in the world economy. *American Economic Review, 70*, 291–299.

Findlay, Ronald. (1993). International trade and factor mobility with an endogenous land frontier: Some general equilibrium implications of Christopher Columbus. In Wilfred J. Ethier, Elhanan Helpman, & J. Peter Neary (Eds.), *Theory, policy and dynamics in international trade*. Cambridge: Cambridge University Press

Findlay, Ronald. (1995). *Factor proportions, trade, and growth*. Cambridge, MA: MIT Press.

Findlay, Ronald, & Lundahl, Mats. (1994). Natural resources, 'vent-for-surplus', and the staples theory. In Gerald M. Meier (Ed.), *From classical economics to development economics*. New York: St. Martin's Press.

Findlay, Ronald, & Wellisz, Stanislaw (Eds.). (1993). *The political economy of poverty, equity, and growth: Five small open economies*. Oxford: Oxford University Press.

Fisher, Allan G. B. (1939). Production, primary, secondary and tertiary. *Economic Record, 15*, 24–38.

Frank, Andre Gunder. (1969). *Capitalism and underdevelopment in Latin America. Historical studies of Chile and Brazil.* (rev. and enlarged ed.). New York: Monthly Review Press.

Frankel, S. Herbert. (1938). *Capital investment in Africa.* London: Oxford University Press.

Furnivall, J. S. (1957). *An introduction to the political economy of Burma* (3rd ed.). Rangoon: People's Literature Committee & House.

Furtado, Celso. (1970). *Economic development of Latin America. A survey from colonial times to the Cuban revolution.* Cambridge: Cambridge University Press.

García, Rigoberto. (1989). *Incipient industrialization in an 'underdeveloped' country. The case of Chile, 1845–1879.* Stockholm: Institute of Latin American Studies.

Gaspar, Jeffrey Casey. (1979). *Limón: 1880–1940: Un estudio de la industria bananera en Costa Rica.* San José: Editorial Costa Rica.

Gerschenkron, Alexander. (1952). Economic backwardness in historical perspective. In Bert F. Hoselitz (Ed.), *The progress of underdeveloped areas.* Chicago: University of Chicago Press.

Gunnarsson, Christer. (1978). *The Gold Coast Cocoa Industry, 1900–1939. Production, prices and structural change* (PhD thesis). Lund: Department of Economic History, Lund University.

Gunnarsson, Christer. (1983). *Malaysian rubber production: Patterns of growth 1900–1975.* Mimeo. Lund: Department of Economic History, Lund University.

Haberler, Gottfried. (1959). *International trade and economic development.* Cairo: National Bank of Egypt.

Hall, A. R. (1968). *The export of capital from Britain 1870–1914.* London: Methuen.

Hansen, Bent. (1979). Colonial economic development with unlimited supply of land: A Ricardian case. *Economic Development and Cultural Change, 27*, 611–627.

Harbison, Ralph W. (1970). Colombia. In W. Arthur Lewis (Ed.), *Tropical development 1880–1913. Studies in economic progress.* London: George Allen and Unwin.

Hatton, Timothy J., & Williamson, Jeffrey G. (1994). International migration 1850–1939: An economic survey 1850–1939. In Timothy J. Hatton & Jeffrey

G. Williamson (Eds.), *Migration and the international labor market*. London/New York: Routledge.

Hatton, Timothy J., & Williamson, Jeffrey G. (1998). *The age of mass migration: Causes and economic impact*. New York/Oxford: Oxford University Press

Hill, Polly. (1963). *Migrant cocoa-farmers of southern Ghana: A study in rural capitalism*. London/New York: Cambridge University Press.

Hillman, John. (1994). The emergence of the tin industry in Bolivia. *Journal of Latin American Studies, 16*, 403–437.

Hlaing, Aye. (1964). *A study of economic development of Burma, 1870–1940. Mimeo*. Rangoon: Department of Economics, University of Rangoon.

Holmes, A. Baron. (1970). The Gold Coast and Nigeria. In W. Arthur Lewis (Ed.), *Tropical development 1880–1930: Studies in economic progress*. London: George Allen and Unwin.

Horna, Hernán. (1992). *Transport modernization and entrepreneurship in nineteenth century Colombia: Cisneros and friends*. Stockholm: Almqvist & Wiksell International.

Horwitz, Ralph. (1967). *The political economy of South Africa*. London: Weidenfeld and Nicolson.

Houghton, Desmond Hobart. (1971). Economic development, 1865–1965. In Monica Wilson & Leonard Thompson (Eds.), *The oxford history of South Africa, vol. II: South Africa 1870–1966*. Oxford: Oxford University Press.

Houghton, Desmond Hobart. (1976). *The South African economy* (4th ed.). Cape Town: Oxford University Press.

Ingram, James C. (1971). *Economic change in Thailand, 1850–1970*. Stanford: Stanford University Press.

Innis, Harold A. (1930). *The fur trade in Canada: An introduction to Canadian economic history*. New Haven: Yale University Press.

Innis, Harold A. (1940). *The cod fisheries: The history of an international economy*. New Haven: Yale University Press.

Jeeves, Alan. (1975). The control of migratory labor on the South African gold mines in the era of Kruger and Milner. *Journal of Southern African Studies, 2*, 3–29.

Jefferson, Mark. (1926). *Peopling the Argentine pampa*. Port Washington/London: Kennikat Press.

Kenwood, A. G., & Lougheed, A. L. (1992). *The growth of the international economy 1820–1990* (3rd ed.). London/New York: Routledge.

Kindleberger, Charles P. (1962). *Foreign trade and the national economy*. New Haven/London: Yale University Press.

Kirsch, Henry William. (1973). *The industrialization of Chile, 1880–1930* (PhD thesis). Gainesville: University of Florida.

Klein, Herbert S. (1986). Bolivia from the war of the Pacific to the Chaco War, 1880–1932. In Leslie Bethell (Ed.), *The Cambridge history of Latin America. Volume 5, c. 1870 to 1930*. Cambridge: Cambridge University Press.

Kravis, Irving B. (1970). Trade as a handmaiden of growth: Similarities between the nineteenth and twentieth centuries. *Economic Journal, 80*, 850–872.

Kuznets, Simon. (1966). *Modern economic growth: Rate, structure and spread.* New Haven/London: Yale University Press.

Lal, Deepak. (1983). *The poverty of 'development economics'.* London: The Institute of Economic Affairs.

Lal, Deepak, & Myint, Hla. (1996). *The political economy of poverty, equity, and growth: A comparative study.* Oxford: Clarendon Press/Oxford University Press.

Lamartine Yates, Paul. (1959). *Forty years of foreign trade.* London: George Allen and Unwin.

Landes, David S. (1969). *The unbound Prometheus. Technological change and industrial development in Western Europe from 1750 to the present.* Cambridge: Cambridge University Press.

League of Nations. (1945). *Industrialisation and foreign trade.* Geneva: League of Nations.

Lewis, W. Arthur. (1954). Economic development with unlimited supplies of labour. *Manchester School of Economic and Social Studies, 22*, 139–191.

Lewis, W. Arthur (Ed.). (1970). *Tropical development 1880–1913: Studies in economic progress.* London: George Allen and Unwin.

Lewis, W. Arthur. (1978). *Growth and fluctuations 1870–1913.* London: George Allen and Unwin.

Lipton, Merle. (1985). *Capitalism and apartheid. South Africa, 1910–84.* Aldershot: Gower.

Lougheed, A. L. (1968). International trade theory and economic growth. *Australian Economic History Review, 8*, 99–109.

Maddison, Angus. (1995). *Monitoring the world economy 1820–1992.* Paris: OECD.

Maddock, Rodney, & MacLean, Ian. (1984). Supply side shocks: The case of Australian gold. *Journal of Economic History, 44*, 1047–1067.

Mamalakis, Markos J. (1971). The role of government in the resource transfer and resource allocation processes: The Chilean nitrate sector, 1880–1930. In Gustav Ranis (Ed.), *Government and economic development.* New Haven/London: Yale University Press.

Mamalakis, Markos J. (1976). *The growth and structure of the Chilean economy: From independence to Allende*. New Haven/London: Yale University Press.

McGreevey, William Paul. (1985). The transition to economic growth in Colombia. In Roberto Cortés Conde & Shane J. Hunt (Eds.), *The Latin American economies: Growth and the export sector 1880–1930*. New York/London: Holmes & Meier.

McLean, Ian W. (1989). Growth in a small open economy: An historical view. In Bruce Chapman (Ed.), *Australian economic growth*. Melbourne: Macmillan.

Meier, Gerald M. (1953). Economic development and the transfer mechanism: Canada, 1895–1913. *Canadian Journal of Economics and Political Science, 19*, 1–19.

Monteón, Michael. (1982). *Chile in the nitrate era: The evolution of economic dependence, 1880–1930*. Madison: University of Wisconsin Press.

Myint, Hla. (1954–55). The gains from international trade and the backward countries. *The Review of Economic Studies, 22*, 129–142.

Myint, Hla. (1967). The inward and outward –looking countries of Southeast Asia. *The Malayan Economic Review, 12*, 1–13.

Nattrass, Jill. (1981). *The South African economy: Its growth and change*. Cape Town: Oxford University Press.

North, Douglass C. (1956). International capital flows and the development of the American West. *Journal of Economic History, 16*, 493–505.

North, Douglass C. (1966). *The economic growth of the United States 1790–1860*. New York: Norton.

O'Brien, Thomas F. (1982). *The nitrate industry and Chile's crucial transition: 1870–1891*. New York/London: New York University Press.

O'Rourke, Kevin H., & Williamson, Jeffrey G. (1997). *Globalization and history: The evolution of a 19th century Atlantic economy*. Mimeo. Cambridge, MA: Department of Economics, Harvard University.

Ocampo, José Antonio. (1991). The transition from primary exports to industrial development in Colombia. In Magnus Blomström & Patricio Meller (Eds.), *Diverging paths. Comparing a century of Scandinavian and Latin American economic development*. Washington, DC: Inter-American Development Bank.

Perloff, Harvey S., Dunn, Edgar S., Jr, Lampard, Eric E., & Muth, Richard F. (1960). *Regions, resources, and economic growth*. Baltimore: Johns Hopkins Press.

Phongpaichit, Pasuk, & Baker, Chris. (1995). *Thailand: Economy and politics*. Kuala Lumpur/Oxford: Oxford University Press.

Pope, David H. (1990). Australia's payments adjustment and capital flows under the international gold standard, 1870–1913. Working Papers in Economic History, no. 141, Australian National University, Canberra.

Pope, David, & Withers, Glenn. (1994). Wage effects of immigration in late-nineteenth-century Australia. In Timothy J. Hatton & Jeffrey G. Williamson (Eds.), *Migration and the international market, 1850–1939*. London/New York: Routledge.

Prebisch, Raúl. (1950). *The economic development of Latin America and its principal problems*. New York: United Nations Economic Commission for Latin America.

Ranis, Gustav. (1991). Towards a model of development. In Lawrence B. Krause & K. Kim (Eds.), *Liberalization in the process of economic development*. Berkeley: University of California Press.

Reynolds, Lloyd G. (1985). *Economic growth in the Third World, 1850–1980*. New Haven/London: Yale University Press.

Robertson, Dennis H. (1938). The future of international trade. *Economic Journal, 48*, 1–14.

Rostow, Walt W. (1960). *The stages of economic growth: A non-communist manifesto*. Cambridge: Cambridge University Press.

Sachs, Jeffrey D. (1996). *Resource endowments and the real exchange rate: A comparison of Latin America and East Asia*. Mimeo. Cambridge, MA: Harvard Institute for International Development.

Sachs, Jeffrey D., & Warner, Andrew M. (1995). *Natural resource abundance and economic growth*. NBER Working Paper Series, Working Paper 5398. Cambridge, MA: National Bureau of Economic Research.

Singer, Hans W. (1950). The distribution of gains between investing and borrowing countries. *American Economic Review, 40* (Supplement), 473–485.

Snodgrass, Donald R. (1966). *Ceylon: An export economy in transition*. Homewood: Richard D. Irwin.

Stein, S. J. (1957). *The Brazilian cotton manufacture: Textile enterprise in an underdeveloped area 1850–1950*. Cambridge, MA: Harvard University Press.

Stovel, John A. (1959). *Canada in the world economy*. Cambridge, MA: Harvard University Press.

Stover, Charles C. (1970). Tropical exports. In W. Arthur Lewis (Ed.), *Tropical development 1880–1913: Studies in economic progress*. London: George Allen and Unwin.

Szereszewski, R. (1965). *Structural changes in the economy of Ghana, 1891–1911*. London: Weidenfeld and Nicolson.

Taylor, Alan M. (1992). External dependence, demographic burdens, and Argentine economic decline after the Belle Époque. *Journal of Economic History, 52*, 907–936.

Taylor, Alan M. (1994). Mass migration to distant Southern shores. Argentina and Australia, 1870–1939. In Timothy J. Hatton & Jeffrey G. Williamson (Eds.), *Migration and the international market, 1850–1939*. London/New York: Routledge.

Taylor, Alan M. (1996). *International capital mobility in history: The saving-investment relationship*. Working paper 5743. Cambridge, MA: National Bureau of Economic Research.

Taylor, Alan M., & Williamson, Jeffrey G. (1994). Capital flows to the new world as an intergenerational transfer. *Journal of Political Economy, 102*, 348–371

Turner, Frederick Jackson. (1921). *The frontier in American history*. Tucson: University of Arizona Press.

Viner, Jacob. (1953). *International trade and economic development*. Oxford: Clarendon.

Watkins, Melville H. (1963). A staple theory of economic growth. *Canadian Journal of Economics and Political Science, 29*, 141–158.

11

Lampião and the Colonels: On the Political Economy of Banditry

'A volta de Lampião é cruel.'

As Eric Hobsbawm has demonstrated in a classic book, banditry is a ubiquitous phenomenon in pre-modern societies. 'Social banditry', he writes 'is one of the most universal social phenomena known to history, and one of the most amazingly uniform' (Hobsbawm 1985, p. 18). Hobsbawm deals almost exclusively with social bandits, i.e. people who are regarded as outlaws by the state but who are seen as heroes by the local society in which they live because they fight for some vaguely defined just cause. The protagonists of our story, the Brazilian *cangaceiros*, are treated as social bandits by Hobsbawm, and by a large number of other authors. This is a dubious procedure, however. Not all bandits are social. Many have taken up bandit life for other reasons. One of these is economic. Given the means at their disposal and the characteristics of the society in which they operate, being a bandit is conducive to higher income and social status than being an ordinary citizen. As it seems, this was to a very large extent also the case of the *cangaceiros*. The existing literature is in no way coherent. It contains highly contradictory views, ranging

---

Thanks are due to Thaïs Machado-Borges for help with some tricky Brazilian terminology.

Original chapter for the present volume by Ronald Findlay and Mats Lundahl.

R. Findlay, M. Lundahl, *The Economics of the Frontier*,
DOI 10.1057/978-1-137-60237-4_11

from full moral support for the bandits to total condemnation of them. The explanations of their behavior often leave a lot to be desired. Some romanticize and excuse. Others treat them as simple crooks, hardly worthy of analysis.

The purpose of the present chapter is to bring some economic reasoning to bear on the story of Brazilian banditry. Our piece is an exercise in the economics of the frontier. The more well-known *cangaceiros*, not least the most famous of all, Lampião, were able to operate for long periods of time across very wide geographical territories without being seriously bothered by the police or the military. In a sense they were able to carve out their own private 'empires'. In order to understand why this was possible it is necessary to bring in all the principal actors of their habitat, northeast Brazil, not only the bandits themselves but also the police and the military, the local political bosses known as *coronéis* (colonels), the politicians at the state level, the general population, and in the end the modern centralized state that emerged in Brazil from 1930. Their interaction can be analyzed with the aid of some economics. Let us, however, begin with an account of the isolated physical environment in which the activities of the Brazilian bandits took place, of the geography of drought of northeast Brazil.

The Physical Setting

The northeast is the poorest area of Brazil. Most of it is plagued by a harsh climate. The region is the location of the dry and hostile sertão portrayed in the classic works of, for example, Euclides da Cunha (1944) and Josué de Castro (1966). The sertão extends across parts of the territory of the states of Piauí, Ceará, Rio Grande do Norte, Paraíba, Pernambuco, Alagôas, Bahia and Maranhão, and marginally touches Sergipe and northern Minas Gerais. It is literally a hinterland, alternatively qualified as the 'quadrilateral of hunger' and the 'polygon of drought', a backland hidden behind a narrow fertile coastal band blessed by plentiful rainfall. In the sertão, water is scarce (Lima 1965, p. 4):

> The winds that blow don't refresh the environment and they aggravate the erosion of the soil, lifting dust clouds, the only clouds that during certain

> periods rise towards the clear skies. [...] The river beds are empty. Pebbles extend across immense distances. Cauldrons without water. No chances of rain. Mere puddles at great distances from one another, league after league, innumerable, without anything, and don't even dream of finding artesian wells.

The semi-arid landscape is mainly gray, dry, poor and sandy, earth, naked or with spots of low, spiny xerophytic vegetation: cactuses and bromeliads under a relentless sun (Castro 1966, p. 23), 'long, silent sleeping lands of lapis-lazuli. A geography of fulgurations' (Macêdo 1968, p. 14).

The heart of the sertão is the *caatinga*, the scrub land with thorny bush vegetation, which is more prone to drought than other parts and which exhibits desert-like characteristics when the dry spells occur. There, only the hardiest plants survive, the trees shrink to the size of bushes in the scorched landscape and the rivers dry up completely in the dry season (Castro 1966, p. 37). Euclides da Cunha (1944, p. 30) describes the impression that the *caatinga* makes on the traveler:

> The caatinga ... stifles him; it cuts short his view, strikes him in the face, so to speak, and stuns him, enmeshes him in its spiny woof, and holds out no compensating attractions. It repulses him with its thorns and prickly leaves, its twigs sharp as lances; and it stretches out in front of him, for mile on mile, unchanging in its desolate aspect of leafless trees, of dried and twisted boughs, a turbulent maze of vegetation standing rigidly in space or spreading out sinuously along the ground, representing, as it would seem, the agonized struggles of a tortured, writhing flora.

In the sertão it normally rains only in the winter, some time during a five to six-month period beginning from December to March, depending on the particular locality. The beginning and the end of the winter may, however, vary from place to place and so may the highly erratic distribution of the rain. The entire precipitation of a year may be concentrated to a few days or weeks, or it may come at the beginning or the end of the winter season (Chandler 1978, p. 6).

When it rains in the sertão, the latter undergoes a metamorphosis. The backlands of the northeast, writes da Cunha (1944, p. 40), 'are barbarously sterile, marvellously exuberant'. When the rains come they become 'one vast garden', but once they are over, things immediately go back to their 'natural' state: 'The days of torture return; the atmosphere is asphyxiating; the soil is hard as rock; the flora is stripped bare; and on those occasions when summer meets summer without the intermittency of rain—the dreadful spasm of the drought' (Cunha 1944, p. 41). Dry spells are a constant and credible threat, and they occur periodically. Limiting ourselves to the period of relevance for the present chapter, severe droughts took place in 1877–79, 1888–89, 1898, 1900, 1902–04, 1907–08, 1915, 1919 and 1930–32 (Castro 1966, p. 49; Souza 1972, p. 120; Mello 2004, p. 55).

The harshness of the climate of the sertão makes it unsuitable for agriculture. Already the early Portuguese colonists turned to cattle-raising instead, and animal husbandry continued to dominate the life of the *sertanejos* for centuries to come, although the relative isolation of the region forced families everywhere to cultivate for subsistence purposes. The result of the periodic droughts was starvation, out-migration by tens of thousands and severely inflated death rates, not just from hunger, thirst and intake of unsuitable foodstuffs, but also from epidemic diseases of various kinds.

Believers and *Cangaceiros*

The sertão is an area which at various times during the history of Brazil has given birth to movements which in different ways were perceived as challenges or threats to the established order. Robert Levine (1992) lists seven religious (millenarian) movements in the northeast between 1817 and the late 1930s. Two of these stand out in terms of the attention that they attracted from the outside.

The first is the Canudos movement (Cunha 1944; Levine 1992) (the movement that inspired Mario Vargas Llosa's (1981) novel *La guerra del fin del mundo*), headed by Antônio Vicente Mendes Maciel, alias Antônio Conselheiro, who between 1893 and 1896 attracted thousands of families who withdrew with him from the secular world and founded a holy city at Canudos in northeastern Bahia, following a cruel drought between

1888 and 1892. The entire subsistence base was threatened and the population was in a state of flux. Antônio Conselheiro and his apocalyptically tinted message thus found a ready market.

Antônio Conselheiro attracted the attention of both religious and secular authorities. Local *fazendeiros* [landowners] were afraid of losing their authority in the eyes of the population, and the Canudos people were depicted as backward and barbarian enemies of the Republic. At the end of 1896 the first of a series of four police or military expeditions was dispatched to cope with the movement. It failed. So did a second expedition of almost 550 army and police troops and a third of 1,000 well-equipped soldiers, both in 1897. It took a fourth expedition and more than 8,000 men to finally wipe the population of Canudos and their 5,200 houses out, between July and October the same year, after a massacre on of the faithful and more than 15,000 dead.

The second religious movement was the one headed by Padre Cícero (Cícero Romão Batista) in the southeastern corner of the present-day state of Ceará, in the Carirí valley, in the hamlet of Juàzeiro (Macêdo 1961; Morel 1966; Cava 1970). On 1 March 1889, he was administering communion to one of the *beatas* [pious women] of his flock, who fell to the ground while the white host in her mouth became red with blood, an event which was repeated each Wednesday and Friday of Lent for the next two months (Cava 1970, p. 31). The miracle at Juàzeiro attracted large numbers of pilgrims. The hamlet grew rapidly, from less than 2,500 inhabitants in 1890, to over 15,000 in 1909 (Cava 1970, p. 250). The hierarchy of the Catholic Church, however, labeled Maria de Araújo an impostor. Padre Cícero was drawn into a life-long conflict with the church officials and in 1896 was suspended from priesthood.

The Canudos and Juàzeiro episodes both occurred during one of the most difficult periods in the history of the Brazilian northeast. Between 1877 and 1879 one of the worst droughts on record took place in the area. Ceará was declared a national disaster area. In mid-1880, around 300,000 people, or one-third of the population of Ceará, had either emigrated to other states or died (Cava 1970, p. 66). Eight years later another, very severe, drought unfolded, followed by three more, in 1898, 1900 and 1915. In twelve of the years between 1877 and 1915, agriculture was severely hit and almost half a million people left the region during this period (Cava 1970, p. 88).

The influx of people to Juàzeiro continued until the death of Padre Cícero in 1934, mostly poor farm hands, *vaqueiros* (cowboys) and landless *rendeiros* (tenant farmers), illiterate and impoverished (Cava 1970, p. 85). The entire Carirí valley, a region of natural fertility, in bright contrast to the surrounding sertão, underwent an economic transformation in less than twenty years. Juàzeiro became 'a burgeoning agricultural, commercial, and artisan emporium of the Northeastern backlands' with spread effects extending to the entire Carirí valley, which became known as the 'breadbasket of the Northeastern *sertão*' (Cava 1970, p. 4). Padre Cícero entered politics and became one of the most influential chiefs in the northeast of Brazil (Cava 1972, pp. 133–34).

The movements led by Antônio Conselheiro and Padre Cícero were 'social', movements which attracted poor people during difficult times and tried to improve their situation. The present chapter is about a different type of movement in the same geographical area: the *cangaço*,[1] Brazilian banditry. The *cangaceiros* constitute one of the most classic of all bandit varieties, right out of the motion picture screen, as it were: 'Most of them could be identified by a colorful kerchief and a leather hat … whose brim, usually decorated, was turned upwards at the front; numerous cartridge belts, worn over the shoulders (crossing each other over the chest) and around the waist, added to the striking appearance' (Chandler 1978, p. 5).

As is well known from the writings of Eric Hobsbawm (1959, 1985), bandits may also be 'social': avengers of past injustices who settle accounts, or Robin Hoods stealing from the rich and giving to the poor, 'considered by their people as heroes, as champions, avengers, fighters for justice, perhaps even leaders of liberation, and in any case as men to be admired, helped and supported' (Hobsbawm 1985, p. 17). Much of the literature on Brazilian banditry portrays the *cangaceiros* as social bandits, notably the *literatura de cordel*, the popular pamphlets written in verse and telling more or less romantic stories about the life of the great Lampião, but also

[1] The term apparently derives from *canga* or *cangalho*, yoke. The *cangaceiros* carried their guns across their shoulders like an ox carries a yoke (Chandler 1978, p. 5).

more scholarly works (e.g. Hobsbawm 1985; Macêdo 1968; Mello 2004; Maciel 1985a, b, c, 1987a, b, 1988; Torres 1994; Lins 1995). This is, however, is a 'truth' with many modifications, if, indeed, it can be called a truth at all (Chandler 1978; Lewin 1979). Clearly, other elements than altruism were present in the picture, and we will argue that they were the dominant ones.

The early *cangaço* was connected to kinship and limited its actions to a local, area, but with time the bands grew into larger and professional organizations active across a much wider territory. Their activities included the invasion of estates and the plunder of villages and towns, sometimes with the aim of damaging a particular individual or group (frequently from the ruling class) as revenge for real or imagined injustices (Fausto 1986, pp. 805–06).

Banditry in the northeast began in the mid-nineteenth century, as a result of demographic growth in combination with sporadic droughts, from around 1845 (Cava 1970, p. 141). When the great drought of 1877–79 took place, the hitherto unorganized individual highwaymen began to form groups of five to twenty people, 'assuming terrifying *noms de guerre* by which history now remembers them', in pursuit of personal gains 'but not infrequently for the welfare of their drought-stricken and helpless compatriots' (Cava 1970, p. 142). As the drought came to an end, however, so did the social aims of the *cangaceiros*. With the advent of the Republic and the consequent delegation of power to the local level, the *cangaço* acquired new strength, as part of the power struggle among local *chefes*. The apogee came with the arrival of professional banditry in the 1920s. No statistics seem to exist with respect to the number of *cangaceiros* active at any one time, but Fernando Pernambucano de Mello (2004, pp. 190–92) has identified, 'with certainty' 44 different gangs that operated at different times between 1919 and 1927, before the *cangaço* entered its phase of decline.

The most famous *cangaceiro* at the beginning of the twentieth century was Antônio Silvino (born in in 1875 as Manuel Batista de Morais), who had the reputation of being the Robin Hood of Brazil (Lewin 1979). Silvino was active from 1897 to 1914, when he was caught in Lagôa do Lages, Pernambuco. He operated in four states, mainly in Paraíba and Pernambuco, but also in eastern Ceará and southern Rio Grande do

Norte, in a territory of approximately 100,000 square kilometers, housing a population of about 1 million.

Antônio Silvino became a bandit in 1897 after his father had been murdered. He learned the tricks of the trade for two years in the band of his godfather Silvino Aires de Cavalcanti e Albuquerque, 'the doyen of the preceding generation of *cangaceiros* who had incredibly eluded his pursuers for a quarter of a century' (Lewin 1979, p. 123), and when the latter was imprisoned, Antônio replaced him as band leader. Thereafter, until 1914, he roamed the sertões, in a series of assaults, robberies, killing of enemies and destruction of their property (Lewin 1979, p. 123). After his capture, Antônio spent twenty-three years in prison in Recife, before being pardoned by President Getúlio Vargas in 1937. He died in poverty in 1944.

The Greatest of Them All: Lampião

The greatest *cangaceiro* of all times, however, was Lampião ('The Big Lamp').[2] Based on the description by reporter from the daily newspaper *O Ceará* Billy Jaynes Chandler (1978, p. 67), the author of the most scholarly biography of Lampião, offers the following portrait of him (cf. Fig. 11.1)[3]:

> Lampião was … a thin, well proportioned man of medium stature, with dark skin and thick black hair. His clothing, of an ordinary type, included a felt hat of regular formation (not the highly decorated hat with turned-back brim that the cangaceiro often wore) and a pair of leather sandals of the type worn by area cowboys. Around his neck he wore a green scarf, held secure by a diamond ring. Six additional rings of precious stones—a ruby, a topaz, an emerald, and three diamonds—adorned his fingers. He was armed with a rifle, a pistol, and a long knife of close to twenty inches in

[2] The following account of the life of Lampião builds mainly on the works of Chandler (1978), Maciel (1985a, b, c, 1987a, b, 1988) and Grunspan-Jasmin (2001).

[3] Maciel (1988) goes into great (and slightly romanticized) detail about the looks and personality of Lampião.

Figure 11.1 Lampião during his visit to Padre Cícero in Juàzeiro in 1926

> length. Lampião—as was the cangaceiro ideal—was well adorned and well armed.
>
> … Lampião's right eye had been injured … when a piece of a tree branch had penetrated it, causing the development of leukoma (white opacity) of the cornea. Over the years, the condition worsened, and he became almost totally blind in that eye. He frequently wore colored glasses, not only to conceal the defective eye, but also, apparently, because he suffered from an intolerance to light in the other eye.

Lampião was probably born in 1897 or 1898 in the Pajeú area in the state of Pernambuco, in the dry sertão (Grunspan-Jasmin 2001, pp. 30–31).[4] His real name was Virgulino Ferreira da Silva. The Ferreira family were cattle raisers and farmers. Why Lampião chose to become an outlaw is not completely clear (Chandler 1978, p. 34), but at the bottom

[4] Grunspan-Jasmin (2001, pp. 30–32) lists a dozen suggested birth dates ranging from 1893 to 1905 and six different birth places.

was a conflict between the Ferreira family and José Saturnino, a neighbor related to the Nogueiras, a local elite family. The issue began in 1916 with unclear allegations of trespassing and thefts of animals. It soon escalated into violence, and the Ferreiras were forced to sell their ranch and leave the area.

At the new residence, Nazaré, in the neighboring Floresta county, the trouble continued. The family had to move for the second time, to Agua Branca in Alagôas, around 1920, having lost most of their cattle. Virgulino, together with his two older brothers attacked José Saturnino's ranches and a ranch owned by the Nogueiras in nearby Serra Vermelha, which led to clashes with the local police. Again, the family had to move, which caused the death of Virgulino's ailing mother. The brothers then attacked the Pariconhas village in Agua Branca, an event which produced the death of José Ferreira, their father, in a charge by the police in May 1921.

This was a decisive event. 'Whatever chance there had been that the lives of the Ferreira boys could be directed into peaceful avenues was shut off' (Chandler 1978, p. 34). The feud had placed Virgulino outside the law, and with time he would turn into a full-scale bandit. His professed aim was to avenge his father's death at the hands of the police, and this is, of course, also the aim that looms large in the folklore and myth surrounding the Lampião figure. However, the two men whom the Ferreiras blamed for their father's death were never killed but outlived the brothers by several decades (Chandler 1978, p. 35).

The three Ferreira brothers allied themselves with other *cangaceiros* on a makeshift basis, until, in 1922, Lampião became the most prominent bandit of the northeast. For the next few years his group survived on plunder and more or less 'voluntary' contributions from the local population. It appears as if he refrained from the worst excesses, neither plundering indiscriminately nor murdering without reason. 'He normally did not choose his victims at random' (Chandler 1978, p. 40). Often, the motive was revenge.

Most of the time, the police showed no more than a lukewarm interest in pursuing Lampião, and, like all other *cangaceiros*, he had his protectors and helpers: *coiteiros*, as they were known. These were of two different kinds. First, there were the prestigious and wealthy political bosses of counties, or even regions, who preferred to stay on good terms with Lampião, in order to avoid damage to their property. Some of them even had personal ties to him or to his friends or at least had enemies in common with him. The mass of the *coiteiros*, however, came from a far more modest background, from rural areas, small proprietors, tenant farmers or *vaqueiros*, who acted more or less as agents for Lampião, providing him with necessities and feeding him information that made it possible to stay out of the way of the police (Chandler 1978, pp. 86–87).

Between 1923 and 1926, Lampião enjoyed a close degree of coexistence with the population and the political bosses of the northeast, subject to less police persecution than at any other time of his life (Chandler 1978, p. 47). Towards the end of this period he came close to returning to a regular life. The occasion was a visit to Padre Cícero in Juàzeiro. The background was the following. In early 1926 the so-called Prestes Column, a remnant from an unsuccessful military revolt in São Paulo in July 1924, was on the move into the northeast, headed by Luís Carlos Prestes, later the leader of the Brazilian communist party.[5] In January 1926, the column was about to enter Ceará. Congressman Floro Bartolomeu, the man who had been running the real political show in Juàzeiro with Padre Cícero as the front, felt that the defense of Ceará could not be left to the notoriously inefficient police and the local political bosses, so he decided to recruit Lampião, who was at the time in Pernambuco. At the beginning of March, when the Prestes Column was in Bahia, Lampião saw Padre Cícero and received a commission (of doubtful legality) as a captain in the Patriotic Batallions. He also promised the priest to end his crimes, and that 'once the insurgents were expelled, he would leave the Northeast to live, honestly, away from his enemies' (Padre Cícero, quoted by Chandler 1978, p. 70). The Pernambuco police, however, continued to pursue him. Lampião decided to return to Juàzeiro and meet Padre Cícero again, but the latter refused, presumably under pressure from his supporters, who did not want to see a protector of bandits running for the federal Chamber of Deputies. Lampião was furious and went back to his old ways.

[5] The column numbered 3,000 men (Queiroz 1968, p. 91).

As it seems, Lampião's attitude to violence had undergone a change. The local newspapers began to report more unprovoked killings, rape incidents, etc., and he and his band began to kill all soldiers and police officers whom they happened to lay their hands on. The authorities, in turn, decided to step up the fight against banditry. At the end of November 1926 Lampião, accompanied by some 100 *cangaceiros* fought a protracted battle against 295 soldiers at Serra Grande near Vila Bela in Pernambuco. This battle inaugurated a period of more vigorous pursuit. A meeting between the police chiefs of Paraíba, Rio Grande do Norte, Ceará, Alagôas and Bahia produced a joint pledge to cooperate and allow troops to cross state borders when pursuing bandits. Lower-level *coiteiros* were beginning to be jailed.

In June 1927, Lampião attacked Mossoró, the most important city of the interior of Río Grande do Norte, with no more than some 60 people under his command, after requesting a ransom of no less than 500 contos,[6] subsequently reduced to 400, but failing to obtain it. The city defended itself, and fought off Lampião and his men. He had attempted too much. 'Mossoró, the most ambitious and most foolish undertaking of his career, was a mistake. He was not to make that kind of mistake again' (Chandler 1978, p. 99). The attack set a tri-state police force almost 500 troops after Lampião. With less than 50 men, he was ambushed by some 400 soldiers, including 50 cavalrymen, at the hill of Macambira, but managed to escape.

Lampião's activities thereafter subsided until the end of the year, and through most of 1928 he continued to keep a low profile. He was under heavy pressure from the police, and the size of his band was reduced until it consisted of a mere five *cangaceiros*. Towards the end of August he crossed the São Francisco river into Bahia from Pernambuco. There, he was by and large left in peace. It was not until the end of December that the first serious clash with the police took place. After a second clash, at the beginning of 1929, Lampião's activities waned again. He stayed in Bahia for a few months, assaulting villages and ranches, and again ran into a police force in April. During the rest of the year, his band grew. In October he attacked a road construction gang and in November he

[6] 1 conto (de réis) = 1,000 milréis = 1 million réis.

crossed the border into Sergipe, where he requested a contribution of twenty contos from the town of Capela and got six. A month later he obtained twenty-three contos from Queimadas in Bahia, after occupying the police station. Before leaving with two of his men, he shot the seven soldiers who had been locked up in the station.

During the first three months of 1930 little was heard from Lampião. He was active across a wide territory in both Bahia and Sergipe. In July two more encounters with the police took place, the last one at the Mandacaru ranch near Tucano in Bahia, where five policemen were killed. In October and November, an uprising in Rio Grande do Sul put an end to the first Brazilian republic, and the troops chasing *cangaceiros* were retired to the capital areas for political reasons. Lampião then moved into Pernambuco and Alagôas assaulting ranches and demanding contributions, increasing his power in the region, aided by the fact that the new political regime in Brazil began a policy of disarming the population in the backlands, especially those who had resisted the revolution. The result was that Lampião could continue his activities relatively undisturbed by the authorities throughout 1931.

In September that year 400 contos were allocated by the federal government to the campaign against bandits in Bahia. The campaign, however, got off to a bad start at Maranduba, on the Sergipe-Bahia border at the beginning of January 1932 when a detachment of soldiers was defeated by Lampião and his men. Around this time, a plan devised by Captain João Miguel, the officer in charge of chasing bandits in Bahia, which consisted in evacuating the population from areas known to be infested with *cangaceiros*, was put into effect—to little avail. The year 1932 turned out to be one of severe drought and cattle herds had to be more or less abandoned. '… everybody suffered, but Lampião' (Chandler 1978, p. 175), who moved on to areas with more water. In the end, the scheme had to be abandoned, and Miguel was demoted. The troops pursuing the *cangaceiros* were not particularly active during the first half of the year, and from then until the end of the year, only three battles took place.

Lampião spent the first half of 1933 in Sergipe and Bahia, but his activity level was low, until the beginning of July, when he entered the village of Oliveira, west of Juàzeiro, in the far interior of Bahia, cleaning it out in two hours, leaving with a booty of 70 contos. After a number of encounters with the police during the remainder of the year, Lampião gradually withdrew from Bahia, to Sergipe and Alagôas, where he remained during 1934, limiting himself to incursions into the border area of Bahia. The campaign against him declined accordingly. In mid-1934, some 900 troops were after him. At the end of the year, the figure had fallen to some 250. Funds for the campaign were late and this led to demoralization of the soldiers. Eight combats took place in 1934, against 15 in 1933.

In early 1935 Lampião assaulted ranches and extorted money in Alagôas, before he moved into Pernambuco in mid-year, engaging in combat with the police in May and July. Between October 1935 and February 1936 he oscillated between Bahia, Sergipe and Alagôas, moving thereafter into Pernambuco, covering a vast territory between the Alagôas and Paraíba borders. In September his gang appeared in Bahia and Alagôas, where the town of Piranhas was attacked. 1937 was 'a fairly busy though unspectacular period' (Chandler 1978, p. 195) for Lampião, who dedicated himself mainly to extortion, with 16 battles against the police, mainly in Sergipe and the border areas of Bahia and Alagôas.

The beginning of 1938 was less conspicuous, until, in April, Lampião and his men went on a pillage spree in Alagôas, before disappearing once more from sight until July. By then the Alagôas authorities were determined to get rid of him. In 1937 President Getúlio Vargas had proclaimed his *Estado Nôvo*, the New State, a measure which had increased the power of the central government. During his dictatorship from 1937 to 1945, all political parties were outlawed and the central government tightened its hold on the federal system (Souza 1972, p. 129). Possibly, Vargas had also personally ordered that something be done about Lampião.

José Lucena, the official in charge of the Alagôas state campaign against banditry, chose João Bezerra to carry out the elimination. Bezerra located Lampião with some 50–60 men at Angicos, a ranch on the Sergipe side of the São Francisco River, opposite Piranhas in Alagôas. On the morning of 28 July, Bezerra and his 45 soldiers attacked. The attack was over after some 20 minutes. Eleven *cangaceiros* had been killed, among them Lampião himself, and his fiancée, Maria Bonita. Their bodies were decapitated and exhibited to the public. The heads of Lampião and Maria Bonita were sent to Salvador de Bahia where they were kept in a museum until given burial in 1969. With that, of the more well-known of Lampião's men, only Corisco and Ângelo Roque ('Labarêda'), were left. Roque surrendered in April 1940, and Corisco was killed in battle in May. The *cangaço* had come to an end.

The Bandits: Income Versus Strength Maximization

The two most outstanding facts about Lampião's career is the length of it, almost 20 years, and the size of the territory that he managed to control, around 300,000 square kilometers in seven states, an area almost the size of Italy. This he did with the aid of a band whose size varied between a mere handful and about 100. In 1925, the diary *A Tribuna* (Petrolina, Pernambuco) called him the 'governor of the backlands' (Chandler 1978, p. 81), and following the battle at Serra Grande, in November the following year, Lampião sent a letter to the governor of Pernambuco, suggesting a division of that state between the governor and himself. He recommended that he would govern the portion west of Rio Branco (present-day Arcoverde), while the governor would keep the eastern part (Chandler 1978, p. 85; the text is reproduced in Assunção 2007, pp. 69–70). In the rest of this chapter we will analyze the mechanisms that allowed *cangaceiros* like Antônio Silvino and Lampião to operate in a vast geographical territory for decades without being caught and, at least in the case of Lampião, exert a certain degree of control over that territory for almost two decades.

According to Amaury de Souza (1972, p. 128), the average size of Lampião's band was eighty men, who were divided into twelve-man raiding units which operated a maximum of 200 miles from the core unit led by Lampião himself. 'This was the band's exclusive territory, within no other band was allowed to operate.' But the band as a whole moved across a much wider territory. How could a bandit like Lampião with between five and a hundred people, dominate 300,000 square kilometers in spite of the presence of military and police chasing him all the time, for a period of almost twenty years? Why were the military inefficient?

The answer to these questions will be sought with the aid of some simple economic theory.

We will look at each of the principal actors in turn. During the heyday of the *cangaço* the northeast contained four different groups which interacted with each other in various ways to produce the economic and political equilibrium which allowed banditry to persist: the *cangaceiros*, the local political bosses known as *coronéis*, the population at large and the police and *volante* units fighting the bandits.

Let us begin by a look at the protagonists, the *cangaceiros* themselves. In *Bandits*, Eric Hobsbawm includes Lampião in the 'avenger' category of bandits. 'In the sertão, he who does not take revenge is morally dead', wrote Gustavo Barroso in his book on heroes and bandits, published in 1917 (quoted by Mello 2004, p. 63), and Hobsbawm (1985, p. 58) agrees: 'They are not so much men who right wrongs, but avengers, and exerters of power; their appeal is not that of the agents of justice, but of men who prove that even the weak can be terrible.' Hobsbawm goes on to quote some of the folk poetry about Lampião to substantiate his point. The point is a doubtful one, however. Frederico Pernambucano de Mello (2004, p. 126) points to the apparent contradiction between words and deeds. 'The cangaceiro held out his condition as an avenger but did little or nothing to concretize his revenge.' In the 1980 postscript to the second edition of his book, Hobsbawm (1985, p. 142) himself shows clear signs of doubt with respect to his categorization of Lampião:

> Lampião never actually did anything to revenge himself on the two men claimed to be his deadly enemies. [...] ... Lampião and indeed any backwoods bandleader who wished to survive and flourish, had to manage their alliances and enmities primarily in terms of the oligarchic politics of the region. The protection of a suitable, and perhaps changing, selection of the powerful 'colonels' was more vital ... than the support of the poor. Were the great *cangaceiros* primarily rebellious victims of society? In the anarchic and virtually stateless *sertão* ... brigandage was also a promising career for tough young men, and Lampião himself as well as others saw it as a profession or business. When asked in 1926 by the newspaper *O Ceará* why he did not give up banditry, he pointed out that nobody running a successful business (*negocio*) would think of giving it up.

Here, Hobsbawm clearly favors an 'economic' explanation of the *cangaço*. So does Estácio de Lima: 'Nobody will think of the interpretation of a human behavior in terms of a single cause [...] But the influence of the physical environment is real' (Lima 1965, p. 6). This is precisely where we have to begin the explanation. The physical environment of northeast Brazil was described in the opening section of the chapter, and it weighs heavily. 'If the physical characteristics of the land inhabited by Lampião appear to be unduly emphasized, let it be said that the society of which he was a not atypical member was molded in part by these physical factors', states Chandler (1978, pp. 7–8).

Northeast Brazil in the late nineteenth and early twentieth century was much like Mongolia during the times of Chinggis Khan (Findlay and Lundahl 2006). The marginal product of labor was a function of the forbidding natural environment in both cases. The harsh natural conditions made for a low marginal return to agriculture in particular but also to cattle-raising. Few people in the sertão owned large land tracts. On the contrary, the absolute majority lived in dire poverty, and it was from the poor that many of the bandits came (Chandler 1978, p. 9). Most owned very little, and even rich families could look forward to gradually falling incomes. The landed estates were fragmented over time, as a result of the division that took place among the heirs as soon as an owner died, but ranching was an activity that required a large land area, so as the properties grew smaller and smaller, incomes declined as well. Add to this periodic droughts and whatever other misfortunes that might occur, and the owners would have to sell out and join the rural proletariat. 'Two years of drought turned out to be enough to destroy the work of ten', writes Mello (2004, p. 42) laconically. As dispossessed workers, the *sertanejos* had difficulties finding employment, since ranching needed few hands, so over time a surplus population was being built up. Agriculture did not constitute any realistic alternative either. The sertão was ill-suited to farming, and the fragmentation process pulverizing the cattle ranches had a similar impact on the farms (Chandler 1978, pp. 10–12).

Under these circumstances, banditry stood out as a realistic alternative in pure income terms. 'Banditry had grown into an enterprise', writes Amaury de Souza (1972, p. 112), 'and it was carried on as such' (Souza 1972, p. 125). 'Lampião turned the cangaço into a way of life, nay, a profession', states Élise Grunspan-Jasmin (2001, p. 15). While it is certainly true that many bandits were driven into the *cangaço* for reasons of social tension, family rivalry, feud or vengeance, an economic component was definitely present, especially during bad times when incomes were lower than normal (Fausto 1986, pp. 805–06). The regular *cangaceiros* were recruited among the poorer strata of the rural population: the poor, the hungry, the dark—people with no interest in politics. 'For them, "turning *cangaceiro*" offered the traditional incentive of better work at higher pay' (Lewin 1979, p. 139).

Mello (2004, p. 89) makes a distinction between three different types of *cangaceiros*: the professionals, represented by Lampião and Antônio Silvino, the avengers, or 'noble' *cangaceiros* and those who joined the *cangaço* looking for protection because they were persecuted and had no alternative. The quantitatively most important category was the first one (Mello 2004, p. 140). The professional bandits also tended to be active for longer periods than the avengers and their operations covered a larger territory (Mello 2004, p. 146). Even Chandler, who by and large prefers to seek the causes of the *cangaço* directly in the communities where banditry was rampant, does not fail to stress the importance of economic matters. They created banditry, and once the latter was in place it readily absorbed poor people when times turned from bad to worse. Factors like the abrupt fall in the demand for Brazilian cotton when the American Civil War came to an end, a depressed sugar market and the end of the Amazon rubber boom in the 1910s and 1920s, in combination with a population increase in the backlands of the northeast all contributed to the same end (Chandler 1978, pp. 13, 15–16).

To this has to be added the droughts, which made banditry flare up. Even though banditry was present also under 'normal' conditions, suggests Chandler, the increased frequency of severe droughts during the late nineteenth (especially the 1870s) and the early twentieth century made for an uncommonly high level of sustained banditry. 'Indeed, the drought of 1919 seems to have inaugurated the worst of it' (Chandler 1978, p. 16). Mello (2004, p. 187) agrees: 'With the 1919 drought, professional cangaceirismo entered the phase of its most vertiginous expansion.' He identifies, 'with certainty', 44 different bandit groups that were active between 1919 and 1927 (Mello 2004, pp. 190–92).

In the concrete case of Lampião, economic factors may very well have been directly behind his desire to take vengeance on the enemies of his family. The family had been driven away from its ranch in Vila Bela and forced to go to Nazaré, and from there it was forced on to Agua Branca in Alagôas around 1920. By then, the economic situation of the Ferreiras had undergone a change for worse. Most of their cattle had been lost and they were 'reduced to making their living from subsistence agriculture and the mule team' (Chandler 1978, p. 29). Lampião himself had been an *almocreve* (mule driver) (Maciel 1985a, pp. 94–96) and a merchant (Macêdo 1968, p. 111):

> The rude and strenuous work of the mule driver was carried out by the small boys, the sons of Zé Ferreira [Lampião's father], almost always, taking turns traveling. [...] The wage they were paid was more or less miserable. Twelve or fifteen thousand milréis for exhausting yourself lifting up and putting down twice a day bundles of 75 or 80 kilos, in the laborious work of loading and unloading the pack animals, for 10, 15 or 20 days! There was not much of a choice between a life like that and entering the cangaço and die in the first skirmish.

Estácio de Lima (1965, p. 22) quotes the mood prevailing in wide circles among the peasants of the northeast during Lampião's times: 'The cangaceiros at least do not die of hunger. And to die of hunger is worse than dying at knife point or at the mouth of a rifle.' When Lampião and his 49 men were interviewed by a reporter from the newspaper *O Ceará* during their stay in Juàzeiro in 1926, the *cangaceiros* without exception stated that the profession was good (Chandler 1978, p. 68). Lampião never seemed to lack money (Chandler 1978, p. 110). In a sense, the *cangaço* provided an alternative avenue of social advancement in general, open to anyone from the rural masses (Souza 1972, pp, 124–25). At any rate, once the decision to join the *cangaço* had been made, for whatever reason, there was no way back. The Ferreira brothers had to live on what their banditry brought.

Antônio Silvino attacked whoever was known to possess money, jewels, guns and other attractive goods, not least merchants who had to keep cash for their business (Lewin (1979, p. 137):

> Silvino's' robberies or extortions were not undertaken for the principal purpose of redistributing rural income but as a means of securing the personal income necessary for maintaining himself and his men as *cangaceiros*. It has been estimated that he and his band earned between six and ten *contos* per month, exclusive of more lucrative booty, which also suggests that they allocated only a small portion of their 'collections' to the poor. For example, when Silvino 'collected' one *conto* eight hundred *mil réis* in the celebrated robbery in Pilar, he distributed only a modest tithe, approximately two hundred *mil réis*, to the poor.

Lampião was quite adamant about the purpose of what he was doing. When he had been designated captain in Juàzeiro in 1926 he gave an interview: 'Banditry is a means of livelihood. If I were to fire on all the *macacos* ["soldiers" or "policemen"] I come across, I would have been dead long ago' (Lampião, quoted by Souza 1972, p. 127). '... this trade [of mine] allows me to live well, and up to now I have not had any intention to leave it' (Lampião, quoted by Grunspan-Jasmin 2001, p. 86). This interview, one of the few that Lampião ever offered, 'reveals a man obsessed with accumulating riches in order to become a merchant or a *coronel* in the future', comments Moacir Assunção (2007, p. 131).

Let us proceed to how the above can be analyzed. This is shown in Figure 11.2. Let us assume that we have a bandit chief who derives revenue

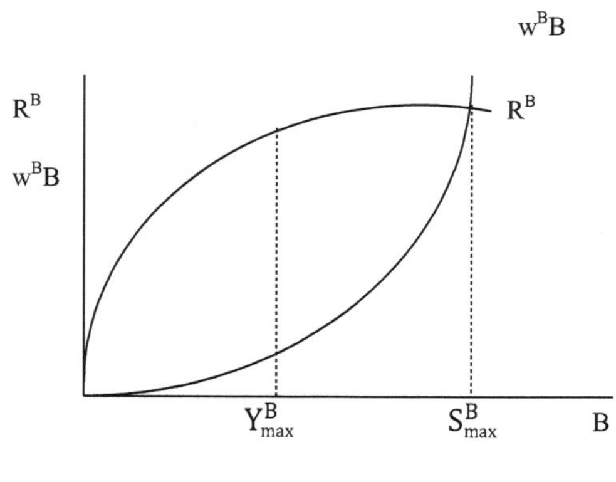

Figure 11.2 Income and strength maximization by the bandits

from more or less voluntary contributions by the population which he controls with the aid of his bandits, and in addition from people who buy his services. His net income is the difference between his gross revenue and his cost. It is reasonable to postulate that his gross revenue is a function of the number of bandits that he employs. This revenue is subject to diminishing returns. Bandits are in turn available only at an increasing wage rate. Mello (2004, p. 145) makes the observation that desertions were frequent among the professional *cangaceiros*. Hence the turnover of bandits was high, and this, in turn, required band leaders to pay constant attention to recruitment activities.

The striking power of the bandit chief is also an increasing function of the number of men at his disposal, given the military technology of the gang. This power as well exhibits diminishing returns to gang size. The bandit leader has a choice between maximizing his net income and maximizing his striking power. The maximum income is reached when the marginal contribution of recruitment to revenue equals the marginal cost of recruiting gang members. Maximizing the strength of the gang, on the other hand, requires that the entire revenue be spent on recruitment, i.e. going beyond the point which marks the maximum difference between marginal revenue and marginal cost. It is readily seen that income maximization renders a sub-optimally small gang size from the strength point of view. This, in turn, contributes to the explanation of why Lampião managed to remain for almost two decades in the *cangaço*. Most of the time, his activities were carried out on a relatively small scale, a scale which was not large enough to call forth a powerful response from the powers that be.

It is in the light of the above that the following statement by Chandler (1978, pp. 135–36) must be interpreted:

> In actuality, Lampião's basic key to success was simple. He normally preferred to run and hide rather than confront the police. For this, the police often taunted him as being cowardly, but for Lampião it was a tenet of survival. His aim was not to engage the police in open and sustained warfare, for, given the inequality of forces, he could not have long survived. However much he hated the police, he sought to engage them only when the advantages lay heavily with his side. He murdered them when there was

> no immediate risk, as in Queimadas, or he attacked them when he could scarcely lose, as in Favelas and … [Mandacaru]. And in the latter instances, he attacked only when they were closely pursuing him, interfering with his operations and posing a direct threat to him. By the 1930s, it was becoming clear that he preferred not to do battle at all. He would have been much happier had the police just left him alone. The mature Lampião probably would have been content to settle down as a backlands sultan, doing only what was necessary to keep his subjects in line and the tribute flowing into his coffers.

Portraying the *cangaceiros* as income maximizers explains why they preferred to keep the level of violent activities low.

The *Coronéis*

While a low level of violence may be a necessary condition for bandit survival over a long period, it is definitely not a sufficient one. Bandits interact with the surrounding society, and it is necessary to look at the forms of this interaction if we want a deeper understanding of the survival process. Eric Hobsbawm (1985, pp. 91–92) explains the longevity of Lampião by the fact that he had powerful political friends. His main allies were big ranchers, businessmen and political bosses (who often combined all three roles) who provided Lampião with money and other necessities against being left alone by him. They had good political contacts and were hence not bothered by the police (Chandler 1978, p. 164).

The political system of the Brazil from the beginning of the (First or Old) Republic in 1889 until the revolution of 1930 was based on the so-called *coronéis* ('colonels'), local political bosses, usually large landowners, who controlled the rural population in their respective *municípios*. They were the representatives of a 'private' form of power, 'a local power monopoly' (Pang 1973, p. 65). Their basic function was that of furnishing the votes demanded by the next political level and it was precisely this ability that allowed them to stay in power (Pang 1973, p. 79). They were part of a larger hierarchy which in the end extended across the entire country. The formal, organized, state government was strong on the coast, but in the sertão informal *coronelista* rule prevailed and the skilful *coronéis* managed to be in good standing with both the state government and the federal president (Pang 1973, pp. 72–73).

After the fall of the empire, an extremely decentralized system of government was adopted in Brazil (Pang 1973, p. 69). Client *coronéis* delivered votes, frequently through ballot fraud, to incumbent state officials in exchange for licence to run their local communities as they pleased. In return for votes, the *coronéis* in favor obtained jobs, investment and sometimes also political offices from the state oligarchies (Fausto 1986, p. 789; Pang 1973, p. 82). As a rule they controlled the local judges and could get away with crimes while the members of the opposition had to count on arbitrary 'justice' being dispensed. (Levine 1992, p. 94)

During the presidency of Manuel Ferraz de Campos Sales (1898–1902), local power was further strengthened, by the so-called *política dos governadores*, which 'granted complete independence to the regional oligarchies', which in the case of the northeast meant dynastic clans or personalist cliques (Pang 1973, p. 71). Clientelistic relationships prevailed, especially in rural areas, where a tiny minority of landowners controlled both the productive resources and politics, most of the time with one *coronel* in charge of each *município*. Alliances were often temporal and lasted as long as both parties benefited from them.

The balloting system during the Old Republic was not secret, but the voters had to stand before a board of local town elites and sign their names overtly under the appropriate column in the election book. Often, elections were not even held in public, and the literacy requirement for voting was dispensed with by paying people to vote for the 'right' candidate. As could be expected, imagination knew no limit when it came to ensuring a high number of votes (Pang 1973, pp. 83–84):

> Imaginative coronéis hired forgers, usually ambidextrous men, to fill the books by privately signing the names of absent townspeople. Others blatantly padded the voter[s] listed by adding names of nonexisting persons and even of the diseased. Such ghost voters were known in the electoral jargon of the time as *fósforos* and *fantasmas*. This type of fraudulent election, called the *bico de pena* [pen and ink], was a standard fixture of coronelismo in the Northeast. When bico de pena was not sufficient, the

> coronel mobilized his jagunços [workers-gunmen loyal to a particular patron] and even hired a temporary contract army of cangaceiros (or state police, if the coronel was a member of the 'in' party) to win the election. After all these steps had been taken, the books were forwarded to the state of federal legislature for final scrutiny. At this point the governor and federal congressional leaders took over. The selective procedure of granting recognition to their supporters and refusal to their foes constituted the final phase of the electoral process ... at no time during the Old Republic were election results in the Northeast automatically accepted and recognized as first reported. What coronéis were unable to do was done by governors, and vice versa.

Ralph della Cava (1970, pp. 93–94) describes how the system worked in Ceará at the end of the nineteenth and the beginning of the twentieth century:

> ... political power ... recognized the structural changes introduced by the Republic: each state was now made responsible for education, public services, administration, and its own financial solvency. As a consequence, the *município* became a critical thread in the web of government: it was the chief source of resources, necessary to maintain the essentially bureaucratic expansion of state government. To assure the steady flow of 'legal tribute,' the state oligarchy would reward municipal chiefs not only with federal and state employment and local patronage, but also with a larger share of local revenues. It was this marked increment of local power and wealth, rather than the mere continuation of time-honored local rivalries between prominent families, that unleashed throughout the backlands the violent struggles for municipal power in the first decades after the proclamation of the Republic.

Nowhere was the *coronelista* system stronger and more autonomous than in the territory of the *cangaceiros*. On both sides of the river São Francisco whole 'nations of *coronéis*' were present who controlled their respective territories with the aid of their private armies, united in their efforts by the existence of trade networks in Bahia, Goiás, Pernambuco, Piauí and Maranhão which in turn forged alliances across state boundaries (Fausto 1986, p. 791).

In the northeast, no party managed to establish a permanent power monopoly, and this had consequences for *coronel* behavior. 'The high turnover and short-lived party rule not only discouraged coronéis from identifying too vigorously with any one faction, but also encouraged them to play with all factions.' What mattered was to maintain a dominant position in the *município*, not to secure a long-time relationship with the incumbent state party, and this was not too difficult. 'The sertão offered relative security through geographical isolation and difficult communication so that many coronéis "out of favour" with the state government effectively remained in power' (Pang 1973, p. 76).

Relations between the *coronéis* and the ruling parties at the state level were both complicated and uneasy. In some states, the governors made use of the state police resorted to violence (*policía militar*) to impose their political will on reluctant *coronéis*, which in turn tended to spur an equally violent response from the latter, based on personal armies of *jagunços*, *capangas* [paid gunmen], and possibly also *cangaceiros* (Pang 1973, p. 74). Thus, a 'symbiotic' tradition evolved between *coronéis* and *cangaceiros*, one of convenient 'constant reciprocal assistance' (Mello 2004, p. 87). For the *coronéis*, the *cangaceiros* constituted an important political weapon in a situation where there were many contenders for power. The *coronéis*, in turn, represented the dominant forces in the sertão and it was convenient for the *cangaceiros* to be able to count on their support, a support which went further than that which could be provided by ordinary people, in terms of e.g. shelter and ammunition (Fausto 1986, p. 806).

The *coronéis* were the main factor responsible for the long duration of the *cangaço* in the northeast. This included Lampião, who was generally thought to provide important services for his powerful friends 'attacking, for example, a ranch of one of their enemies or killing someone they wanted dead' (Chandler 1978, p. 46). Lampião's own confessor, Father José Kherle, in an interview published in 1972 stated that he 'was always protected by political bosses and large landowners. From them he received arms and supplies in exchange for certain "favors"' (quoted by Mello 2004, p. 317).

Antônio Silvino was also known to be a gun for hire, sometimes to the point where he destroyed his own business. In Campina Grande two merchant-landowner families were fighting for control over the cotton trade for several decades after 1889. Both factions hired bandits to support them. Silvino made the mistake of offering his services to both sides, sometimes simultaneously, which in the end turned both factions off and led to an unusually strong effort to capture or kill him by the authorities (Lewin 1979, p. 134).

Analytically, the *coronéis* attempt to maximize the number of votes they will get, by employing bandits, because in this way they also maximize their income from the state government. The more *cangaceiros* the *coronel* hires, the more votes will he attract from the dependent population, because the *cangaceiros* constitute a credible threat against those who choose not to side with the *coronel* in the elections. This we may call the threat effect (subject to diminishing returns). On the other hand, some ordinary people may be turned off by the presence of threat and choose to vote for someone else instead, if they think they can get away with it, and this we may call the repulsion effect. Thus, the *coronel* may be losing some votes, probably at an increasing rate as the number of *cangaceiros* increases. In practice, however, the latter effect was weak: '… the typical coronel was more than willing to go beyond normal preparations to win votes. Any refusal of the townspeople to support his chosen candidates was apt to be a personal affront that should be prevented even with violence' (Pang 1973, p. 80). The maximum impact of hiring bandits for the *coronel* is obtained when the marginal threat effect equals the marginal repulsion effect. This determines the number that he wants to hire.

Coronel revenue is a function of the net *cangaceiro* contribution to the number of votes that he receives, which in turn depends on the number of bandits around. However, we must also take the cost of recruiting bandits into the picture. The marginal cost for the *coronel* of obtaining bandits increases with their number. Exactly like the bandit chief, the *coronel* obtains his maximum net income when the marginal revenue from employing more bandits coincides with the marginal cost of doing so.

One problem remains. It is not certain that the optimum number of bandits from the point of view of the *coronel* coincides with the optimum number as viewed by the *cangaceiro* chief. Assume that in the first round the optimum number of bandits for the *coronel*, the number demanded, exceeds the number supplied. This excess demand cannot exist in equilibrium. The *coronel* will then increase his offers to the bandits. As a result their revenue will increase, and by the same token so will the cost for the coronel, until the excess demand is wiped out and an equilibrium number of bandits is reached where both the bandits and the *coronel* balance their marginal revenues and costs.

It should also be noted that the fact that Lampião's activities were carried out on a relatively small scale suited not only Lampião, but also the *coronéis*, who in this way could employ the *cangaceiros* for their own purposes without running the risk of being pointed to as outspoken bandit supporters, with all the political risks that this would have entailed.

Possibly, Lampião's relationship with the *coronéis* of the northeast can even be described as that of a price discriminating monopolist vis-à-vis his customers. As Chandler (1978, pp. 170–71) has pointed out, in the 1930s the only bandit gangs that were still around were those controlled by Lampião. The 'King of the Cangaceiros' even issued passports with his picture on, to guarantee freedom from attacks by his people. '… Sergipe was so infested with Lampião's bandits, a newspaper in that state complained in 1936, that such a passport was a necessity for traveling and doing business in the interior counties' (Chandler 1978, p. 171).

The *cangaceiros* were not stationary. On the contrary, they had no fixed point whatsoever, but moved from area to area as the circumstances called for it, equalizing the marginal net benefits from actions in different states. The dependence of the *coronéis* on bandits varied from area to area, i.e. their respective demand for bandits displayed different price elasticities. Lampião was in the position to supply what they needed, and since the various markets for his services were geographically distant from each other, they could be separated. The maps in Frederico Bezerra Maciel's books provide an eloquent demonstration of how widely he moved across the sertão region, showing up with his men at different times in different places, receiving pecuniary and other favors from the *coronéis* in return.

In order to maximize his profits, a price-discriminating monopolist bandit selling his services in two markets equates his total marginal revenue (obtained by the horizontal addition of the marginal revenue curves for the two markets) with his marginal cost and equating the marginal revenues in the two markets. The prices charged for bandit services differ according to the price sensitivity of demand, with the less elastic market paying the higher price.[7] In practice, the bandits did not appear at the same time everywhere, but Lampião's gang was an itinerant, roving one, appearing sequentially and randomly (at least when viewed from the outside) in different areas. We would also expect the number of bandits demanded to differ in different territories, which in turn helps to explain why the size of Lampião's gang varied over time.

The General Population

The *cangaceiros* were aided and protected not only by *coronéis*. There was a second group of *coiteiros* as well, common people like *vaqueiros* and small tenants, small and medium-sized farmers or ranchers, traders and store owners, people who could not count on any sympathy from the police and who would hence not hesitate to misinform the latter (Chandler 1978, pp. 164–65). Instead they would serve as messengers and informers for the *cangaceiros* and provision him with whatever goods they needed. 'For all this, Lampião paid well, for the cooperation of his protectors … was indispensable to his well-being' (Chandler 1978, p. 47). When the police chiefs of the states of Pernambuco, Paraíba, Rio Grande do Norte, Ceará, Alagôas and Bahia met in Recife in late 1926 to coordinate their pursuit of Lampião, they agreed that one of the major problems was the support that the bandit received from the general population of the sertão (Chandler 1978, pp. 85–86).

For the common man, the calculation of benefits and costs was simple. Lampião made a point of demonstrating that he was on the side of the population at large, as when he was in the state of Bahia in September 1928 (Chandler 1978, p. 115):

---

[7] $MR = \partial TR/\partial Q = \partial(PQ)/\partial Q = P + Q(\partial P/\partial Q) = P(1 + 1/\varepsilon)$, where MR denotes marginal and TR total revenue, P price, Q quantity and $\varepsilon = (\partial Q/\partial P)/(Q/P)$ the elasticity of demand for the service. In the case of two markets we have: $MR_1 = P_1(1 + 1/\varepsilon_1) = MR_2 = P_2(1 + 1/\varepsilon_2) = MC$. Since the price elasticities (the ε:s) are negative, it follows that if $\varepsilon_1 > \varepsilon_2$, then $P_2 > P_1$. The price discriminating monopolist will not sell at all in markets where the demand is inelastic, i. e. where the value of ε lies between 0 and − 1, because this will make his marginal revenue negative. The elasticity of demand must be between − 1 and − ∞.

> He was building the reputation of being a kind and generous man. In September in Barro Vermelho and Patamuté, he gave money to the poor and passed out drinks to the thirsty. He traveled by car between the two towns, generously paying the chauffeur and his assistant. On ranches and in villages, he attended wedding parties, on occasion purchasing a pretty dress for the bride or furnishing the drinks. In Canché, he drank with the small contingent of soldiers that managed the police station and exchanged a rifle with one of them. Lampião was on good behavior. He was also doing a good job at public relations. The visits of the legendary bandit thrilled the backlanders. No doubt, too, he and his men were enjoying themselves. At the same time, the knowledge of the region that Lampião was gaining and the contacts and the friends that he was making would serve him well in the future.

But Lampião also exacted contributions from time to time. Billy Jaynes Chandler's and Frederico Bezerra Maciel's books are full of accounts of how Lampião descended on different *fazendas* and of how much tribute he exacted on each occasion.

The contributions paid to the *cangaceiros* were not the only ones exacted from the population. The police too preyed on the *sertanejos*, imposing a second cost on them. When the *volante* troops were in the field, their commanders were authorized to purchase food, usually *rapadura* [brown sugar], *farinha* [manioc meal] and meat. *Rapadura* and *farinha* were usually purchased in villages or ranches. The third item was different. Cattle, sheep, and goats were simply taken when found. If the owner was lucky, he was around and in the best case he was paid as well. If he was away, he could usually forget about compensation (Chandler 1978, p. 141). When the *volantes* needed horses they simply took them and frequently made no effort to give them back to their owners. In the worst case they simply killed the animals when they had no more use for them (Chandler 1978, p. 165).

The common man also had to take into account the severity of the punishment if detected by the military and the probability of detection, since *cangaceiros* and policemen were seen as '*meal from the same bag*' (Lins 1995, p. 92). The police were known to be almost as harsh as the bandits and a search of a house could easily end with its destruction and with the mistreatment of the dwellers (Chandler 1978, p. 30). Chandler reports that police brutality had been generalized for a long time, that it was a major complaint in Pernambuco, Paraíba, Ceará, and Alagôas and that it became a big problem also in Bahia and Sergipe after 1928 (Chandler 1978, pp. 165–67). Violence—'beatings, maimings and sometimes deaths' (Chandler 1978, p. 166)—was frequently used deliberately against those who were suspected of aiding the bandits by police and soldiers who did not think much of it, brutal, illiterate men who were not made to change their ways once they were in the police force and had to face the harsh reality of the campaigns against the bandits.

Police brutality was a fact of life, to be reckoned with by the *sertanejos*. But how important was it? The benefits and costs of siding with the *cangaceiros* must be compared with those of the alternative: supporting the military. The profit that could be obtained by siding with the military consisted of the difference between no reward whatsoever minus the sum of three losses. The low pay of the soldiers often made them loot the properties of those assumed to be friendly with the *cangaceiros* and enemies of the state governments (Lima 1965, p. 239). The first two items are thus the same as in the case of supporting Lampião: the contributions that Lampião might require on the one hand, and on the other hand whatever the military might lay their hands on when they appeared. Should Lampião decide on a visit, there was no choice, and the need to feed and provision the soldiers was basically the same whatever the constellation of the forces.

Far more important, however, was the expected punishment from the bandits—which at least in the case of Lampião would typically be very high, involving the loss of lives or severe mutilation, much more so than in the case of the military (Chandler 1978, p. 87). Not to incur the enmity of Lampião was a major factor in the calculations (Chandler 1978, p. 47):

> All in all, it must be said that the rural population in general cooperated with Lampião because to refuse him a favor was an invitation to an almost certain reprisal. In doing so, they risked incurring the displeasure of the police, and many people suffered at the hands of the *volantes*, who were feared almost as much as the bandits. But, when all was said, Lampião was

> a more real and persistent threat than were the authorities. The actions of the authorities and whatever protection they offered were erratic and temporary; they offered neither a permanent threat nor permanent security.

The odds were strongly in favor of Lampião. Common people were afraid of his vengeance, since he did not limit himself simply to killing suspected informers but also tortured and humiliated them in different ways. 'Conditions virtually dictated that the people in the countryside became the enemies of the police, since to become their collaborators was an invitation to the terrible vengeance of the cangaceiros' (Chandler 1978, p. 169).

The vast majority of the rural inhabitants would thus conclude that it paid more to associate with Lampião than with the military. Lampião was known to be cruel. He was also known to pay well for whatever services he needed. This, for ordinary people was enough to tip the scales in his favor, even though punishment by the military was a real possibility. Small landowners with no influence were easily beaten up by the police. (For the larger landowners, what presumably mattered most was that the punishment meted out by the police was low, very close to zero in many cases. A large, influential landowner with good political connections had little to fear from the police.) Nevertheless, it seems as if Lampião had a satisfactory relationship also with the common people in the backlands, a relationship which helped ensure his survival, while the police and the general population virtually found themselves on opposite sides (Chandler 1978, p. 172). For the population at large, living in peace with Lampião made sense. In societies where the system of public order is weak or inexistent, and banditry hence rampant, appealing to distant authorities makes no sense, 'all the less so as such an appeal will quite likely bring along an expeditionary force of troops, who will lay the countryside waste more surely than the local bandits' (Hobsbawm 1985, p. 89). This was clearly the case in Brazil (Chandler 1978, pp. 164–65):

> This [second] class of coiteiros—the poorer among them were often called the 'barefoot coiteiros'—suffered more at the hands of the police than they did from the bandits. In actuality, the great majority of them feared the bandits more and, had they been given effective protection, would have

> cooperated with the police. But policing every village and rural homestead was an impossible task, and, as a result, the ever-present threat of Lampião's arrival and the terrible consequences of his retaliation for disloyalty brought most of the population to deny the police the information they so badly needed to wage their war effectively. An inevitable consequence of this situation was the wave of violence it left in its wake. Only by brutal methods, it seemed, could they induce the backlanders to inform on the bandits.

In the end, the problem of the general population may thus be reduced to a cost comparison. The more support you give to the bandits, the lower the damage they inflict on you and the higher the damage inflicted by the police. The problem is one of equalizing the value of the marginal damage inflicted by the *cangaceiros* (taking into account that Lampião on occasion might yield some benefits as well) and the value of the marginal damage caused by the police. The optimum entailed considerable support to the bandits and considerably less to the police.

The Police and the *Volantes*

The above is fine as far as it goes. However, the analysis has so far not taken into account the fact that Lampião's gang was chased by the military and the police during its entire existence. Why did these forces not move in and wipe the *cangaceiros* out? To answer this question we must look at the behavior of the police.

It was not necessarily advantageous for the police to kill Lampião. The various state governments did not have much of an interest in coming to grips with banditry. They 'looked away, permitting the *coronéis* to maintain order any way they wished. In return, the local bosses allied to the incumbent machine delivered votes by means of fraud and iron-fisted intimidation and provided dutiful tribute when requested' (Levine 1992, p. 97). The state oligarchy should be seen as vote maximizers. Strong efforts against banditry were not undertaken, since they would have weakened the *coronéis* and led to a loss of votes. Also, the money to finance efforts on a major scale was lacking, to the extent that Chandler calls it 'a chronic problem in Brazil', which during the depression years of the early 1930s 'probably was insurmountable' (Chandler 1978, p. 143). The forces in the field were inadequately financed. Their pay was late, uniforms were lacking and after their incursions into the bush, many soldiers returned practically without clothes, simply to be faced with the fact that they had to pay their commander for their food (Chandler 1978, p. 141).

As a result, the police were usually undermanned (Chandler 1978, p. 44). They were posted in towns and cities and did as a rule not patrol rural areas. The main units fighting bandits were the ones known as *volantes* [flying squads], semi-mercenary units whose actions had little to do with their name (Chandler 1978, p. 45):

> Despite their name, speed was not one of their characteristics, for, like the bandits, they usually went on foot. The police generally were not furnished with horses, since they were expensive [...] The main disadvantage of the volantes, however, was inadequate manpower. The backlands of Pernambuco in 1922 and 1923, for example, had only one volante of 20 men and one officer devoted to fight against banditry, and these were the years when not only Lampião but also numerous other bands were operating. A state might put a much larger force than this into the field in response to a major attack, as Alagôas did after Lampião's raid on Agua Branca, but such an effort was rare.

The enthusiasm for fighting Lampião was low among the untrained troops who had to spend weeks trailing the bandits on foot and who were given inadequate and irregular pay and provision. They were easy enough to corrupt and were known to sell ammunition to Lampião to increase their incomes. Many avoided combat contact if they could and fought only when they were forced to. Lampião had little to fear from the police as long as he limited his raids to isolated villages and ranches (Chandler 1978, pp. 45–46).

The volantes did not serve the interest of the population at large (Alcino Alves da Costa, quoted by Assunção 2007, pp. 39–40):

> It is a soft-brained ingenuity to think that the volantes chased bandits in order to give peace and quiet to the sertão, to guarantee lives and families

> or to put an end to the gloomy suffering. No. Pure and happy deceit. No volante ever, not even those who acquired name and fame, acted resolutely and fearlessly out of altruism to serve the sertanejo community well.

This view is corroborated by an interview with João Bezerra, the man who led the police force that killed Lampião, by the *Diario de Pernambuco* in 1959, where he stated that the police gained very little trying to perform its task. What was paid had very little to do with the budget voted every year in every *município* of the northeast (Grunspan-Jasmin 2001, pp. 234–35).

Economic factors clearly played an important role shaping the behavior of the police. Young men chose to become police officers just in order to get a regular job, for few others were available. Others were more or less forced to join, under threats (Chandler 1978, p. 167). 'These police units, far from exterminating banditry, encouraged it', writes de Souza (1972, p. 112), and Frederico Bezerra Maciel (1987a, p. 169) is quite explicit about the attitude of the police in the case of Lampião. He was protected by *coronéis* and *coiteiros*, but he was also 'permanent and secure business [*mamata*]'[8] in the game of securing promotions and salaries for the police.

The situation of the police is thus analogous to that of the bandits. They may also be thought of as income maximizers. The police chief receives a revenue which increases with the size of the force used to combat bandits. If the local *volante* commanders are free to contract, soldiers are available at an increasing wage rate. Then we have the income and strength functions for the police corresponding to those of the *cangaceiros*.

The sizes of the police force which maximize income and strength, respectively, are determined in the same way as in the case of the bandits. Again, income maximization leads to sub-optimal striking power. This, in turn leads directly to the central message of the model: a police commander who chooses to maximize income instead of striking power may be severely weakened, and even if the bandits at the same time choose not

[8] Maciel's choice of word is interesting. *Michaelis dicionário prático inglês-português, português-inglês* (1993, p. 676) translates *mamata* as 'enterprise or administration of which favoured persons take pecuniary advantage' and also as 'shady business, theft'.

to forego income to maximize strength, the result may easily be that the police is not strong enough to wipe out the bandits.

Furthermore, with an administratively set wage rate, if the rate is too low, the local commanders may not even be able to contract enough people to reach their income maximum. The number of soldiers may fall short not only of the maximum strength level but also of the maximum net income level. On the other hand, the *volante* commander may find that the wage level imposed is higher than what is required for maximizing income, and that, in addition, he has to recruit precisely the number willing serve at that wage. In the worst case he must recruit the number of soldiers that maximizes his striking power. Since that would wipe out his profit, however, he may attempt to reduce other costs, like those of ammunition and transportation (horses). The soldiers will still not fight but choose to remain in some safe place and do next to nothing.

Alternatively, the behavior of the police may be portrayed as security maximization. The police then may be thought of as having a likelihood of survival function with three arguments: the strength of the unit, the danger to which it is exposed, and in addition, of course, the military technology. The strength of the unit will increase with the number of soldiers, but at a decreasing rate. The danger to which a unit is exposed may also be assumed to increase with the number of soldiers, because with more soldiers the likelihood increases that they have to be involved in actual combat.

The result is the same as in the case of income maximization. The strength of combat of the police force falls short of the maximum. Again the reasoning assumes that the *volante* commander is not constrained by income concerns or by the wage level. If that is the case, he may have to stop recruiting before he even reaches his security maximum.

Hobsbawm (1985, p. 90) observes that in societies where bandits play an important role it may be better to come to a tacit agreement with them:

> Local officers who want to carry out their jobs quietly and without fuss—as which of them do not?—will keep in touch and on reasonable terms with them, or else risk those painful local incidents which give unwelcome publicity to a district, and cause superior officials to take a poor view of their

> subordinates. This explains why in really bandit-infested areas campaigns against banditry are so often carried out by special forces brought in from the outside. [...] Even the locally stationed soldiery and police may prefer to keep crime—by tacit or overt agreement with the bandits—below the threshold which will attract the attention of the capital, which leaves plenty of room for banditry, for in the pre-industrial period the eye of central governments does not penetrate too deeply into the undergrowth of rural society, unless its own special interests are involved.

This was definitely the case in Brazil. Dedication was lacking. The police was afraid and would avoid getting into outright battle whenever possible (Chandler 1978, p. 44). This attitude was most apparent in the case of Ceará where the authorities offered Lampião refuge as long as he limited his activities and did not launch any major assault or murder local people. 'He seemed to restrict himself to requesting money and occasionally seizing someone for ransom', as Chandler (1978, p. 92) writes when commenting on Lampião's activities in early 1927. When, at the end of June the same year, Lampião with only 50 men at his disposal had to engage in combat with 50 cavalrymen and 350 foot soldiers, the police forces sounded the bugle and began firing long before any real contact with the bandits was possible. 'It may have been ... that the police, as Ceará's newspapers continually charged, preferred to fire at Lampião from a safe distance and, if possible, give him adequate warning of their approach, so that he could withdraw. If that was their attitude, it was one shared by many a soldier who fought Lampião at other times and at other places' (Chandler 1978, p. 104).

Generally, police forces were concentrated to the major towns, in order to guarantee their safety, and this left few people actually on Lampião's track for most of the time. When a campaign against him was launched in Bahia, after Christmas 1929, with 1,200 police soldiers and 36 officers, the equivalent of one-third of the entire Bahia police force, these troops were deployed in a way that made it impossible to catch the bandit. They were responsible not only for pursuing Lampião but also for law and order in general. To this end, but also to prevent bandit attacks on the larger population concentrations, police forces were concentrated to the towns (Chandler 1978, p. 140):

> Less than 150 troops ... were available to man the volantes that actually pursued the bandits in the field. Each volante normally having from 20 to 30 men, 150 troops provided for five or six units charged with pursuing from one to three bands of criminals over an area of not much less than 50,000 square miles.

When it came to actual fighting, the police as a rule performed poorly. Souza (1972, p. 126) states that of 'thirty-seven incidents in Pernambuco and Bahia alone, during a period of fifteen years', Lampião won two of three encounters with the police.

The Extension of the Territory

We are now in a position where we can determine the size of the territory of bandit operations. For this, we may invoke the Findlay (1996) model of the limits of empire. In that model the extension of an 'empire'—what in the present case corresponds to the territory under the control of Lampião—is determined by the relative strength of two opposed factions, who compete for the same territory, as given by their numbers (and their military technologies). The equilibrium which yields the territory under empire control is given by two reaction functions (curves), in a duopoly fashion, which depict how each of the factions respond to an increase in the size of the army of the other faction. The equilibrium division of the contested territory is obtained by the intersection between the curves, which gives the optimum size of each army.

In the present case, as we have seen, however, the size of both the bandit gang and the police force, and hence their striking power, is determined by income considerations in the case of the bandits and income, administrative constraints or security in the case of the police. With given technologies then, the extension of the territory dominated by the bandits is determined by the relative strength of the bandits and the *volantes* as given by income or security considerations. The reluctance of both the *cangaceiros* and the police to maximize their strength and enter into serious battle made it possible for the bandits to hold an immense area in the

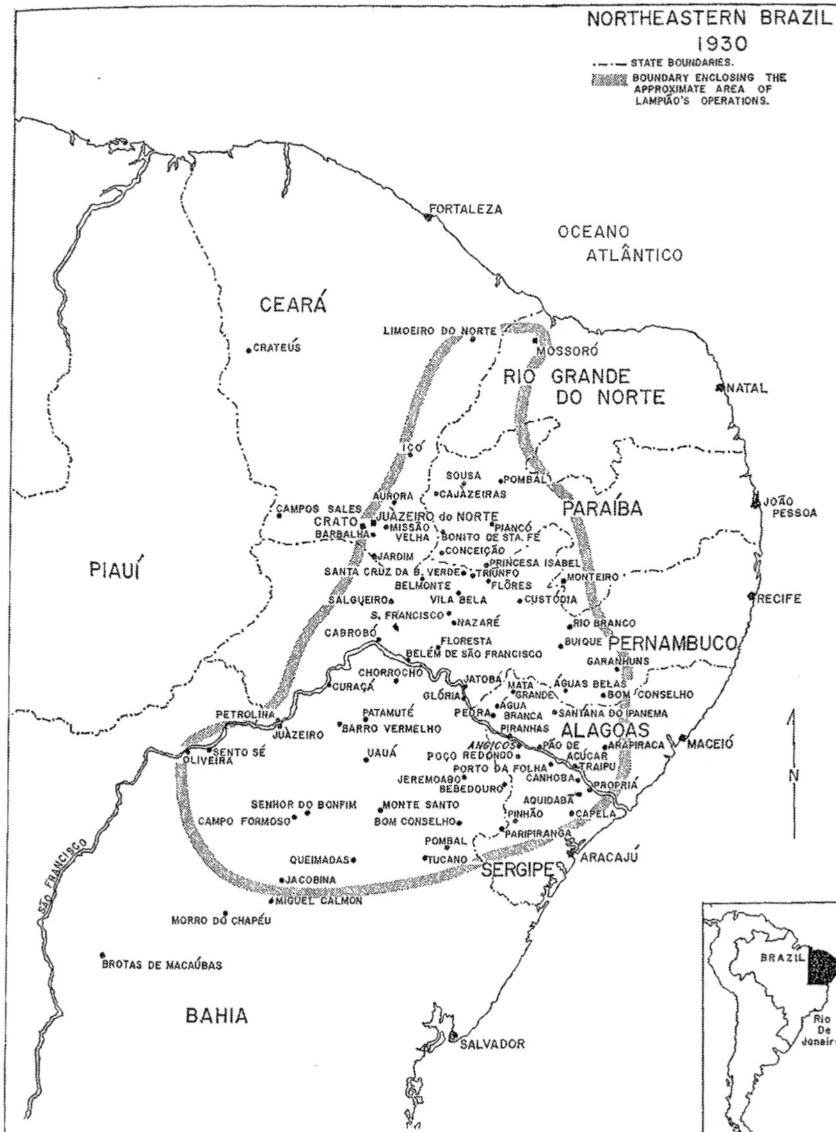

Figure 11.3 The territory of Lampião (*Source*: Chandler (1978), p. 57. ©Texas A&M University Press. Reprinted by permission)

interior of northeast Brazil for close to 20 years. The maximum extension of this territory is shown in the map in Figure 11.3.

The End of the *Cangaço*

Billy Jaynes Chandler has suggested that the fact that the *cangaço* survived until the end of the 1930s was essentially due to the leadership qualities of Lampião. If it had not been for them, the Pernambuco campaign in the late 1920s which almost put an end to banditry in that state would have finished him too, but he crossed the São Francisco river into Bahia and Sergipe and managed to prolong the *cangaço* for almost a decade (Chandler 1978, p. 234).

Lampião himself is, however, only part of the explanation. With or without him, the *cangaço* would not have survived the advent of the modern society to the sertão. Banditry had been able to survive for almost a century thanks to the physical and political isolation of the interior of the northeast. As long as the sertão had been more or less cut off from the outside world and as long as the central power and the state power preferred not to intervene directly in local political affairs, the *coronéis* continued to run the show, and as we have demonstrated, it was in their direct interest to have the *cangaceiros* around.

The advent of a strong, autonomous central state capable of acting without the support of local bosses, on the other hand, was conducive to modernization. This modernization took two routes. One was social and economic. At the time of the 1930 revolution, Brazilian society was on the threshold of economic and social change. The 1920s had been a decade of social ferment, with occasional outbreaks of violence (Poppino 1968, p. 253):

> In retrospect it is apparent that the root of the trouble was the inability of Brazil's tradition-bound political leadership to respond to the changing needs and aspirations of the growing urban, commercial-industrial society ... federal and state administrations ... tolerated change only to the extent that it complemented the established rural economy and did not pose an added burden on official revenues.

During the next decades, southeastern Brazil embarked on a process of industrialization, and with time, although mainly from the 1940s onwards, this would act as a magnet also on the population of the northeast. The industrialization process to a large extent was the result of the political change that took place in 1930. From the fall of the empire in 1889 up to World War I, Brazilian politics had been dominated by coalitions or federations of local state-level oligarchies which, in turn, rested on the *coronéis*. Geographically, initially two states, São Paulo and Minas Gerais, dominated (the so-called *café com leite* alliance), and they were joined after 1910 by Rio Grande do Sul. Around 1920, these three states accounted for more than half the value of the agricultural and industrial production of Brazil (excluding the Federal District) (Fausto 1986, p. 795). From the beginning of World War I, the hegemony of the traditional oligarchies was to an increasing extent challenged by the urban middle class, by younger army officers (the so-called *tenentes*) advocating a stronger role for the central government, and on the geographical level the *café com leite* alliance had to cope with the opposition of other states.

When the time arrived for the 1930 presidential elections, the oligarchic system was in crisis. A split ensued between the São Paulo political group and those of Minas Gerais and Rio Grande do Sul. The sitting president was Washington Luís from São Paulo, and the *Paulistas*—contrary to the established rules of rotation—were unwilling to let the presidency go. The onset of the Great Depression and the abrupt fall of the coffee prices, however, made the Paulista coffee oligarchy politically vulnerable, and the other two states launched Getúlio Vargas, the governor of Rio Grande do Sul, as their candidate. The *Paulista* candidate, Júlio Prestes, however, won the election, characterized by extensive fraud on both sides, in March 1930. Discontent spread among the urban population, and after the assassination of Vargas' candidate for the vice presidency, João Pessoa, from Paraíba, an armed revolt broke out in October, in Minas Gerais, Rio Grande do Sul and the northeast, and one month later, Getúlio Vargas was sworn in as provisional president. This finished the old oligarchic system which had cemented the hegemony of the *Paulista* coffee bourgeoisie (Fausto 1986, p. 828).

A new era in Brazilian politics had dawned. Vargas saw the political potential of both the middle class and the working class and forged an alliance with them, to the detriment of the rural oligarchy, an oligarchy which was under pressure as a result of the Great Depression. The pattern of power changed with Vargas. 'Under his aegis many groups—civilians and military, bureaucrats, technicians, professionals, and industrialists, bourgeois and proletariat—emancipated Brazil from the absolute control of the coffee interests' (Burns 1980, pp. 419–20).

As a result, important economic and social changes took place in the country. Economic policy gradually focused on the promotion of industrialization, social policy concentrated on the protection of urban workers and the armed forces were given a leading role both in the maintenance of internal order and as a support for the industrialization process. Vargas pushed industrialization not just backed by the alliance of the industrial bourgeoisie and the urban working class but also by a state apparatus supported by the army. 'The plan for industrialization came more from the Government's technocrats than it did from the industrialists' (Fausto 1999, pp. 196–97).

The new economic and social forces were seen by some contemporary observers as important agents of change also in the northeast. After the death of Corisco in 1940, a Rio de Janeiro editorial called the *cangaço* an anachronism that had no place in the new Brazil characterized by schools, airplanes and the Ford. This—the entry of the northeastern backlands into the twentieth century—was what had propelled the destruction of banditry (Chandler 1978, p. 234).

Chandler (1978, p. 235) is, however, sceptical to the idea that modernization was instrumental in the process that led to the demise of the *cangaço*:

> Roads were constructed in the backlands in the 1930s, some of them for the specific purpose of facilitating the campaign against Lampião. But such roads were only primitive dirt trails built by human and animal labor, and vast areas continued to lie outside their reach. Trucks for transporting soldiers, moreover, were few, and those that were furnished often could not be used, either because they so frequently broke down or because the roads were impassable from rains and washouts. For that matter, motorized transport remained a novelty in the backlands throughout the 1930s for soldiers and civilians alike. In Bahia, for example, no more than two or

> three trucks and automobiles existed in each of the backlands counties; some counties had none at all. The fact is that most of the war against the bandits continued to be waged mostly on foot. Governor Magalhães of Bahia stated in 1937 that, while the new roads made greater vigilance against the bandits possible, the bandits' main incursions into the state were being made in places like Bebedouro and Paripiranga, where there still were no roads. Of course, trucks were useful, where and when conditions permitted their use, in transporting soldiers between major towns and in the more rapid formation of a force—as, for instance the one that attacked Angicos. It would be injudicious to deny that improved communications hastened the end of the cangaço, but it should be kept in mind that improvements were not extensive.
>
> Other signs of material progress in the backlands during the 1930s would be difficult to uncover ... Airplanes were not used against the bandits; schools, even of the lowest elementary grades, were almost unknown outside of sizable towns, and many county seats had none that regularly functioned. If material improvements had reached the backlands, they were not much in evidence in places like Bebedouro and Poço Redondo.

The above is true, but, whichever way you look at it, time was running out on the *cangaceiros*. Not least the improvement of communications that made possible the physical penetration of the interior made it impossible for the bandits to survive. Modest as it may have been during the last years of Lampião, this improvement would sooner or later have acquired the momentum that would have made troop penetration on a major scale a reality. It was simply a matter of time before the *cangaço* would come to an end under the pressure of successive modernization.

Lampião clearly felt the pressure of modern society. As Chandler (1978, p. 121) himself recognizes, he understood the threat posed to his activities by improved transportation facilities which destroyed the isolation on which banditry thrived and facilitated the penetration of military units. Hence, he made a point of attacking highway constructions, realizing that an effective road network could become the end of him and his band (Chandler 1978, pp. 121–23, 136, 180, 196). Antônio Silvino had employed similar tactics thirty years before, combating the gradual extension of the rails of the Great Western in the Cariris Velhos in

Paraíba. 'During the entire year of 1906 he persecuted engineering crews, hindered work, pulled out sleepers, cut telegraph lines, took people for ransom, destroyed already constructed lines, stopping trains and charging passage fees from terrified passengers' (Mello 2004, pp. 298–99).

The backlands were shrinking, not so much in terms of material and social progress, but in political terms. The end of the bandits was bound to come sooner or later in a centralized country where there was no room or role for them. What matters is not that a small force of forty-five *volantes* overtook some fifty to sixty bandits at Angicos (Chandler 1978, Chap. 12). This in a sense was pure coincidence. It could have happened anywhere, at any time. What was not coincidental was that the *cangaceiros* were being forced to act in a political environment that had no need for them. The second route to modernization in Brazil was political, and this was the route that had more of an immediate impact. When Getúlio Vargas rose to power, the balance between the central government and the local politicians shifted in favor of the former. The new government made a strong effort to centralize not only economic and financial decisions but also decisions that directly affected the constellation of political interests. The regional oligarchies lost power. They did not disappear, nor did the patron-client system, but it gradually became clear that in the Brazil of the 1930s there was a single patron: the central state. It was this state that conferred as much political power on its peripheral clients as it wished—not vice versa (Fausto 1999, p. 196).

All legislative bodies from the national Congress all the way down to the municipal assemblies were abolished. With the exception of the governor of Minas Gerais, all governors were dismissed in 1930 and replaced by centrally appointed *interventores*, and the following year a new law was promulgated which limited their sphere of power and subordinated it to the central government. '… after 1933 coronelismo in the Northeast began to lose its deinstitutionalized, personalized, and prepolitical characteristics, for it was forced to operate within a new structural relationship to the state and central governments. No longer were coronéis individual power brokers, able to pick and choose their clients' (Pang 1973, p. 88). The remaining, single client had been converted into a patron state. The power of the latter increased gradually, and in 1937, after Vargas' proclamation of the *Estado Nôvo* and the abolition of the political parties, it was complete. Vargas became the strongest president that Brazil had ever had, with a power that extended across a wider area than any of his predecessors, 'emperors not excluded' (Burns 1980, p. 419). And he dealt a severe blow to the old political order. Vargas immediately proceeded to minimize the autonomy of the *coronéis*. Those who had supported President Luis in October 1930 were disarmed and neutralized, and henceforth the federal government appointed all mayors, directed the local police and monitored the use of the municipal budgets (Burns 1980, p. 414).

The destruction of the *coronelismo* was, however, not immediate. For a time, the *coronelista* system managed to adapt to the new corporative political system and clientilism continued to be part of it, notably because the 1930 revolution did little to change production relations in the countryside (Fausto 1986, p. 828). In the end, however, the system would crumble. The transformation of Brazilian political life after the proclamation of the *Estado Nôvo* would be both deep-going and irreversible. At the end of the *Estado Nôvo* in 1945 the social base of politics in Brazil was no longer the one it had been in 1930. Industrialization accompanied by economic development was on its way and with that increased urbanization and literacy. Urbanization in, turn, shifted the political balance towards the Belo Horizonte, Rio de Janeiro and São Paulo triangle with large numbers of voters with interests that differed radically from those of the representatives of the old, rural-based, order. 'There were still large areas of Brazil where the old-style "clientilistic" politics persisted, but national politics, if and when free elections were held, would inevitably become a more open and less predictable game' (Skidmore 1967, p. 33).

Mello (2004, p. 312) is emphatic. It was the *Estado Nôvo* that killed Lampião. In the end, the Brazilian state apparatus monopolized the use of violence, in the Weberian fashion, and in that process, there was no room for the *cangaço*. The process which changed Brazilian politics after World War I, and in particular after 1930, had a gradual impact also in the backlands of the northeast. It came at different times in different places, but in the late 1920s the process began which would end with the demise of the old order. The *coronéis* were no longer left to their own devices in exchange for votes (Chandler 1978, p. 236):

The war against the bandits and their coiteiros in Pernambuco in the late 1920s stands as evidence of the onset of the trend. The changes wrought by Getúlio Vargas' regime during the next decade, but especially after 1937, demonstrate – however haltingly, at times – the continuity of it. Parts of the old order and the new existed side by side, of course. For example, authorities in Alagoas in 1938 were moved to take drastic steps to ensure the elimination of the cangaceiros, while Interventor Eronides in neighboring Sergipe remained able to offer them the traditional protection. But, as uneven as the manifestations of the trend were, when we view the history of the backlands from early in the century to 1940, it is clear that incidences of more effective governmental authority during the last fourteen years or so of that period contributed measurably to the passing of the cangaço.

For Getúlio Vargas, a bandit like Lampião was a threat not only to local law and order in the northeast, but to the entire process of centralization which constituted the very core of his political ideology. After 1937, Lampião and his *cangaceiros* were seen as 'extremists' (Grunspan-Jasmin 2001, p. 216), that is, as enemies of the Nation. The 'new' state that was emerging in the Brazil of Getúlio Vargas did not tolerate any competitors for the monopoly of violence pertaining to the modern state, and it went to considerable length to demonstrate its point of view. Many of the events that we described in the section on the life of Lampião must be seen in the light of this fact (Souza 1972, pp. 129–30):

Backed by the Army and freed from local political interferences, the police forces embarked on a war of extermination of the *cangaço*. Commanded by the chief of police of Bahia, a pool of four northeastern state police troops was formed, some of which remained stationed at state borders, and all of which were organized into mobile forces equipped with radio transmitters. Repression of banditry was now a formidable enterprise; the evacuation of certain areas of the backlands, in … [1932], exemplifies this point. This plan expressed the police assumption that the rural population's support was the main factor in the survival of banditry, thereby, under the supervision of Captain J. Miguel, an area within the range of almost three hundred miles from Paripiranga, in Bahia, was evacuated by the police, and some twelve thousand people were moved to villages and cities outside this

> range. From 1931 on, thousands of bandits were arrested or executed, and in 1938 Lampião was killed. The remaining bandits surrendered to the police, with the exception of Corisco, killed in 1940. The government was careful to dissuade the re-emergence of banditry; the bandits were decapitated and their heads exhibited throughout the backlands. The mummified heads rested until recently at the Nina Rodrigues Institute, in Salvador, as an example of the state's intolerance of private violence.

The end of the *cangaço* was inevitable. By the 1940s the military presence in the Brazilian backlands rested on a much more effective and technically well-equipped army than hitherto, and on a good system of access roads and communication based on radio transmission and aerial surveillance (Lewin 1979, p. 144). The technology at the disposal of the police had changed and with that the balance between police and bandit forces. Already at Angicos, Lampião's fate was sealed by the technichal superiority of his adversaries. '... [I]t was not in vain that the volante force counted with the support of four machine guns, situated in different places and shooting in converging trajectories' (Mello 2004, pp. 281–82; for details see pp 280–81).

And hand in hand with the demise of the *cangaço* went the creation of the myth of the good bandit (Fausto 1986, p. 806):

> The disintegration and ultimate extinction of the *cangaço* resulted from a process by which the intervention by the state, with its growing ability to punish and patronize, reduced the instability of the local elite, and transformed the *cangaceiros* into mere bandits, whose actions were no longer of any use to their erstwhile protectors. There remained the mythology rooted in the figure of the *cangaceiro*, who is the personification of a supreme physical violence which the poor, under the oppression of their local potentates, cannot hope to emulate.

Conclusions

The Brazilian *cangaceiros* have often been portrayed as social bandits. Many of the authors of the major works on the *cangaço* have been unable to resist the temptation to romanticize the lives and deeds of the bandits.

The present chapter offers a different interpretation—one that runs in terms of economic calculations made by the various groups involved in the struggle between the 'cops' and the 'robbers'. Analyzing the activities of Lampião and other bandits, as well as the activities of the police chasing him, as economic activities allows us to advance a plausible explanation of why Lampião was able to mock the efforts to come to grip with him for two decades, exerting a certain control over a territory as large as Italy.

The conflict was a low-intensity conflict where neither party was interested in doing battle, where the bandits were an essential ingredient in local politics and where the population at large stood to gain more from siding with the *cangaceiros* than with the forces of the law. Banditry survived as long as *coronelismo* did. Once political power was centralized it no longer stood any chance. The key word when it comes to understanding the *cangaço* is 'backlands'. Banditry thrives under conditions conducive to the physical and political isolation. Once modernization sets in, it is wiped out.

References

Assunção, Moacir. (2007). *Os homens que mataram o facínora. A historia dos grandes inimigos de Lampiño*. Rio de Janeiro: Editora Record.

Burns, E. Bradford. (1980). *A history of Brazil* (2nd ed.). New York: Columbia University Press.

Castro, Josué de. (1966). *Death in the northeast*. New York: Random House.

Cava, Ralph della. (1970). *Miracle at Joaseiro*. New York/London: Columbia University Press.

Cava, Ralph della. (1972). The entry of padre Cicero into partisan politics, 1907–1909: Some complexities of Brazilian politics under the old republic. In Ronald H. Chilcote (Ed.), *Protest and resistance in Angola and Brazil*. Berkeley/Los Angeles: University of California Press.

Chandler, Billy Jaynes. (1978). *The Bandit King. Lampião of Brazil*. College Station/London: Texas A&M University Press.

Cunha, Euclides da. (1944). *Rebellion in the Backlands (Os Sertões)*. Chicago/London: University of Chicago Press.

Fausto, Boris. (1986). Brazil: The social and political structure of the First Republic, 1889–1930. In Leslie Bethell (Ed.), *The Cambridge history of Latin America, Volume V: c. 1870 to 1930*. Cambridge: Cambridge University Press.
Fausto, Boris. (1999). *A concise history of Brazil*. Cambridge: Cambridge University Press.
Findlay, Ronald. (1996). Towards a model of territorial expansion and the limits of empire. In Michelle R. Garfinkel & Stergios Skaperdas (Eds.), *The political economy of conflict and cooperation*. Cambridge: Cambridge University Press.
Findlay, Ronald, & Lundahl, Mats. (2006). The first globalization episode: The creation of the Mongol empire, or the economics of Chinggis Khan. In Göran Therborn & Habibul Haque Khondker (Eds.), *Asia and Europe in globalization. Continents, regions and nations*. Leiden: E. J. Brill.
Grunspan-Jasmin, Élise. (2001). *Lampião, vies et morts d'un bandit brésilien*. Paris: Presses Universitaires de France.
Hobsbawm, Eric J. (1959). *Primitive rebels: Studies in archaic forms of social movement in the 19th and 20th centuries*. Manchester: Manchester University Press.
Hobsbawm, Eric J. (1985). *Bandits* (2nd ed.). Harmondsworth: Penguin.
Levine, Robert M. (1992). *Vale of tears: Revisiting the Canudos Massacre in Northeastern Brazil, 1893–1897*. Berkeley: University of California Press.
Lewin, Linda. (1979). The oligarchical limitations of social banditry in Brazil: The case of the "Good" thief Antonio Silvino. *Past and present*, no. 82.
Lima, Estácio de. (1965). *O mundo estranho dos cangaceiros*. Salvador: Editôra Itapoã.
Lins, Daniel Soares. (1995). *La passion selon Lampião. Le roi des cangaceiros*. Paris: Éditions du Seuil.
Macêdo, Nertan. (1961). *O padre e a beata*. Rio de Janeiro: Leitura.
Macêdo, Nertan. (1968). *Capitão Virgulino Ferreira da Silva: Lampião. Seguido do Cancioneiro do Lampião* (2nd ed.). Rio de Janeiro: Ediçóes O Cruceiro.
Maciel, Frederico Bezerra. (1985a). *Lampião, su tempo e seu reinado. I. As origens. Por que Virgulino se tornou Lampião*? Petrópolis: Editora Vozes.
Maciel, Frederico Bezerra. (1985b). *Lampião, su tempo e seu reinado. II. A guerra de guerilhas (fase de vinditas)*. Petrópolis: Editora Vozes.
Maciel, Frederico Bezerra. (1985c). *Lampião, su tempo e seu reinado. III. A guerra de guerilhas (fase de domínio)*. Petrópolis: Editora Vozes.
Maciel, Frederico Bezerra. (1987a). *Lampião, su tempo e seu reinado. IV. A campanha de Bahia (Maria Bonita, Ezequiel e Virgínio)*. Petrópolis: Editora Vozes.

Maciel, Frederico Bezerra. (1987b). *Lampião, su tempo e seu reinado. V. O apogeu do dominio. A tragedia de Angico. A coroa do rei.* Petrópolis: Editora Vozes.
Maciel, Frederico Bezerra. (1988). *Lampião, su tempo e seu reinado. VI. Lampiônidas. A imagen de Lampião (volumen complementar e analítico).* Petrópolis: Editora Vozes.
Mello, Frederico Pernambucano de. (2004). *Guerreiros do sol: Violencia e banditismo no Nordeste do Brasil* (2nd ed.). São Paulo: A Girafa Editora.
Michaelis dicionário prático inglês-português, português-inglês. (1993). São Paulo: Melhoramentos.
Morel, Edgar. (1966). *Padre Cícero – O santo do Juàzeiro* (2nd ed.). Rio de Janeiro: Editôra Civilização Brasileira.
Pang, Eul-Soo. (1973). Coronelismo in Northeast Brazil. In Robert Kern (Ed. with the assistance of Ronald Dolkart), *The Caciques. Oligarchical politics and the system of Caciquismo in the Luso-Hispanic World.* Albuquerque: University of New Mexico Press.
Poppino, Rollie. (1968). *Brazil. The land and the people.* New York: Oxford University Press.
Queiroz, Maria Isaura de. (1968). *Os cangaceiros. Les bandits d'honneur brésiliens.* Paris: Juillard.
Skidmore, Thomas E. (1967). *Politics in Brazil 1930–1964. An experiment in democracy.* London: Oxford University Press.
Souza, Amaury de. (1972). The Cangaço and the Politic of Violence in Northeast Brazil. In Ronald H. Chilcote (Ed.), *Protest and resistance in Angola and Brazil.* Berkeley and Los Angeles: University of California Press.
Torres, Luiz Wanderley. (1994). *Lampião e o cangaço.* São Paulo: EDICON.
Vargas Llosa, Mario. (1981). *La guerra del fin del mundo.* Barcelona: Seix Barral.

Epilogue: Frontiers—Theory and History

The time has come to wind up and summarize. As stated at the outset, the ten chapters of this book were all written separately, the earliest (Chapter 8) in 1993 and the latest (Chapter 2) in 2016. They also vary in style and content with Chapters 4, 5, 6, 7 and 8 being for the most part formally analytical in their approach whereas the lengthy Chapter 2 is an extended historical narrative. While all the chapters are unified in terms of all being concerned in one way or another with the concept of a 'frontier', the reader might well ask how they are connected more specifically and concretely to one another rather than just being separate individual instances of the study of frontiers.

Concepts and History

The book has three foundations for the study of frontiers. First, in the introduction, we deal with concepts and definitions, such as the distinction between natural and artificial frontiers. Frontiers are rarely natural but they are determined by political and military factors—factors which

Original chapter for the present volume by Ronald Findlay and Mats Lundahl.

R. Findlay, M. Lundahl, *The Economics of the Frontier*,
DOI 10.1057/978-1-137-60237-4

in turn rest on economic considerations. The territory of a nation state is not given once and for all. It can expand and it can contract—for example, as a result of more or less violent conquest.

Second, in Chapter 2 directly, but in all the other chapters as well, there is a wealth of reference to the historical experience of frontiers. In Chapter 2, which is entirely historical—its purpose is to pinpoint the importance of the frontier concept—we stated that we did not have any ambitions to be exhaustive in our choice of historical examples of frontiers and empires. The purpose was simply to indicate that the frontier is a concept which is ubiquitous in time and space and that it lends itself to economic analysis. Still, within Chapter 2 the particular frontiers studied are chosen not just as a collection of particularly interesting examples but are connected in a sequence.

The Roman Empire, in what eventually became its Eastern or Byzantine section, embraced North Africa and the Middle East, what was to become the core area of the Islamic world in the seventh and eighth centuries. The Arab conquests and the associated Islamic empire that they created were therefore in an important sense a 'successor state' to the Roman Empire, as was the Latin Christendom of Western Europe. The Spanish and Portuguese *Reconquista* can thus be seen as a struggle between the two successor states over which of them should gain dominion over the Iberian Peninsula. The crusading fervor that gripped Western Europe in response to the threat of Islam was then also turned against the surviving pagan peoples of eastern Europe in the Northern Crusades.

As we saw in Chapter 2, in all of these four cases, what we have called the 'conquest frontier' and the 'settlement frontier' moved together and interacted in producing the actual historical outcome. Ernest Gellner (1988) identifies Plow, Sword and Book, i.e. production, coercion and cognition, as being the fundamental driving forces of 'the structure of human history'. He states emphatically: 'Basically, you own what you can defend' (Gellner 1988, p. 145), in other words the land that you cultivate with the Plow is only safe if you can defend it with the Sword, but the converse is also true. Frontiers can be established by the Sword, but when it comes to consolidating and keeping them the Plow has been more important. As several of the examples in the present volume demonstrate, any land you have taken with the Sword will not be of any use unless it is put to the Plow. They are examples of how frontiers are established by the interaction of these two prime movers of history. In order to convert a no-man's land into national territory, settlement and cultivation is necessary. This is exactly why we say that the conquest and settlement frontiers always tend to move together, whether at the Duero or the Vistula. But what determines the extent and durability of each of these frontiers? To answer this question we deploy the resources of economic theory—our third foundation—in Chapter 4 on conquest, drawing on the insights of Owen Lattimore (1940, 1962), and in Chapter 8 on settlement, following the lead of Guido Di Tella (1982). Thus, Chapters 2, 4 and 8 are all firmly tied together analytically and historically.

What about the Book? Human beings have to base their lives not only on food and security but also on some system of thought that enables them to give meaning to their lives in relation to both nature and society, what Gellner (1988, p. 23) calls 'codified, scriptural belief-and-legitimation systems'. The pagans of northeastern Europe had variants of the rich Norse mythology that provided this for them, without being literate, but just as they had in the end to submit to the superiority of the German Sword and the German Plow they had also to submit to the written Word of him whom they called the 'German God', Jesus Christ. Similarly the pagans of North Africa and Central Asia had to submit to another literary embodiment of an Abrahamic religion. The 'frontier of faith' moved just as inexorably as the frontiers of conquest and settlement. In Iberia the two Holy Books clashed for seven centuries until one had to give way.

We have not aimed at completeness in our selection of cases. It would hardly have made any sense. Still, in retrospect, we may argue that there is some method in our madness, for there is a historical and chronological connection between our examples. Our broad sweep begins with Rome, the Empire with a capital E. It grew out of insignificant beginnings, aggressively establishing itself in the Italian Peninsula before its superior military force turned the Mediterranean world and its surroundings into a coherent political and economic area. In the end, however, Rome grew too big. The centrifugal forces overwhelmed the centripetal ones. The frontier, as it were, moved inwards.

The Roman Empire split into two halves, the western one of which proved to be relatively short-lived. The eastern half, on the other hand, turned into a new—less powerful—empire: the Byzantine one. This empire rapidly came under stress too. The Plague of Justinian in the mid-sixth century weakened it to the point where it was overtaken by the emerging force of Islam, moving west from its Arabian heartland. The historical story of the expansion of Islam is told in Chapter 2. The economics of the plague, the expansion of Islam and its clash with Byzantium are analyzed in Chapter 5 which also deals with the emergence of what in the longer run would turn out to be the superior player in the frontier game: Western Europe. As we show, the interaction and territorial competition of the Byzantine Empire, Islam and Western Europe had consequences that extended until the advent of the next great plague in the mid-fourteenth century.

Before that, both Europe and Islam would suffer the onslaught of the Mongols, another military machine that emerged on the barren steppes of northern Central Asia. Exactly like in the case of Rome, it took a period of unification and stabilization within the core Mongol area before a concerted expansion effort could begin, but once that point had been reached no foes proved strong enough to stop the Mongol horsemen before they had penetrated deeply into Europe in the west and taken China in the east. Again, exactly like in the Roman case, the Mongol Empire proved to be too big. It split into four parts before it began to dissolve. The story is told and the underlying economic forces, as predicted by the model of the optimum size of empires in Chapter 4, are brought out in Chapter 6.

Islam would be pushed back on more fronts. Four crusades did little to rout the Arabs out of the Middle East, but the spirit of the crusades carried over into Europe proper. The forces of the Prophet had swept all of North Africa, from Egypt to the Atlantic at the beginning of the eighth century, and in 711 the Strait of Gibraltar was crossed. Chapter 2 gives the details of what took place during the next 800 years. The frontier that was pushed almost to the Pyrenees during the first century of conquest was gradually rolled back thereafter, as the Christian states were established, consolidated and united. Settlement followed upon conquest in an interior crusade, and in spite of occasional bursts of Arab military energy, by the mid-thirteenth century all that remained in Arab hands was Granada in the far south. By the beginning of the sixteenth century all of Spain and Portugal was in Christian hands. The European crusader mentality was brought to bear on the frontier not only in the southwest but in the northeast as well. Chapter 2 tells the story of how the Cross and the Sword joined hands in the christening and conquest of the territories around the Baltic in a series of 'crusades' launched by Germans, Danes and Swedes. The Middle Ages was a period when Europe expanded its borders in all directions.

Modeling History

The third foundation of the present book is economic theory. The conquest model of Chapter 4 has many implications that are consistent with the historical experiences recounted in Chapter 2. One of these is the difference between a single expanding empire confronted by disorganized 'barbarian' tribes and the situation when two expanding empires collide. The Romans did not advance far across the Rhine or the Danube not because they encountered a rival empire, but because it was not in their own interest to push their frontier any further. The same was the case with the Arab conquests in Central Asia. But the Roman expansion to the east did have to confront the Sasanian Empire, resulting in a zone of separation that kept the two sides apart in an uneasy equilibrium. This situation was replicated in Iberia with the Caliphate of Córdoba on one side of a no-man's land and the Christian kingdoms of Castile-León and Aragón on the other. Similarly, the Teutonic Knights expanded the eastern frontier of Latin Christendom until they were stopped by a confrontation with the Grand Duchy of Lithuania, allied after 1386 with the Kingdom of Poland, with their union forming another expanding conquest state.

Chapter 6 is a detailed analysis of what was perhaps the most remarkable example of an empire in history, the Mongol Empire of Chinggis Khan and his descendants. We adapt the model of Chapter 4 to explain the remarkable feat of Chinggis Khan in unifying the Mongol tribes, turning their energies outward to conquer the rich borderlands to east and west instead of dissipating them on fruitless internal conflicts. Anatoly Khazanov (1993) has pointed out the remarkable similarity, as well as the differences, between the Prophet Mohammed and Chinggis Khan as builders of world empires. The empire was divided into four parts: the Chagatai Empire in the original Mongol homeland in the steppes of Central Asia; the Yuan Dynasty directly administering China with its capital at Beijing; the dynasty of the Ilkhans, also directly ruling over Iran, with its capital at Tabriz; and the Golden Horde, which exercised suzerainty over the Russian principalities while remaining camped out on the steppe. Perhaps not surprisingly, because it continued to pursue the rugged nomadic way of life, the Golden Horde lasted till 1562 whereas the Yuan and the Ilkhans both lost their vigor by absorption into the more sophisticated sedentary civilizations of their subjects, with both empires falling around the middle of the fourteenth century.

Chapters 5 and 7 were each originally written to deal with analyzing the economic impact of a plague, the sixth-century Plague of Justinian in the first case and the fourteenth-century Black Death in the second. What do plagues have to do with conquest, settlement and frontiers? Quite a lot, it turns out. The sixth-century plague seriously weakened the Byzantine and Sasanian Empires, enabling the Arab conquests of the next century to push the former out of Syria, Palestine and Egypt and to not only occupy the lands of the latter but to extinguish it completely. The demographic recovery from the effects of the plague, predicted by the Malthusian mechanism incorporated in the model of Chapter 5, benefited both the Byzantine and the Islamic Empires but it especially favored Roman Catholic Europe, leading to the burst of energy and religious fervor resulting in the crusades against the Muslims in both the Holy Land and the Iberian Peninsula and the assault on the pagans of the northeast.

An important feature of the model of Chapter 7 is that one of the two production sectors is for a commodity 'silver' that is also used as a unit of account, store of value and medium of exchange, in other words it is 'money', as was true of almost all monetary systems all over the world before the adoption of 'fiat' currencies in the twentieth century. The output of silver depends, in addition to labor, on the capacity of the 'mines' from which it can be extracted, which is taken as given. When the demographic shock of the Black Death occurs we trace the response not only of population, labor supply and other variables but also the evolution of the money supply and the price level (of goods in terms of silver). We show that the economy of Europe experiences a drain of silver to the east, what monetary historians have termed the 'bullion famine of the fifteenth century', resulting from the rise in demand for 'eastern luxuries' due to the transitory rise in per capita income caused by the effect of the plague. This trade was facilitated by the expansion of the Mongols, through the creation of the Pax Mongolica, securing the east-west trade routes. The very same expansion was also instrumental in bringing the bubonic plague from Asia to Europe.

We next go on in Chapter 7 to consider the effect on 'Europe' of the discovery in 'America' of virgin silver mines such as the 'silver mountain' of Potosí. We show that the output of silver expands in both Europe and America, to which some of the European population emigrates. Europe exports goods to America and imports silver, some of which is retained to augment the money supply, raising the price level, while the rest is exported to Asia in exchange for 'Eastern luxuries', raising the price level there. As Chapter 2 shows, this is exactly what happened in the New World during the sixteenth century, while Chapter 7 itself cites a voluminous literature on the global impact of the American treasure, including the famous thesis of the historian Earl Hamilton (1934) on American silver and the 'Price Revolution' of the sixteenth century.

The European or 'Old World' section of Chapter 2 came to an end with the triumphant entry of Ferdinand and Isabella into Granada in 1492. Was it just coincidence that the other famous event associated with *Los Reyes Católicos* also happened in the same year? Surely, the 'closing of the medieval frontier' within Europe itself and the opening of the 'early modern frontier' in the New World were closely interrelated historical processes. As we insist in Chapter 2, the Spanish expansion in the Americas was a direct continuation of the *Reconquista*. The mixture of religious and economic motives was the same in both cases. When Francisco Pizarro was scolded by a priest for being brutal to the Indians instead of attempting to convert them to Christianity, he replied 'I have not come here for any such reasons. I have come here to take away from them their gold' (Hanke 1949, p. 7). However, while the frontier in America was initially a mining frontier it was with time converted into a settlement frontier. Animal husbandry and cultivation defined the extent of European domination, with the demand for the export goods determined in Europe, which also supplied most of the people who extended the frontier.

This brings us to Chapter 8 and what we have called the 'Christopher Columbus model'. This chapter was first published in 1993, earlier than any of the others and so in a sense it is the '1492' moment for the project of this book. Here 'Europe' is the source of labor, capital and manufactured goods, while a newly discovered 'America' is just a wilderness but one in which arable land can be cleared at a rising marginal cost, on which both food and a plantation crop such as sugar or cotton can be grown, which is in turn an input into the production function for manufactures in Europe. The return on clearing an acre of land is the marginal value product of that land in terms of either commodity grown on it, while the price of that acre is the marginal cost of clearing it from the wilderness, which is an increasing function of the amount of land cleared. The extent of the frontier is endogenously determined by the equality of the rate of return in clearing land with an exogenously given rate of time preference. The model determines all relative product and factor prices, the outputs of all three goods and the amount of emigration from Europe to America. Exogenous increases in population or technological efficiency can generally be shown to expand production on both continents and extend the settlement frontier in America. Thus the model can account, at an abstract level, for all the historical developments recounted in the New World sections of Chapter 2.[1]

One major issue not dealt with in the present volume is the whole question of slavery and the Atlantic slave trade. The plantation crops of sugar and cotton were produced with African slave labor throughout the New World. The economic analysis relevant to the study of this problem is provided in Findlay (1990), which is not included in this book because it does not deal with the issue of frontiers. Thus the model of Chapter 8 has frontiers without slavery, while Findlay (1990) has slavery without frontiers. It would not be too difficult to construct a model embracing both slavery and frontiers but we have not yet done so and neither, to our knowledge, has anyone else.

The extension of the settlement frontier to a large extent is the story of staples production. This hardly comes as a surprise, for a staple is defined as a product in high international demand with a weight or volume per unit which is low enough to allow for overseas transportation. Once this demand materialized, production factors began to move across national

[1] See also Findlay (1995, Chap. 5) for further extensions and applications of the model.

boundaries as well, in the historical perspective from Europe to the other four continents. Labor, capital, technology and entrepreneurship from the Old World spread to the rest of the world during the 'golden age' of Heckscher-Ohlin factor-based trade from the 1970s to World War I, in a non-Marxian fashion—not triggered by an excess supply of goods at home, but by an excess demand. In America, Asia, Australia and Africa, as the model of Chapter 9 and the historical sequences of Chapters 2, 9, and 10 demonstrate, this served to extend the frontier, linking their economies to those of Europe.

Chapter 9 uses the concept of an endogenous land frontier developed in Chapter 8 to formalize and elaborate the very useful 'vent-for-surplus' approach to the opening up of international trade introduced by Adam Smith and creatively extended and applied by Hla Myint (1958) in the papers cited in that chapter. This model is then applied to the 1870–1914 experience of the exchange of manufactured goods from Europe for the primary products exported by the developing economies of Latin America, Africa and Asia in Chapter 10. The model is particularly applicable to such famous episodes as the 'colonization of the delta' of the Irrawaddy River in Burma after the opening of the Suez Canal in 1869 to export rice and the response of the Akwapim people to the opportunity for the export of cocoa from the Gold Coast, what is now Ghana (Adas 1974; Hill 1963).

The final act in all frontier episodes is that of the closing of the frontier. Sooner or later empires either clash with other empires or expand to the point where Owen Lattimore's centrifugal forces swamp the imperial centripetal ones. Rome was split, the Byzantine Empire clashed with Islam and the Arabs were halted both in the west and in the east. The Mongol Empire expanded beyond the point where it could be centrally administered. Alternatively, countries or empires find that there is no more land to be had. In the latter case, as demonstrated by the Spanish and US experiences, a solution may be found in overseas expansion, but sooner or later that too will have to come to an end. Settlement has its limitations as well. A product which is a staple at a given time may later turn into an ordinary good with a demand that is not strong enough to provide growth and frontier expansion impulses to the economy. This happened in many of the cases that we examine in Chapters 9 and 10.

The final episode in the book, the 'interior' frontier of northeast Brazil in the 1920s and 1930s, may seem a bit of an outlier in comparison with the rest of our cases, but it is not. It provides an illustration of the usefulness of the basic model of the optimum extension of empire, discussed in Chapter 4, as do several of the other episodes that we deal with. It also illustrates the fact that territorial expansion has a limit—in this case given by the encounter with a superior force intent on finishing the contender: the modern state in Brazil. Also, if given a 'presentist' reading, in the spirit of Eli Heckscher (1904, pp. 184–85), it may provide some lessons for today, for the analysis of the rise of a state within the state in the Middle East: the Islamic State which has gradually established itself over the past decade. In the same way as the authorities in Brazil tolerated the existence of banditry, keeping the extent of direct confrontation on a low level, the international society has so far refrained from wiping out the self-proclaimed caliphate in Syria and Iraq. Mechanisms have been at work which have contributed to keeping Western striking power well below its maximum potential, presumably until further provoked.

References

Adas, Michael. (1974). *The Burma delta: Economic development and social change on an Asian rice frontier, 1852–1941*. Madison: University of Wisconsin Press.

Di Tella, Guido. (1982). The economics of the frontier. In Charles P. Kindleberger & Guido Di Tella (Eds.), *Economics in the long view: Essays in honour of W. W. Rostow* (Vol. 1). London: Macmillan.

Findlay, Ronald. (1990). *The 'Triangular Trade' and the Atlantic economy of the eighteenth century: A simple general equilibrium model*. Essays in International Finance, no. 177. Princeton: International Finance Section, Department of Economics, Princeton University.

Findlay, Ronald. (1995). *Factor proportions, trade and growth*. Cambridge, MA: MIT Press.

Gellner, Ernest. (1988). *Plough, sword and book: The structure of human history*. Chicago: University of Chicago Press.

Hamilton, Earl J. (1934). *American treasure and the price revolution in Spain*. Cambridge, MA: Harvard University Press.

Hanke, Lewis. (1949). *The Spanish struggle for justice in the conquest of America.* Philadelphia: Pennsylvania University Press.
Heckscher, Eli F. (1904). Ekonomisk historia: några antydningar. *Ekonomisk Tidskrift, 24*, 67–198.
Hill, Polly. (1963). *Migrant cocoa-farmers of Southern Ghana: A study in rural capitalism.* London/New York: Cambridge University Press.
Khazanov, Anatoly M. (1993). Muhammad and Jenghiz Khan compared: The religious factor in world empire building. *Comparative Studies in Society and History, 35*, 461–479.
Lattimore, Owen. (1940). *Inner Asian frontiers of China.* New York: American Geographical Society.
Lattimore, Owen. (1962). *Studies in frontier history. Collected papers 1928–1952.* London/New York: Oxford University Press.
Myint, Hla. (1958). The classical theory of international trade and the underdeveloped countries. *Economic Journal, 68*, 317–337.

Index

Note: Page numbers followed by "n" denote notes.

R. Findlay, M. Lundahl, *The Economics of the Frontier*,
DOI 10.1057/978-1-137-60237-4

C

F